CW00345865

Church and State

**The Contribution of the Church of England Bishops
to the House of Lords during the Thatcher Years**

STUDIES IN CHRISTIAN HISTORY AND THOUGHT

A full listing of titles in this series appears at the close of this book

Church and State

The Contribution of the Church of England Bishops to the House of Lords during the Thatcher Years

Andrew Partington

Foreword by George Carey

Paternoster:
thinking faith

First published 2006 by Paternoster
Paternoster is an imprint of Authentic Media
9 Holdom Avenue, Bletchley, Milton Keynes, MK1 1QR, U.K.
and
PO Box 1047, Waynesboro, GA 30830-2047, USA

12 11 10 09 08 07 06   7 6 5 4 3 2 1

British Library Cataloguing in Publication Data
A catalogue record for this book is available from the British Library.

ISBN-10 1–84227–334–5
ISBN-13 978–1–84227–334–0

Typeset by Profile, Culmdale, Rewe, Exeter

Printed and bound in Great Britain
by Nottingham Alphagraphics

Series Preface

This series complements the specialist series of *Studies in Evangelical History and Thought* and *Studies in Baptist History and Thought* for which Paternoster is becoming increasingly well known by offering works that cover the wider field of Christian history and thought. It encompasses accounts of Christian witness at various periods, studies of individual Christians and movements, and works which concern the relations of church and society through history, and the history of Christian thought.

The series includes monographs, revised dissertations and theses, and collections of papers by individuals and groups. As well as 'free standing' volumes, works on particular running themes are being commissioned; authors will be engaged for these from around the world and from a variety of Christian traditions.

A high academic standard combined with lively writing will commend the volumes in this series both to scholars and to a wider readership.

Series Editors

To Michaela

Only a church which is taking seriously the need for its own inner life to express the Kingdom and its righteousness can speak to the public domain with a right to be taken seriously.

Duncan Forrester

Contents

Foreword

In this extremely thorough study of the role of bishops in the House of Lords, Andrew Partington has chosen to focus his attention on the Thatcher years to assess their contribution and effectiveness. He does so at a time of uncertainty facing the Second Chamber of Parliament. Prime Minister Tony Blair declared his intention in 1997 to reform the House of Lords and the place of bishops will be determined in due course.

In many respects it is an extraordinary anomaly that, in a secular society, bishops sit in Parliament and participate in the affairs of state. This is entirely due to the vicissitudes of history. Before the Reformation, bishops, along with abbots, were a significant element in the House of Lords and were among the monarch's most influential advisers. At the Reformation, bishops, now of the reformed Church of England, were allowed to continue as Lords Spiritual in a House that included a larger number of lay peers.

Today, the proportions are entirely different. Only 26 bishops, out of 750 peers, sit in the House of Lords and are able to intervene in, and contribute to every bill that passes through Parliament.

Dr Partington has chosen the Thatcher period as offering a unique window on the exercise of Christian ministry of busy bishops who were confronted by an adversarial politician with clear-cut views on most issues, driven by her desire to get 'Britain back to work and back on its feet'. He shows that, although the bishops were often heroic in their intentions and backed by the remarkable document 'Faith in the City', their contributions were 'insignificant, inefficient and indistinct'.

As Archbishop of Canterbury in the period directly following that turbulent decade, I wish to offer three reflections on Dr Partington's thesis from my perspective.

Dr Partington draws attention to the problem of pressure on bishops who often have to travel long distances to get to London. That bishops are extremely busy, no one doubts. That they are expected to turn up regularly to the House of Lords to participate in debates, which are usually only known a week or two prior to the business of the House, makes it very difficult for people whose diaries are formed a year ahead. As Archbishop I usually tried to pop into the House of Lords once a week to take my seat and be visible, but it was exasperating to find that I would be out of the country when critical debates were tabled. Yes, presence is very important but fleeting presences simply suggest that we are visitors rather than members bound together in a common task to oversee the way the nation is run. Over 150 years ago Archbishop Tait commented that so many of his bishops 'made so little of their parliamentary opportunities'. Things have not changed much, except that life has become more frantic for bishops in the exercise of their ministries.

I find it intriguing that bishops interviewed by Dr Partington argued that they were not in Parliament as bishops of the Church of England but as individual Lords of Parliament, implicitly asserting independence. Whilst this is technically correct, it is dangerously disingenuous and has led to many problems for the Church of England. In my time as Archbishop, bishops who had previously disagreed with the majority opinion of the House of Bishops and General Synod, have later argued for their own position in the House of Lords. Whilst they have every right to do so, the net effect was to undermine the collegiality of bishops and weakened the public view of the Church's stance on national issues. Thus Bishop Montefiore in his interview sadly comments that when he introduced a bill on abortion Roman Catholic peers were supportive but 'I didn't have much support from my fellow bishops'.

Dr Partington offers important reflections on the theological and biblical content of the speeches given by bishops during this period and argues that, without intending to do so, their cautious and feeble commitment to scripture undermined the public relevance of the bible. This may of course indicate the theological background of the majority of the bishops at the time. On the other hand, the rejoinder may come: 'You don't have to quote the bible to be biblical'. That, as Dr Partington does readily acknowledge, is true. Indeed, some of the bishops' interventions register high on the prophetic scale. Nevertheless, Dr Partington's comments warrant serious reflection, making one wonder if the failure of Christian leaders to refer to Scripture outside of the church context is due to an embarrassment which impoverishes their witness.

Interestingly, Bishop Maurice Wood scores highest in his use of scripture and in his pastoral care of others, ending his time in the House of Lords as one of the most effective bishops. However, according to this book, he was also one of the most supportive of Margaret Thatcher's policies, although not uncritically so.

This is a fascinating and powerfully argued book. Of its relevance I have not doubt. This analysis is unsettling reading for all bishops and demands an urgent appraisal by the Church of England of the role of bishops in the House of Lords. Although, toward the end of my active ministry, I led a delegation to argue the case for no change in the number of bishops in the House I recall, at the time, being troubled by the argument to retain 26 bishops. My discomfort was caused by the fact that the evidence shouted that the majority of bishops have not considered the House of Lords among their highest priorities. I certainly do believe that bishops have a continuing role to play in a reformed House, but I am now convinced that a much smaller, dedicated group of bishops, who give substantially of their time to the second most important Chamber in the land, would serve the gospel and church more effectively.

George Carey

Acknowledgements

Few research students can have completed their thesis without feeling a profound sense of their dependence upon the support, encouragement and guidance of a whole host of individuals and groups. This one is no different. I trust that all who have in any way contributed to the production of this thesis will be pleased with the end result.

I have been privileged to study under the astute supervision of Rev Dr Derek Tidball. I am certain the whole process would have been far more laborious were it not for his skill and commitment. I am particularly thankful to him for responding to my self-doubt with belief, not just during the course of this project, but during my time as an undergraduate at London School of Theology (formerly London Bible College). There can be few whose spoken commitment to mentoring is underscored by such consistent and effective practice. For any academic or vocational success that I may achieve, I owe him a considerable debt. I would like to acknowledge the contribution of Rt Hon Sir Brian Mawhinney MP. He initiated the whole project and provided me with access to the House of Commons Library and the House of Lords Record and Information Office. A number of other individuals should be acknowledged in appreciation of their willingness to take the time to guide an apprentice in his work: Mr David Beamish, Clerk of the Committees and Clerk of the Overseas Office at the House of Lords; Professor Kenneth Medhurst; Richard Cracknell of the House of Commons Library; Canon Michael Saward; and Dr Steve Walton at London School of Theology. The staff of the British Library, Lambeth Palace Library, the House of Commons Library and London Bible College Library all deserve my thanks. I am heavily indebted to Myra Imhoff for typing-up the transcripts of my interviews and to Mary Conroy, Chris Short and Anne-Marie Tate for their diligent proof-reading. My mother-in-law, Colleen Hancock, deserves special thanks. She worked feverishly over the Christmas of 2002, casting the eyes of a skilled English teacher over the whole manuscript.

The insights of a number of bishops who served in the House of Lords during the Thatcher years have added depth and colour to my thesis. I should like to thank the Rt Revs Michael Baughen, Hugh Montefiore, David Say and John Taylor for their willingness to reflect with me on their experience as Lords Spiritual during the 1980s. Talking with them was the highlight of the research process. I am particularly grateful to David Say for entrusting to me his original copies of a number of articles and letters, and to John Taylor for using his business diaries to write-up a typical month's bishop's diary for me. I must also express my appreciation to Bishops David Halsey and David Jenkins for corresponding with me by post in response to particular questions raised by my investigations and, of course, to the Rt Rev and Rt Hon Lord Carey of Clifton for his very gracious Foreword.

Another long list is required to pay tribute to those who have given financial support to my endeavours. The Gardner family, the Norman Evershed Trust, the Bible Society, the Laing Trust, and the Tidball family have all invested in me, and I am deeply grateful. I must also say thank you again to Chris Short, this time for giving me a home to live in during my first-year of study. I benefited tremendously from his generosity, but far more from his friendship. I am also thankful to my parents-in-law, Mike and Colleen, for their very generous practical support during my period of full-time research – just one expression of their care and commitment to me over the past ten years.

My final period of study was undertaken whilst working as part of a team discipling young people in preparation for missionary service at The King's Lodge, a Youth With A Mission training base in Nuneaton (formerly Lindley Lodge, the preparatory school attended by Archbishop Geoffrey Fisher). The King's Lodge leadership team were unswerving and selfless in their commitment to my research, providing ample space for me to study and taking a keen interest in my progress. I offer them my thanks.

Only as I have experienced the joys and the pressures of parenthood for myself do I fully realise how privileged I am to have been nurtured in a loving, supportive and godly family. My Mum and Dad deserve abundant thanks in relation to this thesis for providing me with the foundations, particularly in character, needed to complete such a task. More than anyone my beautiful wife, Michaela, deserves my thanks. She is a constant source of love, friendship and encouragement and has sacrificed much in support of this project. A faithful refuge, an inspiration and a wonderful Mother to our precious children, Daniel and Jemimah, this thesis is dedicated to her. For each of the people listed above I give thanks to God. For all of the financial provision we have received I thank God. I attribute to Him every moment of 'luck' I have had in relation to this research, every moment of inspiration. It is to Him that I give the ultimate thanks and the ultimate credit for this thesis.

Andrew Partington
January 2006

List of Figures

The Bishops and the Bible

List of Tables

CHAPTER ONE

Introduction

1.1 Introduction

A research thesis could be written about the contribution of the twenty-six bishops to the House of Lords since the war – the period during which I have myself been a member of the House. The years of Mrs Thatcher's government alone provide plenty of material.[1]

Lord Longford's call for research, issued in 1986, remained largely unanswered during the 1980s and 1990s. Throughout this period consideration of the contribution of the bishops to the legislative and deliberative work of the Upper House was to be found within wider studies of the House of Lords, the Church of England, and the relationship of Church and State, but rarely in academic enquiry focused exclusively on the Lords Spiritual. This work endeavours to respond to the absence of data on, and analysis of, the bishops' role in British political life by exploring the contribution of the bishops to the House of Lords during the Thatcher years.[2]

The period from May 1979 to November 1990[3] was chosen for scrutiny in this thesis for two primary reasons. On the one hand it represents a relatively coherent unit of history, both politically and ecclesiastically. The Conservative Party remained in power with Margaret Thatcher as Prime Minister throughout the period and no attempt was made at the reform of the House of Lords. In the Church of England Robert Runcie was Archbishop of Canterbury from March 1980 to January 1991, his tenure at Lambeth Palace paralleling Thatcher's at 10 Downing Street to a remarkable degree. On the other hand the Thatcher years are widely considered, not least in the media, to have been the low-point in the post-war relationship between Church and State. Historically there is, therefore, much to be gained from investigating what was said and done by the Lords Spiritual, the primary constitutional interface between Church and

---

1   F. Longford, *The Bishops: A Study of Leaders in the Church Today* (London: Sidgwick & Jackson, 1986), 113.
2   J. Campbell, *Margaret Thatcher: The Grocer's Daughter* (London: Jonathan Cape, 2000), xi.
3   We will refer to this period both as 'the Thatcher years' and 'the 1980s', using the two terms synonymously.

State, during this period.

This analysis of the contribution of the Church of England bishops to the House of Lords during the Thatcher years has four main purposes. The first is to place the topic in its political and ecclesiastical context. For an author born in the late 1970s, and therefore belonging to a generation whose political awareness was in its infancy when Mrs Thatcher's premiership ended on 22nd November 1990, this is primarily a task in contemporary history. The second purpose is to generate a comprehensive body of empirical data on the attendance, voting and speech-making of the Lords Spiritual during the 1980s with which future research can engage. Few observers of the Church of England have been able to resist the temptation to make claims about what the Lords Spiritual have, or more often have not, done. These claims are not to be dismissed lightly. Very often they have been based on many years of experience, observation, and valuable anecdotal evidence. However, it remains the case that there has been a dearth of facts against which the validity of these claims can be measured. This book seeks to provide new facts which can be employed to both substantiate and challenge claims which are made in relation to the contribution of the bishops to the House of Lords. The third purpose of this study is to analyse and interpret this body of data in conversation with the literature which exists on the contribution of the bishops to the Upper House. The fourth purpose is to reflect on this data in the light of the process of House of Lords reform initiated by the Labour Government's January 1999 White Paper *Modernising Parliament: Reforming the House of Lords*, and in so doing to consider afresh how the Church of England can best facilitate the service of its bishops in Parliament. Finally, it should be stated explicitly that that the purpose of this work is not to critique theologically episcopal involvement in British Parliamentary government. Instead it examines in detail the outworking of one aspect of the Church of England's theological understanding of both itself and its mission, and of the 'governing authorities'.[4]

The remainder of this introductory chapter describes the methodology employed in this study. Methodological issues relevant to each particular aspect of the book will also be tackled in the introductions to chapters four, five, six, seven and eight. Chapters two and three place our subject into its political and ecclesiastical context. Chapter Two considers the British political scene and the life of the Church of England before examining the nature of the Church-State relationship during the 1980s. Chapter Three looks at the role of the

---

4   Romans 13:1 (New International Version).

bishops within the Church of England and the work of the House of Lords, before exploring the particular role of the Lords Spiritual. The following five chapters present empirical data on, and analysis of, the contribution of the bishops to the Upper House. We consider the bishops' attendance at the Palace of Westminster (Chapter Four), their voting record (Chapter Five), the extent of their speech-making (Chapter Six), and the content of the speeches that they made (Chapter Seven). Chapter Eight then gives special attention to the bishops' use of the Bible in their speech-making. Chapter Nine concludes by presenting a summary of the empirical data presented and reflects, in the light of this data, on how the Church of England's approach to the bishops' service in the Lords can evolve to best serve both Church and nation.

1.2 Methodology

The first task of the research process was to engage with the published literature of relevance to a consideration of the contribution of the bishops to the House of Lords during the 1980s. Material which focused directly on this subject does not, as mentioned above (Section 1.1), abound. The only research available which has this particular topic as its sole focus is Francis Bown's article, 'Influencing the House of Lords: the role of the Lords Spiritual 1979-1987', published in Political Studies during 1994.[5] Otherwise our dependence has been on material contained within wider studies on related topics to which frequent reference will be made. Of particular value were Kenneth Medhurst and George Moyser's *Church and Politics in a Secular Age*; Donald Shell's *The House of Lords*; Henry Clark's *The Church Under Thatcher*; and Simon Lee & Peter Stanford's *Believing Bishops*. In contrast there was considerable material with which to engage in order to place our interpretation of the contribution of the Lords Spiritual during the Thatcher years in its political and ecclesiastical context.

The second task of the research process was to gather data on the contribution of the bishops to the House of Lords direct. Data on the attendance of the bishops was taken from the House of Lords *Sessional Statistics* (compiled by the House of Lords Journal and Information Office) for each Parliamentary session for which Margaret Thatcher was Prime Minister. Data on the voting record of the bishops was drawn from House of Lords *Hansard*, the official record of

---

5   We will engage with Bown's article in detail in below (Chapters Four, Five, Six and Seven).

House of Lords debates, and cross-checked against lists compiled by the House of Lords Journal and Information Office recording each of the House of Lords divisions in summary. Data on the extent of the bishops' speech-making was taken from House of Lords *Hansard* – with the exception of data on whether Bills were sponsored by the Government or a Private Member. This information was gleaned from the House of Commons *Weekly Information Bulletin*. Data on the content of the bishops' speeches was based on a thorough analysis of 123 volumes of House of Lords Hansard. The involvement of the bishops in House of Lords Select Committees was not included in this research process due to the limitations imposed by a finite time-frame for research.

The third task of the research process was to conduct interviews with a selection of bishops with experience of serving as Lords Spiritual during the 1980s. Interviews with four bishops representing a cross-section of churchmanship were undertaken during May and July 2002. In line with the approach used by Medhurst and Moyser, a similar set of open-ended questions (Appendix 1) was posed to each interviewee in order to afford ample opportunity for the respondents to think aloud, to volunteer otherwise unavailable information, and also to ensure a degree of comparability between the interviews.[6] Three of the four interviewees were given a copy of the interview questions a number of weeks in advance of the interview date. Unfortunately, the date for one interview was arranged at such short notice that this was not possible. It was intended that giving advance notice of these questions would prompt the interviewees to reflect afresh on their experiences in the House of Lords during the 1980s in advance of the interview and in relation to the specific issues to be discussed in the interview. In so doing it was intended that the interviewees would be better able to give considered and detailed answers to the questions posed, as well as to recall anecdotal evidence with which to illustrate their comments. The interviewing approach employed was also similar in tone to that adopted by Medhurst and Moyser:

> In our particular approach the tendency was to veer in the direction of the more deferential or polite approach. This was partly a matter of personal inclination but more importantly it was because

---

6   K.N. Medhurst & G.H. Moyser, 'Studying a Religious Elite: the Case of the Anglican Episcopate', in G.H. Moyser & M. Wagstaffe (eds.), *Research Methods for Elite Studies* (London: George Allen & Unwin, 1987), 93.

of the particular elite involved. Virtually from the outset, it was apparent that they normally operated within a consensual and eirenic frame of reference.[7]

The decision was made during the course of the research process to follow, for the most part, Adrian Hastings's approach to labelling bishops according to their churchmanship: 'It would be hopeless,' he argues, 'to try and sort out "Evangelicals", "Anglo-Catholics" and "Liberals" among these men. The terms are just too simple. They characterize the young but seldom the mature. Good bishops outgrow such labellings.'[8] They also grate against the tendency among many bishops themselves to eschew such theological pigeon-holing, largely as due to their role in the diocese as 'the effective symbol of unity':[9]

> As symbols of unity within their dioceses, bishops have tradition-ally been expected to gravitate toward 'centrist' theological positions and to avoid the more militant postures of the differing ecclesiastical parties... The overwhelming majority of modern bishops... have had a psychological and spiritual make-up which has made it possible for them to embrace a significant measure of doctrinal latitude.[10]

Throughout the thesis, therefore, a general sensitivity to episcopal churchmanship has been maintained and occasional references to churchmanship[11] have been made (as Towler and Coxon note these labels are 'a useful shorthand description of different types of churchmanship').[12] No attempt, however, has been made to perform

---

7   *ibid*, 95.

8   A. Hastings, *Robert Runcie* (London: Mowbray, 1991), 66.

9   P. Avis, *The Anglican Understanding of the Church: An Introduction* (London: SPCK, 2000), 28.

10   K.N. Medhurst & G.H. Moyser, *Church and Politics in a Secular Age* (Oxford: Clarendon Press, 1988), 88-89. When one of the bishops interviewed by Medhurst and Moyser was asked whether he felt there was any sense in which he had become more moderate or had moved toward the centre theologically since becoming a bishop, he replied: 'I do not see how it could not be so... clergy open their hearts to you and you see the inside of the faith of the man of a quite different tradition from what you have known. Things that have never rung a bell for you... you can see them ringing powerfully for other people. I don't see how you could have that position for any length of time and not be influenced by it...' Medhurst & Moyser, *Secular*, 89-90.

11   For example in Chapter 8, 'The Bishops and the Bible'.

12   R. Towler & A.P.M. Coxon, *The Fate of the Anglican Clergy: A Sociological Study* (London: Macmillan, 1979), 106.

detailed analysis which is dependent upon the categorization of each bishop by his churchmanship.[13]

---

13   An attempt was made, early in the research process, to categorize each bishop by his churchmanship. Following the precedent of Towler & Coxon's *The Fate of the Anglican Clergy*, churchmanship was attributed on the basis of the theological college attended by each bishop. This assessment was then subjected to the critique of Dr Steve Walton of London School of Theology and Canon Michael Saward. This process confirmed to the author the difficulty of dividing the bishops in this way. Reference to theological colleges will always be an uncertain tool for attributing churchmanship, particularly with clergymen largely in their 60s, because of the possibility that the theological position of the individual concerned will have shifted since his theological training. Moreover, in conversation with Michael Saward and Steve Walton it became clear how difficult it is to attribute churchmanship in a satisfactory manner. To refer once more to Hastings: 'Good Bishops outgrow such labellings.'

CHAPTER TWO

Church and State during the Thatcher Years

2.1 Confrontational Politics

2.1.1 Consensus to Confrontation

'Consensus', writes Dennis Kavanagh, 'is not an ideal term because, although it is a firmly established concept, it is used in so many different ways.'[1] He proceeds to explain three meanings intended by its use within the study of politics:[2]

1) 'A high level of agreement across the political parties and governing elites about the substance of public policy.'
2) 'A high level of agreement between the political parties and governing elites about the nature of the regime or about the rules of the political game.'
3) 'The political style by which policy differences are resolved – namely a process of compromise and bargaining and a search for policies which are acceptable to the major interests.'

Our emphasis will be upon the first and third of these meanings.[3] Consensus in both of these senses is accepted by most who write within the political and social sciences as a helpful concept when describing the shape of British politics during the post-war era.[4] Basic agreement over the substance of public policy and the methods by which disputes should be resolved emerged during Clement Attlee's 1945-51 Government[5] and remained in place, with slight modifications, during the 13 years of Conservative Government

---

1   D. Kavanagh, *The Reordering of British Politics: Politics After Thatcher* (Oxford: Oxford University Press, 1997), 9.
2   *ibid*, 9-10.
3   Consensus in the second sense is assumed *de facto*. 'Institutional change in Britain has been incremental, and over the past sixty years there has been little popular support for proponents of comprehensive constitutional change.' Kavanagh, *Reordering*, 9.
4   A. Seldon, 'The Rise and Fall of the Post-War Consensus', in Jones et al., *Politics UK* (London: Philip Allan, 1991), 41.
5   The genesis of this consensus, however, is to be found in the war years of 1939-1945. Seldon, 'Consensus', 41, Kavanagh, *Reordering*, 30-32.

which followed.[6] This consensus remained from 1955 into the 1970s – a period which Anthony Seldon describes as the 'high noon of the consensus'.[7] The consensus was constructed around the twin pillars of the welfare state and the mixed economy. There was also agreement on the need to construct foreign policy around NATO and the nuclear deterrent.[8]

> The new consensus did not entail detailed State economic planning; rather, both parties embraced Keynesian ideas concerning macro-economic management. Tax, credit, monetary, and other measures were used in an attempt to manage overall levels of demand and to avoid the depression and unemployment that had characterised the 1930s. Under such auspices, the 1950s saw not only economic recovery but also a period which, measured in absolute terms, brought unprecedented prosperity to most sections of British society.[9]

More precisely the post-war period saw the railways, gas, and electricity taken into public ownership. Government both increased its aid for, and its regulation of, private enterprise.[10] The welfare state was expanded to include a National Health Service and the provision of sickness, unemployment, and retirement benefits.[11] The expansion of the welfare state occurred, Henry Clark suggests, for a number of reasons, including the influence of a new social philosophy, English Ethical Socialism.[12] Additionally the trade unions were 'brought into both formal and informal contact with the Government in a continu-

---

6   Seldon, 'Consensus', 45-46. Seldon outlines the reasons for the Conservative's continuance of the policies of the Attlee Government, amongst them the particular influence of Churchill. 'His policy preferences, his appointments and his very presence were central to the consolidation of consensus.'

7   Seldon, 'Consensus', 48.

8   Medhurst & Moyser, *Secular*, 34.

9   *ibid*, 35.

10   D. Kavanagh, *British Politics: Continuities and Change* (Oxford: Oxford University Press, 1985), 52-53.

11   *ibid*, 53.

12   Henry Clark gives the following reasons for the expansion of the welfare state: 'The first was the result of advances in social science (particularly Keynesianism, most especially Keynesian doctrine as assimilated into the thinking of a new generation of political leaders such as Beveridge and Macmillan). The second was the appearance of a new social philosophy which stressed individual rights and denounced the extremes of class stratification and economic inequality which had been more or less accepted for centuries in most European countries before the nineteenth century. The third was the historical experience of the British people in the twentieth

ing relationship' and policies (including heavy progressive taxation) pursued to reduce economic inequalities.[13] Between the main parties 'arguments persisted about the exact nature or extent of State responsibility, but the concepts of the welfare state and of the mixed economy continued to command general assent.'[14]

A thorough re-examination of the policies of the post-war consensus came during the 1970s due to the persistence of certain economic and social problems. Domestically, '[t]he promise of sustained economic growth had been disappointed and no obvious alternative basis remained upon which to rebuild confidence.'[15] Internationally, shrinking military power, an inability to maintain international defence commitments, the loss of Empire, and diminishing economic competitiveness heightened the pressure for new policies and approaches to British government. Britain, dismissively labelled the 'sick man of Europe', was in crisis and political remedies were in high demand. The post-Callaghan Labour Party continued to propose the extension of state powers to engineer economic recovery and protect Britain's international economic interests. This continuation and extension of Keynesian economic policies was combined, perhaps fatally, with support for unilateral nuclear disarmament.[16] The Conservative Party led, from 1975, by Margaret Thatcher favoured a radical break with current economic policies involving a massive reduction in state activity and manipulation of the economy, alongside the fostering of an environment conducive to entrepreneurial wealth creation.[17] Wealth redistribution was abandoned in favour of the 'trickle-down' effect and the pursuit of the ideal of equality abandoned in the belief that an enterprise economy needed the incentive of varying wage levels.[18] The SDP-Liberal Alliance shared the Labour Party's desire to 'reforge a consensual pattern of politics' and sought to steer a 'middle course between prevailing Conservative

---

century, particularly the hardships of the Great Depression and the frightening but exhilarating challenges of the Second World War.' H. Clark, *The Church Under Thatcher* (London: SPCK, 1993), 2.

13 Seldon, 'Consensus', 43.

14 Medhurst & Moyser, *Secular*, 35.

15 *ibid*, 39-40.

16 *ibid*, 43.

17 Peter Hennessy wryly observes the impact of Thatcher's leadership upon the post-war consensus: 'Heath was not alone when he called on the Queen on 4th march 1974. The post-war consensus, too, when with him to resign.' P. Hennessy, *The Prime Minister: The Office and its Holders since 1945* (London: Penguin, 2001), 356.

18 Seldon, 'Consensus', 53.

and Labour orthodoxies'[19] but failed to achieve electoral successes after 1982.[20] The only policy area in which a real consensus remained into the 1980s between the main political parties was the welfare state.[21]

With the election of Michael Foot as Leader of the Labour party in 1980, 'both parties had their most left- and right-wing leaders respectively since 1945.'[22] Under these leaders there was a shift in the British political landscape in which diametrically opposed responses to national concerns were pitted against one another. Where the hallmark of the political process had been consensus, it was now confrontation.[23]

2.1.2 Thatcherism and the New Right

Until 1979, then, the British ideal was that the 'haves' would help the 'have-nots', with the government as the most reliable middle-man. The arrival of Margaret Thatcher destroyed that consensus. She took on the forces of paternalism – the wets in her own party, the BBC, the Church of England, the universities, even on occasion the House of Lords and the Royal Family – and set out to crush socialism, declaring the trade unions nothing less than 'the enemy within'. The Thatcherite vision proclaimed that government would no longer act as a vast steamroller, levelling the playing field of life. The rich would have less of their income redistributed to the poor via taxes and the welfare state.[24]

Where the post-war consensus rallied around English ethical socialism in part justification for its economic policies and Conservatism traditionally operated on the basis pragmatism, eschewing ideology,[25] the Thatcherite politicians who came to dominate the Conservative Party of the 1980s, increasingly saw politics as a contest between opposing and mutually exclusive ideas. Thatcherism

---

19   Medhurst & Moyser, *Secular*, 44.
20   Kavanagh, *Reordering*, 183.
21   Seldon, 'Consensus', 54.
22   Kavanagh, *Reordering*, 67.
23   'The last few years', wrote R.H. Preston in 1983, 'have seen an astonishing change in public opinion in this country in the area of economics and politics. The broad consensus which was called Butskellism, from the time when R.A. Butler and Hugh Gaitskell were leading figures in the Tory and Labour parties respectively, has almost disappeared.' See R.H. Preston, *Church and Society in the Late Twentieth Century: The Economic and Political Task* (London: SCM Press, 1983), 59.
24   J. Freedland, *Bring Home the Revolution* (London: Fourth Estate, 1998), 134.
25   B. Jones, 'Conservatism', in Jones et al., *Politics UK*, 125.

drew its guiding ideology from the seminal New Right thinkers Frie-
drich Von Hayek and Milton Friedman and the various think-tanks,
especially the Institute of Economic Affairs and the Centre for Policy
Studies, who espoused and applied their ideas.[26] Clark summarises
the central tenets of New Right thinking:[27]

1) Poverty must only be measured in 'absolute quantitative
   terms'.
2) Political freedom is the 'supreme human and social value'.
3) The laws of the market cannot be contravened by human
   action.
4) 'There is no injustice without the malicious intent on the part of
   some evildoer.'
5) People of 'extraordinary merit rise to the top, and they deserve
   the handsome rewards they get.'
6) People who are 'losers in the market game should be stigmatised
   by public disapproval, for only if driven to desperation will the
   best of them do whatever they must to become winners.'

Thatcherism, notes Kavanagh, 'was a matter of both style and policies'.[28] Kavanagh proposes four main principles upon which Thatcherite policies were constructed.[29] Firstly, the priority of halting the
growth of the money supply as a method of tackling the crippling
inflation of the 1970s. Secondly, the reduction of the size of the public
sector and the aim of creating a free-market-oriented economy. This
culminated in the return to private ownership of large swathes of
the public sector industry and service provision, and the withdrawal
of Government support for loss-making industries. Taxes were cut
(funded by public spending reductions) and regulations dismantled
so as to improve the environment for entrepreneurial enterprise and
economic growth. Thirdly, the deconstruction of the trade-unions'
suffocating control of the labour market. Fourthly, the re-establish-
ment of governmental authority, involving increasing funding for
the Armed Forces and the Police. 'In all, the four themes married the

---

26 Kavanagh, *Reordering*, 90-91.
27 Clark, *Under*, 6.
28 Kavanagh, *Reordering*, 25.
29 *ibid*, 25-26. Brendan Evans asserts the importance of seeing Thatcherism
    within the historic development of Conservatism: 'There were no Thatcher-
    ite values which could not be discovered in previous Conservative history.
    Social conservatism, social order and discipline, the free market, fiscal pru-
    dence, patriotism, effective central government, a strong leader, the defence
    of property and privilege have all been elements of Conservative political
    history.' B. Evans, *Thatcherism and British Politics 1975-1999* (Stroud: Sutton,
    1999), 246.

values of a strong state and a free economy.'[30]

Upon every side the structure of the welfare and semi-socialist state was to be chipped away in favour of the extension of individual or capitalist initiative – in education, health, the social services, the wider concern for the environment, the infrastructure of local government, the ownership of the means of production.[31]

2.1.3 The Crusading Prime Minister

That the term 'Thatcherism' even exists is indicative of Mrs Thatcher's personal impact upon the British political landscape.[32] Her impact, however, was more far-reaching than the political arena:

> Mrs Thatcher was not only Prime Minister for longer than any other holder of the office this century: she was a hyperactive and interventionist Prime Minister who was closely involved in practically everything that happened in Britain – and much that happened throughout the world – during the 1980s. Even where she was not directly responsible she nevertheless personified the decade... The years 1979 to 1990 will always be the Thatcher years...[33]

So much of Thatcher's impact was the result of what Brendan Evans calls the 'Thatcher factor' – her leadership style, her dominant personality and the subtle use she made of her femininity.[34] From the Cabinet Room[35] to the European Council her approach was 'entirely adversarial',[36] making it inevitable that the political culture of the 1980s would be one of conflict and polarization, not compromise and

---

30 Kavanagh, *Reordering*, 26, dependent upon A. Gamble, *The Free Economy and Strong State* (London: Macmillan, 1994).

31 A. Hastings, *A History of English Christianity: 1920-1985* (London: William Collins, 1986), 594.

32 K. Minogue, 'Introduction: The Context of Thatcherism', in K. Minogue & M. Biddis (eds.), *Thatcherism: Personality and Politics* (London: Macmillan, 1987), x-xii.

33 Campbell, *Thatcher*, xi.

34 Evans, *Thatcherism*, xi.

35 John Major provides a window on a Thatcher Cabinet meeting, contrasting it to his own more consensual approach: 'Margaret had often introduced subjects in Cabinet by setting out her favoured solution: shameless but effective. I, by contrast, preferred to let my views be known in private, see potential disasters ahead of the meeting, encourage discussion, and sum up after it... Margaret had been at her happiest confronting political dragons; I chose consensus in policy-making, if not always in policy.' J. Major, *The Autobiography* (London: Harper Collins, 1999), 209.

36 H. Young, *One of Us: A Biography of Margaret Thatcher* (London: Macmillan 1989), 149. Peter Hennessy notes the significance of the Falklands War for the

bargaining. This strong, almost aggressive persona was perceived from afar, as well as at home, prompting the Soviet Army Newspaper, *Red Star*, to christen her 'The Iron Lady'.[37]

The political style [of Thatcherism] – emanating from Mrs Thatcher herself – vigorously challenged many established beliefs and interests, boldly expressed personal and often right-wing views, and did not compromise on many deeply held political principles.[38]

Henry Clark describes Thatcherism as a 'religious crusade',[39] pointing to Thatcher's famous 'speech-cum-sermon' to the Scottish Kirk in May 1988 as the primary justification for his judgement.[40] Clark also looks to Hugo Young's observation that a 'sense of moral rectitude' was an essential characteristic of her leadership.[41] John Campbell makes the same point as Young, going on to argue that it was her 'crusading spirit which was Thatcher's unique contribution to the counter-revolution which ultimately bore her name':[42]

> More than anything else in her political makeup, it was her fierce confidence that she knew right from wrong – even if what was right was not always immediately attainable – which marked her

---

development of her style: '[I]t was the Falklands War which remains her own abiding memory of her premiership and certainly the fulcrum around which her power and her style most significantly revolved... The Falklands War was the defining event of her premiership.' Hennessy, *Prime Minister*, 412.

37 I. Gilmour & M. Garnett, *Whatever Happened to the Tories: The Conservatives Since 1945* (London: Fourth Estate, 1998), 303.

38 Kavanagh, *Reordering*, 25.

39 Thatcher herself used the term 'crusade' to desribe her political mission. Speaking to the 1976 Conservative Party Conference she gave a rousing appeal to stir the hearts of her ground-troops: 'I call the Conservative Party to a crusade. Not only the Conservative Party. I appeal to all those men and women of goodwill who do not want a Marxist future...' Cited by Campbell, *Thatcher*, 382. It is worth digressing to note that, from 1978 onwards, Conservative Party Conferences were organised by Harvey Thomas, the man who staged rallies for the American evangelist Billy Graham. Campbell, Thatcher, 345.

40 Clark, *Under*, 10. On the importance of the speech to the Scottish Kirk within Thatcher's 'zealous and puritanical Reformation' see J. Raban, *God, Man and Mrs Thatcher* (London: Chatto & Windus, 1989), 67-68.

41 Young, *One*, 543.

42 Campbell, *Thatcher*, 187. The phrase 'crusader' is also used by Michael Biddis to describe Thatcher: 'Even before General Galtieri gave her the opportunity to become quite literally so, there was something of the crusading leader in Mrs Thatcher.' M. Biddis, 'Thatcherism: Concept and Interpretations', in K. Minogue & M. Biddis (eds.), *Thatcherism: Personality and Politics* (London: Macmillan, 1987), 3-4.

out from contemporary politicians. She believed absolutely in her own integrity and habitually disparaged the motives of those who disagreed with her. This rare moral certainty and unreflective self-righteousness was her greatest political strength in the muddy world of political expediency and compromise; it was also her greatest weakness.[43]

As a child Margaret Thatcher attended the local Wesleyan Methodist Church[44] to which her parents belonged.[45] Under the influence of her father, lay-preacher and Alderman Alfred Roberts, she was fed on a diet of theology which focused on personal salvation and personal holiness, and in which a social gospel which stepped beyond personal acts of generosity was unknown.[46] As an adult, partly as a result of her marriage to a divorcee, she only maintained 'an irregular association' with the Church of England.[47] Her chief religious influences, however, lay elsewhere. Victorian virtues[48] and a superficial understanding of Old Testament ethics, more than the Christian gospel itself, shaped Margaret Thatcher's religious world view. In her account of her tenure as Prime Minister she comments thus:

> I do not, as a Christian, believe that the Old Testament – the history of the Law – can be fully understood without the New Testament – the history of Mercy. But I often wished that Christian leaders would take a leaf out of Britain's wonderful Chief Rabbi, Immanuel Jackobovits, and indeed that Christians themselves would take closer note of the Jewish emphasis on self-help and acceptance of personal responsibility.[49]

When Mrs Thatcher won the Finchley constituency in 1959 it was

---

43   Campbell, *Thatcher*, 31. See also Young, *One*, 544. Campbell provocatively describes the 'iconography of Grantham' as being 'almost as familiar as the manger in Bethlehem'. He goes on: 'The problem with this iconography is that it originates with Mrs Thatcher herself... she has successfully controlled the presentation of her life story as an improving morality play, illustrating the rewards – personal and national – of hard work, self-reliance, family values and practical Christianity.' Campbell, *Thatcher*, 1-2.

44   A tradition of Methodism distinct from the wider body of nonconformity normally associated with left-wing politics. Campbell, *Thatcher*, 16.

45   *ibid*.

46   *ibid*.

47   Young, *One*, 6, 36.

48   M. Thatcher, *The Downing Street Years* (London: Harper Collins, 1993), 627. Thatcher explains the reason for her 'great regard' for the Victorians with reference to their 'civic spirit' and their distinction between the 'deserving' and 'undeserving' poor.

49   *ibid*, 510. This unqualified dichotomy between the Law and Mercy reveals something of the naiveté of her theological outlook.

20% Jewish,[50] initiating an association with the Jewish faith which remained significant throughout her years as Prime Minister. Hugo Young goes so far as to argue that, particularly as a result of his critical response to the *Faith in the City* report of the Archbishop's Commission, Jackobovits was, 'in effect, the spiritual leader of Thatcherite Britain.'[51] Jackobovits provided her with the religious justifications for her policies, fuelling the moral superiority which dominated her dealings with enemies both inside and outside her own party.

2.1.4 Her Majesty's Opposition

'The legitimacy of the activity of political opposition,' writes Dennis Kavanagh, 'is reflected in the statutory duty levied on the Speaker to designate the leader of the largest party not in government as Leader of Her Majesty's Opposition.'[52] A strong political opposition is essential to good government. During the 1980s the Labour Party, under the leadership of Michael Foot (1980-83) and Neil Kinnock (1983-1992), was a weak and divided challenge to the Thatcher Governments.[53] Thatcher's mean satisfaction rating for her 11 years in power makes her the second least popular Prime Minister of the post-1945 era.[54] Nevertheless between 1979 and 1997 the Labour Party experienced its longest period of opposition since it became a national party in 1918.[55]

From 1951 to 1979 the Labour Party experienced a dramatic decline in electoral support[56] with its vote share shrinking from 47% in 1966 to 37% in 1979.[57] After 1979 alternative responses to the crisis were given by the left- and right-wings of the Labour Party, with the left-wing view prevailing in official policy. This proved disastrous for the Party's attempts to regain electoral support. The memory of

---

50 Young, *One*, 40.
51 *ibid*, 424. Young also points to Thatcher's relationship with Anglo-Catholic Bishop Graham Leonard as an indication of the extent to which her true allegiance lay apart from mainstream Anglicanism. Young, *One*, 420.
52 Kavanagh, *British*, 231.
53 Evans, *Thatcherism*, 53-54.
54 On the basis of the results of the monthly Gallup poll, undertaken since 1945, asking the question: 'Are you satisfied or dissatisfied with x as Prime Minister?' Mrs Thatcher's mean satisfaction rating for her 11 years in power was 39%. Gallup, as cited by Kavanagh, *Reordering*, 133.
55 *ibid*, 171.
56 'By 1979 Labour had undergone the most spectacular electoral decline of any socialist party in the post-war period. Between 1951 and 1979 it lost vote share at every general election bar 1966...' Kavanagh, Reordering, 175.
57 *ibid*.

the left-wing policies of the Heath Government which had conspicuously failed to alleviate economic and social problems were etched
onto the consciousness of the electorate and, of course, New Right
rhetoricians. 'No alternative' lines of argument prevailed, repeatedly handing electoral success to the Conservative Party. The Labour
Party was further weakened by the alliance of the Social Democratic
Party and the Liberal Party at the beginning of the 1980s which 'acted
as a siphon for disillusioned Labour supporters and as a reminder of
the party's "extremism".'[58]

2.2 A Consensus-driven Church

2.2.1 Diversity and Decline

The UK Anglican Church, like all other institutional Churches in
the UK has seen decline in recent years – though not as sharp as, for
instance, attendance at football matches or membership of trades
union. But the hinterland around every Anglican Church is still
full of nominal Anglicans, who are fundamentally well-disposed
to the Church of England.[59]

Grace Davie, writing in 1994, concludes that 'the dominant impression of Anglicanism remains a rather depressing, though regionally
varied, statistical profile, alongside an increasing fragmentation in liturgy and worship.'[60] The same features of diversity and decline characterized the Anglican[61] Church during the 1980s. Between 1980 and
1990 Anglican Church attendance dropped from 967,000 to 916,700[62]
as part of a decline which saw average weekly Church attendance in
England drop from 12% of the population in 1979 to 10% in 1989.[63]
It was fitting, therefore, that the 1988 Lambeth Conference decided
to christen the 1990s the 'Decade of Evangelism'.[64] Anglican leaders

---

58 *ibid*, 224.
59 Peter Brierley, as cited by D. Rogers, *Politics, Prayer and Parliament* (London:
    Continuum, 2000), 113.
60 G. Davie, *Religion in Britain Since 1945: Believing Without Belonging* (Oxford:
    Blackwell, 1994), 55.
61 Davie notes that the term 'Anglican' includes the Church of England, the
    Church in Wales, the Episcopal Church of Scotland, and the Church of Ire-
    land. The Church of England accounts for 80% of Anglican membership.
    ibid, 51.
62 P. Brierley & H. Wraight (eds.), *UK Christian Handbook*, 1996/97 Edition
    (London: Christian Research, 1995), Table 11.
63 P. Brierley, 'Religion in Britain 1900 to 2000', in P. Brierley & D. Longley
    (eds.), *UK Christian Handbook*, 2000/01 Edition (London: Christian Research,
    1999), 26.

were left seeking justification for their political involvement in the Church's large nominal membership (estimated at 25.8 million in 1990)[65] and in the Church's claim, as the English national church, to minister not only to those who regularly attended Church services, but to the whole community in each of its 13,000 parishes.[66] During the 1980s, as today, the situation looked bleak. There is, however, a need to keep the present situation in perspective:

> [T]he weaknesses of the Church can be exaggerated by those with a romantic view of its past, or ignorance of its present life. Diminished in numbers and distanced from Westminster, it is still the largest network of voluntary associations for social well-being in this country. Time and again it is this network, mostly staffed by the laity, that nudges the government. Above all, the Church still provides a nationwide meeting place for people of otherwise differing opinions to seek and find divine inspiration.[67]

Decline in Church attendance was accompanied by growing diversity within the Church:

> Divisions, which have hitherto been mainly contained, are now becoming so critical that a consensus can no longer be sustained. The old familiar splits persist, such as those discerned between Catholic and Reformed (Evangelical). The two wings, however, seem to unite in the face of another grouping – 'the liberal establishment'.[68]

Added to this there were factions which developed to lobby for gay rights, the ordination of women and the protection of the Book of Common Prayer. Yet throughout the 1980s a measure of unity (or consensus) was sustained. It was, as is 'par' for the course, a strained consensus, involving every bit as much politicking as existed in the national politics of post-war Britain. It was also a consensus of style more than substance, where conflicts were resolved through 'a proc-

---

64 It should, however, be noted that the impetus at the 1988 Lambeth Conference for the Decade of Evangelism came not from the English bishops, but from the African bishops.

65 Brierley & Wraight (eds.), *Handbook*, 1996/97 Edition, Table 11.

66 The Archbishops' Council, *The Role of the Bishops in the Second Chamber*, GS Misc 558 (London: Church House Publishing, 1999), 3.

67 Robert Runcie, speaking on Church and State to the Coningsby Club, London during 1984 as cited by D. Say, 'Nudging the Government: Runcie and Public Affairs', in S. Platten (ed.), *Runcie: On Reflection*, (Norwich: Canterbury Press, 2002).

68 Wesley Carr, 'Is there a future for the Church of England?', in W. Carr (ed.), *Say One for Me: The Church of England in the Next Decade*, cited by M. Furlong, C of E: The State It's In (London: Hodder & Stoughton, 2000), 227.

ess of compromise and bargaining'[69] in order to protect the superficial unity of the Church.

2.2.2 Synodical Government

Synodical government is 'an essentially democratic process'[70] which provides a forum congenial to consensus style decision-making.[71] At the top of its pyramidal structure is General Synod consisting of the House of Bishops, the House of Clergy and the House of Laity. The members of the Houses of Clergy and Laity are re-elected once in five years.[72] There were two primary reasons for the shift to Synodical government.[73] The first was to reduce the control that Parliament had over the affairs of the Church, creating more freedom for the Church and more space in the Parliamentary programme. The second was to create a system which facilitated lay and clerical, as well as episcopal, input into the Church's policy-making. Indeed, with the advent of Synodical government in 1970, the hierarchical authority of the episcopate was reduced.[74] Within Synod the bishops are 'only one part of the decision-making body, and regularly the House of Bishops vote in a different direction to the Houses of Clergy and Laity.'[75] Nevertheless, the historic authority of the bishops has not been entirely subsumed within the democratic structures of Synodical government and alongside Synod there continues to exist a source of authority which is 'traditional, pastoral, and hierarchical' and which 'finds its fullest expression in the – largely undefined – authority of bishops'.[76] As the Catholic and Reformed traditions

---

69   Kavanagh, *Reordering*, 10.
70   Davie, *Religion*, 172.
71   Prior to 1970 the government of the Church of England was performed by two sets of bodies: the Convocations of Canterbury and York (the oldest legislative bodies in England) and the Church Assembly (which came into being as a result of the Enabling Act (1919)). P.A. Welsby, *How the Church of England Works* (London: Church Information Office, 1985), 49.
72   Hastings, *Robert Runcie* (London: Mowbray, 1991), 67.
73   *ibid.*
74   K.A. Thompson, 'The Church of England Bishops as an Elite', in P. Stanworth & A. Giddens (ed's.), *Elites and Power in British Society* (Cambridge: Cambridge University Press, 1974), 206.
75   J. Whale, *The Anglican Church Today: The Future of Anglicanism* (Oxford: Mowbray, 1988), 41.
76   J. Habgood, *Church and Nation in a Secular Age* (London: Darton, Longman & Todd, 1983), 115. Habgood is dependent here on Thompson, *Bureaucracy and Church Reform* (Oxford: Clarendon Press, 1970).

continue to co-exist theologically within the Church of England so the two traditions also continue to co-exist organizationally.[77] Thus organizationally and theologically we see consensus and compromise at work maintaining the unity of the communion.

With the shift to Synodical government the importance of the social and political aspects of the Christian mission were written into the structures of the Church of England, giving it both a greater legitimacy and a greater claim on the human and financial resources of the Church.[78] In his essay 'The General Synod and Politics', Giles Ecclestone notes the General Synod mandate to 'consider and express their opinions on any other matters of religious or public interest.'[79] In particular the decision of each Synodical government to set up a Board for Social Responsibility as one of its principal Advisory Committees (with terms of reference 'to promote and co-ordinate the thought and action of the Church in matters affecting man's life in society') has ensured that since the 'inception of Synodical Government... the Church's voice has been regularly and systematically heard in public on matters affecting society as a whole.'[80] Indeed, every meeting of the General Synod has involved a minimum of one debate on these kinds of issues and press coverage of their deliberations has been encouraged.[81] Hugh Montefiore points to the increasing number of General Synod debates on matters of social concern during the late 1980s, arguing that there was an additional reason why social concern rose up Synod's agenda:

> [T]he chief reason lies in the ending by Mrs Thatcher's successive administrations of the political consensus which has grown up between the parties on social questions after the Second World War. New policies have been brought forward. This, I think, is the explanation for the increase in such debates in the General Synod in the last six or seven years compared with the initial period some

---

77 Davie, *Religion*, 172.
78 G. Ecclestone, 'The General Synod and Politics', in G.H. Moyser (ed.), *Church and Politics Today: The Role of the Church of England in Contemporary Politics* (Edinburgh: T & T Clark, 1985), 111.
79 Article 6b of the Constitution of General Synod, as cited by Ecclestone, 'Synod', 110.
80 As cited by Ecclestone, 'Synod', 110-111. Hugh Montefiore describes himself as being under 'some pressure, while Chairman of the Board for Social Responsibility, to produce a subject for discussion at each Group of Sessions, to prevent Synodical discussion from becoming too inward looking.' H. Montefiore, *Christianity and Politics* (London: Macmillan, 1990), 76.
81 Ecclestone, 'Synod', 112.

sixteen years ago. The Church and its chief spokesmen have had a positive duty to subject those new policies to Christian scrutiny...[82]

2.2.3 Transformer of Culture

The centrality of social and political issues to the Church of England's agenda after 1970 was the structural outworking of a long-term shift to the left in Christian social theology:[83]

> The Church of England as a whole, and its corporate leadership in particular, has indisputably shifted its centre of gravity to the left (in conventional secular terms), and to some degree raised the priority accorded to its social and political engagement.[84]

Medhurst and Moyser highlight certain features of the Christian attitudes resultant from this shift.[85] There was a growing:

1) Disengagement from alliances with those forces which 'legitimate traditional, hierarchically structured forms of social organisation'.
2) Questioning of 'inherited Church-State alliances'.
3) Emphasis on the servanthood nature of the Church's role.
4) Willingness to 'associate the Church with the victims rather than the beneficiaries of economic, social, or political inequalities'.
5) Theological recognition of the 'sometimes destructive effects of impersonal social structures and... a Christian responsibility for transforming them'.

A comparison of the central tenets of the New Right thinking which underpinned the Thatcherite agenda with this list (particularly the fourth and fifth features) exposes the extent to which the social philosophies of Church and State were opposed during the Thatcher years (Section 2.1.2 above).

The shift which has taken place within Anglican socio-political thought is essentially a shift from Niebuhr's 'Christ in Culture' model of Christian cultural engagement (the 'Christendom model' in which Christianity is equated with particular cultural, social, and political frameworks) towards his 'Transformer of Culture' model (in which Christianity works within existing cultural, social, and political frameworks in order to 'promote change').[86] '[T]he rise of

---

82   Montefiore, *Politics*, 76.
83   Medhurst & Moyser, *Secular*, 65 and Preston, *Church and Society*, 75-92.
84   G.H. Moyser, 'The Church of England and Politics: Patterns and Trends', in Moyser (ed.), *Today*, 22.
85   Medhurst & Moyser, *Secular*, 65-66.
86   *ibid*, 355-357. Exponents of the 'Transformer of Culture' model (referred to by Niebuhr as 'conversionists') are described by Niebuhr thus: 'The

social Christianity manifested itself in Anglican thought and practice, changing the Church of England from a relatively docile supporter of the established order to resolute foe of injustice.'[87] Medhurst and Moyser are sagacious, however, in remaining concerned to emphasize factors which 'militate against' a full shift to the 'Transformer of Culture' model.[88] These include the Church's established status which ensures that, irrespective of the strength of their 'radical impulses',[89] the Church's leaders can never fully extricate themselves from the need to stand alongside, as well as to bring prophetic challenge to, those in positions of political authority.[90]

2.2.4 Ecumenism

Grace Davie asserts that 'the shift from mutual hostility towards active co-operation – never mind toleration – on the part of most, if not quite all, of the churches in contemporary Britain is one of the most remarkable stories of the post-war decades.'[91] Ecumenism has fostered a considerable change in the religious atmosphere of the nation whilst itself coinciding with, and feeding off, a general increase in toleration as a popular virtue within Western liberal-democratic cultures. At a national and local level the British Council of Churches, inaugurated in 1942, has provided the focus for ecu-

---

conversionist, with his view of history as the present encounter with God in Christ, does not live so much in the expectation of a final ending of the world of creation and culture as in awareness of the power of the Lord to transform all things by lifting them up to himself. His imagery is spatial and not temporal; and the movement of life he finds to be issuing from Jesus Christ is an upward movement, the rising of men's souls and deeds and thoughts in a mighty surge of adoration and glorification of the One who draws them to himself. That is what human culture can be – a transformed human life in and to the glory of God.' Niebuhr writes of the influential Anglican F.D. Maurice whose thought was at the core of English Ethical Socialism: 'In Maurice the conversionist idea is more clearly expressed than in any other modern Christian thinker and leader.' H.R. Niebuhr, *Christ and Culture* (London: Faber & Faber, 1952), 197.

87 Clark, *Under*, 2.
88 Medhurst & Moyser, *Secular*, 358-359.
89 *ibid*.
90 The significance of the established status of the Church of England will be considered in more detail below (Section 2.3.1).
91 Davie, *Religion*, 164. For the pessimistic view see B. Wilson, *Religion in Secular Society: A Sociological Comment*, (London: C.A. Watts, 1966), 128. For the optimistic view see B. Till, *The Churches Search for Unity*, (Harmondsworth: Penguin, 1972), 26-31.

menical dialogue and endeavours. Internationally, the driving force behind this ecumenical shift has been, since 1948, the World Council of Churches which Anglicans have played a prominent role in creating, staffing, and financing.[92] Both organizations are inclusivistic, holding together (albeit precariously) and facilitating the co-operation of the complete rainbow of Christian worldviews through consensus style decision-making.

Ecumenism is explained by some sociologists as a response to growing strength and confidence within the Churches, by others as a sign of a level of weakness which has made interdenominational co-operation essential.[93] Whatever the explanation, one outworking has been a growing co-operation between the Christian denominations in the public realm which is widely held to have benefited the causes of the Churches. Medhurst and Moyser rightly assert that, when seeking to influence Government policy-making, 'ecclesiastical leaders who can claim to speak authoritatively for Christians at large seem more likely to command attention than those speaking from a narrower base.'[94] One of the main ways in which the public voice of the Churches is co-ordinated is through the Churches Main Committee, which was set up in 1941 by the Churches in response to the provisions of the first War Damage Bill.[95] Most of the mainline Churches are members of the Churches Main Committee. It provides a forum for the exchange of views and the reaching of a united position of any secular matter (with the exception of education) which is of interest to its members.

The ecumenical movement has also played a part in the leftward shift of Anglican socio-political thought, particularly in fostering a theological recognition of the 'sometimes destructive effects of impersonal social structures and... a Christian responsibility for transforming them.' Medhurst and Moyser describe the emergence of indigenous Third World Churches (and the resultant shift in the internal balance of power of the World Council of Churches) as resulting, within the international Christian community, in 'a heightened awareness of the often negative consequences of industrialization and of post-colonial international economic arrangements.'[96]

---

92 Clark, *Under*, 20 and P.A. Welsby, *A History of the Church of England 1945-1980* (Oxford: Oxford University Press, 1984), 78-80, 86-87.

93 Davie, *Religion*, 164.

94 Medhurst & Moyser, *Secular*, 365.

95 J.S. Peart-Binns, *Graham Leonard: Bishop of London* (London: Darton, Longman & Todd, 1988), 243.

96 Medhurst & Moyser, *Secular*, 67.

2.2.5 The Anglican Clergy

The Church of England (one of Kavanagh's 'governing elites') gave assent to the policies of the post-war political consensus and the consensus style of doing business. This was an entirely natural development since the English ethical socialism which underpinned the post-war political consensus had been 'deeply influenced by the Christian faith'.[97] Indeed, the post-war consensus 'to a substantial degree embodied the measures which the more socially conscious inter-war churchmen had long advocated' and there was little for the Church to criticize.[98] This post-1920s support for the liberal-left consensus from the clergy of the Church of England has, however, 'surfaced most dramatically since the political consensus broke up into radical right and radical left in the mid-1970s.'[99] One indicator is to be found in the support given by more than half the clergy of the major denominations (as opposed to only a quarter of the electorate) to the SDP-Liberal Alliance.[100] Another is offered by Medhurst and Moyser who, writing in 1988, note that in their interviews with bishops they found 'a general perception that the bulk of their colleagues could be broadly identified with centrist to moderate left-of-centre political postures.'[101]

As the Thatcher years marched on the dissenting voice of senior churchmen against the substance of Government policy, and the New Right social philosophy which was used to justify it, became both comprehensive and detailed. Grace Davie describes it as one aspect of an 'unravelling of... solidarities' in which the Church, but also the BBC and the universities 'emerged as the defenders of the old-left liberal consensus and the politics of welfare...'[102] Conservative Ministers were enraged, the media were enthralled,[103] and the confrontational style of the political debate – something the Church strongly objected to – extended beyond the main political parties to include the Church itself.

---

97 S. Lee & P. Stanford, *Believing Bishops* (London: Faber & Faber, 1990), 20. See also Kavanagh, *British*, 15.

98 Medhurst & Moyser, *Secular*, 47.

99 D. Martin, 'The Churches: Pink Bishops and the Iron Lady', in A. Seldon & D. Kavanagh (eds.), *The Thatcher Effect: A Decade of Change* (Oxford: Clarendon Press, 1989), 336.

100 *ibid.*

101 Medhurst & Moyser, *Secular*, 127.

102 Davie, *Religion*, 150, dependent upon Martin, 'Pink', 340.

103 Lee & Stanford, *Believing*, 21.

2.2.6 The Diplomatic Archbishop

Robert Runcie, the 102nd Archbishop of Canterbury, was enthroned in 1980 in a service reflecting his liberal-Catholic churchmanship. Paul Welsby, writing in 1984, assesses Runcie in relation to his post-war predecessors:

> The new archbishop is a marked contrast to his three predecessors. He lacks the administrative flair of Dr Fisher, the deep scholarship, the creative intellect, and the spiritual other-worldliness of Dr Ramsey and the earnest evangelizing spirit of Dr Coggan. Yet he is an able administrator, a person of deep spirituality and committed to the reconciling power of the Gospel.[104]

Above all Robert Runcie was a diplomat.[105] His style was to 'preside rather than to lead'.[106] In this sense Hugh Montefiore (Bishop of Birmingham) gave the following description of Runcie to Humphrey Carpenter:

> He was an intelligent archbishop, but he was a great sitter on the fence... Until he saw which way the wind was blowing, he wouldn't commit himself. He did in the end, but not very strongly. I must say, I always felt this was constitutional. It wasn't his fault, and no one could blame him... He always thought diplomatically rather than theologically.[107]

Arguably diplomacy was essential to the archiepiscopal role, especially amidst the changes of the 1980s. However, a diplomatic character coupled with a liberal-Catholic churchmanship proved less helpful in Runcie's relations with Thatcher and her Government. 'His eye for moral complexity, coupled with his staunch refusal to espouse an extreme position on any part of the agenda with which the Tories presented him,' notes Hugo Young, 'marked him out as

---

104 Welsby, *History*, 284.

105 Hastings, *History*, 613 and Hastings, *Runcie*, 102-103.

106 'The Most Rev Lord Runcie', Obituary, *The Times*, 13th July 2000. Adrian Hastings draws the same conclusion with regard to Runcie's involvement in General Synod: 'While Ramsey too often simply looked bored... and while Coggan preached, Runcie truly presides. He has influenced it a great deal by the care he has given to it, his loyalty to its decisions, his lack of partisanship and willingness (perhaps over-willingness) to admit that while he will vote one way, he has considerable sympathy for the other point of view too.' Hastings, *Runcie*, 70.

107 Hugh Montefiore in an interview with H. Carpenter, *Robert Runcie: The Reluctant Archbishop* (London: Hodder & Stoughton, 1996), 142.

a man destined for ever to irritate them.'[108] Adrian Hastings agrees, whilst recognising that their working relationship was by no means hijacked by their essential differences:

> He has probably irritated her far more than she has irritated him because she cannot stand disagreement within the establishment while he takes it for granted. Their styles are different... Nevertheless no Archbishop in this century can have had easier access to the Prime Minister. They have had to co-operate continually over the appointment of bishops and, perhaps still more closely, of deans. They have done so without significant disagreement, despite the fact that Mrs Thatcher paid a lot of attention to the appointment of bishops, in which she personally took great interest... Runcie's archiepiscopate has, nevertheless, been more profoundly affected by a single Prime Minister than any before him. Her sense of the Church and religion as a force for the reinforcement of personal morality is rather different from his. His conviction of having a political responsibility, and his frequent participation within what can be called the public-secular field in a non-Thatcherite way have been in consequence the underlying cause of much of the vituperation he has suffered.[109]

Runcie's character and convictions could simply never support brash, black-and-white Thatcherite solutions to complicated, long-standing problems – especially when there was an immediate social cost for which to budget.[110] Runcie was a consensus-man in style and substance[111] leading a consensus-driven Church. Thatcherism

---

108 Young, *One*, 421. Adrian Hastings suggests another factor may also explain some of the tension inherent in the Runcie-Thatcher relationship during the 1980s: 'While Lang was chosen by Baldwin, Temple and Fisher by Churchill, Ramsey by Macmillan and Coggan by Wilson, Runcie had not been chosen by Mrs Thatcher but by a Commission of the Church, including several of his fellow bishops. Mrs Thatcher had merely accepted their choice, by no means the same thing.' Hastings, *Runcie*, 46.

109 Hastings, *Runcie*, 52.

110 Runcie gave expression to this approach during his enthronement service: 'The cry is "the church must give a firm lead". Yes, it must – a firm lead against rigid thinking, a judging temper of mind, the disposition to over-simplify the difficult and complex problems. If the church gives Jesus Christ's sort of lead it will not be popular.' Cited by Lee & Stanford, *Believing*, 16.

111 Martin refers to an interview with *The Times*, 28th September 1984, describing Runcie's comments as being critical of 'divisive policies, the erosion of the middle ground, and vituperative politics.' Martin, 'Pink', 338.

was a crusade, pushed forward on a wave of moral rectitude, which sought to turn on its head the policies which successive Labour and Conservative governments, supported by the Church of England, had put into place within the broad terms of the post-war consensus. The result could be nothing but conflict between Church and State; a conflict of contrasting ideologies and contrasting personnel. The paradox is irresistible: a Prime Minister on a religious crusade against the Welfare State and the mixed economy, challenged by an Archbishop seeking a diplomatic solution to protect the innocent victims.

2.3 Church and State: Strained Relations

2.3.1 Establishment

'Establishment', writes sociologist Grace Davie, 'refers to the complicated but definable links between the Church of England and the state.'[112] The 1970 Chadwick Commission described establishment as meaning 'the laws which apply to the Church of England and not to other churches.'[113] Above all, to understand establishment it must be recognized that establishment is not one thing. It is a relationship which can, and historically has, taken many different forms.[114] It is the practical outworking of the 'unity of Church and Nation under the Crown'.[115] Establishment is, in Grace Davie's words:

[A] particular state of affairs bequeathed to us by history, and like most historical legacies it has some advantages and some disadvantages. Nor is the situation a static one; the nature of establish-

---

112 Davie, *Religion*, 139.
113 Archbishop of Canterbury's Commission on Church and State, *Church and State* [The Chadwick Report], (London: Church House Publishing, 1970), 2.
114 'There are shades and degrees of establishment. It is not a univocal concept. But at its lowest establishment involves some kind of recognition of a church by the state and corresponding obligations on the part of the church.' P. Avis, *Church, State and Establishment* (London: SPCK, 2001), 21.
115 P. Cornwell, 'The Church of England and the State: Changing Constitutional Links in Historical Perspective', in Moyser (ed.), *Today*, 34. Cornwell quotes Canon A7: 'We acknowledge that the Queen's most excellent majesty, acting in accordance to the laws of the realm, is the highest power under God in this kingdom, and has supreme authority over all persons in all causes, as well ecclesiastical as civil.' He does, however, note that 'we are not dealing with the exercise of personal regal power but with a constitutional monarchy, the Queen in Parliament.' In turn, as we shall discuss further, Parliament has increasingly devolved its powers over the Church to representative Church bodies.

ment has, like everything else, shifted and adapted over time and will continue to do so.[116]

It is widely accepted that the Church of England's special relationship with the State carries with it attendant 'rights and privileges' and 'restrictions and limitations'.[117] Davie alerts us to the inextricable link between the two. She points, as an example, to the right of 26 Church of England bishops to sit in the House of Lords, setting it alongside the restrictions imposed because the State therefore expects to have a role in the appointment of bishops.[118] Today, as a result of a series of modifications to the Church-State relationship since the 1960s, the Church has greater freedom from restrictions and limitations than it did in the first half of the century.[119] For example, in the context of the appointment of bishops, Bernard Palmer observes that 'the sting has largely been removed with the setting up of the Crown Appointments Commission. The State, through the Prime Minister, may still nominally appoint the bishops, but it has retained the shadow without the substance.'[120] Julian Rivers goes further than Palmer, arguing that the restraints imposed upon the Church by establishment are now so minimal that there is little that a 'spiritually vigorous' Church of England could not achieve.[121] However, the mission of the Church of England in the public realm remains a difficult one to manage. Whilst present formal restrictions and limitations placed on the Church as a result of its established status are few, the dual role it faces as a national church seeking to both encourage and criticize those in authority will always makes its mission a difficult one.

The relaxation of ties binding Church to State has opened up space within which the Church seems freer than before to articulate a relatively distinctive view of political matters. Nevertheless, continuing State links keep alive a special claim to minister to all sectors of society and, not least, to the powerful whom the Church may sometimes be disposed to criticize. Such criticism clearly entails the possibility of alienating groups, in Church and State, to

---

116 Davie, *Religion*, 140. See also Cornwell, 'Constitutional', in Moyser (ed.), *Today*, 35.
117 Welsby, *How the Church of England Works*, 45 and Davie, *Religion*, 141. See also Cornwell, 'Changing', 33 and Avis, *Establishment*, 36.
118 Davie, *Religion*, 141.
119 B. Palmer, *High and Mitred: A Study of Prime Ministers as Bishop-Makers 1837-1977* (London: SPCK, 1992), 1-2. See also Furlong, *C of E*, 236-237.
120 Palmer, *Mitred*, 2.
121 J. Rivers, 'Disestablishment and the Church of England', in M. Schluter (ed.), *Christianity in a Changing World: Biblical Insights on Contemporary Issues* (London: Marshall Pickering, 2000), 79.

whom ecclesiastical leaders have traditionally felt obliged to offer encouragement. Not least, their alienation may result in Church leaders' loss of access to the powerful and the loss of opportunities for informal exercises of influence. On the other hand, public silence could sometimes be construed as offering tacit support for the status quo in ways likely to damage the Church's integrity or to harm its standing amongst critics and victims of official policy. Delicate political judgements have to be made concerning the appropriate balance to be struck between the Church's commitment to encourage those in authority and its obligation to criticize them.[122]

Judging correctly the balance that needs to be struck will, as far as Medhurst and Moyser are concerned, 'inevitably inhibit radical impulses.'[123] Grace Davie argues that this may not necessarily be the case.[124] She refers to the response of the bishops in the House of Lords to the so-called permissive legislation of the 1960s[125] and the debates which surrounded the *Faith in the City* report[126] as evidence to support her claim that some forms of protest will not be hindered by the Church's established status. Davie seems to over-emphasise the extent to which Medhurst and Moyser are negative about a national Church offering a genuine critique of the ruling authorities. They are pointing to the limitations imposed by the system or climate within which any national Church, by definition, operates which conspire to make criticism of the State unlikely. They do not deny that the weather within that climate may become stormy for a season, or that national-church status can during these seasons, benefit prophetic critique of the state by the Church or 'at least a small minority of Church leaders'.[127] Within *Church and Politics in a Secular Age* there is full recognition of the conflicts which existed between the Thatcher Governments and the Church of England bishops during the 1980s.[128] In fact, Davie herself comments that within the *Faith in the City* report, '[c]ritique there certainly was, but critique restrained

---

122 Medhurst & Moyser, *Secular*, 290. Also J. Sleeman, 'The Church and Economic Policy', in Moyser (ed.), *Today*, 275.
123 Medhurst & Moyser, *Secular*, 358.
124 Davie, *Religion*, 150.
125 Davie, *Religion*, 150 citing C. Davies, 'Religion, Politics and the "Permissive" Legislation', in P. Badham (ed.), *Religion, State and Society in Modern Britain* (Lampeter: Edwin Mellen Press, 1989), 319-340.
126 Davie, *Religion*, 153.
127 Medhurst & Moyser, *Secular*, 131.
128 *ibid*, 131-140.

by the system'.[129] Peter Hinchcliff assesses the situation helpfully:

> Historically, establishment has tended to make the Church, at least in some respects, the servant of the state. It might be thought, then, that the Anglican tradition would have been one which was conservative politically and disinclined to challenge the government. This has not, however, been the universal pattern... even in England in recent years the Church has been prepared to criticize the political party in power.[130]

Above all it should be emphasized that, whilst the Church's established status has the potential to hinder the Church in issuing prophetic challenges to the Government, a tremendous number of opportunities are available to the Church to offer constructive criticism of the Government precisely because of its established status. David Rogers, reflecting on the benefits of establishment to the Church of England's role as a campaigning organization reminds us that:

> It has the things which other charities and lobbying groups value and work to obtain: a brand name which is instinctively recognised; royal patronage; access to opinion-formers, decision-makers and government; a professional staff at Church House and Lambeth Palace – many of whom come from the ranks of the civil service, who understand the business of government; a network of local organizations and an army of volunteers willing to do the drudgery work. Thanks to the fact that it is an established church, it has a leader, the Archbishop of Canterbury, who can be effective on the world stage, in a way that is out of proportion to the actual numbers in the church.[131]

Having considered the nature of the Church of England's established status and its influence upon the socio-political witness of the Church today we need to briefly question whether establishment is any longer appropriate or beneficial in a plural society, either for the Church of England or the UK's other faith communities. Fierce debates on this topic are a part of the Church of England's ecclesiological furniture. Davie captures their heart, and the response most often used to defend and protect the status quo:

> The established nature of the Church of England requires... that some, if no longer all, decisions of the General Synod are them-

---

129 Davie, *Religion*, 153. Davie does concede that Medhurst and Moyser are 'perhaps, partly if not wholly correct in their assertion that there are inevitable limits on what a national church can or cannot say.'

130 P. Hinchcliff, 'Church-State Relations', in S. Sykes & J. Booty (eds.), *The Study of Anglicanism* (London: SPCK, 1988), 363.

131 Rogers, *Parliament*, 142.

selves subject to approval (or very occasionally disapproval) by Parliament.[132] And how is it possible to justify the continuation of this system when Parliament itself is made up of an enormous variety of individuals, of different faiths and none, most of whom have no interest in the internal affairs of the Church of England?[133] The answer can only be a pragmatic one: that the system – curious though it may be – rarely causes a major problem, though the unexpected check to Synodical policy can and does occur. On a more theoretical level the argument becomes more difficult.[134]

Within the Anglican Church the restrictions and limitations resultant from the Church's established status are generally not perceived to outweigh the rights and privileges which come with it. Few would disagree with Paul Avis's claim that '[g]iven proper vigilance, establishment can be one of the ways in which the Church exercises its mission in the great community that is the nation.'[135] There is also, according to Richard Harries (Bishop of Oxford), little support for disestablishment amongst the UK's other faith communities (those who appear to be most disadvantaged under existing arrangements):

> It is paradoxical that the most outspoken defenders of the establishment are now the Chief Rabbi and the leading Muslim spokesman, Dr Zaki Badawi. The Chief Rabbi has argued that the Church of England provides a kind of umbrella under which all the major religions can make their contribution to public life. Dr Badawi has said that, where you don't have an established Church of the broadly tolerant kind like the Church of England, you get either a fanatical secularism, as in France, or a fanatical extremism, as in the United States.[136]

Grace Davie quotes Adrian Hastings (a Roman Catholic),[137] Modood (a Muslim),[138] and Jonathan Sacks (the Chief Rabbi)[139]

---

132 The role of the Prime Minister in the appointment of Bishops is another issue which evokes the same questions.

133 Furlong notes: 'Nowadays the gap between the aspirations of the Church and the comprehension and involvement of MPs grows ever wider.' Furlong, *C of E*, 235.

134 Davie, *Religion*, 144.

135 Avis, *Establishment*, 36.

136 R. Harries, 'Why we need faith in the Lords', *Church Times*, 24th May 2002.

137 'The establishment of the Church of England remains, then, in contemporary terms somewhat anomalous – both in regard to English society and in regard to the Christian church elsewhere. But as both English society and the world church are full of anomalies, it is not to be rejected on account of that. It remains adequately but not overwhelmingly defensible on the grounds of doing quite a lot of good and very little harm, on being part

to make the same point as Harries.[140] The perspective offered by Modood is outlined in an article published in the *British Political Quarterly*. He writes:

> I have to state as a brute fact that I have not come across a single article or speech or statement by any minority faith in favour of disestablishment. This is quite extraordinary given that secular reformers make the desire to accommodate these minorities an important motive for reform.[141]

It would seem that, for all who maintain a religious worldview in what, at the very least, to many people feels like an increasingly secular context, the established status of the Church of England acts as an assurance that a faith perspective on the world will receive widespread and ongoing protection.

2.3.2 Secularization

Love it or loathe it, most people until the last generation or so knew roughly what Christianity was about and what it stood for. The comments about religion by journalists in the press and on television, as they attempt to deal with religious information, suggest that even basic Christian ideas are no longer understood by university-educated people, still less by others. Indeed even churchgoers can reveal an ignorance of the main elements of Christian belief. Some huge erosion of a central and common body of ideas and beliefs has taken place.[142]

There is a strong case for concluding that Britain feels less religious today because it actually is less religious than it has been in the past. A process of secularization has occurred 'whereby religious thinking, practice and institutions lose social significance.'[143] Among the changes which, it is argued, have taken place as part of the secularization process is the disengagement of society and religion whereby the latter has a decreasing impact on the former. The result is religion

---

of the wider symbolic culture of the nation which we would be fools to dismantle, and of requiring for its termination a quite excessive amount of time and energy.' A. Hastings, *Church and State: The English Experience* (Exeter: Exeter University Press, 1991), 75-76.

138 Modood, 'Ethno-religious minorities, Secularism and the British State', in *British Political Quarterly* (1994), 61-65.

139 Sacks, *The Persistence of Faith* (London: Weidenfeld, 1991), 68.

140 Davie, *Religion*, 146-147. See also Medhurst & Moyser, *Secular*, 365.

141 Modood, 'State', 65.

142 Furlong, *C of E*, 3.

143 Wilson, *Society*, xiv.

which is, to use Peter Berger's phrase, 'privately engaging, but publicly irrelevant.'[144] Medhurst and Moyser support the secularization theory,[145] it is assumed by Lee and Stanford,[146] and the Church of England's submission to the Wakeham Commission on the reform of the House of Lords states that society has become 'more secular'.[147]

In contrast, whilst accepting some aspects of the general theory of secularization,[148] Grace Davie argues that the general theory is 'getting harder and harder to sustain', arguing that religion in modern Britain is marked by 'believing without belonging'.[149] She describes an 'increasingly evident mismatch between statistics relating to religious practice and those which indicate levels of religious belief... the marked difference between two types of variable in the measurement of religiosity.' She continues:

> On the one hand, variables concerned with feelings, experience and the more numinous aspects of religious belief demonstrate considerable persistence in contemporary Britain...; on the other, those which measure religious orthodoxy, ritual participation and institutional attachment display an undeniable degree of secularization... both before and during the post-war period.[150]

Another dissenting voice is that of Robin Gill who challenges the historian E.R. Norman's politicization thesis[151] which claims that the Church has declined because it has responded to the secularization of Western society by translating its theological beliefs into secular moral and political values.[152] Writing at the beginning of the Thatcher years, Gill argues that Norman and many sociologists are wrong to base their analysis of Christianity and Western politics on the assumption that Western society is essentially secular and Chris-

---

144 P. Berger, *Noise of Solemn Assemblies* (Garden City, NY: Doubleday & Co., 1961), 37-38.
145 Medhurst & Moyser, *Secular*, 18.
146 Lee & Stanford, *Believing*, xv.
147 Council, *Role*, 11.
148 See Davie, 'From Obligation to Consumption: Patterns of Religion in Northern Europe at the Start of the 21st Century' (Forthcoming).
149 Davie, *Religion*, 5.
150 *ibid.* 4-5.
151 As presented in his 1978 Reith Lectures and published as *Christianity and the World Order*.
152 E.R. Norman, *Christianity and the World Order* (Oxford: Oxford University Press, 1979), 13.

tianity is today 'politically insignificant'.[153] He builds upon Max Weber's theory of the transposition of religious values arguing that 'Western society is embedded in Christian values and concepts to such an extent that it can scarcely even detect these values.'[154] As an example Gill points to the fundamental political values of 'peace' and 'justice' as having their roots in Christianity.[155] He goes on:

> A thoroughgoing transposition view-point would suggest, in contrast to the politicization thesis, that if the churches do, at times, seem to be adopting their values from society at large, rather than setting values for society to follow, this may be because Western society has already been radically christianized and that its apparent secular values are not really secular.[156]

Gill's work continues to have an important contribution to make to any analysis of impact of religion in the modern world. It warns us against placing the 'Christian' and the 'secular' into entirely distinct categories and assuming that a value cannot be considered to be 'Christian' unless an explicit theological link is made. Christianity has been feeding into Western society, and particularly the development of democracy, since the Edict of Milan (313) and the gradual emergence, under the Emperors Constantine and Theodosius, of Christianity as the 'unitive religion of the unitary Roman state'.[157] Christian values do inform the assumptions of society as whole. Gill's work, however, does not warrant a wholesale abandonment of the secularization thesis as a tool for the analysis of the changing relationship between Christianity and Western society. We might argue that the numerical decline of Christian Church within the UK, whilst not totally removing the influence of Christian thinking from those individuals who once attended church regularly (because Christian values have been transposed into their fundamental values), does suggest a lessening of the Christian influence upon these individuals and the communities to which they belong which may result in

---

153 R. Gill, *Prophecy and Praxis* (London: Marshall, Morgan & Scott, 1981), 44. Both defenders and critics of the secularization theory, he argues, start from this point. Critics of the theory positing either that there was no previous 'golden age' of religiosity from which the present deviates or that the present decline in religion is only a short-term process, a part of the ebb and flow of societal development.

154 *ibid*, 46.

155 *ibid*.

156 *ibid*, 55.

157 S.L. Greenslade, *Church and State from Constantine to Theodosius* (London: SCM Press, 1954), 33 as cited by J.W. De Gruchy, *Christianity and Democracy* (Cambridge: Cambridge University Press, 1995), 58.

thinking and behaviour which is less in line with Christian values.

This is largely the position taken by George Moyser in relation to the secularization thesis. He does accept that secularization is driving religion off the political agenda but agrees with Gill that the new values which are displacing Christianity are those of humanism, not militant atheism, which are to an extent 'indebted to and arising out of earlier Christian perspectives.'[158] In relation to the political sphere in Britain he argues that whilst the secularization process has been at work it has taken place under the veneer of the establishment, meaning that a significant religious presence continues to exist within public life. Moyser identifies five constituent parts of this process.[159] His explanations for each part are worth quoting in full:

1) *Constitutional Secularization.* '[T]he process whereby the official character and goals of the state ceased to be defined in religious terms, or whereby religious institutions cease to be given special constitutional recognition.'
2) *Policy Secularization.* '[T]he process whereby the state ceases to regulate society on the basis of religious criteria, and expands the policy domains and service provisions of the state into areas previously the reserve of the religious sphere.'
3) *Institutional Secularization.* '[T]he process whereby religious structures lose their political saliency and influence as pressure groups, parties and movements.'
4) *Agenda Secularization.* '[T]he process whereby issues, needs and problems deemed relevant to the political process cease to have overtly religious content, and whereby solutions developed to resolve those issues are no longer constructed on the basis of religious principles.'
5) *Ideological Secularization.* '[T]he process whereby the basic values and belief systems used to evaluate the political realm and to give it meaning cease to be couched in religious principles.'

The establishment shows no immediate signs of eroding and as such the total (or near total) secularization of the political realm is nowhere near to becoming a present reality, even though it has undergone a process of secularization in each of the five areas outlined above. The January 2000 report of the Royal Commission on the Reform of the House of Lords, *A House for the Future*, gave no indication whatsoever that the place of religious representation in the House is likely to end, or even diminish as a result of the current

---

158 Moyser, 'Patterns', 17.
159 Moyser, 'Modern', 14-15. His five-fold breakdown is employed by J. Haynes, *Religion in Global Politics*, (London: Longman, 1998), 3.

process of reform (Section 3.3.3 below).[160] The report asserts that:

> In the reformed second chamber, as in the present House of Lords, individual members will bring their own deepest convictions to bear whether their basis is religious or secular. Any formal representation for religious bodies should be seen as an acknowledgement that philosophical, moral and spiritual insights are a significant factor in many debates and that a variety of such contributions are welcomed. Religious belief, however, is an important part of many people's lives and it is desirable that there should be a voice, or voices, in the second chamber to reflect that aspect of people's personalities and with which they can identify. It would be consistent with our overall views on the composition of the reformed second chamber that it should be in a position to view public policy issues from a range of points of view, including, specifically, the philosophical, moral and spiritual.[161]

2.3.3 The Media

Nowadays it seems impossible to open any national newspaper, or follow the news on any television or radio channel, without somewhere finding a bishop preaching to millions on a subject about which he seems singularly ill-equipped to pontificate. No longer are our leading churchmen content with an occasional supporting role on the inside pages, being literally a Godsend to picture editors because of their fancy dress. Today it is the bishops who are making the headlines, even dominating the front pages.[162]

Writing in 1990, Lee and Stanford, capture the extent to which the Media played a crucial role in the Church-State relationship during the Thatcher years. The same theme is taken up by David Martin who observes: 'Anyone observing the media at the beginning of 1989 would have been struck by the increased salience of news about religion in Britain...'[163] Such was the volume of media coverage of the

---

160 Recommendation 109 of the report states that: 'The Appointments Commission should ensure that at any one time there are at least five members of the second chamber specifically selected to be broadly representative of the different non-Christian faith communities.' Recommendation 110 of the report states that: 'The total number of places in the reformed second chamber for members formally representing the various Christian denominations throughout the United Kingdom should be 26.' Royal Commission on the Reform of the House of Lords, *A House for the Future*, Cm 4534 (London: The Stationery Office, January 2000), 192.
161 *ibid*, 151 (15.4 & 15.5).
162 Lee & Stanford, *Believing*, 19.
163 Martin, 'Pink', 330.

Church over the early part of the 1980s that George Moyser, in his article 'The Church of England and Politics: Patterns and Trends', points to the media interest, day by day, in the involvement of religion in public life and is persuaded that secularization has not marginalized religion within modern Britain to the extent that it is no longer considered to have anything of significance to contribute to the political sphere.[164]

Media interest in the Church was the result of the genuinely newsworthy tensions between the Church of England and the Thatcher Government. Convinced of the value of the welfare state and economic policies which contained an immediate and obvious bias to the poor, the Church issued repeated prophetic challenges to the Government during the 1980s. The furore surrounding Archbishop Runcie's Falklands Thanksgiving sermon, the apparent official Church support for unilateral nuclear disarmament contained in *The Church and the Bomb*, the *Faith in the City* report, the Chequers meeting with the bishops which Thatcher organized (which the media only became aware of some months after it happened) are amongst those events which warranted serious media coverage. As Lee and Stanford state:

> It is not simply the fact that the bishops have entered or re-entered the political debate in the Thatcher years that has angered Ministers and prompted widespread media attention; rather it is the comprehensive and detailed nature of the bishop's rejection both of the substance of government policy and of the philosophy that underpins it.[165]

Mrs Thatcher herself was far from satisfied with the Church of England,[166] and particularly the bishops,[167] but she rarely entered the

---

164 Moyser, 'Patterns', 1-2. See also Lee & Stanford, *Believing*, 19.

165 Lee & Stanford, *Believing*, 21.

166 It cannot be insignificant in understanding Margaret Thatcher's own feelings towards the Church that the Index to *The Downing Street Years* contains only one reference to 'Church of England' (as opposed to four for 'Catholic Church' and two for 'Church of Scotland') no references to 'Runcie' (as opposed to one for 'Jackobovits'), and no references to *'Faith in the City'*. Thatcher, *Downing*, Index.

167 Reflecting on the work of Sir Richard O'Brien who whilst Chairman of the Manpower Services Commission was also Chairman of the committee which advised the Prime Minister on the appointment of Donald Coggan's successor as Archbishop of Canterbury, Thatcher comments: 'In view of my later relations with the hierarchy, I could wish that Sir Richard had combined his two jobs and established a decent training scheme for bishops.' Thatcher, *Downing*, 31. Perhaps it was good that Thatcher's wish did not come true.

front-line of the Church-State battleground.[168] There was, however, a silent endorsement from No.10 of the Media attacks on the Church's political interventions. Robert Runcie, in an interview with Humphrey Carpenter, recollects: 'I remember Jim Prior used to say to me, "It's not that she initiated the attacks on you in the papers, but she could have called them off at a moment's notice."'[169]

There was also a sense in which the tense relationship between Church and State was the product of the media's need for news, views and personalities which the Labour opposition were not providing. John B. Taylor (Bishop of St Albans), having been asked if there was ever a point at which the bishops ever made a conscious decision to become more active in providing an opposition voice in response to the Conservative Government, answered:

> No. It was just a vacuum and therefore people were wanting another voice and then they turned to a bishop. I mean Runcie was a very good media man and he was much sought after and he had a good number of people around him. And the BBC suddenly got the idea that bishops were available, bishops were articulate, bishops had a degree of authority. Michael Foot had none at all and Neil Kinnock not very much. So that was the weakness, there was no opposition of that sort and therefore you didn't want to get in a half-baked politician. You didn't want an opposition point of view, you wanted a different point of view.[170]

Media interest in the Church created significant opportunities for the exercising of the Church's ministry to the nation as a whole, allowing it, at its best, to be the voice for the voiceless on a far grander scale than would have otherwise been possible.[171] It also gave the public an artificial image of its spokesmen (generally the bishops)

Sir Richard O'Brien was also Chairman of the Archbishop of Canterbury's Commission on Urban Priority Areas which produced the *Faith in the City* report which so infuriated Thatcher and her Ministers during 1985.

168 Hugo Young writes: 'She made her opinions known on every controversial subject on which the Church intervened... But she rarely indulged, herself, in the most venomous attacks. Some kind of gut respect, for the Church if not churchmen, held her back. The knife tended to be wielded instead by successive chairmen of the party, in which role John Selwyn Gummer, who believed in God and belonged to the Church Synod, played hardly less aggressively than Norman Tebbit, whose relationship to organised religion was altogether different.' Young, *One*, 421-422.

169 Carpenter, *Runcie*, 219-220.

170 John B. Taylor (Bishop of St Albans) in an interview with the author, 29th July 2002, Appendix 5.

171 See Clark, *Under*, 78.

which itself generated some of the public perception of an unhappy Church-State relationship because, as Hugh Montefiore notes, 'the Church is only news on those comparatively few occasions when a critical stance on these matters has been adopted: silence or positive approval goes unnoticed...'[172]

The televising of the House of Lords (which came before the proceedings of the Commons were broadcast) was a key factor in raising the profile of the bishops and enhanced the Church-State tensions of the 1980s yet further.[173] The impact of the televising of the Lords on the Lords Spiritual is considered in John Whale's article (entitled 'The Right Reverend Magpies of the Upper House') in the August 1985 edition of *The Listener*, inspired by the fact that '[i]t so happens that no group in the Lords shows up so well as the bishops on television'.[174] Whale concludes his article with a sober and balanced assessment of the impact of the bishops within the House, noting the role played by the media in enhancing their impact:

> The peers spiritual are not a powerful group. When they feel obliged to stand together against easy divorce or Sunday shopping, they achieve little. They depend now on the weight of their individual abilities, not on the weight of their office. But those individual abilities are considerable and increasing, and television will reflect them, and establishment will be to that extent accidentally strengthened.[175]

2.3.4 The Thatcher Years

We come now to look at the particular issues which dominated the Church-State agenda during the Thatcher years; years in which the Church of England, though shrinking in real terms, maintained a high public profile because of 'outspoken collisions between its most prominent leaders and the Government'[176] and the eagerness of the media to report and comment upon these collisions. We will be limited, at this stage, to a brief overview of each issue. Our discussion will focus upon the policy differences of Church and State on each issue rather than the specific occasions on which they were expressed.

---

172 Montefiore, *Politics*, 1.
173 A point supported by David Say (Bishop of Rochester) in an interview with the author, 29th May 2002, Appendix 4.
174 Whale, 'Bishops in the Lords', in *The Listener*, 8th August 1985.
175 *ibid*.
176 G.I.T. Machin, *Churches and Social Issues in Twentieth-Century Britain* (Oxford: Clarendon Press, 1998), 212.

John Sleeman in his essay 'The Church and Economic Policy' asks whether it is fair to speak of 'an' Anglican economic policy, noting that within the Church there can be found the complete spectrum of socio-political views. The same question, and Sleeman's response, could be applied to each of the issues we shall consider below. He responds thus: '[T]hough we cannot claim that there is 'an' official Church of England, or Anglican, economic doctrine, this does not mean there are not distinguishable predominant economic philosophies which can be regarded as characteristic of the most influential Anglican circles.'[177] It is to this influential sector of the Church of England, essentially found within the three Houses of the General Synod, to which we refer throughout this discussion when we look at the views of 'the Church'.

2.3.4.1 The Economy

At the heart of the Thatcherite agenda lay matters of economic policy, matters which also lay at the heart of the Church-State relationship during the Thatcher years. John Keegan, writing in *The Daily Telegraph* during April 1988, offers a fair description of the Church's response to the Government's economic agenda, accompanied by an endorsement of the 'Jewish' attitude to wealth creation, so admired by Thatcher.

> The bishops of the established church, almost without exception, are today critics of the economic system. They are frequently heard to condemn the iniquities of financial inequality and the injustice of the market. The prevailing attitude to economic reality in the English Roman Catholic Church is equally short-sighted.... Judaism alone among the great religions seems to see no conflict between profit and virtue.[178]

In reality the Church did not see a conflict between profit and virtue. In the Board of Social Responsibility publication by E.R. Wickham, *Growth and Inflation* (1975) the goodness and importance of wealth creation is asserted. It is, however, accompanied by what Clark summarises as a 'two-pronged moral proviso'.[179] Firstly, the goodness of wealth creation is dependant upon attention being paid to the social and morally-convincing objectives that must serve the good of society. Secondly, that wealth creation should give priority

---

177 Sleeman, 'Economic', in Moyser (ed.), *Today*, 257.

178 J. Keegan, *The Daily Telegraph*, 8th April 1988, cited by B. Mawhinney, *In the Firing Line: Faith, Power and Forgiveness* (London: Harper Collins, 1999), 231-232.

179 Clark, *Under*, 36.

to the needs of the economically weak members of society. Wickham wrote:

> There is a persistent biblical warning against the dangers of wealth and the sin of avarice, but it is not the only or even the first word of guidance to man in his handling of material things... It is a primary biblical word that gives providential significance to the great enterprise of science and technology, industry and work, and the creation of wealth... we should not allow the cancerous excesses and the failures of the growth society to blind us to positive social and economic realities. The threats are real enough – and we need public accountability and structured vigilance to check them – but there is no evidence that the rejection of growth simply removes them. What we do know is that without growth it is not possible to meet the competing demands on our resources, and substantially they are proper demands. There is the understandable demand for higher standards of living by the masses of ordinary people... It is crucially important to understand that a more egalitarian society implies a wealthier society – unless very considerable social controls are imposed.[180]

Hugh Montefiore (Bishop of Birmingham until 1987), writing at the very end of the Thatcher years gives expression to this approach:

> [W]ealth needs to be created before it can be distributed; and the structures of society must permit this. At the same time the basic needs of the poor must be met, regardless of the effect on the economy, because people are our most important resource, and they should live with sufficient dignity as children of God. It is particularly important for Christians to insist on this at a time when the official opposition to the government seems weak. It is generally recognised that the Church has nothing to gain by political intervention. Indeed it often suffers obloquy by speaking out.[181]

It was the proclamation of this two-pronged moral proviso which formed the essence of the Church's economic message to each of the Thatcher governments. It was the proclamation of this same message which formed the essence of the message of the eighth-century BC Israelite prophet Amos to an Israel whose affluence was not shared with the poor and vulnerable.

Throughout the 1980s the Church continued to consider a strong welfare state essential to caring for the economically weak members of society, and on this basis persisted to denounce Conservative tax-cutting budgets[182] and reductions in public spending.[183] Though not

---

180 E.R. Wickham, *Growth and Inflation* (London: Church Information Office, 1975), 4,6.

181 Montefiore, *Politics*, 17-18.

182 Young, *One*, 424.

183 Board for Social Responsibility, *Not Just For The Poor: Christian Perspectives*

uncritical of the weaknesses within the welfare state, the Church offered unwavering support for the social security system, the National Health Service, and public housing provision.[184] Aware of arguments concerning the long-term benefits of New Right economic policies for all sectors of society, the Church nevertheless refused to acquiesce with the short-term sacrifices demanded to indulge the economic dreams popularized for Thatcher by Keith Joseph, Alfred Sherman and John Hoskyns. For the Church's spokesmen moral 'ends' could never justify immoral 'means'.

2.3.4.2 Unemployment

Unemployment was, to all intents and purposes, one of the 'means' which the Church denounced during the Thatcher years. Carpenter quotes from an interview that Runcie gave to *The Times* on 7th October 1984, shortly after the miners' strike had begun, in which he offered support to the Thatcherite aims of economic growth, higher pay, and the recovery of national pride, but insisted that, 'if the human consequences of such aims mean unemployment on an unprecedented scale, poverty, bureaucracy, despair about the future of our communities, inequitable sharing of the sacrifice called for, then the objectives must be called into question.'[185]

Henry Clark distils several Board for Social Responsibility position papers[186] on the subject of work, which contain the policy recommendations that the Church consistently pressed upon the Government during the 1980s, as follows:

The policy recommendations set forth in these publications include support for full employment as a crucial social policy goal, an affirmation of technological innovation, a suggestion that the traditional work ethic needs to be supplemented by a life ethic which affirms that one may achieve dignity and worth without holding a conventional job, and a tentative endorsement of work-sharing (conditional upon existing rates of pay and no loss of wage income). In addition, two publications have explored questions pertaining to union-management relationships. One sets forth in a surprisingly tentative and almost apologetic way the case for the legitimacy of the closed shop;

---

on the Welfare State (London: Church House Publishing, 1986), 78, 115.

184 Clark, *Under*, 41-42.

185 *The Times*, 7th October 1984, cited by Carpenter, *Runcie*, 273.

186 Clark cites *Power Sharing in Industry* (1975); *Work or What: A Christian Examination of the Employment Crisis* (1977); *Understanding Closed Shops* (1977); *Work and the Future* (1979); *Winters of Discontent* (1981); *Perspectives on Economics* (1984); *Growth, Justice and Work* (1985); *And All That is Unseen* (1986).

the other tries to explain why strikes are sometimes inevitable and are infrequently a legitimate expression of grievances or demands which cannot and should not be suppressed.[187]

2.3.4.3 Education

Education policy marked the only significant battleground between Church and State in which the Church had a measure of self-interest.[188] Unlike the activities of the Church with regard to other areas of social policy '[t]he Church actually *implements* policy through its own involvement as a partner in the system.'[189] Education reforms were part of the Government's legislative agenda during 1980 and 1988. The Church's input revolved around protecting the place of Christian worship and religious education in schools. In relation to the 1988 Education Reform Bill the Bishops, led by Graham Leonard (Bishop of London), 'used their status and block vote in the House of Lords to persuade – and where necessary compel – the Secretary of State for Education [Kenneth Baker] to show a great deal more devotion to religious education than he had envisaged in his core curriculum'.[190]

2.3.4.4 Foreign and Defence Policy

Perhaps the lowest-point in Church-State relations during the Thatcher years came after a service of thanksgiving in St Paul's Cathedral after the Falklands War (26th July 1982) during which Runcie[191] preached 'an excessively even-handed sermon'[192] which included a call for the congregation to share in the grief of the Argentinian as well as British mourners.[193] Afterwards Denis Thatcher is reported to have remarked that 'the boss was spitting blood'[194] (though Run-

---

187 Clark, *Under*, 49.
188 '[T]he churches have long realised that control of schools and a role in educating young minds is at the base of their power and authority.' Lee & Stanford, *Believing*, 108-109.
189 R. Waddington, 'The Church and Educational Policy', in Moyser (ed.), *Today*, 225.
190 Lee & Stanford, *Believing*, 109.
191 Robert Runcie was able to deliver his sermon with the authority which came with being the only Archbishop of Canterbury since the Middle Ages to have fought in a war and only one to have been awarded the Military Cross. *ibid*, 28.
192 Young, *One*, 417.
193 'There was nothing at all triumphalistic or militant in the sermon, no trace of jingoism, of a "God on our side" mentality.' Hastings, *Runcie*, 89.
194 Furlong, *C of E*, 129.

cie's sermon was apparently 'better than expected').[195] Frank Field, Labour MP for Birkenhead, marks the fact that the service was not allowed to become a nationalistic victory celebration as the Anglican episcopate's only victory in a 'head-to-head' conflict with the Thatcher Government.[196]

'[R]eturning with unflinching, perhaps pleasurably masochistic, fortitude for another dose of punishment'[197] the Church challenged the government's refusal to apply economic sanctions against South Africa as a means of compelling its Government to abandon apartheid policies. Thatcher herself refused to sanction their imposition, arguing that they would not serve their intended purpose[198] and the their worst effects would be felt by the Black South African population. Church leaders, including Desmond Tutu (the Archbishop of Capetown), disagreed.[199] Their thinking reflected that outlined in the Board for Social Responsibility report *Facing the Facts: The United Kingdom and South Africa* (1982) which called for a gradual disengagement from the South African economy coupled with increased aid provision for independent states in Southern Africa.[200]

The *Church and the Bomb* (1982), the report of a working-party of the Board for Social Responsibility, was widely understood to advocate British unilateral nuclear disarmament. John Elford argues that this was misrepresentation of the report,[201] and its recommendations certainly never became official Anglican policy.[202] It was, however, enough to add further fuel to the fires of dispute with a Government whose leader made clear her position on nuclear disarmament at the Lord Mayor's Banquet of 1984: 'The fact is that nuclear weapons have prevented not only nuclear war but conventional war in Europe for forty years... That is why we depend and will continue to depend on nuclear weapons for our defence.'[203]

---

195 Young, *One*, 282.

196 Reported, but uncited, by Lee & Stanford, *Believing*, 28.

197 Young, *One*, 425.

198 Thatcher, *Downing*, 513.

199 David Sheppard reports that Tutu '...believed that it was in the best interests of a peaceful future for South Africa that sanctions should be adopted, even if that meant in the short term suffering for the poor.' D. Sheppard, *Steps Along Hope Street: My Life in Cricket, the Church and the Inner City* (London: Hodder Stoughton, 2002), 281.

200 Ecclestone, 'Synod', 115-116.

201 J. Elford, 'The Church and Nuclear Defence Policy', in Moyser (ed.), *Today*, 196.

202 Young, *One*, 418.

203 Thatcher, cited by Young, *One*, 480.

2.3.4.5 Immigration and Race Relations

Riots on the streets of British towns and cities including London, Manchester, Nottingham, Reading, and even Cirencester, between 1981 and 1985 were a 'graphic demonstration' that race relations were no longer a marginal political issue.[204] The Church's relations with the Conservative Government on immigration and race relations were handicapped before they began. Margaret Thatcher spoke on Granada Television's *World in Action* programme in January 1978 about the fears that the British race might be 'swamped' by the 'alien' influx of black people, arguing for an to end immigration.[205] Some months later a number of bishops felt compelled to issue a strong statement (printed, among other places, in the *Church Times* on 30th November 1979) accusing political leaders of making racism respectable. The statement made specific reference to Margaret Thatcher, by then Prime Minister.[206]

The Church continued to collide with the Government on these issues throughout the 1980s, most notably with regard to the Nationality Bill (1981). The General Synod passed a motion that the Bill 'may lead to treatment of individuals which is not in keeping with Christian teaching and which could be racially divisive or socially inequitable' by 198 votes to one before the Bill began its passage through Parliament.[207] After the Nationality Act had come into force another General Synod debate during February 1984 voted overwhelmingly in favour of a motion highly critical of the Act.[208]

2.3.4.6 Sunday Trading

The 'Keep Sunday Special' campaign was run during the mid-1980s and elicited wide support from amongst the full range of Christian denominations. 'The massive organizational structure of the Churches and the almost total commitment of its local leaders – priest, minister and lay preachers – to the Keep Sunday Special cause was a powerful weapon aimed at a single target.'[209] That target was the

---

204 M. Phillips and T. Phillips, *Windrush: The Irresistible Rise of Multi-Racial Britain* (London: Harper Collins, 1998), 363-364, 368.

205 Granada Television, *World in Action*, 31st January 1978.

206 Kenneth Leech lists the signatories as the Bishops of Birmingham, Bristol, Chelmsford, Lewes, Lichfield, Lincoln, Liverpool, London, Manchester, Namibia in exile, Newcastle, Ripon, Southwell, Sherborne, Stepney, St. Albans and the retired Michael Ramsey. K. Leech, 'The Church and Immigration and Race Relations Policy', in Moyser (ed.), *Today*, 213.

207 Leech, 'Immigration', 214.

208 *ibid*, 217.

209 F. Bown, 'The Defeat of the Shops Bill, 1986', in M. Rush (ed.), *Parliament and Pressure Politics* (Oxford: Oxford University Press, 1990), 217.

efforts of the Thatcher Government to deregulate economic activity on Sundays. The Church of England's approach was to argue against a total deregulation of Sunday trading laws which would 'open up the high street and change, in a significant way, the public face of Sunday' whilst avoiding an extreme Sabbatarianism which makes Sunday 'a burden to be endured' rather than a 'delight'.[210] A crucial aspect of the Church's argument against total deregulation related to freedom. Having asserted the importance of freedom as a human value, *Sunday Trading*, an unpublished Board for Social Responsibility document, then asserts:

> The emphasis on the freedom of the individual to consume, trade or work has nevertheless to be measured against other freedoms, ...laws which govern society must somehow reflect the concerns of individuals in their totality not in their partiality.[211]

2.3.4.7 'Faith in the City'

The Archbishop of Canterbury's Commission on Urban Priority Areas was set up in the wake of the 1981 Brixton riots and reported in the 1985 report *Faith in the City: A Call for Action by Church and Nation*. Clark describes it as 'by far the most important action taken by the Church of England bishops' during the 1970s and 80s.[212] Lord Scarman, author of the earlier Government report on the Brixton riots, asserts that:

> Whether or not one agrees with its proposals, or with all or any of them, it is the finest face-to-face analysis and description of the problems of the inner-city and of other urban priority areas. In the long run it will take its place, I believe, as a classic description of one of the most serious troubles in British society.[213]

Lee and Stanford provide a useful summary of the report's content:

> The 1985 report *Faith in the City* spent half its time criticizing the church for being out of touch with life in the inner city and the other half of its time attacking Government policy, calling for a higher child benefit and welfare payments and more investment in job creation for the inner cities. Most controversially, the Archbishop of Canterbury's commission declared that those who were suffer-

---

210 Unpublished Board for Social Responsibility report, *Sunday Trading*, para. 105, as cited by Clark, *Under*, 55.
211 *ibid*, para. 90.
212 Clark, *Under*, 79.
213 Lord Scarman, contributing to a House of Lords debate on 12th February 1987 as cited by Hastings, *Runcie*, 95.

ing in the inner cities were suffering *because* of Thatcherism – or, as the report put it, modern conservatism – in its emphasis on individualism rather than the post-war consensus of collectivism.[214]

A surprise supporter of the report came in the form of the *Financial Times*.[215] Unsurprisingly, it was not, however, well received by the Conservative Government, being denounced as 'pure Marxist theology' by one unnamed cabinet Minister in the *Sunday Times*.[216] Thatcher 'declared herself "absolutely shocked" at one aspect of the Commission's report, namely that it failed to make any proposals whatsoever for developing the role of individuals and families in setting standards for society.'[217] The negative reaction (Hastings describes it as a 'gut reaction'[218]) was counter-productive. The arguments surrounding *Faith in the City* received front-page treatment in national newspapers for four days,[219] ensuring that the combined sales of the full and abridged versions of the report reached 83,000 copies. As Davie justifiably points out, '[t]he Church of England... achieved what the Labour Party had so conspicuously failed to do; that is, to push issues of deprivation – and in particular urban deprivation – to the top of the political agenda.'[220] Indeed, a new concern with the inner cities was to be found in the Conservative Party's 1987 General Election campaign.[221] Medhurst and Moyser comment thus:

> It could... at least for a while, have been construed as a matter of the Church's leaders being constrained to accept the role of a surrogate political opposition. The divided and sometimes self-preoccupied nature of anti-government political forces, struggling in the wake of successive and substantial electoral defeats, have sometimes seemed to leave the Government without formidable critics upon whom the victims of official policy could rely.[222]

---

214 Lee & Stanford, *Believing*, 104.

215 'A Church Not Very Militant', *Financial Times*, 3rd December 1985.

216 *Sunday Times*, 1st December 1985 as cited by Carpenter, *Runcie*, 276.

217 Lee & Stanford, *Believing*, 105.

218 Hastings, *Runcie*, 94.

219 Sheppard, *Steps*, 250.

220 Davie, *Religion*, 152. See also T. Beeson, *The Bishops* (London: SCM Press, 2002), 170.

221 Hastings, *Runcie*, 95-96. Such was Mrs Thatcher's personal awareness of the needs of the inner-cities that they were on her mind at the central office victory party where Mrs Thatcher said: 'We have a big job to do in some of those inner cities... to help the people get more choice and politically we must get back in there'. Quoted by Evans, *Thatcherism*, 100.

222 Medhurst & Moyser, *Secular*, 297. The same point is made by Clark, *Under*, 64 and Lee & Stanford, *Believing*, 99.

2.4 Conclusion

The re-election of the Conservative Party in 1987 'locked the Thatcher era into place as a phase in Britain's political evolution'.[223] It was an era in which the crusading Prime Minister, resolute and confident in her own moral rectitude, dominated the political landscape.[224] The polite consensus of the post-war period was replaced by confrontational politics as Thatcher, leaning heavily on New Right ideas and Victorian Values, prescribed the various treatments for her sick nation; treatments which were given the name 'Thatcherism'. The response of Her Majesty's Opposition was weak and ineffectual.

The Church of England during the 1980s was a consensus-driven Church: consensus-driven (though chronically divided) internally; consensus-driven (though, as a result, conflictual) in its socio-political vision; and consensus-driven in its relations with other Christian denominations. At the apex of its pyramidal structure sat an Archbishop every bit as consensus-driven (by necessity and inclination) as the Church he led and represented.

The Church-State relationship during the Thatcher years was characterised by tension and polarization. Over economic policy, unemployment, education, foreign policy and defence, immigration and race relations, and over the *Faith in the City* report, Church and State, working from contrasting philosophical foundations, came into conflict. Indeed, it can be persuasively argued that the Church of England provided much-needed political opposition during the 1980s more effectively than the Labour Party.[225] Such conflict gives the impression of a Church becoming more and more left-wing politically during the course of the 1980s. In reality the Church's political instincts remained in essentially the same place as they had done since 1945.[226] However, during the 1980s the political playing-field became waterlogged with right-wing political solutions.[227] The

---

223 Young, *One*, 518.
224 Writing in 1986, Peter Hennessy noted: '...she has put Cabinet government temporarily on ice.' Hennessy, *The Prime Minister*, 436.
225 Davie, *Religion*, 39. Hugh Montefiore takes this line: '[W]e were the only opposition. Labour were hopeless at that stage, I really did think that, they didn't seem to have any cutting edge and the Liberals were very feeble too.' Hugh Montefiore (Bishop of Birmingham) in an interview with the author, 21st May 2002, Appendix 3.
226 See Section 2.2.5 above.
227 This interpretation is also proposed by Haynes, *Global*, 71. Hugh Montefiore makes a similar point: 'The natural position for the Church of England is a *via media*, but even the middle way is anathema to an administration which regards as "wet" those Tories who take up a traditional Conservative position.' Montefiore, *Politics*, 73-74.

Church's voice sounded radical and appeared increasingly left-wing because the context into which it spoke had changed.

The bishops who sit in the House of Lords act as a crucial junction between Church and State. They perform a role which is at the very centre of this relationship. The main focus of this book is the discovery of what characterized their performance of this role during the tense years of the 1980s. In order that this analysis operates with due sensitivity to the full political and ecclesiastical of its subject we now turn to consider the role of the bishops within the Church of England, the work of the House of Lords, and the precise role of the Lords Spiritual within the Second Chamber.

CHAPTER THREE

Lords Spiritual

3.1 The Bishops of the Church of England

3.1.1 From Princes to Pastors

The Church of England bishop has two main roles. He is a pastor and a prophet.[1] Robert Runcie, instructing a young Korean bishop at a consecration service in Taejan during 1987, reflects on the prophetic responsibility:

> A bishop is inescapably a public figure, and he has a unique responsibility to prevent the Church from becoming an exclusive club concerned only for its own spiritual welfare. He must see the wider scene, identify the major issues of the day, and be ready to speak the unpopular word of warning. He may well be called to be a voice of the voiceless and a spokesman for the weak. He will know that the God with whom Christians have to do is the God who inspired the prophets, and demanded social justice for his people.[2]

George Carey, Robert Runcie's successor as Archbishop of Canterbury, gave the following three definitions of the role of the Church of England bishop in an interview with Lee and Stanford, broadly capturing both the pastoral and the prophetic aspects of the episcopal role:[3]

1) the bishop is 'a teacher of faith'.
2) the bishop is 'a leader and in particular must lead his mission'.
3) the bishop is 'a pastor – he must care for the flock of Christ entrusted to him'.

The role of the bishop today is the result of centuries of evolution and change. Medhurst and Moyser chart the development of the episcopal role within the Church of England over the last 300 years describing three main eras. The eighteenth and early nineteenth century was the era of the 'Prince' bishop during which bishops:

> [E]xercised something akin to absolute monarchial authority which

---

1   Lee & Stanford, *Believing*, xiii, 125-126.
2   Robert Runcie as cited by Hastings, *Runcie*, 97-98.
3   George Carey in an interview with Lee & Stanford, *Believing*, xiii.

owed more to social assumptions, nurtured in feudal society, than to theological insight. They were regarded as integral parts of one relatively cohesive governing class; though not always drawn from aristocratic families, they certainly came to be closely associated with the landed aristocracy and therefore tended to be seen as remote from the generality of parsons and parishioners.[4]

The era of the bishop as 'Prelate' traversed the late nineteenth and much of the twentieth century. During this time, in the context of an industrialized society, 'clerics tended to be driven back in the direction of their "core" ecclesiastical functions and so became more socially marginal figures.'[5] The third era, from the 1960s to the present, sees the bishop primarily as 'the Pastor'.[6] Overall, Medhurst and Moyser describe this development as being a movement from the bishop 'being an omni-competent decision-maker' to the bishop thinking of himself as '"the animator", "the enabler", "the supporter", or "encourager" within his diocese.'[7] In practice this development means that 'for most contemporary bishops, pastoral activity in the diocese rates rather higher than national involvement' (be that in the central organs of the Church or within Parliament).[8] The establishment of the Crown Appointments Commission in 1977 played a crucial role in creating this shift to a diocesan focus by giving, as it did, the diocese far greater involvement in the selection of its bishop. Owen Chadwick describes the input of diocesan representatives in the selection of their bishop:

> Normally the diocese asked for someone who was a good pastor and physically fit and therefore not too old. Quite often they would ask for someone of an ecumenical spirit who would not disturb the good relations between the denominations in that diocese... [Q]uite often they would ask for someone who would not be too involved in outside commitments. They wanted a diocesan pastor

---

4   Medhurst & Moyser, *Secular*, 78.

5   *ibid*, 79.

6   *ibid*, 78-82.

7   *ibid*, 113. John Whale presents a similar analysis, emphasising the modern managerial aspects of a modern bishop's role: 'Besides being representatives, they are managers, particularly of their clergy.' Whale, *Anglican*, 43. See also Beeson, *Bishops*, 1.

8   Medhurst and Moyser, 'Lambeth Palace, The Bishops and Politics', in Moyser (ed.), *Today*, 77. Research by Towler and Coxon into the careers of bishops prior to their appointment supports this analysis by identifying a 'swing... towards the placing of greater importance on the parochial ministry' between 1930 and 1973. Towler & Coxon, *Fate*, 185.

rather than a national figure.[9]

Medhurst and Moyser argue that today most bishops devote very little of their time to exerting social and political influence. They ascribe this to four factors.[10] Firstly, it is due to a revised theological understandings of the role of the bishop as 'pastor and servant rather than prince and hierarchical superior'. This has caused the bishop's focus to be upon facilitating the Christian service of his congregation within the political realm, not on acting as 'the Church's chief or sole authoritative spokesman.' Secondly, theologically and culturally there are 'constraints pointing clerical leaders towards a quest for consensus and harmony rather than confrontation and conflict'. Thirdly, there are constraints placed upon bishops by the changing demands of their office.[11] Amongst other things the introduction

---

9 Chadwick, *Michael Ramsey: A Life* (Oxford: Clarendon Press, 1990), 129-130. See also Beeson, *Bishops*, 45.

10 Medhurst & Moyser, 'Lambeth', 79-82.

11 J.H.R. Moorman (Bishop of Ripon, 1959-75) provides an insight into the workload of the diocesan bishop which is worth quoting extensively: 'A bishop will find himself fully occupied. He observes no hours. Archbishop Benson started work each day at 6.15am and finished after midnight. A bishop has no weekend relaxation and not much in the way of summer holiday, as he must always be accessible... The daily correspondence will take up a good deal of the bishop's time. He will write about twenty to twenty-five letters every day, some of them dealing with matters of considerable importance - at any rate to the recipient... In addition to all his spiritual and pastoral work, a bishop is also a public figure in the district where he lives, and, as such, will be expected to attend public dinners and make entertaining speeches at them, to give away prizes at schools and address the children and parents who attend those functions, and even perhaps to give lectures to a university or college...'
Moorman also notes the responsibility of the bishop to care for around 300 priests under his care, for the selection and ordination of candidates for the ministry and for visiting the parishes in his diocese. 'He will find the preparation for these visits very costly of his time', he notes, 'for he will be required to preach a sermon which the people will expect to be better than what they normally get from their parson... To preach at least three times a week means a lot of time at his desk...'
The bishop also has duties beyond the diocese: 'He is often called away from his diocese to meet his fellow bishops, or to look after some central concern of the Church both at home and abroad. No council or governing body is thought to be complete without a bishop serving on it, probably as chairman. And, in this jet age, this may mean constant travels abroad, taking up a considerable part of his time. In England most of the bishops have the additional duty of sitting in the House of Lords... He is provided

of Synodical government has increased the bishops workload and decreased the authority with which they can lead the Church's contribution to public debate. Fourthly, bishops are without the appropriate resources, particularly at the local level, needed for them to 'discharge their task with suitably high levels of information or expertise.' At the same time the process of episcopal disengagement from the society's ruling hierarchies has also given rise to:

> [A]n episcopal bench to some degree more at odds with traditional social and political arrangements and more disposed to take critical or even radical political stands or to be favourably disposed towards those in their immediate pastoral care who might do so. This is not to say that the overall level of political involvement of the Church has necessarily increased much as a result. But it is to say that the style and content of episcopal political contributions is shifting in ways which certainly give the impression, through their historical novelty, of a greater degree of political concern and activism.[12]

In summary, while the pastoral bishop is likely to be less involved in national political business than many of his predecessors, the content of his involvement when it does occur is more likely to be the critique of the prophet than the legitimation of the pastor. It could be argued that there is a logical flow from one to the other. The Church's episcopal leaders, due to shifting emphases in their own role within the Church of England and as part of the general disengagement of Church and State, increasingly come to political debate as unpoliticized 'outsiders' whose Christian worldview has had little part, implicitly or explicitly, in the formulation of the policies they are discussing. It stands to reason that they will therefore be less satisfied with these policies and will be eager to make full use of the opportunities exert their influence and the Christian perspective they represent.[13]

---

with a chauffeur as he travels, on average, about 50 miles a day, often late at night.' J.R.H. Moorman, 'The Anglican Bishop', in P. Moore (ed.), *Bishops: But What Kind?* (London: SPCK, 1982), 119-122. See also Council, *Role*, 10; Furlong, *C of E*, 249 and Hastings, *Runcie*, 85.

12   Moyser, 'Patterns', 20.

13   Jeff Haynes makes much the same point in relation to trends throughout Western Europe: 'The concern of institutional religious elites to make public pronouncements on social and political issues is a growing feature in much of Western Europe. It is, in effect, an attempt to deprivatize religion from where the process of secularization seems to be sending it: to socio-political marginality. It also reflects growing disquiet at the direction which modern

3.1.2 The Archbishop of Canterbury

If the workload of a diocesan bishop is overbearing then the work-load of the Archbishop of Canterbury demands that the holder of the office must, first and foremost, have an other-worldly capacity for work, not a deep spirituality.[14] 'Throughout the twentieth century it was acknowledged,' writes Trevor Beeson, 'whenever the primacy fell vacant, that the archbishopric of Canterbury was an impossible job which nonetheless someone needed to undertake.' He continues:

> In 1998 Archbishop Carey spent three weeks presiding over the Lambeth Conference, visited 30 countries, delivered 140 sermons, speeches and addresses, made more than 50 broadcasts, contributed ten articles to journals and books, spent many hours in the House of Lords and on other state affairs, gave innumerable interviews and dealt with a mountain of letters, e-mails and faxes. His car was equipped with a telephone and a computer to enable such work to be uninterrupted by journeys, and it was reported that he rose at 6.30 am or earlier, rarely went to bed before midnight and took one weekend off every six weeks.[15]

When it comes to the major public debates in the House of Lords on matters of 'particular concern to the Church, there is a general presumption that the Archbishop will take the lead in making the Church's contribution.'[16] Such archiepiscopal contributions are virtually guaranteed to receive media coverage. The role of the Archbishop (the first subject of the realm)[17] is unique and he remains politicized to a greater extent than the other bishops, '[h]e still expe-

---

society seems to be taking: away from the teachings of Christianity towards an increasingly amoral, selfish conception of what is appropriate. The result is what Hunter calls an "aggressive promulgation of these ideals in the public sphere".' Haynes, *Global*, 68.

14 Robert Runcie, in his Foreword to Edward Carpenter's biography of Archbishop Fisher, betrays the fact that a workaholic temperament is a normal part of a bishop's make-up: 'His capacity for work was staggering, setting perhaps unfortunately high standards for other senior churchmen: not all workaholics can stand the pace as long as he did.' R. Runcie, 'Foreword' in E. Carpenter, *Archbishop Fisher: His Life and Times*, (Norwich: The Canterbury Press, 1991), vii.

15 Beeson, *Bishops*, 6.

16 Medhurst & Moyser, 'Lambeth', 91.

17 Hastings, *Runcie*, 51. The Archbishop ranks above the Prime Minister and Lord Chancellor in order of precedence and is the first subject to be introduced to foreign Heads of State.

riences the "establishment" as a constant reality in his life.'[18] The tensions felt between the established Church's pastoral and prophetic role towards the State come into 'particularly sharp focus' in the experience of the Archbishop of Canterbury.[19] He, more than any other Christian leader, is 'actually and symbolically associated with established authority' and yet he also 'functions in a national and international ecclesiastical environment characterized by a growing radicalism'.[20] Adrian Hastings dispels the myth that this 'double-edged' role of the Archbishop (and, to a lesser extent, all the bishops involved in the House of Lords) is a recent development:

> To collaborate with the Government in strengthening peace and good order, but also on occasion to criticize Government for not doing these things – these tasks are not new. They are certainly not the product of some twentieth-century rethink of political theology; equally they are not the product of "Establishment", as a creation of the sixteenth century Reformation... They are characteristics of the role of the Archbishop of Canterbury over a far longer period. They are, one can claim, part of the unwritten constitution of the country.[21]

3.2 The House of Lords

3.2.1 Membership, Functions and Powers

Arguably second chambers are becoming more rather than less significant in the contemporary world... The relative significance of second chambers may be enhanced by the apparently diminished significance of first chambers.[22]

[T]he House of Lords was not established to meet the requirements of any particular theory of politics; it was not created by any national conventions; it does not owe its existence to some paper scheme drawn up by politicians, academics or constitutional lawyers. Rather it is a product of history. It has not been made, it has grown.[23]

---

18   Hastings, *Experience*, 68.
19   Medhurst & Moyser, *Secular*, 291.
20   *ibid*.
21   Hastings, *Runcie*, 33.
22   N.D.J. Baldwin & D.R. Shell, *Second Chambers* (London: Frank Cass, 2001), 1.
23   Baldwin, 'The House of Lords: Behavioural Changes - A New Professionalism and a More Independent House', in P. Norton (ed.), *Parliament in the 1980s* (Oxford: Basil Blackwell, 1985), 98.

The history of the House of Lords is the story of an evolving body. Indeed its willingness to acquiesce in change, sometimes with great reticence, has been the key to its survival.[24] Our interest is in the House of Lords during the period from 1979 to 1990 in which no attempts were made at reforming the Lords. Throughout the 1980s the House had over 1,000 members made-up of the two archbishops and twenty-four bishops of the Church of England, royal peers, peers by succession (64.2 per cent of the House in May 1990), up to 11 serving Law Lords, and life peers (30.2 per cent of the House in May 1990).[25] Donald Shell, writing in 1992, gives the following account of the membership of the House of Lords:

> In part, the House has become a meritocratic chamber where leading figures in various walks of life mingle with politicians. In part it is a representative chamber, not according to any elective principle but simply through accidental membership, as it were, of doctors, practising dentists, bee-keepers, opticians, accountants, lecturers, social workers, journalists, retailers, and so on. In part the House remains an aristocratic chamber, some of its most active members being there because of peerages awarded to their forebearers, and a high proportion having grown up in families marked by privilege or conspicuous success.[26]

The Lords is busier than any other legislature in Europe except the House of Commons.[27] The House of Lords briefing paper 'The Work of the House of Lords – Its Role, Functions and Powers' offers the following description of the role of the House of Lords:

> The House of Lords is the second chamber of the United Kingdom Parliament. It plays an important part in revising legislation and keeping a check on Government by scrutinising its activities. It complements the work of the Commons, whose members are elected to represent their constituents. Members of the Lords are not elected and are unpaid. They have a wide range of experience

---

24 D.R. Shell, *The House of Lords* (London: Harvester Wheatsheaf, 1992), 8. Shell describes the key events of this evolution from the Tudor Period, including: The Reform Act (1832) by which the democratic element (The House of Commons) within the government recognised as pre-eminent; The Parliament Act (1911); The Parliament Act (1949); The Life Peerages Act (1958) which introduced Life Peerages and an expense allowance for attending peers; The Peerage Act (1963) which enabled peers by succession to renounce their peerages for life and permitted women to who had inherited peerages to sit in the Lords. Shell, *Lords*, 7-24.

25 *ibid*, 30-36.

26 *ibid*, 63.

27 *ibid*, 126.

and provide a source of independent expertise. The House also has a judicial role as the final Court of Appeal.[28]

The same document distinguishes between those functions of the House of Lords which are performed 'on the floor...' of the chamber and those which are performed 'off the floor...' of the chamber. On the floor of the chamber the legislative functions of the House, which are considered to be its most important task,[29] are performed. Government Bills introduced into the Commons are considered once they have completed their passage through the Lower House and an increasing number of non-controversial Government Bills are introduced into the Lords. Each Bill, wherever it begins its passage, receives a First Reading, Second Reading,[30] Committee Stage, Report Stage, and finally a Third Reading. The deliberative functions of the House are also performed on the floor of the chamber through Starred Questions (non-debatable questions), Unstarred Questions (questions which lead to short debates), debates on topics of general concern, and through the consideration of Government statements on important or urgent matters.

Off the floor of the chamber the peers' specialist expertise is deployed in its two permanent investigative select committees: The European Communities Committee was set up in 1974 to scrutinize proposed European legislation and identify those proposals which should be considered on the floor of the House.[31] The Select Committee on Science and Technology began functioning from 1979 to consider the whole range of issues relating to science and technology.[32] Further committees are set up on an *ad hoc* basis. The reputation that the House of Lords committees have earned for the high-quality and independence of their work has added to the overall reputation of the House.[33]

Law and convention place limitations on the powers of the House

---

28 House of Lords Briefing Paper, 'The Work of the House of Lords - Its Role, Functions and Powers', (October 1998).

29 Shell, *Lords*, 128.

30 Shell notes that the Second Reading is generally taken to be the opportunity for consideration of the principle of the Bill. *ibid*, 135.

31 P. Norton, 'The House of Lords and Parliamentary Reform', in Jones et al., *Politics UK*, 364.

32 Since 1990 two further permanent investigative select committees have been added: the Economic Affairs Committee and the Constitutions Committee.

33 *ibid*, 366.

of Lords.[34] The Parliament Acts of 1911 and 1949 define the powers of the Lords in relation to public Bills. Bills defined as Money Bills (concerning taxation and public expenditure) always begin life in the Commons. The Lords is able to impose a delay of one month on their passage but has no right of amendment. Other Bills can be delayed by the House of Lords for a maximum of one year. The Parliament Acts do not apply to Bills prolonging the length of a Parliament over five years, Private Bills, Bills sent to the Lords less than a month before the end of a session, and Bills which start life in the Upper House. The Salisbury Convention, which emerged during the Labour Government of 1945-51, ensures that the House of Lords allows any Government Bill whose provisions appeared in an election manifesto to receive its Second and Third Readings. Within this constitutional framework it is intended that the House of Lords plays a complementary role to the House of Commons:

> Paradoxically, the value of the House of Lords in the legislative process appears to lie precisely in its complementarity to the Commons, based as it is on the former's non-elected (and undemocratic) character. It is the less party political character of the House which is the single most important factor differentiating its legislative role. Some peers at least approach any item of legislation devoid of a party stance, while many who basically subscribe to government or main opposition party views do so with considerably greater flexibility that their Commons counterparts. The expert, the political and the truly lay contributors all mingle in the House of Lords, and in so doing almost invariably seek to exert influence over legislation rather than contest power.[35]

3.2.2 The Thatcher Years

There seems something paradoxical in a Conservative government experiencing real difficulties in the House of Lords. After all, hereditary peers out-number created peers by almost two to one, and the Conservative Party remains far and away the largest single party in the House. Yet by Summer 1984 it was apparent that Mrs Thatcher's legislation was more at risk in the Lords than in the Commons.[36]

Even with its inbuilt Tory majority Mrs Thatcher's ascendancy

---

34 This section is dependent upon the House of Lords Briefing Paper, 'The Work of the House of Lords' (October 1998).
35 Shell, *Lords*, 176-177.
36 D.R. Shell, 'The House of Lords and the Thatcher Government', in *Parliamentary Affairs*, Vol. 38, No. 1, 16.

was never reflected in the Lords.[37] 'The sheer continuity of the Upper House ensured that the Party there was less "Thatcherite" and remained more tempered by the old paternalistic Tory tradition.'[38] During the 1980s the volume of Lords business grew and it would appear that, as a result of the one-party domination in the House of Commons, peers felt an added sense of responsibility for the thorough scrutiny of government policy.[39] Philip Norton comments:

> In the 1980s the House became especially active. The average daily attendance exceeded 300. Almost 800 peers attended one or more sittings each Session.[40] Late-night sittings became a regular feature. In the session of 1985-86 the House sat after ten o'clock on almost one hundred occasions. The House also became a more visible body, having admitted... the television cameras in 1985.[41]

Consequently, during the 1980s the role of the Lords in getting detailed changes made to Bills also increased.[42] Throughout her premiership, though particularly during her first two terms, Thatcher was regularly obstructed by the House of Lords, occasionally on major issues, such as the Education (No.2) Bill (1980), the 'Right to Buy' legislation, and the Local Government (Interim Provisions) Bill (1984) relating to the abolition of the Greater London Council.[43] In total, between 1979 and 1990 the Lords voted down Government legislation on more than 150 occasions.[44] This readiness to challenge the government led to a growing influence in real terms for the House of Lords during the Thatcher years which has made them more responsive to public concerns and lobbying:[45]

> There is clear evidence that Conservative government concern over not being able to secure the passage of particular items of legislation in a particular session has been at least a factor in persuading ministers to accept unpalatable amendments and to reach compromises on a number of occasions during the post-1979 period.[46]

---

37   Shell, 'Thatcher Government', 31.
38   Shell, *Lords*, 27.
39   *ibid*, 26-28. See also Norton, 'Lords', 356.
40   These figures are in line with those in the House of Lords *Sessional Statistics* produced by the House of Lords Record and Information Office.
41   Norton, 'Lords', 357.
42   *ibid.*, 178.
43   Shell, *Lords*, 168-169.
44   Norton, 'Lords', 356.
45   *ibid*, 365.
46   Baldwin, 'Behavioural Changes', 101.

3.3 The Bishops in the House of Lords

3.3.1 *The Constitutional Perspective*

The bishops of the Church of England are officially eligible to sit in the House of Lords as individual Lords of Parliament, not peers. The distinction dates back to the 15th century when the Lords Temporal became known as 'peers'.[47] The Lords Spiritual did not take on the same title due to the fact that they could not be put on trial by their peers or take part in such trials 'because canon law forbade their participation in judgements of blood'.[48] The bishops are not present in the Upper House as corporate representatives of the Church of England. Hugh Montefiore states it plainly: '[y]ou see you're not there in the House of Lords as a representative of the Church. It's a very important point... you are not chosen to go to the House of Lords because you are a representative. You go in your own right as a bishop, a rather important distinction.'[49] The bishops are issued with the following writ of summons:

> Whereas our Parliament for arduous and urgent affairs concerning Us the state and defence of Our United Kingdom and the Church is not met at Our City of Westminster We strictly enjoining command you upon the faith and love by which you are bound to Us that considering the difficulty of the said affairs and dangers impending (waiving all excuses) you be personally present at Our aforesaid Parliament with Us... to treat and give your counsel upon the affairs aforesaid...

The presence of the bishops in the House of Lords is one significant aspect of the establishment between Church and State but it is not essential to the established status of the Church of England. The Wakeham Report on the Reform of the House of Lords is unequivocal in its assertion that '...there is no direct or logical connection between the establishment of the Church of England and the presence of the Church of England bishops in the second chamber', noting that while the Church of Scotland is established it has no rep-

---

47 House of Lords Briefing Paper, 'History of the House of Lords' (May 1997).
48 F. Bown, 'Influencing the House of Lords: the Role of the Lords Spiritual 1979-1987', in *Political Studies*, XLII (1994), 105.
49 Hugh Montefiore (Bishop of Birmingham) in an interview with the author, 21st May 2002, Appendix 3. See also Medhurst & Moyser, *Secular*, 97 and Bown, 'Influencing', 105.

resentation in the House of Lords.[50] The report contains a succinct summary of the historical development of episcopal representation in the Lords:

> The origins of the bishops' role as members of the House of Lords go back to the early Middle Ages, when they, along with abbots, represented some of the powerful landed interests in the country and were among the Monarch's chief advisers. Until the Reformation the Lords Spiritual usually outnumbered the lay members of the House of Lords. They remained a significant minority of the House of Lords until the mid 19th century, when their number was capped at 26 and the number of new lay peerages soared. This trend continued and was reinforced by the introduction of life peerages in 1958.[51]

The basic constitutional facts are well rehearsed. The incumbents of the dioceses of Canterbury, York, London, Durham, and Winchester sit by right in the Lords. The remaining twenty-one places are filled on the basis of seniority, measured from the date of first appointment to a diocesan See.[52] The only bishops who are ineligible to sit in the Lords are the Bishop of Sodor and Man (who sits in the House of Keys on the Isle of Man) and the Bishop of Gibraltar.[53] The appointments are *ex officio* and as such when a bishop retires he loses his seat. Statutory retirement at the age of 70 means that the length of any individual's involvement in the House is often short, particularly in the context of the lifelong membership of all other members of the House. Shell reports that in 1990 only three of the twenty-six sitting bishops had been members of the House for ten years or more.[54] The Lords Spiritual always sit on the Government side of the House on the Bench of Bishops '...with its lower armrest designed to accommodate their cassocks and surplices'.[55] They are the only members of the House whose wives are not able to call themselves 'Lady'.[56]

---

50 Royal, *Future*, 152 (15.8). Paul Avis makes the same point, arguing that '[i]f the representation of Church of England bishops in the second chamber were significantly reduced (or even abolished altogether), the establishment of the Church of England would not be affected in principle.' Avis, *Establishment*, 21.

51 Royal, *Future*, 150 (15.1).

52 Shell, *Lords*, 30.

53 *ibid.*

54 *ibid*, 31.

55 J. Wells, *The House of Lords* (London: Sceptre, 1997), 2. For Robert Runcie's colourful explanation for the armrests on the Bench of Bishops see Hastings, *Runcie*, 80.

56 Rogers, *Parliament*, 58.

3.3.2 The Church of England Perspective

The Role of Bishops in the Second Chamber (1999) was the Church of England's submission to the Wakeham Commission on the reform of the House of Lords. Its content provides some insight into how the Church of England sees its role as a contributor to the socio-political life of the nation, including its involvement in the House of Lords. In response to the question 'What does the Church of England contribute?' the submission states that:

> The Church believes that its potential arises out of its belief in God and the moral law, and its concern to establish how that moral law should be worked out in human life. It follows that its instinct is to bring a thoughtful concern with ethical principles to all public as well as personal issues. This concern runs seamlessly with the whole of life, and this therefore leads the Church to be deeply and unshakeable involved in the social and – in an entirely non-partisan way – also with the political issues of the day. That is why bishops are not merely ecclesiastical but also regional and national figures.[57]

By extrapolation from the fact that the Church considers its work to be 'directed to the entire community and not just those who attend church services' it considers its membership of the House of the Lords 'to flow not from a status representative of the Church as an organization but, rather, from a function lying at the core of the spiritual, ethical and social dimension of the nation's life.'[58] It is argued that in their contributions to the House of Lords the bishops speak from a vein of personal experience in the dioceses which enables them 'to draw with a special authority on the realities of life in their parishes, including in areas abandoned by other institutions.'[59] Michael Baughen (Bishop of Chester), describing his involvement in the famous bishops' meeting with Margaret Thatcher at Chequers, provides an example of this approach in operation: in the wider context of the bishops' contribution to the political life of the nation:

> [I]t was an honest thing and I said to her... "if you really came to see what the Church is doing in these areas and you came to Birkenhead in my diocese, or Wallasey... where they are in the inner city, they are the only professionals who live there after 5.30 at night or on the weekends. There is no doctor, no policeman, no administra-

---

57 Council, *Role*, 6.

58 *ibid*, 3.

59 *ibid*, 7. Francis Bown notes: 'The Lords Spiritual are, after all, the only members of the House who can make any serious claim to an element of regional representation.' Bown, 'Influencing', 116.

tive person from the council and no teacher, nobody lives there. They all come in. The only people who live there are the clergy and their families and they know what's going on and this is why our network is picking up what's going on, it's honest and real. It isn't from an outsiders point of view."[60]

The Church's submission to the Wakeham Commission also makes the justifiable claim that 'bishops will be found speaking not just for the Church of England but for its partners in other Christian Churches, and for people of other faiths and of none'[61] and emphasises the independence of each diocesan bishop, rather than the collegial leadership of the bishops:

The bishops are not members of a cabinet headed by the archbishops and serving under a yoke of temporal collective responsibility but primarily independent local leaders whose service is to the whole of their communities regardless of creed, race or gender.[62]

3.3.3 A Political Role

Bishops in the House of Lords suggests the Church in politics. That idea at once creates a tension. Christians find in themselves an instinctive sense that Christian political activism is both fitting and unfitting.[63]

By their sheer existence the Churches are caught up in politics. It is a fact of history that once Churches have become a significant presence in the life of a particular society they had to face the question of their relationship with those who exercise authority in that society.[64]

The established status of the Church of England dictates a considerable level of Church involvement in State affairs and State involvement in Church affairs. However, debate persists amongst social ethicists, theologians, sociologists and all manner of lay observers about the extent to which the Church's official contributions to the socio-political sphere should be 'political' in character. We will con-

---

60 Michael Baughen (Bishop of Chester) in an interview with the author, 21st May 2002, Appendix 2.
61 Council, *Role*, 4. See Section 7.3 below which shows the bishops making considerable use of arguments based on the views of 'the Churches' to support the points made in their speeches.
62 *ibid*, 6.
63 Whale, *Anglican*, 58.
64 G. Ecclestone, *The Church of England and Politics* (London: Church House Publishing), 3.

sider the four most commonly held positions.[65]

1) Stay Out of Politics

There is a body of opinion, popular amongst Conservative politicians during the 1980s,[66] which argues that the Church should stay out of politics stating only, at the most, the rudiments of Christian standards in the public realm.[67] This was the position advocated by E.R. Norman in his 1978 Reith Lectures[68] and crisply illustrated by the approach to the 1978-79 Miners' strike outlined by Alexander Grey in an article in *Crucible* (the Board for Social Responsibility journal):

> [T]he right approach for the Church is to get above the conflict by stating clearly the Christian standards and ideals to be followed, and below it by personal example in helping to relieve the distress and hardship caused to individual miners and their families. The stuff in the middle – the wheeling and dealing that has to be part of government – should be avoided.[69]

Henry Clark rightly criticises this approach for its theological limitations, presenting as it does, a very limited understanding of the Christian faith and a 'pseudotransformationism' which is 'hope-

---

65 This breakdown is taken from Clark, *Under*, 22-27.

66 John B. Taylor recalls the prevalence of this view amongst members of the Thatcher Government: 'They didn't like the opposition to the Sunday Trading Bill in particular. I remember being taken to task by Lord Hailsham in a long letter because I happened to say that when that came forward that I could no longer give my support to the Government who attacked the institution of the Sunday... It was at a time when they were always telling the bishops not to meddle with politics, to which my reply was, "well let the politicians not meddle with religion".' John B. Taylor (Bishop of St Albans) in an interview with the author, 29th July 2002, Appendix 5.

67 This view has recently received fresh support from Brian Mawhinney who argues that the Bishops should be making 'Thus saith the Lord...' style proclamations of Christian values in the political arena. He criticises the Church for setting out 'policies which they think will resolve the matter with which they say God is displeased.' Mawhinney, *Firing Line*, 224-225.

68 See particularly Norman, *Order*, 78, 80. Norman became something of a guru to Mrs Thatcher. She even hailed him as 'a prophet'. His *Church and Society in Modern England*, 'developed the idea of a natural congruence between Christianity and Conservatism, based on the moral superiority of the free market.' Campbell, *Thatcher*, 372.

69 Alexander Grey, 'Establishing Church and State Ethics', *Crucible* (1982), 52ff as cited by Clark, *Under*, 23.

lessly unrealistic'.[70] We might also criticise this approach for ignoring the fact that silence, as well as words and actions, have political implications.[71] Theologically this approach also shows weakness by making a dualistic distinction between the sacred and the secular:

> Religion has not to do with an eternal deprived of temporal roots, nor has politics to do with a temporal stripped of its trans-temporal repercussions... A religion for our times must be political, and thus cannot keep itself on the edge of problems of injustice, hunger, war, exploitation, the power of money, the function of the economy, armaments, ecological questions, demographic problems, etc.[72]

The stay out of politics approach also falsely dichotomises between social service and social action.[73] John Stott, using one of Thatcher's favourite parables,[74] argues that:

> It seems clear, then, that genuine Christian social concern will embrace both social service and social action. It would be very artificial to divorce them. Some cases of need cannot be relieved at all without political action... To go on relieving other needs, though necessary, may condone the situation which causes them. If travellers on the Jerusalem-Jericho road were habitually beaten up, and habitually cared for by Good Samaritans, the need for better laws to eliminate armed robbery might well be overlooked... So if we truly love our neighbours, and want to serve them, our service may oblige us to take (or solicit) political action on their behalf.[75]

Additionally, an approach which considers political comment to be beyond the remit of the Church represents a radical break with the historic witness of the Church. Bringing critique and challenge to the State was not a theological or ecclesiological innovation of the

---

70 Clark, *Under*, 29. Pseudotransformationism is an American term used to describe 'the stoutly held (but pathetically naive) assumption that society will automatically be transformed if Churches concentrate on promoting the redemption of individuals.'

71 Montefiore, *Politics*, 23.

72 R. Pannikar, 'Religion or Politics: The Modern Western Dilemma', in P.H. Merkl & N. Smart (eds.), *Religion and Politics in the Modern World* (London: New York University Press, 1983), 46, 55.

73 John Stott defines social action for us: 'Social action is not only a question of winning the public debate, but of securing legislation which makes public life more pleasing to God. Not that every sin should be made a crime, and all duty buttressed in legal sanctions.' J.R.W. Stott, *Issues Facing Christians Today* (London: Marshall Pickering, 1990), 57.

74 Campbell, *Thatcher*, 17.

75 Stott, *Issues*, 12.

1980s.[76] Indeed, as Michael Fogarty observes, '[t]he Churches have never been absent from involvement in public policy.'[77]

2) Make Pronouncements only on 'Moral Issues'

Other writers assert that Christian leaders should make pronouncements only on 'moral issues' in the socio-political sphere. This position is built upon two considerations. Firstly, that it is only on moral matters that bishops have an expert knowledge and are therefore competent to speak. Secondly, that it avoids idolatry.

> The argument concerning idolatry is that no secular cause, programme, party or person is good enough to be baptized as (fully or perfectly) 'Christian'. To appear to urge church people to support some partisan endeavour... is to proclaim a religious duty where none can rightly be said to exist...[78]

While rightly recognising the danger of idolatry inherent when Christian leaders speak politically this approach is open to criticism for its limited assessment of the competence of Christian leaders, many of whom have experience which is far more broadly based than is often recognised. Such logic also falls prey to the assumption that on any and every subject the comments of all, except the accredited 'expert', should be gagged – an assumption which is as dubious in relation to morality as it is in relation to politics.[79] Most significantly, however, Clark justifiably condemns this approach on the basis of the impossibility of classifying a specific set of issues as 'moral issues'.

3) Present Middle Axioms

The middle axioms approach originated with J.H. Oldham, was developed by William Temple, and has subsequently been widely accepted within Anglican socio-political thought. Medhurst and Moyser describe the middle axioms approach as the attempt to:

---

76 Richard Bauckham observes: 'Many Christians have recently been rediscovering the political dimension of the message of the Bible. This is really a return to normality, since the notion that biblical Christianity has nothing to do with politics is little more than a modern Western Christian aberration, which would not have been entertained by the Church in most periods and places of its history. R. Bauckham, *The Bible in Politics: How to Read the Bible Politically* (London: SPCK, 1989), 1.

77 M. Fogarty, 'The Churches and Public Policy: The Case for a Review', in *Policy Studies*, 9.4 (1989), 43.

78 Clark, *Under*, 24.

79 See the comments of John Whale below relating to the middle axioms approach.

[I]nterpose between very general propositions and mundane daily practice a mediating body of principles capable of providing Christian political activists with general yet relatively unspecific pointers, albeit pointers falling short of detailed policy recommendations. The latter, it is maintained, are best left to practitioners with appropriate expertise.[80]

The middle axiom approach is greeted more warmly by Clark than the previous two positions. He does, however, argue that in an age in which the Christian foundations of the nation are being eroded the Church's spokesmen may need on occasions to push beyond middle axioms in search of a more potent weapon of witness.[81] We might also challenge that aspect of the middle axiom approach which argues that the Church is not entitled to apply those middle axioms 'to advocate specific remedies' in the political sphere. This, it is argued, should be left to politicians with the expertise necessary to execute such a task.[82] Politicians do, of course, have a tremendous wealth of experience and resources which rightly puts them in the centre of public-policy making but, as John Whale argues vividly and persuasively:

That argument will not silence Christian political recommendations, nor does it deserve to. It suggests that a principle can be separated from its application. In fact, though, a principle can be intelligently stated only in its application. Otherwise it floats free, unattached to human experience. It cannot be seen to be applicable unless the application is examined.[83] This distinction between principle and application is in fact a claim that politics should be left to politicians. But that is not a statement of the same order as that flying airliners should be left to airline pilots. It posits a degree of expertise in politicians as a class that is not borne out in their performance; nor could it be. Politics is an inexact science of vast range, dealing constantly with the hitherto unknown. In a properly

---

80   Medhurst & Moyser, *Secular*, 293. See also Montefiore, *Politics*, 28.
81   Clark, *Under*, 29. See also Montefiore, *Politics*, 30 and D.B. Forrester, *Beliefs, Values and Policies* (Oxford: Clarendon Press, 1989), 34.
82   W. Temple, *Christianity and the Social Order* (London: SCM Press, 1942), 24, 47.
83   See also Forrester who argues that: '[P]rinciples and middle axioms cannot be understood, elucidated, or assessed except in relation to the policies which might be used to implement them. Principles need to be tested, reconsidered, and modified in the light of the experience of trying to make them operational.' Forrester, *Beliefs*, 33.

run democracy it calls on the best thoughts of every citizen.[84]

Of course the real danger is that the political recommendations made by the bishops will be proven wrong. In the words of William Temple: 'This refusal to adopt a particular policy is partly a matter of prudence, for the policy may turn out to be mistaken... and the Church must not be involved in failure'.[85] American Christian Ethicist, J. Philip Wogaman, discussing the role of the Churches in educating their members on the factual and theological aspects of public issues, demolishes this line of argument:

> It could be objected that the churches run the risk of being wrong in their analysis of particular issues. But they can be wrong about anything, including their own more basic statements of faith, their exegesis of scripture, their portrayals of church history, or the implications of their canon law or liturgies. The church is a fallible human institution, populated and led by sinners of limited intelligence... If the church had to limit itself to actions and proclamations concerning which it could be certain, what could it do or say?[86]

4) The Niebuhrian Model

Henry Clark points to *The Church and the Bomb* (1982) and *Faith in the City* (1985) as successful examples of the Church stepping beyond middle axioms to propose specific policy recommendations.[87] He supports this approach, suggesting that Church spokesmen should pursue what he calls a Niebuhrian Model of socio-political involvement.[88] Such an approach involves 'an analysis of issues from the

---

84 Whale, *Anglican*, 60-61. Andrew Marr shares Whale's assessment of the limitations of politicians, asking: '[I]f the political leaders are so expert, if they are initiates in some hidden science of choosing, why are they so bad at it, and why do they disagree about so many basic questions?' A. Marr, *Ruling Britannia: The Failure and Future of British Democracy* (London: Penguin, 1996), 50.

85 Temple, *Social*, 24.

86 J.P. Wogaman, *Christian Perspectives on Politics* (Louisville, KY: Westminster John Knox Press, 2000), 266.

87 See Section 2.3.4.7 above regarding the apparent influence of *Faith in the City* on the Conservative 1987 General Election campaign.

88 In a footnote Clark explains why he considers the term 'Niebuhrian' to be pertinent: '...it highlights certain assumptions about collective sin, pragmatism, and the need to use power which I see as necessary correctives to the excessive faith in reason and individualism in British ethical theory.' Clark, *Under*, 30. His term has been used in this analysis though others, such as 'Tendering Modest Political Contributions', could be used to summarise the same position.

standpoint of the speaker which ends with tentative recommendations about the kinds of policies which are needed to achieve the
values to which the speaker is committed.'[89] In *Church and Politics in
a Secular Age* Medhurst and Moyser conclude similarly:

> [T]he Church may modestly contribute to the resolution of specific
> policy questions. In this area there is the danger of platitudinous
> moralizing or of technically ill-informed judgements. But this has
> to be set against the danger of too readily abdicating responsibility
> in favour of narrowly based technical specialists. The Church per-
> haps has a distinctive part to play in placing ostensibly technical
> issues within the relevant moral frameworks. Not least, the cred-
> ibility of its own political witness partly depends on contributing
> positive and well-informed policy-proposals. A merely negative
> denunciatory role will not, in the long run, enable the Church to be
> heard in the public arena.[90]

Looking at a similar selection of approaches to those outlined
above, Hugh Montefiore emphasises the importance of the Church
avoiding being limited to using the same approach in every particular situation (though he does exclude the 'stay out of politics'
approach in all circumstances):

> Here, then, are various options from which the Church may
> choose to use its influence and persuasive powers in political mat-
> ters. Which should it choose? It is tempting to say that only one
> should be chosen and the others eschewed. I do not myself find
> this satisfactory.[91]

3.3.4 A House for the Future

During the course of our analysis of the contribution of the bishops
to the House of Lords during the Thatcher years, and in our concluding remarks, we will consider how the Church of England can

---

89   Clark, *Under*, 30.
90   Medhurst & Moyser, *Secular*, 364. See also Ecclestone, *England*, 48.
91   Montefiore, *Politics*, 28. Montefiore did, however, strike a strong note of
     caution with regard to bishops proposing specific policy recommendations
     (the fourth of the approaches he outlines in *Chrstianity and Politics*) in an
     interview with the author: 'I'm doubtful as to whether its appropriate that
     the Church should give detailed recommendations on what a government
     should do in particular situations, though I appreciate in a report like that
     [*Faith in the City*], that unless you had some detailed recommendations, the
     whole thing would collapse and not be taken seriously. But, by and large,
     I am not, I don't approve of clergymen getting involved in political details
     because it's not their job.' Hugh Montefiore (Bishop of Birmingham) in an
     interview with the author, 21st May 2002, Appendix 3.

best facilitate the service of its bishops in the Second Chamber in the future. As we do so our comments need to be sensitive to changes to religious representation in the Second Chamber likely to result from the ongoing process of Lords reform heralded by the Labour Party's 1997 Manifesto commitment:

> New Labour in government will, as we promised, carry out a careful and considered reform of the House of Lords: the immediate removal of the hereditary peerage, and longer-term reform of the House of Lords as a whole. This is a radical and a historic task.[92]

The initial result of that commitment was the publication of a White Paper (January 1999) in which, most significantly, the Government committed itself to legislating to remove the rights of hereditary peers to sit and vote in the House of Lords and to appoint a Royal Commission to make recommendations for a wide-ranging reform of the second chamber.[93] The rights of all but ninety-two hereditary peers to sit and vote in the House were duly removed in November 1999 and a Royal Commission, chaired by Lord Wakeham, with broad terms of reference to consider the role, functions, and composition of the second chamber met from March to December 1999, publishing its report entitled *A House for the Future* in January 2000. The Church of England's submission to the Royal Commission has been referred to above (Section 3.3.2). It pressed for wider representation for the other Christian denominations and faiths which are part of the nation's spiritual life without giving precise suggestions regarding the numbers of representatives that should be involved.[94] With regard to the role of its own bishops in a reformed second chamber the Church's submission argued that: '[r]educing the number of bishops available to the chamber [below the present twenty-six] risks compromising the service of the Church of England by impoverishing the range of contributions – regional and otherwise – that it can offer.'[95]

A House for the Future contained 132 recommendations, nine of which related to the representation of religious faiths.[96] The most significant of these, in relation to the role of the bishops in a reformed House, assert that:

- 'The Church of England should continue to be explicitly rep-

---

92 Government White Paper, *Modernising Parliament: Reforming the House of Lords*, Cm 4183 (London: The Stationery Office, January 1999), iii.

93 *ibid*, 7.

94 Council, *Role*, 9.

95 *ibid*, 10.

96 For these recommendations in full see Royal, *Future*, 191-192.

resented in the second chamber, but the concept of religious representation should be broadened to embrace other Christian denominations, in all parts of the United Kingdom, and other faith communities.' (Recommendation 108).

- 'The Appointments Commission should ensure that at any one time there are at least five members of the second chamber specifically selected to be broadly representative of the different non-Christian faith communities.' (Recommendation 109).[97]

- 'The total number of places in the reformed second chamber for members formally representing the various Christian denominations throughout the United Kingdom should be 26. Taking into account the relative size of the population in each of the nations which comprise the United Kingdom, 21 of these places should go to members representing the Christian denominations in England and five should go to members representing the Christian denominations in Scotland, Wales and Northern Ireland.' (Recommendation 110).

- 'Of the 21 places available for members of the Christian denominations in England, 16 should be assigned to representatives of the Church of England and five to members of other Christian denominations in England.' (Recommendation 111).

- 'The Church of England should review the options for providing formal Church of England representation in the reformed second chamber. Their detailed recommendations should be made to the Government in time for incorporation into whatever legislation is required to implement our own recommendations.' (Recommendation 115).[98]

The House of Lords: Completing the Reform, a second Government White Paper published in November 2001, sets out '...how the Government intends to deliver its 2001 Manifesto pledge to implement

---

97 It should be noted that the report does acknowledge the difficulties inherent to facilitating the representation of the nation's non-Anglican Christian denominations. Royal, *Future*, 153 (15.11-15.13). Until these obstacles are overcome the Church of England bishops are better placed to represent the broad spectrum of religious opinion in the United Kingdom than any other members of the House of Lords.

98 In the context of Recommendation 115 the Wakeham report expresses concern that 'unless the number of eligible bishoprics were reduced, or the basis of Church of England representation altered, bishops would in future need to wait for up to ten years before becoming members of the second chamber and could then only expect to serve for three or four years.' It also indicates a preference for Church of England representatives who would be able to serve a 15-year term in the House of Lords. It leaves the resolution of these issues to the Church of England.

the Royal Commission report "in the most effective way possible."'[99]
It states that: 'The Government acknowledges the force of the Royal
Commission's proposition that religious representation helps in the
recognition of the part that moral, philosophical and theological considerations have to play in debating political and social issues.'[100]
Likewise, the White Paper accepts the Royal Commission's proposal that there should be a formal representation for the Church
of England and that this representation should be reduced numerically, from 26 to 16 places.[101] It does not, however, accept the recommendation that other denominations and faiths should be formally
represented in a reformed second chamber arguing that 'the practical obstacles are simply too great.'[102] Instead the Government White
Paper proposes that the Appointments Commission[103] should '...give
proper recognition to the non-Church of England faith communities
as they seek greater representativeness in the independent membership of the House.'[104]

The Government's invitation for responses to all the proposals
contained in *The House of Lords: Completing the Reform* was accepted
by the Archbishops' Council whose unpublished response was sent
to the Lord Chancellor and the Prime Minister on 31st January 2002.
As expected, the Church's response did not greet warmly either the
Government's intention to reduce the Church of England's representation to 16 or the failure to provide for formal representation for
other denominations and faiths:[105]

> Our belief remains that a total presence of twenty bishops is the
> minimum necessary to maintain the parliamentary service we seek
> to offer. We also continue to believe that there should be a defined
> overall number of places for other Christian churches and other
> faiths. [106]

---

99 Government White Paper, *The House of Lords: Completing the Reform* (London:
   The Stationery Office, November 2001), 4.

100 *ibid*, 29.

101 *ibid*.

102 *ibid*. For an outline of these obstacles see Royal, *Future*, 153 (15.11-15.13).

103 The body responsible for managing the balance and size of the House,
   appointing the independent members of the House, and ensuring the
   integrity of the members nominated by political parties. *ibid*, 7.

104 *ibid*, 29.

105 Archbishops' Council, *Comments from the Church of England on the
   Government's White Paper* (Unpublished: January 2002).

106 *ibid*.

3.4 Conclusion

Constitutionally, the eligibility of the Church of England bishops to sit in the House of Lords is rooted in power and influence in medieval society, not in the establishment of the Church. As such they come to the House as individual Lords of Parliament, not as representatives of the Church of England. Pragmatically, both Church and State increasingly point to the bishops' local experience and leadership to defend their seats. Whilst disagreement persists between Church and State with regard to the numerical strength of the Bench of Bishops in a reformed Second Chamber there is no evidence to suggest that there will be a total removal of bishops from Parliamentary life.

The Church of England bishops who contributed to the business of the House of Lords during the Thatcher years were more diocese-focused and less politicized than their post-war predecessors. It is likely that this gave them a predisposition to respond critically to the Government's policies in the House of Lords. During the same period the House of Lords became increasingly active and independent, obstructing the policies of the Thatcher Government on a regular basis and adding to its reputation as a significant and influential political body.

CHAPTER FOUR

Episcopal Attendance

4.1 Introduction

4.1.1 Introduction

The Church of England's submission to the Wakeham Commission on the Reform of the House of Lords claims that '[b]ishops maintain a constant attendance in the second chamber so that the Church is always in a position to respond to the issues of the day.'[1] Certainly, the staff at Lambeth Palace arrange for a duty bishop to be assigned for every day that the House is sitting. His duty is to lead prayers in the Upper House at the beginning of the day's business.[2] A list is circulated amongst the bishops (the most senior bishops receive it first)[3] for the bishops to sign up for two or three weeks at the House during which, according to John B. Taylor (Bishop of St Albans), they are 'supposed to be there all day for any business right up to closing time at ten o'clock or whenever it is...'[4] Taylor's use of the word 'supposed' suggests that the 'constant attendance' claimed by the Church (a claim heavily dependent on the record of the duty bishops) reflects the intention more than the execution.

Commenting on the attendance of the Lords Spiritual more generally Donald Shell proposes that during the 1980s:

> [B]ishops were not on the whole... regular attenders... Bishops are busy people, and attendance at the House of Lords has to be fitted in around a very full schedule... Some bishops give much more attention to the Lords than others, but very few in recent years have attended more than one-third of the sitting-days.[5]

Adrian Hastings shares Shell's analysis, commenting that 'in general episcopal presence is undoubtedly rather thin'.[6] This analysis is

---

1   Council, *Role*, 8.
2   Hastings, *Runcie*, 85. The five bishops whose eligibility is *ex officio* are exempt from this task.
3   John Taylor (Bishop of St Albans) in an interview with the author, 29th July 2002, Appendix 5.
4   *ibid*.
5   Shell, *Lords*, 54-55.
6   Hastings, *Runcie*, 85.

also supported by the research of Francis Bown into the contribution of the bishops to the House of Lords during the period of May 1979 to May 1987 presented in *Political Studies* during 1994. His figures show the average bishop as being in attendance at the House on just 12% of sitting days.[7]

Medhurst and Moyser note that episcopal attendance is dependant upon the individual personality, experience, expertise and priorities of each bishop.[8] This assessment fits with the submission which the bishops made to the Jellicoe Committee on the working of the House of Lords during 1971. It indicates that a minority of diocesans were simply not keen to be involved in the business of the House of Lords. It also reveals that, for those bishops (the majority) who did see it as a valuable opportunity, it always came below the diocese on their list of priorities.[9] The findings of Francis Bown present the same picture, revealing a variety of individual attendance rates ranging from attendance on 2% to 51% of sitting days.[10]

4.1.2 Methodology

Our analysis of episcopal attendance at the House of Lords during the Thatcher years excludes the whole of the 1990/91 Parliamentary session. Attendance figures for the bishops were gathered from the House of Lords *Sessional Statistics*[11] which only report the attendance of members of the House for each Parliamentary session as a whole, not for individual sitting days or weeks. It was, therefore, considered more helpful to exclude from our analysis the first ten days of the 1990/91 Parliamentary session which were part of the Thatcher years (strictly defined), rather than include some 127 days of the same Parliamentary session which were within John Major's premiership.[12] Throughout this chapter the use of the terms 'Thatcher

---

7   Bown, 'Influencing', 107.
8   Medhurst & Moyser, 'Lambeth', 77. For example, in noting that he has always said that his role in the House of Lords is the 'one part' of his life as a bishop that he misses in retirement, it is obvious why David Say was heavily involved in contributing to the House. David Say (Bishop of Rochester) in an interview with the author, 29th May 2002, Appendix 4.
9   Chadwick, *Ramsey*, 183.
10   Bown, 'Influencing', 107.
11   *Sessional Statistics* have been compiled by the House of Lords Journal and Information Office for each Parliamentary session since 1968.
12   Margaret Thatcher was Prime Minister from 3rd May 1979 to 22nd November 1990. Our analysis begins on 9th May 1979 - the first day of the first Parliament of her premiership.

years' and '1980s' assumes the omission of this ten day period. The word 'attendance' is used to refer to the presence of an individual bishop at the House of Lords for some part of an individual sitting day. There is no way of ascertaining whether an individual was present at the House for the whole of a day's business, or just for a few minutes. The attendance figures given in *Sessional Statistics* do not include swearing-in days and days when the House sat for judicial business only.

4.2 The Extent of the Bishops' Attendance

The Lords Spiritual registered a total of 4384 individual attendances at the House of Lords during the Thatcher years, approximately 38% of which would have been made by the duty bishop assigned to read prayers at the beginning of each sitting day.[13] The greatest number of episcopal attendances (730) were recorded during the 1979/80 Parliamentary session, the least (252) during the 1986/87 Parliamentary session (Figure 4.1).

Figure 4.1
Episcopal Attendance at the House of Lords

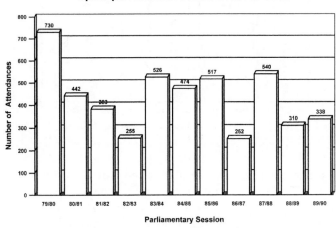

Data Source: House of Lords Sessional Statistics (House of Lords Record and Information Office).

These figures are of negligible value when viewed in isolation from the number of sitting days of the House of Lords in each Parliamentary session. The number of days on which the House sits

---

13 This figure is based on the assumption that a duty bishop was in attendance at some point (even if not for the reading of prayers) during every one of the 1160 sitting days of Parliament. On a handful of occasions this may not have been the case.

during each Parliamentary session varies and so, correspondingly, do the number of opportunities for an episcopal attendance at the House. During the Thatcher years the House of Lords sat for a total of 1660 sitting days at an average of 151 sitting days per Parliamentary session. The greatest number of sitting days took place during the 1979/80 Parliamentary session (206 days during the 18 months between May 1979 and November 1980 immediately after the 1979 General Election), the least during the 1986/87 Parliamentary session (84 days during the six months between November 1986 and May 1987 just prior to the 1987 General Election) (Figure 4.2). A 'normal' Parliamentary session during a non-election year covers a 12-month period from November to November.

Figure 4.2
Number of Sitting Days of the House of Lords

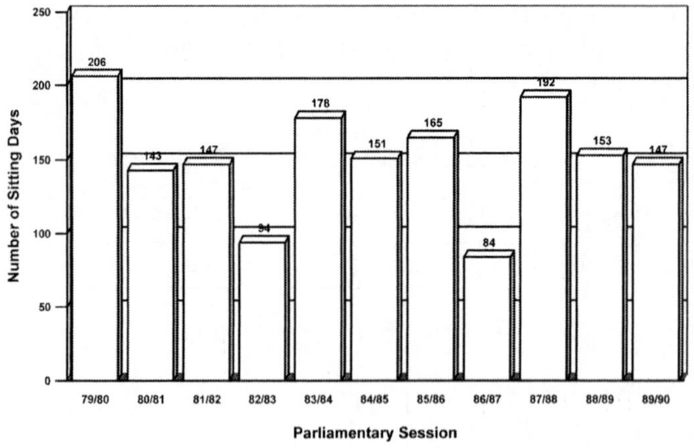

Data Source: House of Lords Sessional Statistics (House of Lords Record and Information Office).

With this vital piece of context taken into account the picture painted of episcopal attendance is more consistent. The average attendance per sitting day during the 1980s was 2.8 bishops per sitting day (11% of the 26 bishops eligible to attend) (Figure 4.3). Such a measurement must be treated with caution because the attendance habits of the bishops were by no means as regular or consistent as an average implies. These figures do not compare favourably with the attendance record of the members of the House as a whole. The House of Lords *Sessional Statistics* lists the total membership of the Lords as averaging 940 during the Thatcher years.[14] The same publi-

---

14 Excluding peers without a writ of summons and peers with leave of
    absence.

cation lists the average attendance per sitting day of the members of the House as a whole during the Thatcher years as 310. Thus, we can say that, on average, 33% of the total membership of the House were in attendance on each sitting day.[15]

Figure 4.3
Average Episcopal Attendance at the House of Lords per Sitting Day

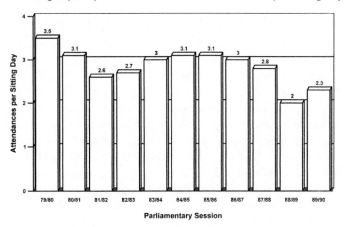

Data Source: House of Lords Sessional Statistics (House of Lords Record and Information Office).

The 1979/80 Parliamentary session experienced the greatest episcopal presence (3.5 bishops per sitting day), the 1988/89 Parliamentary session the least (2.0 bishops per sitting day). The number of episcopal attendances during the 1979/80 Parliamentary session may be explained by the interest aroused by the election of a new government with a passionate commitment to radical reform and under the leadership of the first female Prime Minister in British history – what we might call the 'circus-factor'. This explanation would certainly make sense of the fact that this peak in attendance was not matched by a peak in the number of speeches made by the bishops during the same session (Figure 6.2 below). We can conclude from this contrast

---

15 If we divide up the total membership of the House into those whose membership is 'active' and those who, in the words of Shell, 'belong so loosely that they are scarcely members in any real sense', and exclude the latter from our calculations, then the average attendance of the total membership of the House would be far higher. For example, Shell notes that during the 1989-90 Parliamentary session over 350 peers (more than one third of the total membership of the House) did not attend at all. If we removed these 350 peers from our calculations we would be left with an approximate average of over 50% of the total membership in attendance per sitting day. Shell, *Lords*, 48.

that the bishops attended the House on more occasions for reasons other than to contribute to debates themselves. However, if the 'circus-factor' was responsible for the increased episcopal attendance one would expect that the Lords Temporal would have responded to the change in government in a similar manner. The figures for the daily attendance of all members of the House of Lords do not, however, reveal this to be the case.[16] We must therefore conclude that either the Lords Spiritual were drawn by the 'circus-factor' to attend the House of Lords with extra vigour during the 1979/80 session but that this same influence did not affect their temporal colleagues, or that another explanation exists for their behaviour.

Of particular note are two dips in attendance, during the 1981/82 and 1982/83 sessions and, more markedly, during the 1988/89 and 1989/90 sessions. These dips may not represent an aberration in the attendance behaviour of the bishops. Rather, it could be argued that the higher attendance figures of over 3.0 attendances per sitting day recorded from the 1983/84 to the 1986/87 Parliamentary session represent unusual behaviour amongst the bishops and that the lower attendance rates are the norm. The attendance levels of the members of the House as a whole (as measured between 1959 and 1999) support this assessment, revealing a similar peak in attendance from the 1983/84 to the 1986/87 Parliamentary session.[17] This peak in episcopal attendance may represent a particular episcopal interest in contributing to the House of Lords between 1984 and 1987. Consideration of the extent of episcopal speech-making during this same period (Section 6.2 below) will indicate this is a justifiable interpretation of the attendance and voting data.

4.3 Which Bishops Attended

Attendance at the House of Lords varied considerably amongst the different individual bishops eligible to attend over the course of the Thatcher years (Figure 4.4). Bishops from the provinces of Canterbury[18] and York,[19] relative to their size, made a similar number of visits to the House – in spite of the greater distance of the dioceses within the York province from Westminster. In fact, relative to its size, York undertook a slightly greater proportion of the bishops'

---

16 Royal, *Future*, 19.
17 *ibid*.
18 The province of Canterbury contains 29 dioceses and its bishops made a total of 2934 visits to the House during the 1980s.
19 The province of York contains 13 dioceses and its bishops made a total of 1450 visits to the House during the 1980s.

attendance, with each diocese making, on average, 112 visits to the House as opposed to the Canterbury's 101 visits.

There were individual bishops who made a noticeably high or low number of visits to the House. Intriguingly, the highest level of attendance was achieved by David Halsey (Bishop of Carlisle) who made a total of 596 visits to the House between May 1979 and his retirement in June 1989, even though his See is over 300 miles away from Westminster. The length of his eligibility to attend in part accounts for this but other men such as Eric Kemp (Bishop of Chichester)[20] and David Say (Bishop of Rochester)[21] who were eligible to attend for a similar proportion of the Thatcher years, came from similar types of diocese, and lived far closer to Westminster, did not come close to this level of attendance.[22]

Gerald Ellison (Bishop of London) registered the greatest level of attendance by an individual bishop in one Parliamentary session during the 1979/80 Parliamentary session, visiting the House on 109 occasions. His attendance rate is all the more impressive in view of the fact that, as Bishop of London, he was never required to attend the House as duty bishop. Remarkably, the controversial figure of David Jenkins (Bishop of Durham),[23] who was one of the most publicly recognisable bishops during the 1980s, visited the House of Lords on only 13 occasions.[24] He gives the following explanation for his limited attendance at the House:

> Attendance in the Lords always involved me, if I were to speak, in two days away from the diocese. The notice would also be pretty short-term, so my London visit was bound to clash with some pre-existing engagement locally. This meant that I had to balance the priority between my commitments locally and the likelihood of my appearance in the Lords making any difference there or

---

20 Eric Kemp (Bishop of Chichester) made 163 visits to the House.
21 David Say (Bishop of Rochester) made 382 visits to the House.
22 A fuller discussion of David Halsey's attendance record can be found in Section 5.4 below.
23 The basis for Jenkins' controversial reputation is explained by Bernard Palmer. Several weeks after his appointment had been announced, 'in a television programme, the bishop-designate appeared to cast doubts on the Virgin Birth and the Resurrection, and the flood-gates were opened. Archbishop Habgood... was urged to refuse the alleged heretic consecration; and... he declined to oblige the critics and the consecration went ahead. York Minster was struck by lightning two days later - a sign, so the critics claimed, of the divine displeasure.' Palmer, *Mitred*, 292.
24 Jenkins, as Bishop of Durham, was never required to attend the House as duty bishop.

Figure 4.4
Attendance at the House of Lords by Individual Bishops

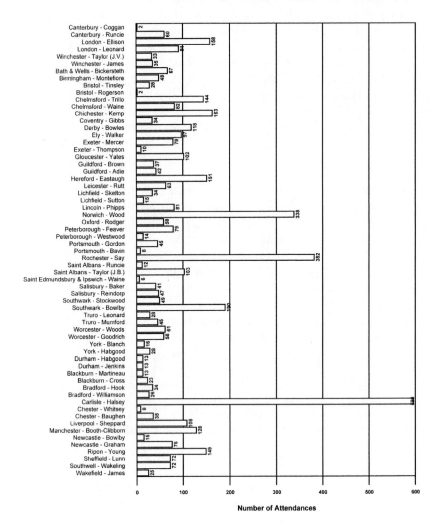

Number of Attendances

Data Source: House of Lords Sessional Statistics (House of Lords Record and Information Office)

elsewhere.[25]

Clearly, Jenkins's limited attendance suggests that he concluded more often than not that an appearance at the House of Lords was unlikely to make any difference in that place or elsewhere.[26] Only

---

25 David Jenkins (Bishop of Durham) in a letter to the author, 13th May 2002.
26 Jenkins also made a limited number of speeches to the House (Section 6.6 below).

Graham Leonard,[27] John Habgood,[28] and Robert Runcie[29] were eligible to attend the House of Lords during the whole of Mrs Thatcher's premiership. Popularized accounts of the period would cast the first as her greatest ally amongst the bishops,[30] and the last as one of her most enduring foes. Leonard attended the House on 28 occasions whilst Bishop of Truro, and on 91 occasions once he became Bishop of London. John Habgood attended the House on just 41 occasions (28 of which were whilst he was Archbishop of York). Runcie attended 12 times whilst Bishop of St Albans, and 60 times as Archbishop of Canterbury. The incumbent of London is traditionally appointed with the expectation that, by virtue of his close proximity to Westminster, he will (alongside the two Archbishops) play a lead role in the central organs of both Church and State. In the light of their particular responsibility in these matters, the attendance rate of Leonard, Runcie and Habgood, whilst respectable, are not as high as one might expect.

4.4 Conclusion

Our analysis of the attendance rates of the individual bishops who were eligible to attend the House during the 1980s supports Medhurst and Moyser's assertion that episcopal attendance is, above all, dependant upon the individual personality, experience, expertise and priorities of each bishop.[31] The sheer variety of the attendance records of the bishops, even taking into account the varying length of their periods of eligibility to attend, can only be accounted for in this way. Such evidence suggests that the present system for selecting bishops to sit in the House of Lords needs reviewing. A strong case exists for considering a system which would ensure a decisive shift away from the present determinative role of seniority to a process of selection which takes into account the individual personality, experience, expertise and priorities of the individuals within the available pool of bishops. Such a change would be unlikely to have a dramatic effect whilst 26 bishops continue to be eligible to attend the Lords (and therefore most diocesan bishops are required to sit on the Bench of Bishops for some part of their time as a bishop). However,

---

27 As Bishop of Truro and London.
28 As Bishop of Durham and York.
29 As Bishop of St Albans and Archbishop of Canterbury.
30 Bill Westwood (Bishop of Peterborough) might have offered Leonard stiff competition for this accolade had he not only become eligible to attend the House of Lords in October 1989.
31 Medhurst & Moyser, 'Lambeth', 77.

in the event of the reduction in the number of places allocated to the Church of England bishops to 16, a change of this type would ensure that those increasingly valuable places would be occupied by individual bishops committed, and able, to make use of the opportunity to contribute to the House. Equally, it would help to ensure that bishops ill-equipped (for whatever reason) to contribute to Parliamentary life are not required to expend their energies away from their calling within the diocese and the national structures of the Church.

Reflecting more generally the evidence reviewed paints a rather negative picture of the attendance levels of the bishops with, on average, just 11% of those bishops eligible to sit in the House of Lords present on each sitting day. This supports the analysis of Shell, Hastings and Bown. Such evidence provides ammunition for those who would call for a review of the structures that govern episcopal involvement in Parliamentary life in order that those bishops who do sit in the House of Lords are able to attend with greater ease. The reform resulting from such a review would necessarily involve a weakening of the link between the bishop and his diocese – whether to a greater extent (through the formation of specialist 'political bishops' who are free from diocesan responsibilities) or to a lesser extent (through growing dependence on suffragan bishops ministering to the diocese). The diocesan link was considered by the Wakeham Commission to be of fundamental importance to the ongoing value of the bishops' presence in the Second Chamber: 'The Church of England bishops have been effective members of the House of Lords, partly because their diocesan responsibilities have given them a valuable insight into a range of social and regional issues.'[32] If no reform is to take place then the Church must give more attention to generating an understanding within Parliament and the Church that the bishops in effect operate as a 'pack' at the House of Lords, whose combined contribution produces the input level of eight or nine 'average' peers.[33]

---

32 Royal, *Future*, 158 (15.27).
33 John Taylor refers to the unofficial leader of the bishops in the House of Lords as the 'pack leader'. Asked whether this was an unofficial term, he replied: 'Certainly I was asked by Robert Runcie: "Would you be one of the pack leaders".' John B. Taylor (Bishop of St Albans) in an interview with the author, 29th July 2002, Appendix 5.

CHAPTER FIVE

Episcopal Voting

5.1 Introduction

5.1.1 Introduction

'It is well understood,' writes Lord Longford, 'that it is almost impossible for bishops to preserve a high record of voting. They remain a minor factor in the politics of the House.'[1] This assessment tallies with the research of Francis Bown which indicates that, between 1979 and 1987, the bishops took part in only 21.4% of the divisions of the House of Lords.[2] Bown's research also reveals that it was exceedingly rare for more than two bishops to vote in the same division, asserting that only 3.9% of the divisions of the House involved more than two bishops.[3] When the bishops are voting Shell points out that they:

> [D]o not appear to show any inhibition in voting against the Government, or even helping to bring about a Government defeat... In the 1980s tensions between the Church of England and Mrs Thatcher's Conservative Government became very obvious, and the bishops in the Lords found themselves voting against the Government much more frequently than in its support.[4]

Bown's research supports Shell's assessment, revealing a ratio of 5:2 between the episcopal votes cast against and in support of the Government. Bown also provides evidence to argue that, 'the differing perspectives and independent views of individual bishops... did not often find expression in a divided bishops' vote'.[5] He records 17 occasions during his period of study (1979-1987) in which bishops voted in opposing lobbies and states that in only one division (on the British Nationality Bill on 29th October 1981) was there more than one bishop in each lobby.[6] He does note, however, that in part this

---

1   Longford, *Bishops*, 114.
2   Bown, 'Influencing', 109.
3   *ibid.*
4   Shell, *Lords*, 54.
5   Bown, 'Influencing', 109.
6   *ibid.*

low number is reflective of the fact that only a little over a third of the total divisions of the House received more than one episcopal vote.

Francis Bown is able to point to just one occasion on which he considers the bishops to have changed the outcome of a division.[7] On the occasion in question two bishops were amongst a group who voted against, and defeated, the Government by 101 votes to 100. Of course, it is entirely a matter of interpretation as to whether it was the vote of one of the bishops which changed the outcome of the division or that of one the other ninety-nine anti-Government voters. Reflecting on this division Bown suggests that, had all twenty-six bishops voted in every division in which a bishop participated during the 1979-1987 period, then the result of sixty-three divisions would have been changed. He rightly dismisses this as 'a somewhat fanciful conjecture' but suggests that it indicates the 'potential effect of the bishops' votes were their behaviour to alter radically'.[8] In response we should note that, even if the bishops were to vote in this aggressive and united manner, it is unlikely that the outcome would be the one that Bown expects. To seek to influence the House in that blunt manner would be futile. As Michael Baughen (Bishop of Chester) points out (in the context of a debate regarding provisions for homeless people living in hotel accommodation in which the debate was 'won' by those speaking against the Government, but which ended in a division at which 'they all appeared' and the Government won): '...even if you had all 26 bishops present what's that against so many?'.[9] Moreover Bown fails to note the fact, that were this radical alteration of behaviour to occur, it would challenge the unwritten assumptions of Parliament to such an extent that it would almost certainly stimulate a hasty and ruthless re-examination of religious representation in the House. Such a re-examination would be likely to result in a drastic reduction of the numerical strength of the bishops.[10]

---

7   A vote on the Housing and Building Control Bill on 10th May 1984 which contained two episcopal votes against the Government and saw the Government defeated by one vote. Bown, 'Influencing', 109.

8   *ibid.*

9   Michael Baughen (Bishop of Chester) in an interview with the author, 21st May 2002, Appendix 2. Hugh Montefiore makes the same point in relation to the Shops Bill: 'They wheeled up all the old Dukes and Earls and they all sat in the bar until it came to voting and then they all voted against it.' Hugh Montefiore (Bishop of Birmingham) in an interview with the author, 21st May 2002, Appendix 3.

10   'I think it would be unfortunate', argues Hugh Montefiore, 'if the bishops turned out en-masse and voted en-masse. I don't think they'd be welcomed

5.1.2 Methodology

Our analysis of episcopal voting in the House of Lords during Margaret Thatcher's premiership excludes, as did our analysis of episcopal attendance, the 1990/91 Parliamentary session.[11] Margaret Thatcher's premiership ended ten days into the 1990/91 Parliamentary session and no votes were cast in the House of Lords during that ten day period. It was therefore considered most helpful to limit our analysis to the 11 full Parliamentary sessions of the Thatcher years. Data on the voting contribution of the bishops was drawn from House of Lords *Hansard*, the official record of the debates and divisions of the Upper House. Alongside *Hansard*, lists compiled by the House of Lords Journal and Information Office recording each division in the House of Lords were used to ensure that no divisions were missed during the process of extracting voting data from 123 volumes of *Hansard*. The divisions of the House are divided into four categories based on the outcome of the division: Government victories, Government defeats, unwhipped divisions (where, by definition, no victory or defeat occurred), and divisions with no quorum (a division on legislation in which fewer than 30 votes were cast). Our analysis will cover each of these four categories of division.

5.2 The Extent of the Bishops' Voting

The Church of England bishops together participated in a total of 476 divisions in the House of Lords during the Thatcher years (Figure 5.1). This represents 23% of the total 2077 divisions which took place in the House of Lords during that period. The vast majority of these divisions (393) resulted in Government victories. The bishops participated in 48 divisions which led to Government defeats, two divisions with no quorum, and 33 unwhipped divisions. Expressed as percentages we can say that 83% of the divisions in which the bishops participated resulted in Government victories, 10% resulted in Government defeats, and 7% were unwhipped divisions and divisions with no quorum.

---

in the House for so doing and I think it might hasten their decline.' Hugh Montefiore (Bishop of Birmingham) in an interview with the author, 21st May 2002, Appendix 3.

11   All references to the 'Thatcher years' and the '1980s' in this chapter therefore do not include the 1990/91 Parliamentary session.

Figure 5.1
Episcopal Participation in Different Types of House of Lords Division

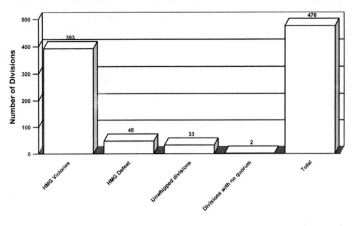

Outcome of Division

This weighting towards episcopal participation in divisions which resulted in Government victories reflects the overall weighting in the outcome of the divisions of the House during the same period. However, in the context of this overall weighting, the bishops show a greater preference for voting against the Thatcher Government than the House as a whole (Table 5.1). The bishops also show a preference for voting in unwhipped divisions.[12] That this should be so is no surprise. The content of legislation whose votes are unwhipped is often related to the ethical and social issues on which the bishops input is widely held to be most valuable and influential.[13]

---

12   Data on the outcome of divisions was taken from the House of Lords Information Office document, *Divisions in the House of Lords since 1970-71*. Unwhipped divisions and divisions with no quorum could not be listed separately from one another because this document categorised them together as 'other divisions'. Figure 5.1 reveals that all but two of the episcopal contributions to divisions which were classified in the House of Lords Information Office document as 'other divisions' were unwhipped divisions, justifying the conclusion that it was unwhipped divisions, and not divisions with no quorum, in which the bishops favoured participation.

13   A scan of the debate titles of the debates in which these unwhipped divisions took place confirms this to be the case: Marriage (Enabling) Bill (1979), Abortion (Amendment) Bill (1982), Video Recordings Bill (1984), Prohibition of Female Circumcision Bill (1985), Suicide Act 1961 (Amendment) Bill (1985), Sunday Sports Bill (1987), Abortion (Amendment) Bill (1989).

Table 5.1
Outcome of House of Lords Divisions

	Divisions resulting in a Government victory (%)	Divisions resulting in a Government defeat (%)	Divisions classified as 'other divisions' (%)
All divisions	88	8	4
Divisions involving episcopal participation	83	10	7

Data Source: Divisions in the House of Lords since 1970-71 (House of Lords Information Office)

Figure 5.2
**Episcopal Participation in House of Lords Divisions
in each Parliamentary Session**

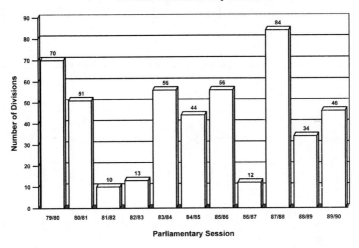

The level of episcopal participation in House of Lords divisions varied considerably over the course of the Thatcher years (Figure 5.2). The bishops participated in the greatest number of divisions during the 1987/88 Parliamentary session, casting votes in 84 divisions. The bishops participated in the least number of divisions during the 1981/82 Parliamentary session, casting votes in just 10 divisions.

A varying number of divisions took place in each Parliamentary session (Figure 5.3). As such a true picture of the voting contribution of the bishops can only be produced when the number of divisions which took place during the course of each Parliamentary session is taken into account (Figure 5.4). When the participation of the bishops in the divisions of the House is viewed in this context the picture which emerges bears some resemblance to the picture which emerged for episcopal attendance (Figure 4.3 above) in relation to the first two Parliamentary sessions of the Thatcher years. A high level of episcopal voting during the 1979/80 and 1980/81 parliamentary sessions is visible. An increase in the participation of the bishops in Lords divisions does fit within the circus-factor explanation of the peak in the attendance of the bishops. It was argued above that the lack of a peak in episcopal speech-making in these same two Parliamentary sessions suggests that the bishops were not primarily at the House to contribute to the debates but to listen to debates. An increase in the voting participation of the bishops during the 1979/80 and 1980/81 Parliamentary sessions does not undermine this argument. An increase in the voting participation in the House is the natural by-product of an increase in attendance. Unlike speech-making, voting requires little additional time or energy from a bishop (or any member of the House) once he is present at the House of Lords.

Figure 5.3
Number of House of Lords Divisions in each Parliamentary Session

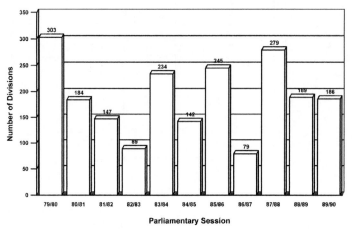

Data Source. Divisions in the House of Lords since 1970-71 (House of Lords Information Office).

In the 476 divisions in which the bishops participated they cast a total of 930 votes. Only 148 (31%) of the divisions in which the bishops participated received more than one episcopal vote. This represents 7% of the total divisions of the House. The duty bishops cast 31% (290 out of 930) of the episcopal votes. The greatest number of episcopal votes were cast during the 1987/88 Parliamentary session during which bishops cast 185 votes (Figure 5.5). The least number of episcopal votes were cast during the 1981/82 Parliamentary ses-

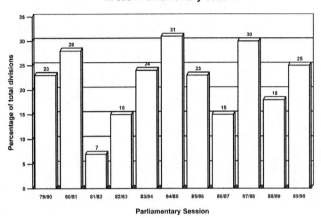

Figure 5.4
**Percentage of Divisions which involved Episcopal Participation
in each Parliamentary Session**

sion during which just 11 votes were cast. To compare fairly the level
of episcopal vote casting over the course of the Thatcher years the
number of episcopal votes cast in each Parliamentary session needs
to be viewed in relation to the number of divisions which took place
during that session. When this is done the broad picture of episcopal
vote casting remains the same, though the 1981/82 Parliamentary
session (not the 1987/88 session) is revealed to have received the
greatest episcopal voting contribution (Figure 5.6).

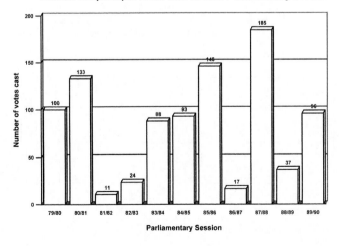

Figure 5.5
Number of Episcopal Votes Cast in each Parliamentary Session

Figure 5.6
Number of Episcopal Votes Cast per Division in each Parliamentary Session

Number of votes cast per division

Session	Value
79/80	0.33
80/81	0.72
81/82	0.06
82/83	0.27
83/84	0.38
84/85	0.66
85/86	0.6
86/87	0.2
87/88	0.67
88/89	0.2
89/90	0.5

Parliamentary Session

5.3 The Nature of the Bishops' Voting

The voting of the bishops was, for the most part, critical of the Thatcher Government. Votes cast in support of the Government accounted for 27% (255 votes) of the total votes cast by the bishops in the House of Lords during the 1980s (Figure 5.7). Votes cast against the Government accounted for 61% (567 votes) of the total votes cast by the bishops over the same period. This represents a ratio of the 2:1 between votes cast against, and votes cast for the Government. A further 11% (105 votes) of the bishops' votes were cast in unwhipped divisions and divisions with no quorum.

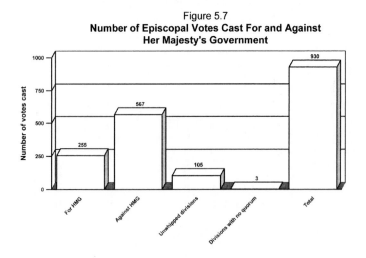

Figure 5.7
**Number of Episcopal Votes Cast For and Against
Her Majesty's Government**

The bishops cast more anti-Government than pro-Government votes in every Parliamentary session except the 1979/80 and 1981/82 sessions (Figure 5.8). The 1985/86 session saw the greatest difference between anti-Government (104 votes) and pro-Government (20 votes) voting. The progress of the Shops Bill (1985) through the House of Lords and the bishops' opposition to it accounts for this ratio of 5:1 between votes cast against, and votes cast for the Government. The 1980/81 session also saw a large number of votes cast against the Government (86 votes) compared to those cast in its support (12 votes). Again, the passage of particular legislation through the House, in this case the British Nationality Bill (1981), accounts for the high number of the anti-Government votes. In fact 76 of the 86 episcopal votes cast against the Government during the 1980/81 Parliamentary session were cast in the divisions on the British Nationality Bill (1981).

Figure 5.8
**Number of Episcopal Votes Cast For and Against
Her Majesty's Government in each Parliamentary Session**

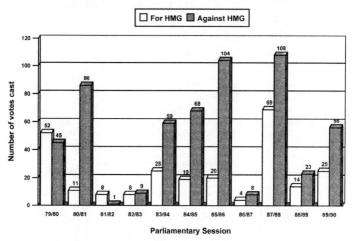

An increased level of episcopal voting against the Government can be clearly seen between the 1983/84 and 1987/88 Parliamentary sessions. The dip in votes cast against (and for) the Government during the 1986/87 session appears to be the result of the very limited number of opportunities (79 divisions) available for participation in divisions during the course of this short Parliamentary session of just 84 sitting days.[14] During these five Parliamentary sessions the

---

14 As the number of opportunities for episcopal participation in divisions decreases so does the likelihood that those divisions which do take place

bishops cast 347 votes against the Government. During the other six
Parliamentary sessions of the Thatcher years they cast just 220 votes
against the Government. This is a similar peak to the one found in
the bishops' attendance at the House during the 1980s (Figure 4.3
above). We will consider the reason for this increased level of voting
against the Government, along with the parallel increase in the bishops' attendance at the House, below (Section 6.2).

These figures also need to be considered in the context of the
number of days on which the House of Lords sat during each Parliamentary session (Figure 4.2). Viewed in this way the voting record
of the bishops in support of the Government can be seen to have
been remarkably consistent throughout the Thatcher years (Figure
5.9). It averaged between 0.05 and 0.17 votes cast in support of the
Government per sitting day except during the 1979/80 'circus factor' Parliamentary session and the 1987/88 Parliamentary session.
That the 1987/88 session was a high-point for vote casting in support, as well as against, the Government can largely be explained
by episcopal support for certain aspects of the Education Reform
Bill (1988) which made its passage through the House of Lords during that Parliamentary session. The bishops cast a total of 31 votes
(45% of the total votes cast in support of the Government during the
1987/88 Parliamentary session) in divisions pertaining to that piece
of legislation.

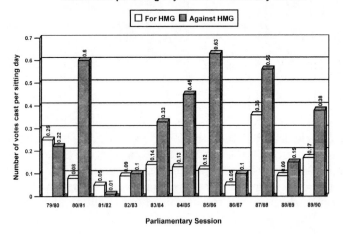

Figure 5.9
**Average Number of Episcopal Votes Cast For and Against Her Majesty's
Government per Sitting Day in each Parliamentary Session**

will be occur on occasions when a bishop is present or will be on matters of
interest to the Lords Spiritual.

In divisions which resulted in Government victories (88% of divisions) the bishops cast 477 anti-Government votes and 249 pro-Government votes (Figure 5.10). This is a ratio of more than 2:1 between votes against and votes for the Thatcher Government. We can therefore say that, more often than not, the bishops failed to back the Thatcher Government's victories in the division lobby. In divisions which resulted in Government defeat (8% of divisions) the bishops cast 90 anti-Government votes and nine pro-Government votes (Figure 5.11). This is a ratio of 10:1 between votes against and votes for the Government. We can therefore assert that the bishops were overwhelmingly supportive of those who sought to defeat the Government in the division lobby.

Figure 5.10
Number of Episcopal Votes Cast For and Against Her Majesty's Government in Divisions which resulted in Government Victories

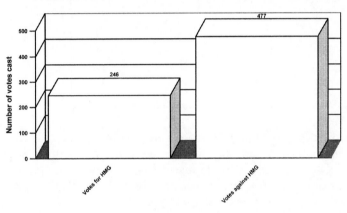

Outcome of Division

In just 18 (4%) of the 476 divisions in which the bishops voted did six or more bishops vote in the same division lobby. On only two occasions, during the Committee stage of the Education Reform Bill (1988), did the multiple votes of the bishops contribute to a Government defeat. The most numerous united episcopal voting occurred in response to the provisions of the Shops Bill (1986). The bishops cast a total of 68 votes against the Government over the course of six divisions at the Second Reading, Committee, and Report stages of the Bill. Two divisions saw 13 bishops enter the division lobby together and in one division, on 2nd June 1986, 18 bishops voted in unison against legislative clauses which provided for the removal of the restrictions on Sunday opening hours for shops. The British Nationality Bill (1981) also saw bishops voting en masse, casting a total of 30 votes against the Government in four divisions. Only once did more than six bishops vote together in support of the Government, in a division at the Report stage of the Government's Employment Bill (1980) relating to secondary industrial action.

In total 27 (6%) of the 476 divisions in which the bishops partici-

Figure 5.11
Number of Episcopal Votes Cast For and Against Her Majesty's Government in Divisions which Resulted in Government Defeats

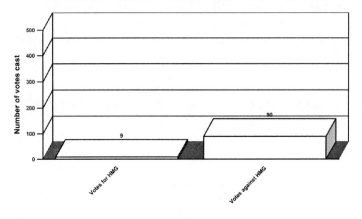

Outcome of Division

pated during the Thatcher years saw bishops voting in opposing division lobbies. Thus, the bishops were united in their voting in 94% of the divisions of the House. This is, in part, the result of the fact that only 148 of the divisions in which the bishops participated received more than one episcopal vote. However, even when this is taken into account, we still find a high level of unity amongst the bishops in the division lobby. The bishops were united in their voting in 92% of the divisions in which two or more bishops voted. Over the course of the Thatcher years there were four occasions when more than one bishop entered each division lobby. Contrary to the data provided by Francis Bown two of these occasions, not one, occurred between 1979 and 1987. The first (which was not recorded by Bown) was a division on the Government's British Nationality Bill which took place on 22nd July 1981 and saw two bishops voting in each lobby in a division. The second occasion was also in a division on the British Nationality Bill, this time on 29th October 1981. As Bown records, two bishops voted in each division lobby. The remaining two occasions saw the bishops divided in their voting response to two Bills which came before the House in 1988. The first occasion, on 2nd February 1988, saw two bishops vote in support of the introduction of Clause 28 of the Government's Local Government Bill (a clause to prohibit the promotion of homosexuality 'by teaching or by publishing material')[15] while three voted against it. The second, on 16th May 1988, again saw five bishops voting, this time in a division on the Government's Education Reform Bill.

5.4 Which Bishops Voted

A comparison between the number of votes cast by bishops from the Canterbury and York provinces reveals that, relative to the number of dioceses within each, the province of Canterbury was responsible for a slightly greater proportion of the bishops' total vote casting over the course of the Thatcher years. Each diocesan within the Canterbury province cast, on average, 24.3 votes during the 1980s whereas each diocesan within the York province cast, on average, 17.4 votes during the same period.[16] The bishops from the Canterbury province also undertook a slightly heavier burden for speech-making in the House (Section 6.6 below). In attendance, however, the two archdioceses's share of the burden was, relative to their size, almost equal (Section 4.3 above). So the picture painted of the bishops from the York province is that they were in attendance at the House as much as their colleagues from the Canterbury province. Once at the House, however, they were less involved in contributing through speech-making and participation in divisions. Clearly the distance of the York dioceses from Westminster hindered the level of contribution that they could achieve at the Upper House. This data suggests that this was not because the York bishops were unable to get to the House of Lords regularly, but that their distance from Westminster hindered the flexibility with which they could attend the House. This lack of flexibility meant that they found it harder to attend the House in response to particular debates and that they were limited in the amount of time they could spend in the chamber when they did make the journey to London.[17]

The specific case of David Halsey (Bishop of Carlisle) supports this explanation. Halsey, as has been noted above (Section 4.3), made

---

15 As cited by Lord Jenkins of Putney, *House of Lords Debates*, 2/2/88, vol. 492, col. 997.

16 The Canterbury province contains 29 dioceses and cast a combined total of 704 votes. The York province contains 13 dioceses and cast a combined total of 226 votes.

17 Due to the lack of data available on length of time spent by each bishop at the House when in attendance the second part of this argument is based on conjecture, not data.

an astounding 596 visits to the House of Lords over the course of the Thatcher years. However, during the same period he only cast 15 votes.[18] His explanation for this imbalance is worth quoting in full:

> When I was informed that my time had come to be introduced into the Lords... I began to consider what in practice I should do about it. I wanted to take it responsibly, and the only way to do that I believed would be to plan ahead and try to attend with some regularity. But Carlisle is some 4-5 hours distant from Westminster and it would be nearly impossible to attend on the spur of the moment. I came to the conclusion that what I should do would be to try and attend on a Wednesday, which... is the usual day for formal debates on important questions... I also served on two Central Church Committees which met mid-week in London and I could slip out of the Lords for part of the time... In addition there was the unplanned advantage that I often arranged to meet someone, usually a clergyman who was considering coming to the Carlisle Diocese over tea in the Lords. This was very convenient because of the long journey (and expense) of coming to see me in Carlisle.[19]
>
> However I had a further problem to face. Protocol demands that if you speak in a debate you are expected to stay to the end for the formal summing-up of the final two speeches. Unfortunately my return train to Carlisle left, as I remember it, about 5.30 from Euston. Debates, which began after questions seldom started before 3.00 or 3.15 and rarely finished before 6.00 or 8.00pm. I was therefore virtually debarred from speaking. So I compromised by asking questions from time to time.

A Bishop of Carlisle finds himself particularly distant from Westminster. However, each of the bishops attending the House of Lords from dioceses distant from London would have been similarly unable to attend the House at late notice in response to specific debates set to take place and similarly restricted by the need to leave London before the end of the afternoon (let alone the evening) debate was complete. Likewise, the need to maximise the opportunity resultant from being in London (and so near to Church House) to perform other engagements away from the House of Lords would have been common to all of the bishops from far-flung dioceses. So too would the allure of a free first-class rail ticket for a long and expensive jour-

---

18   One of the bishops interviewed by the author (who asked for his comments on this matter not to be attributed) noted that Halsey was 'there a great deal'. He commented: '[o]ne must ask oneself... what he did?', responding to Halsey's attendance strategy (of regular Wednesday attendance irrespective of the subject under discussion in the House) with one, loaded word: 'Interesting'.

19   David Halsey (Bishop of Carlisle) in a letter to the author, 27th April 2002.

ney. Halsey was unique amongst these bishops in responding to this inflexibility with such a regimented approach to his role at the House of Lords. In contrast, for many bishops of dioceses in the Canterbury province, attendance at the House for a particular afternoon, or even evening debate, would be entirely practical. Moreover, once

Figure 5.12
Number of Votes Cast by Individual Bishops

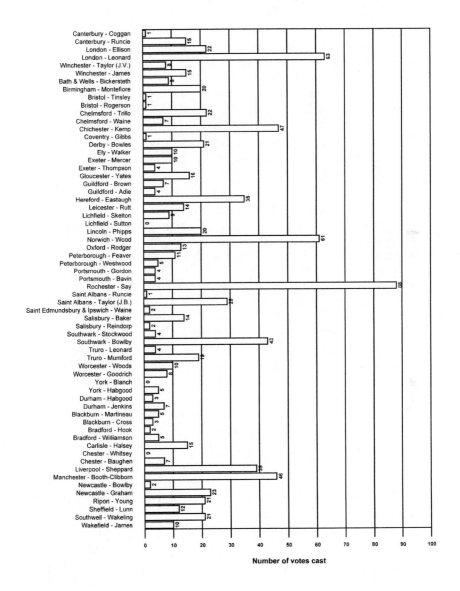

Number of votes cast

at the House of Lords, a bishop from the Canterbury province with reasonable time management skills should be able to ensure that he can focus his time and energy on his parliamentary role.

Analysis of the voting habits of each of the 51 individual bishops who were eligible to attend the House of Lords during the course of the Thacher years reveals a tremendous variety in the extent and the nature of their voting contribution (Figure 5.12). Three bishops who were eligible to vote in House of Lords divisions never took advantage of this opportunity. Included in this group is Stuart Blanch (Archbishop of York) who was eligible to attend the House until the summer of 1983.[20] In view of Blanch's seniority this failure to enter the division lobby even once during the Thatcher years is unexpected. It is with a similar degree of surprise that we observe that Donald Coggan, Archbishop of Canterbury until January 1980 and therefore residing just minutes away from the Palace of Westminster, only voted once at the House of Lords during the Thatcher years. The most prolific episcopal voter over the course of the Thatcher years was David Say (Bishop of Rochester) who cast 88 votes (4% of the total number of divisions of the Lords during the Thatcher years). He was one of a group of just seven bishops who cast 42% (386 votes) of the bishops' votes. This group of seven consisted of:

- David Say (Bishop of Rochester) who cast 88 votes.
- Graham Leonard (whilst Bishop of London) who cast 63 votes.
- Maurice Wood (Bishop of Norwich) who cast 61 votes.
- Stanley Booth-Clibborn (Bishop of Manchester) who cast 46 votes.
- Eric Kemp (Bishop of Chichester) who cast 47 votes.
- Ronald Bowlby (whilst Bishop of Southwark) who cast 43 votes.
- David Sheppard (Bishop of Liverpool) who cast 39 votes.

It is noticeable that Booth-Clibborn and Sheppard were not hindered in their voting by the distance of their diocese from London. Between them, however, Booth-Clibborn and Sheppard did cast 62% of the votes cast by bishops from the York province. The two most senior churchmen eligible to vote in the House of Lords for the majority of the 1980s were Robert Runcie (Archbishop of Canterbury) and John Habgood (Archbishop of York). Both Archbishops used their voting privilege to vote overwhelmingly against Government policies. Runcie voted at a ratio of 6:1 against Margaret Thatcher's Government. Habgood never voted for the Government and voted against it on four occasions.

---

20   During which time he attended the House on 16 occasions (Figure 4.4).

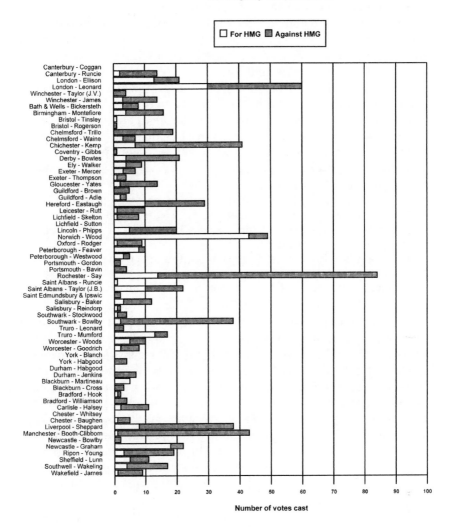

Figure 5.13
**Number of Votes Cast by Individual Bishops For and Against
Her Majesty's Government**

Note: Excludes unwhipped divisions & divisions with no quorum

Only seven of the bishops who cast more than one vote in the House during the 1980s managed to cast more votes in support of the Government than against it (Figure 5.13). These bishops were led in their support of the policies of the Thatcher Government by Maurice Wood (Bishop of Norwich) who cast 43 votes for and just six against the Government. This group also included: Gerald Ellison (Bishop of London until the summer of 1981) who cast 13 votes for and 9 votes against the Government, Alec Graham (introduced to the House as Bishop of Newcastle in November 1985) who cast 18 votes for and just 4 against the Government, and Peter Mumford (also introduced to the House in November 1985 – as Bishop of Truro). However, Graham Leonard (Bishop of London), often considered a supporter of the Conservative Government, registered only 30 votes for and 30 votes against the Government.[21]

The only individual bishops from the group of seven who did not respond negatively to the Thatcher Government in the division lobby were Maurice Wood (Bishop of Norwich) and Graham Leonard (Bishop of London). The remaining five bishops cast their votes in the divisions overwhelmingly against the Government:

- David Say (Bishop of Rochester) who cast 70 of his 88 votes against the Government.
- Stanley Booth-Clibborn (Bishop of Manchester) who cast 42 of his 46 votes against the Government.
- Eric Kemp (Bishop of Chichester) who cast 34 of his 47 votes against the Government.
- Ronald Bowlby (whilst Bishop of Southwark) who cast 36 of his 43 votes against the Government.
- David Sheppard (Bishop of Liverpool) who cast 30 of his 39 votes against the Government.

Between them these five cast 37% (212 votes) of the episcopal votes cast against the Government during the 1980s. A small number of bishops therefore can be seen to have cast a considerable proportion of the total episcopal votes against the Government. However, these figures also indicate that a wide spread of bishops cast anti-Government votes over the course of the Thatcher years and that the bishops as a whole, not just a few active individuals, were overwhelmingly negative in their response to the Thatcher Government in the division lobby. In fact only eight of the 58 bishops eligible to attend the Lords during the 1980s never voted against the Government In contrast there were 19 bishops who never voted in support of the Government.[22]

5.5 Conclusion

The data we have presented on the voting record of the Lords Spiritual supports the assessment of Longford and Bown that the bishops do not maintain a high voting record in the House of Lords. Over the

---

21   Young, *One*, 420.
22   Both of these figures include three individual bishops who failed to vote in the House on any occasion during the Thatcher years.

course of the whole of Margaret Thatcher's premiership, the bish-ops voted in a slightly greater proportion (22.9%) of the divisions of the House than Francis Bown records for the period from 1979-1987 (21.4%). Our research also supports Bown's assertion that it was rare for the division lobbies to receive more than one bishop during a single division, presenting two or more bishops as having voted in 7.1% of the total divisions of the House over the course of the whole of the 1980s (as opposed to the figure of 3.9% provided by Bown for the period up to 1987). The disparity between these two figures does suggest that it became less unusual for two or more bishops to vote in the same division during the latter part of the Thatcher era.

Medhurst and Moyser's observation that episcopal attendance is dependent upon the individual personality, experience, expertise and priorities of each bishop can be fairly applied to episcopal vot-ing habits.[23] Such variety cannot be accounted for by external fac-tors, such as the distance of each diocese from Westminster, alone. Additionally, our analysis indicates that, during the Thatcher years, a core group of seven bishops performed a disproportionately high proportion of the voting of the Bench of Bishops as a whole.

The data presented above provides clear evidence in support of the picture painted by Donald Shell and Francis Bown of a Bench of Bishops with no qualms about voting against the Government, pre-senting a ratio of 2:1 (as opposed to Bown's 5:2) between anti-Gov-ernment and pro-Government vote casting. The evidence outlined above also indicates that Shell is justified in his assertion that the bishops had no inhibitions about supporting a Government defeat in the division lobby. Indeed in divisions which resulted in a Govern-ment defeat the bishops were ten times as likely to vote with those seeking to bring about a Government defeat as they were in support of the Government. In spite of this it would be in no way concurrent with the data on the bishops' voting record during the Thatcher years to argue that they sought to use their voting rights in an aggressive or united manner in an effort to alter the outcome of divisions. In just 4% of the total number of divisions in which the bishops voted did six or more of them vote together providing the level of numerical strength with the potential to alter the outcome of a division. This is not to say that on occasions the bishops did not vote in a manner which makes it clear that they did intend to do their utmost to alter the outcome of the division, such as was the case with the divisions relating to the Shops Bill (1986). Bown's evidence, which indicates that the bishops rarely voted in opposing division lobbies during

---

23   Medhurst & Moyser, 'Lambeth', 77.

the first two terms of the Thatcher premiership, is supported by the
evidence outlined above which reveals the episcopal vote to have
been split on just 18% per cent of the occasions on which two more
bishops voted in same division.

The bishops' approach to voting in the House of Lords during
the Thatcher years reflected, to a very large extent, the approach
proposed by Michael Ramsey in a letter to Donald Coggan during
March 1968. If in a reformed, more democratically credible, Second
Chamber the bishops wish to retain their voting rights they would
do well to continue to vote in same manner and to the same end as
Ramsey suggests:

> The episode [the passing of the Kenya Asians Bill in the House
> of Lords] sets me thinking again about the significance of voting
> in the House of Lords, and I feel that the purpose of our voting
> is to register opinions as a kind of witness and that if we become
> a body which tried to influence legislation by turning up in force
> we should be involved in all sorts of difficulties and our position
> would not be tolerated. I do, however, agree with those who have
> said in our recent discussion that if we are to maintain this kind of
> token voting there must be a good many of us from whom the vot-
> ers can be forthcoming.[24]

---

24 Letter from Michael Ramsey to Donald Coggan, 1 March 1968, cited by
Chadwick, *Ramsey*, 184. Hugh Montefiore makes a similar point: 'It's not
as though everyone there is a Christian, and all you can do is to make them
aware of the spiritual and moral aspects of the situation as you see it and
also through your knowledge in your diocese to make people aware of the
implications of what they are doing to individual people and they have to
make their own decisions... I think it would be unfortunate if the bishops
turned out en-masse and voted en-masse. I don't think they'd be welcomed
in the House for so doing and I think it might hasten their decline.' Hugh
Montefiore (Bishop of Birmingham) in an interview with the author, 21st
May 2002, Appendix 3.

CHAPTER SIX

Episcopal Speech-Making: Extent

6.1 Introduction

6.1.1 Introduction

A bishop (occasionally more than one) will generally speak in a major public debate, including the second readings of Bills on questions of social policy... It is however exceptional for the bishops to engage in sustained political pressure in the Lords for a particular purpose.[1]

This analysis of Giles Ecclestone, former Secretary of the Church of England Board for Social Responsibility, is shared by Medhurst and Moyser who comment that '[t]he contributions of most spiritual peers are spasmodic. In modern times few have been heavily involved in this arena'.[2] Medhurst and Moyser suggest, as discussed above, that the changing episcopal role and the added demands wrought by the introduction of Synodical government are the chief causes of this spasmodic speech-making. In addition we might add that the procedures of the House of Lords itself do not encourage episcopal contributions. Contributors to debates are expected to await official replies, and short official notice of forthcoming business does not allow enough time for bishops to plan their schedules so that they can incorporate preparation for, and attendance at, debates.[3] Uncertainty exists regarding the extent to which the bishops' reading of prayers at the beginning of each day's business affects their speech-making in the House. Donald Shell cites Drewry and Brock, writing in 1971, who found a high correlation between the bishops' contributions to debates and their leading of prayers.[4] Bown indicates, however, that during the period from 1979 to 1987 less than 30% of the

---

1 Ecclestone, *England*, 50-51. Ecclestone points to the bishops' involvement in the progress of the Government's Education Bill through Parliament during the 1979/1980 Parliamentary session as an exception to this trend.
2 Medhurst & Moyser, *Secular*, 274.
3 *ibid*. See also Hastings, *Runcie*, 85 and Longford, *Bishops*, 194.
4 G. Drewry & J. Brock, 'Prelates in Parliament', *Parliamentary Affairs*, 24 (1970-71), 222-250 as cited by Shell, *Lords*, 55.

bishops' spoken contributions were delivered by bishops on prayer duty.[5] He therefore asserts that '...it cannot be argued that the part played by the Lords Spiritual is simply that of the duty bishop "joining-in" when he is obliged to be at the House to say prayers.'[6]

Lee and Stanford assert that, '[i]n general... interventions by bishops tend to be... wide-ranging: delineating legitimate areas of government activity, for example, rather than getting down to the nitty-gritty of clauses in legislation.'[7] Bown also suggests that the bishops concentrate their speeches on the deliberative debates of the House which relate to general principles, rather than detailed legislative discussions. Dividing the House into what he calls the 'House of Discussion' and the 'House of Scrutiny' he indicates that the number of words spoken by the bishops in relation to the former outnumbers the latter by a ratio of nearly 4:1. In terms of the actual number of verbal contributions his data suggests, however, that the ratio was close to 1:1.[8] There is reason to question whether measuring the number of words spoken by the bishops is a helpful measure of their emphases within the House. To contribute verbally to any debate requires that the contributor be present for a reasonable period of time in the chamber. Whether the contributor intends to speak briefly or at length, once or repeatedly, the commitment necessary to attend the House and contribute to the debate is the same.

Donald Shell argues that few eligible bishops never contribute to a House of Lords debate and that 'in almost any area of legislation an episcopal contribution may be forthcoming.'[9] He also suggests that the bishops made speeches in deliberative debates on most occasions where a 'moral dimension was self-evident.'[10] He is, however, critical of low attendance and the limited extent of episcopal contributions to the House during the 1970s and 1980s:

> It is certainly reasonable to argue that, given the fact of their membership (in some strength), more effort should be made to ensure that bishops are present and do contribute on a wider range of issues than at present... One view is that where the Church as a body is publicly critical of the Government, its bishops should be prepared to use the forum of the House of Lords to join debate with government ministers – not spasmodically but in a

---

5   Bown, 'Influencing', 110.
6   *ibid*.
7   Lee & Stanford, *Believing*, 31.
8   Bown, 'Influencing', 112.
9   Shell, *Lords*, 54.
10   *ibid*, 55.

regular and hence more responsible way.[11]

6.1.2 Methodology

Our analysis of both the extent and the content (Chapter 7 below) of the episcopal contribution to the House of Lords begins on the first day of the first Parliament of Mrs Thatcher's premiership (9th May 1979) and continues, uninterrupted, until her final day as Prime Minister (22nd November 1990), over a decade later. House of Lords *Hansard* provided all the information necessary for this analysis, except data on whether the legislation under scrutiny in any particular instance was a Government or a Private Members' Bill. This information was provided by the House of Commons *Weekly Information Bulletin*. A number of explanatory comments must act as gatekeeper to what follows so that reader and author profit from a shared understanding of the terms used and some of the assumptions underlying our consideration of the extent of the bishops' speech-making.

The term 'contribution' is used to refer to an occasion where a bishop makes a speech during a House of Lords debate, such that it is recorded in *Hansard*. Where a bishop interjects in a debate after he has finished his speech to make a point of clarification relating to his original contribution, and where a speech is punctuated by contributions from other peers, no additional contribution is recorded as having taken place. Only a bishop's first contribution each day to the Committee, Report, and Third Reading stages of a Bill is recorded, even though a bishop may have contributed to the debate once or on multiple occasions.[12] Included in this analysis are all the episcopal speeches to the House of Lords which were recorded in *Hansard*, except the rare occasions where a bishop contributed to a Private Bill ('...promoted by bodies outside of Parliament and... concerned with private interests'),[13] a Statutory Instrument, or business and procedural matters.

---

11 *ibid*, 56. Trevor Beeson is also critical of the bishops' record. Having accepted some of the legitimate hindrances to the bishops attending and speaking in the House he notes that: '...the number of them who attend regularly and speak in debates is small. On some important occasions their absence verges on the scandalous.' Beeson, *Bishops*, 65.

12 When a Committee, Report, or Third Reading stage of a Bill goes on for more than one sitting day and a bishop contributes on more than one of these days he is recorded as having intervened once for each of the days on which he verbally contributed to the debate.

13 J.A.G. Griffith & M. Ryle, *Parliament: Functions, Practice and Procedures* (London: Sweet & Maxwell, 1989), 489.

The term 'non-contribution' refers to an occasion where no episcopal contribution was made to a Second Reading debate, a debate on a Motion, or a debate on the Address (the debate which takes place in response to the Queen's speech at the beginning of each Parliamentary session). These types of debates were chosen because they represent the occasions on which important issues are considered at the level of principle and are therefore the occasions which are most likely to warrant an episcopal contribution.[14] They are the occasions on which, if an episcopal contribution is not forthcoming, the bishops are most open to criticism. Recording these non-contributions enables us to place the episcopal contributions to such debates within the context of the number of opportunities available to them for speech-making.

The time of day recorded for each episcopal contribution refers to the start-time of the debate in which the speech was made, not to the specific time of day at which the actual contribution took place. The time of day given to episcopal non-contributions also refers to the start-time of the debate. Convention demands that any peer who intends to contribute to a debate is present for the majority of that debate. As such no peer enters the chamber immediately prior to his own speech and leaves immediately after its conclusion. Thus a record of the start-time of the debate indicates more clearly the time from which the bishop was actively, even if not verbally, involved in the business of the House. It also ensures that episcopal contributions and non-contributions can be compared fairly.

The length of each episcopal contribution is deduced from the timings given in *Hansard* at the start and end of each speech. In most cases this provides an exact timing for the length of the speech. However, very occasionally a timing was found to be missing from *Hansard* or to be incorrect. On these rare occasions an approximate timing was given to the speech by the author. Timings are only given in *Hansard* for speeches to Second Reading debates, debates on Church of England Measures, Unstarred Questions, debates on Motions, and debates on the Address. Notably, therefore, the length of the bishops' speeches at each of the Committee stages of legislation (which can be very time consuming) is not explored in this analysis.

A subject classification scheme was developed in order to facili-

---

14 'The Second Reading is the stage at which the general principles of a Bill are considered.' D. Limon & W.R. Mackay, *Erskine May's Treatise on The Law, Privileges, Proceedings and Usage of Parliament*, 22nd Edition (London: Butterworths, 1997), 468. See also Norton, 'Lords', 361 and Shell, *Lords*, 134.

tate analysis of the variety of subjects on which the bishops spoke in the House of Lords (Appendix 6). The subject classification scheme divides the work of the House into 17 subject groups based on the departments of the Civil Service (as constituted during the 1998/99 Parliamentary session). These subject groups were then divided into the sub-areas of business (subjects) with which each department deals.[15] Every debate in which a bishop spoke (and debates classified as non-contributions) was given one or more subject classification codes relating to particular subjects (such as 'Gambling' or 'Children's Health') which were a part of the debate. It should be noted that the subject classification relates to the debate as a whole, not to the specific content of the speech of the bishop.

6.2 When the Bishops Spoke

The bishops made a total of 768 contributions to the House of Lords during the Thatcher years, speaking in each of the 12 Parliamentary sessions of her premiership (Figure 6.1). The greatest number of contributions were made during the 1983/84 Parliamentary session (105 contributions), the least during the 1982/83 Parliamentary session (39 contributions). On average (excluding the 1990/91 Parliamentary session) the bishops made 66 contributions per session.

Figure 6.1
Number of Episcopal Contributions to House of Lords Debates in each Parliamentary Session

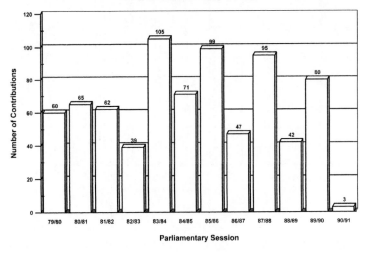

---

15 Full listings of the various Whitehall departments and the matters with which each deals were taken from: *The Whitehall Companion 1998-99*

As with attendance, these figures lack real value until they are expressed in relation to the number of sitting days of the House in each Parliamentary session. Overall the bishops made an average of 0.5 contributions per sitting day during the Thatcher years (Figure 6.2). Thus, on average, the bishops made a contribution to Parliament every other day. The greatest level of episcopal contributions per sitting day were made during the 1983/84 Parliamentary session, the 1985/86 Parliamentary session, and the 1986/87 Parliamentary session. During these sessions there were an average of 0.6 contributions per sitting day. The lowest level of contributions took place during the 1979/80 and 1988/89 Parliamentary sessions during which the bishops averaged 0.3 contributions per sitting day. Averages of this kind can be deceptive though. In fact on 1331 of the 1660 days (80%) on which the House of Lords sat during the Thatcher years no bishop made a verbal contribution. On 142 (9%) of the sitting days of the House one bishop spoke in a Lords debate, on 126 days (8%) the bishops made two contributions, on 36 days (2%) they made three contributions to the House. The most speeches made by the Lords Spiritual on a single day was five. On the 8th April 1981 the bish-

Figure 6.2
Average Number of Episcopal Contributions to House of Lords Debates per Sitting Day in each Parliamentary Session

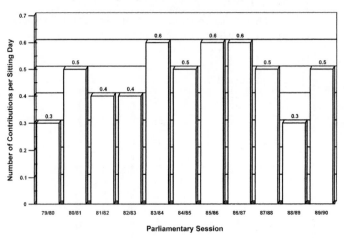

(London: DPR, 1998). The Ecclesiastical Affairs subject group was the only subject group not based on a Whitehall Department. It should be noted that not all of the sub-areas of business included in the subject classification scheme were included in the final analysis of our data and therefore the presentation of results.

ops made two speeches in a debate on Expenditure Cuts and Public Services and three contributions on the Second Reading of Lord Sudeley's Prayer Book Protection Bill. On the 11th April 1984 the bishops made five contributions at the Second Reading of another Prayer Book Protection Bill promoted by Lord Sudeley.

A peak in episcopal speech-making is visible between the 1983/84 and 1986/87 Parliamentary sessions. This suggests that, alongside the peak in interest in the House of Lords indicated by high attendance over this period (Figure 4.3 above) and the high level of voting against the Government (from the 1983/84 to the 1987/88 Parliamentary session) (Figures 5.8 and 5.9), there was also a heightened episcopal interest in contributing to the House. This contrasts with the 1979/80 Parliamentary session during which a peak in attendance was not accompanied by a peak in speech-making. This greater episcopal interest in the House between 1983 and 1987 may well have been the result of the gradual emergence of a distinctly Thatcherite, New Right political agenda (as opposed to the One-Nation Tory agenda which had characterised Conservative policy since 1945).[16] As this programme took shape so, perhaps, did the anxiety of the bishops and their willingness to play their part in House of Lords and its work of scrutinising the Government generally, as well as in relation to specific items of business which were of concern to them. Both David Say (Bishop of Rochester) and Hugh Montefiore (Bishop of Birmingham) deny that the bishops made any kind of conscious decision to increase their response to the Thatcher Government at any point during the 1980s.[17] However, Montefiore indicates that there were individuals on the Bench of Bishops during and after his time in the House (1984-87) who were not in agreement with many of the Thatcher Government's policies and were vocal in their response to them:

> It so happened that there were a lot of local bishops who were more concerned with the distribution of wealth than with its creation. This I certainly found in the urban group of bishops [an informal gathering of the bishops who represented the large conurbations]. Living as I did in Birmingham I was inevitably brought up against

---

16 Of the emergence of this agenda John Campbell writes: 'Even after she achieved power, and a political dominance she could never have imagined in 1975, it still took her the best part of two terms, with the full resources of the civil service at her command, to begin to frame an explicitly "Thatcherite" programme.' Campbell, *Thatcher*, 364.

17 David Say (Bishop of Rochester) in an interview with the author, 29th May 2002, Appendix 4 and Hugh Montefiore (Bishop of Birmingham) in an interview with the author, 21st May 2002, Appendix 3.

the fact that you can't distribute before you can create. But I found that that was rather brushed aside by some of my colleagues and I think that this group of bishops, all of whom went on longer than me, probably were more vocal than you would usually find.[18]

In *Christianity and Politics* (delivered as The Drummond Lectures 1989) Montefiore indicates that the General Synod of the Church of England also saw a rise in the number of debates it held on 'matters of social concern' after 1983. His explanation for this increase supports our explanation for increased episcopal speech-making in the House of Lords:

> [T]he chief reason lies in the ending by Mrs Thatcher's successive administrations of the political consensus which has grown up between the parties on social questions after the Second World War. New policies have been brought forward. This, I think, is the explanation for the increase in such debates in the General Synod in the last six or seven years... The Church and its chief spokesmen have had a positive duty to subject these new policies to Christian scrutiny...[19]

Considering the bishops' level of speech-making in the context of their attendance at the House gives us an indication of the efficiency with which the bishops used their attendance to contribute to the House. The low contribution rate of bishops during the 1979/80 Parliamentary session is then represented more clearly with only 8% of the episcopal attendances yielding a verbal contribution, as opposed to the average of 17% for the whole period (Figure 6.3). This was by far and away the least efficient Parliamentary session in terms of episcopal contributions. The most efficient Parliamentary session was the last full Parliamentary session of the Thatcher years (1989/90) during which bishops contributed on 24% of the occasions on which they attended the House. Attendance at the House dropped close to its lowest level during the 1980s during that Parliamentary session (Figure 4.1 above); nonetheless the number of contributions

---

18 Hugh Montefiore (Bishop of Birmingham) in an interview with the author, 21st May 2002, Appendix 3. David Say makes a similar point. Asked whether there was a growing negative episcopal response to the Thatcher Government from the 1983/84 session onwards he comments: 'I don't think it was a conscious organised thing about opposing Mrs Thatcher... I haven't thought about it before but I think it is just possible that you had a fairly vigorous, well-informed number of bishops, not the total lot, but a number of them, at a time when the leadership in the Commons was not very strong.' David Say (Bishop of Rochester) in an interview with the author, 29th May 2002, Appendix 4.

19 Montefiore, *Politics*, 76.

per sitting day remained steady. Bishops clearly chose to attend the House of Lords only on the occasions when they wanted to make a verbal contribution – the opposite of what happened during the 1979/80 Parliamentary session.

Figure 6.3
**Episcopal Contributions to House of Lords Debates as a
Percentage of Episcopal Attendance in each Parliamentary Session**

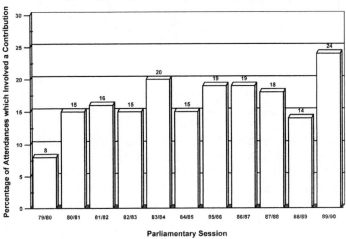

House of Lords *Hansard* records bishops making speeches in the House at the complete range of times of day. The latest contribution by a bishop during the Thatcher years was made in a debate which began at 12.01am. The bishops made the majority (70%) of their contributions during debates which began in the afternoon (2.30pm-4.59pm) whereas just under a quarter of their contributions were made during debates which started during the evening (5pm-9.59pm) (Figure 6.4). We should not be surprised to see bishops contributing more heavily in the two and a half hours of the afternoon period than in the five hours of the evening period. As has already been mentioned (Section 4.3 above) the diocesan responsibilities of a bishop make a same-day return to the diocese after attendance at the House of Lords almost essential and evening contributions to debates too time-consuming to be feasible on a regular basis. In fact time and time again during the 1980s the Church of England bishops began their contributions to the House with an apology for the fact that they were going to be unable to remain at the House until the conclusion of the debate, because of the need to return home in order to be in a position to fulfil their duties in the diocese the next day.

Figure 6.4
Time of Day of Episcopal Contributions to House of Lords Debates

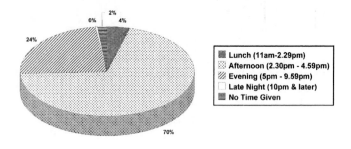

Lunch (11am-2.29pm)
Afternoon (2.30pm - 4.59pm)
Evening (5pm - 9.59pm)
Late Night (10pm & later)
No Time Given

Total Number of Contributions = 768

There were a total of 1066 debates which can be classified as non-contributions ('missed-opportunities') during the Thatcher years (Figure 6.5).[20] The 1979/80 Parliamentary session contained the greatest number (137), the 1986/87 Parliamentary session the least (68). Over the course of the Thatcher years there were an average of 0.65 non-contributions per sitting day (Figure 6.6). If we look at the contributions of the bishops to Second Reading debates, debates on Motions and debates on the Address (those debates included in the non-contribution category), in isolation from their contributions to other debate types, we observe that the bishops made 336 contributions to these types of debate, equating to an average of 0.2 contributions per sitting day (an approximate ratio of 3:1 between non-contributions and contributions). Thus, the bishops contributed to one out of every three House of Lords debates which explored public-policy at the level of principle.

The percentage of episcopal non-contributions to debates beginning in the evening (5pm-9.59pm) was greater (Figure 6.7) than the percentage of contributions made by the bishops at the same time of day (Figures 6.4) whereas the percentage of non-contributions to debates beginning in the afternoon (2.30pm-4.59pm) was less than

---

20 As has been explained (Section 6.1.2) above, a non-contribution is a debate to which the bishops might have been expected to make a speech but did not. The assessment of whether a debate was amongst those at which an episcopal contribution would have been most worthwhile was based on the type of debate, not the specific content of each debate.

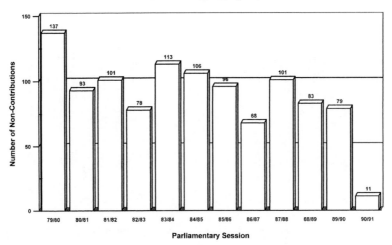

Figure 6.5
Number of Episcopal Non-Contributions to House of Lords Debates in each Parliamentary Session

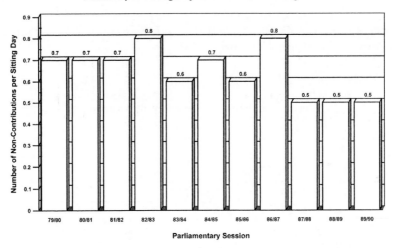

Figure 6.6
Average Number of Episcopal Non-Contributions to House of Lords Debates per Sitting Day in each Parliamentary Session

that for episcopal contributions at the same time of day. This alerts us once more to the fact that the likelihood of a bishop contributing to a House of Lords debate is significantly affected by the time of day at which that debate takes place. If the time of day had no bearing then we should expect to see an equal spread of contributions and non-contributions over each period of the Parliamentary day. The

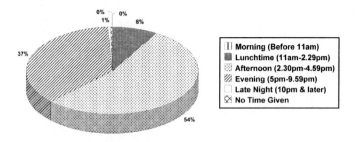

Figure 6.7
**Time of Day of Episcopal Non-Contributions to
House of Lords Debates**

Morning (Before 11am)
Lunchtime (11am-2.29pm)
Afternoon (2.30pm-4.59pm)
Evening (5pm-9.59pm)
Late Night (10pm & later)
No Time Given

Total Number of Non-Contributions = 1066

fact that our consideration of episcopal contributions to the House
has included debate types (such as Statements and Starred Questions which always begin in the afternoon) which are not included
in our analysis of non-contributions makes little difference to the
picture painted of the time of day at which the bishops contributed
to the House. In fact when these types of debate are excluded from
our consideration of the time of day of episcopal contributions (Figure 6.8) remarkably similar results occur as when these debates are
included in our analysis (Figure 6.4).

Figure 6.8
**Time of Day of Episcopal Contributions to Second Reading Debates,
Debates on Motions and Debates on the Address**

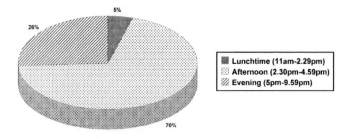

Lunchtime (11am-2.29pm)
Afternoon (2.30pm-4.59pm)
Evening (5pm-9.59pm)

Total Number of Contributions = 336

6.3 The Length of the Bishops' Speeches

In those debates for which a timing is given in *Hansard* the bishops spoke for a total of 4431 minutes (73 hours and 51 minutes) (Figure 6.9). On average (excluding the 1990/91 Parliamentary session) the bishops spoke in Parliamentary debate for six hours and 40 minutes in each Parliamentary session. The vast majority of episcopal contributions (76%) were between six and 15 minutes in length (Figure 6.10). Some 294 speeches were of this length and together they accounted for 3079 minutes of the bishops' contributions to House of Lords debates (Figure 6.11).

The 1985/86 Parliamentary session received the greatest number of minutes of episcopal contribution to the House (585 minutes), the 1982/83 Parliamentary session received the least (267 minutes), a difference of some 318 minutes. When these figures are considered in the context of the number of sitting days of the House the picture which emerges is similar to the picture for the average number of contributions per sitting day (Figure 6.2). The bishops spoke for the shortest amount of time per sitting day during the 1979/80 Parliamentary session (1.8 minutes per sitting day) (Figures 6.12). By far the greatest average length of total contributions per sitting day occurred during the 1986/87 Parliamentary session (4.7 minutes per sitting day). A slight peak in the average length of total contributions per sitting day also exists between the 1983/84 and 1986/87 Parliamentary sessions. Over this period an average of 3.2 minutes of contributions per sitting day occurred, as opposed to an overall average

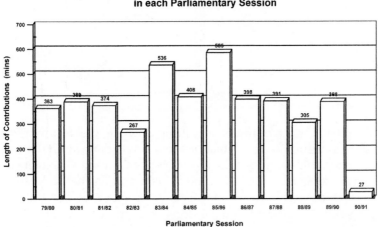

Figure 6.9
**Length of Episcopal Contributions to House of Lords Debates
in each Parliamentary Session**

Parliamentary Session

(Excludes Committee stages, Starred Questions, Tributes and Statements)

Figure 6.10
Number of Episcopal Contributions of Specified Lengths

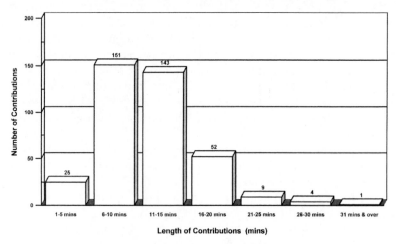

(Excludes Committee stages, Starred Questions, Tributes and Statements)

Figure 6.11
Combined Length of Episcopal Contributions of Specified Lengths
(Excluding Committee stages, Starred Questions, Tributes and Statements)

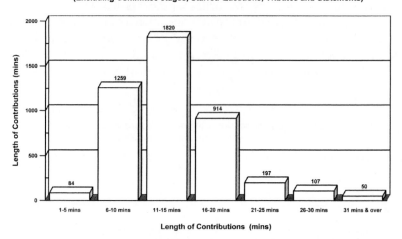

(Excludes Committee stages, Starred Questions, Tributes and Statements)

for the period of 2.8 minutes per sitting day. The greatest number of minutes contributed by the bishops in a single day was 100 minutes on 8th April 1981 during which five bishops spoke. This included a 50 minute speech by John Habgood (Bishop of Durham) during the Second Reading of Lord Sudeley's Prayer Book Protection Bill (1981) which sought protection for the Book of Common Prayer in Anglican worship in the light of introduction of the Alternative Service Book in 1980.

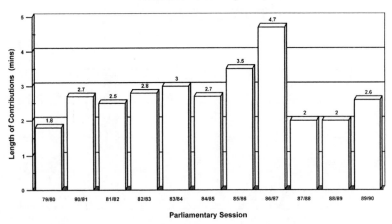

Figure 6.12
**Average Length of Episcopal Contributions per Sitting Day
in each Parliamentary Session**

(Excluding Committee stages, Starred Questions, Tributes and Statements)

6.4 The Type of Debates in which the Bishops Spoke

The bishops contributed to the complete spectrum of House of Lords business during the Thatcher years. They were involved in: the scrutiny of both Government and Private Members' legislation, deliberative debates (debates on Motions, debates on the Address, and Unstarred Questions), responding to Government Statements, the asking of (and contributing to the exchanges surrounding) Starred Questions, the writing of questions for Written Answer by Ministers, the making of Tributes to the deceased or retiring, and debates on Church of England Measures.

The bishops made a total of 230 contributions during debates considering Government Bills (29% of the total episcopal contribution) and 67 contributions during the consideration of Private Members' Bills (9% of their speeches) (Figure 6.13). The number of contributions to Government Bills remained consistently higher than those for Private Members' Bills in every Parliamentary session. When these figures are presented as a percentage of the total number of episcopal contributions during each Parliamentary session it becomes clear that the number of episcopal speeches relating to Government Bills increased during the second half of the 1980s. (Figure 6.14). This increase could be understood to reflect a growing dissatisfaction amongst the bishops with the legislation being put forward by the Thatcher Government. It is apparent though that this increase merely reflects the fact that the proportion of the time which the House of Lords as a whole spent on Government legislation was

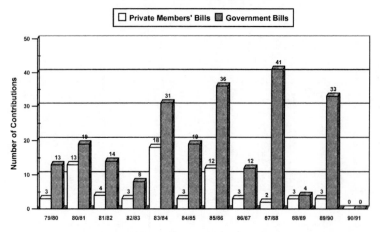

Figure 6.13
**Number of Episcopal Contributions to Private Members' and Government Bills
in each Parliamentary Session**

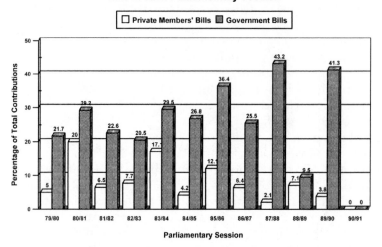

Figure 6.14
**Percentage of Episcopal Contributions to Private Members' and Government
Bills in each Parliamentary Session**

higher in the second half of the 1980s than the first (Figure 6.15).

When the extent of the bishops' contribution to the legislative work of the House is analysed in further detail it becomes clear that at the Second Reading stage, where the principle of a Bill is considered, the number of contributions made (and the total length of those contributions) to Government and Private Members' Bills was broadly similar (Figures 6.16 and 6.17). In contrast, on average just under

50% of the time of the House is committed to the consideration of Government Bills while only 5% is given over to Private Members' Bills (Figure 6.15). Therefore, relative to the amount of time of the House which is given to Government and Private Members' Bills, the bishops' record reveals a preference for contributing to Private Members' Bills over contributing to Government Bills. That this was

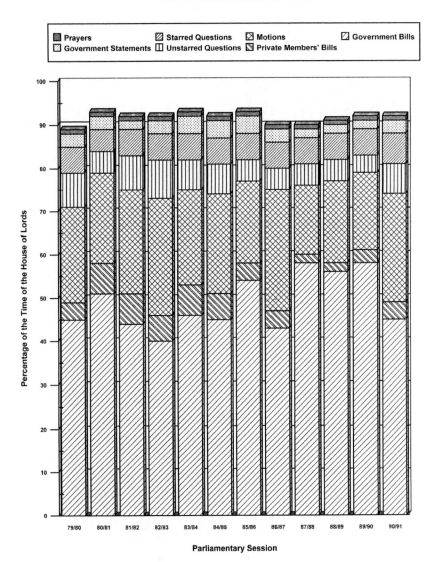

Figure 6.15
The Time of the House of Lords

the case should be no surprise. Private Members' Bills often consider ethical and social issues such as abortion and marriage which are of particular interest to the bishops, and on which the viewpoint of the bishops is often greatly appreciated.

A real difference in the bishops' contribution to the scrutiny of Government and Private Members' Bills is found in the varying rates of contribution to the two types of Bill at the Committee stages

Figure 6.16
**Number of Episcopal Contributions to the Different Stages
of Private Members' and Government Bills**

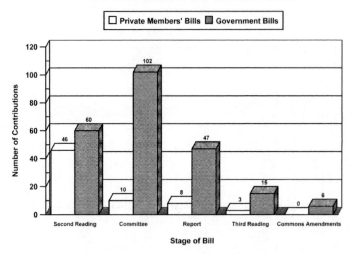

Figure 6.17
**Total Length of Episcopal Contributions to the Second
Reading Stage of Private Members' and Government Bills**

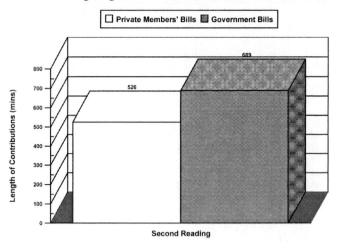

(the Committee, Report and Third Reading). The bishops made 164 speeches at the Committee stages of Government Bills, but only 21 to the Committee stages of Private Members' Bills. These figures are the outworking of two factors. Firstly, the fact that a large minority of Private Members' Bills fail to move beyond their Second Reading in the Lords.[21] Secondly, and more importantly, '...the effect of Commons Standing Order No. 13 is such that no Lords' Private Members' Bill can achieve Royal Assent, unless it is given a Second Reading on the nod [in the House of Commons].'[22] This is not possible when the Bill has come from the Upper House with amendments to be considered. All this means that the Committee stages of a Private Members' Bill in the House of Lords are rarely of significance.[23] Either it must pass through these stages with little discussion and no amendments or it will be discussed and amended but the Bill will never become law. In this context it makes sense that in all but the rarest of cases the bishops declined the opportunity to contribute to the Committee stages of Private Members' Bills.

Ignoring for the moment which types of Bill (Government or Private Members') we turn to an assessment of the types of debate to which the bishops contributed during the Thatcher years. The greatest number of episcopal contributions were made in debates on Motions (201 contributions, 25% of the bishops' total contributions) which took up, on average, 22% of the time of the House[24] (Figures 6.18 & 6.19). The bishops also made a considerable proportion of their contributions to the Committee stages of legislation (191 contributions, 26% of the bishops' total contributions). The smallest number of contributions were made during Tributes (12 contributions, 2% of the bishops' total contributions) and as questions for Written Answer (13 contributions, 2% of the bishops' total contributions). Church of England Measures took up a remarkably small proportion of the bishops time, with only 17 episcopal speeches (2% of the bishops' total contributions) made in debates on Church of England Measures during the Thatcher years. However, this needs

---

21 Shell notes that between 1987 and 1990 25 Private Members' Bills were introduced into the Lords. Of these 16 completed their Lords stages and just four went on to receive Royal Assent. Shell, *Lords*, 153.
22 Griffith & Ryle, *Parliament*, 487.
23 The committee stages of some may be significant, however, such as was the case during the 1960s on abortion and homosexuality.
24 See Figure 6.15. Unfortunately, data on the amount of time the House of Lords spent on the Committee stages of legislation and Tributes is not readily available.

to considered in the context of the fact that Church of England Measures took up an average of just 0.1% of the time of the House as a whole during the Thatcher years.[25]

Figure 6.18
Number of Episcopal Contributions to the Different Debate Types

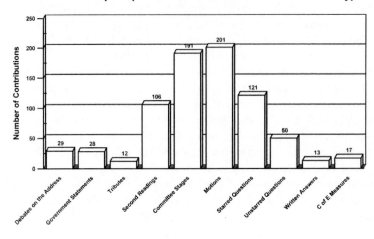

Figure 6.19
Percentage of Episcopal Contributions to the Different Debate Types

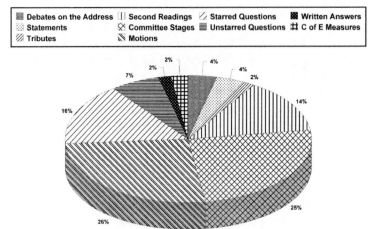

---

25   Data Source: *House of Lords Sessional Statistics.*

That the bishops contributed to the Committee stages of legislation to this extent reveals a willingness to get to grips with the detailed work which is the engine room of the legislative process. This admirable level of involvement in this aspect of the work of the House will have involved not only considerable time at the House of Lords but also considerable preparation time prior to attendance at debates. It will also have demanded a thoroughgoing knowledge of the procedures of the House. Whether contributing at the Committee stages of Bills represents the most efficient use of the bishops limited time is legitimately open to question. Arguably, their contribution would have been more influential if they had focused on contributing to a greater number of Second Reading and deliberative debates at which issues are considered at the level of principle. Nonetheless the influence exerted at the Committee stages of Bills should not be underestimated. Here the bishops are able to apply the principles expounded at the Second Reading and shape the legislation which will finally receive Royal Assent. At the same time, by being present in the House at Committee stage debates, the bishop concerned communicates to the House a depth of concern over the matter in question which he is unable to convey by making a Second Reading speech.

The bishops made 33% of their contributions to the House of Lords during the Thatcher years to the main deliberative debate types (Motions and Unstarred Questions) and 39% of their contributions to legislative debates (the Second Reading and Committee stages) (Figure 6.19). In contrast, the House as a whole gave an average of 28% of its time to debates on Motions and Unstarred Questions and 55% of its time to legislative debates (Figure 6.15). For the bishops the ratio between legislative and deliberative debates is therefore close to 1:1 whereas for the House as a whole the ratio is 2:1 in favour of legislative debates. We can therefore assert that, relative to the House as a whole, the bishops were more committed to contributing to deliberative debates than legislative debates. This is a sensible use of the time and energies of the bishops. In deliberative debates the House performs its intended function as a 'forum for full and free debate on matters of public interest'.[26] Here the bishops have their best opportunity to influence both Government and public opinion through their contribution. Deliberative debates are also often the first occasion on which a subject such as an outbreaking war or a new technology is discussed in Parliament and where new evidence relating to age-old ethical debates is considered, aswell as being used

---

26   Shell, *Lords*, 179 citing the 1968 White Paper on House of Lords Reform.

as a sounding-board for Government policy-makers. Whereas legislation is concerned with the formulation of specific laws to enact policy, it is in deliberative debates that the bishops have an opportunity to contribute to the formulation of the policies which lay behind those specific laws.

Our data on the total length of the bishops' contribution to the different debate types during the 1980s paints the same picture as our figures on the number of episcopal contributions to the House (Figure 6.18) over the same period. The absence of data on the Committee stages of Bills is, however, a hindrance to our analysis (Figure 6.20). The bishops made contributions which totalled 2254 minutes in length to debates on Motions, 1215 minutes to Second Reading debates, and 90 minutes to the discussion of Church of England Measures (which took up, on average, just 0.1% of the time of the House).[27]

Figure 6.20
Total Length of Episcopal Contributions to the Different Debate Types

Debate Type

(Includes all debates for which a timing is given in Hansard)

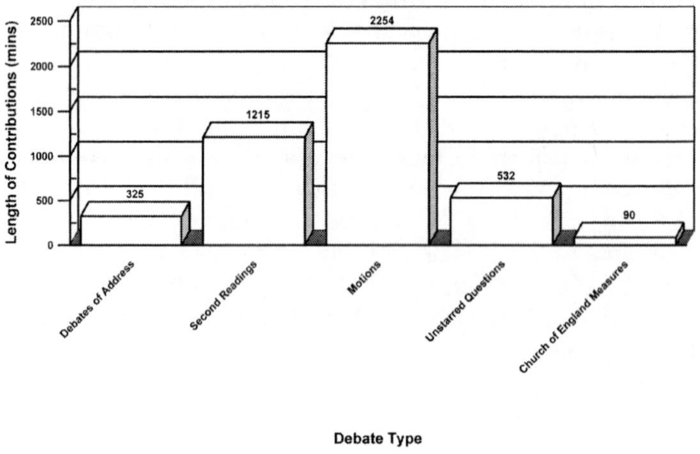

6.5 The Subjects on which the Bishops Spoke

6.5.1 Overview

During the 1980s the Church of England bishops contributed to House of Lords debates which covered a wide-range of subjects (Figure 6.21). The only subject group on which no bishop contrib-

---

27   Data Source: *House of Lords Sessional Statistics.*

uted during the 1980s was the Welsh Office, whose interests are, by definition, beyond the territorial interest of Church of England bishops.[28] A low number of episcopal speeches to debates on Northern Ireland (seven contributions)[29] and Scotland (three contributions) is explained in the same way. Similarly low numbers of episcopal speeches were made to debates on the Agriculture, Fisheries & Food (five contributions) and Lord Chancellor's Department (nine contributions) subject groups. The subject group which received the greatest number of episcopal contributions was the Home Office (208 contributions). The Education and Employment (176 contributions), Environment, Transport & the Regions (138 contributions), and the Foreign & Commonwealth Office (118 contributions) subject groups also received a good number of episcopal contributions. These results reflect, in broad terms, the emphasis one would expect from the bishops in their contribution to the House of Lords.

We now turn to consider the House of Lords debates within each subject group which received no episcopal contribution (what we shall refer to as 'non-contributions or 'missed opportunities'). It must be stressed that we need to be cautious in making comparisons between the number of episcopal contributions and non-contributions. A 'non-contribution' was defined above (Section 6.1.2) as an occasion where an individual did not contribute to a Second Reading debate, debate on a Motion, or debate on the Address. No record was made of the occasions when bishops did not contribute to debates at the Committee stages of Bills, debates relating to Starred Questions, and Unstarred Question debates. In contrast a 'contribution' is recorded whenever a bishop makes a speech to almost any type of House of Lords debate. As such the actual number of debates in which no episcopal contribution occurred (including every debate type) will have been far higher than is indicated by the term 'non-contribution' in this analysis.

It is immediately apparent that the bishops spoke in every debate which covered the subject of Ecclesiastical Affairs (Figures 6.21 and 6.22). This is entirely to be expected, in the same way that one would expect a representative from the Treasury to contribute to all

---

28 The Church in Wales has been an autonomous province within the Anglican Communion since the 31st March 1914 when the Disestablishment Act came into force. J.R. Guy, 'Church in Wales', in J. Cannon (ed.), *The Oxford Companion to British History* (Oxford: Oxford University Press, 1997), 207.

29 The Church of Ireland (which serves both the North and the Republic) was disestablished in 1869. W.M. Marshall, 'Church of Ireland', in Cannon (ed.), *British History*, 210.

debates on matters within its remit. The large number of non-contributions relating to the Home Office (177 non-contributions), the Environment, Transport & the Regions (272 non-contributions), and the Foreign & Commonwealth Office (115 non-contributions) subject groups puts the bishops' high number of contributions to these subject groups into some perspective, indicating the sheer volume of business which came before the House during the 1979-90 period relating to these three subject groups. In contrast the low number of episcopal non-contributions to the Education and Employment (53 non-contributions) and, to a lesser extent, International Development (10 non-contributions) subject groups indicate that the bishops were particularly committed to involvement in the Parliamentary debates on these subjects during the Thatcher years.

The bishops missed 206 opportunities to speak in debates which fell within the Trade & Industry subject group and 133 opportunities to speak in debates which fell within the H.M. Treasury subject group. In view of the fact that one of the Church of England's primary areas of disagreement with the Thatcher Government was over economic policy this is a remarkably high number, especially in the context of the limited numbers of episcopal contributions to the same subject groups (Trade & Industry: 56 contributions, H.M. Treasury: 29 contributions). The House of Lords is not the only medium through which the Church may bring challenge and critique to the Government but, nevertheless, where the opportunity existed for the bishops to contribute to Parliamentary debate regarding an economic policy of which they were publicly critical it should have been grasped more thoroughly than our data suggests was the case.

We shall consider the contribution of the bishops to debates on the particular subject groups in more detail below. The following subject groups have been excluded from further analysis because the number of contributions made by bishops was not great enough to warrant this level of analysis or to provide significant contrast and comparison between each individual subject within them: Agriculture, Fisheries & Food, the Lord Chancellor's Department, Northern Ireland, the Scottish Office, the Welsh Office and Ecclesiastical Affairs.

6.5.2 Culture, Media and Sport

The bishops' contributions to debates within this subject group were dominated by the subject of Broadcasting (Figure 6.23). The 39 contributions to debates which covered this subject account for just over half of the total contributions within this subject group. Of these 39 contributions, 25 were made in debates on Government Bills. Of these

Figure 6.21
Number of Episcopal Contributions: Total for Each Subject Group

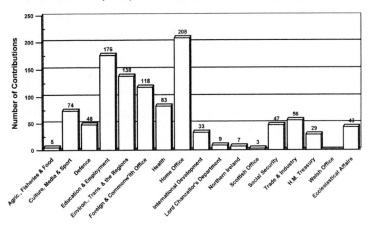

Subject Group

Figure 6.22
Number of Episcopal Non-Contributions: Total for Each Subject Group

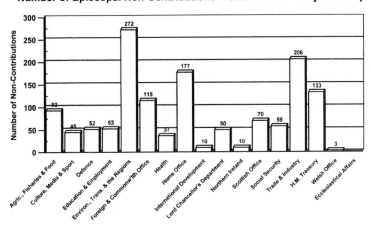

Subject Group

25 contributions to Government Bills, 21 were made at the Committee stages of the Bill implying a particularly high level of episcopal commitment to Broadcasting as a subject. The subject of Films and Videos also received a good number of contributions by the bishops (ten contributions). Of the ten contributions registered for the subject of Historic Buildings and Ancient Monuments eight related, directly or indirectly, to Cathedrals. It was surprising to discover that the

bishops made only one speech on the subject of a National Lottery. However, consideration of the opportunities to contribute to debates relating to the Culture, Media & Sport subject group which the bishops did not take, indicates that this was the only occasion on which the matter of a National Lottery came up for discussion in the House during the Thatcher years (Figure 6.24).

Figure 6.23
Number of Episcopal Contributions: Culture, Media & Sport

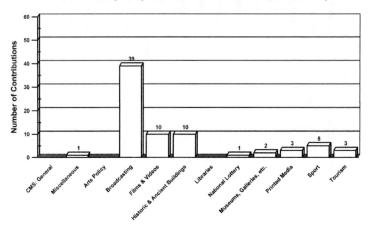

Subject

Figure 6.24
Number of Episcopal Non-Contributions: Culture, Media & Sport

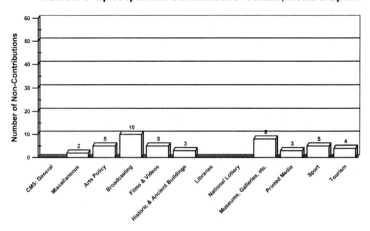

Subject

6.5.3 Defence

In each of the Parliamentary sessions, except the 1979/80 and 1987/88 sessions, the bishops made a contribution to the debate on the Address which gave attention to those parts of the Queen's Speech which referred to the subject of Defence. Indeed, 12 of the 14 contributions made by the bishops to debates covering the subject Defence: General were made in debates on the Address. (Figure 6.25). Each of the bishops' 14 speeches on Non-Conventional Weapons were made in deliberative debates, the bulk of which (11 of the 14) were made between the 1979/80 and the 1984/85 Parliamentary sessions, during which time nuclear disarmament was a crucial international foreign-policy issue for the nuclear powers. The fact that there were ten non-contributions on Non-Conventional Weapons suggests that the high episcopal contribution rate was partly the result of the extent to which the subject caught the attention of the House during the 1980s, as well as an area of particular interest to the bishops (Figure 6.26).

Figure 6.25
Number of Episcopal Contributions: Defence

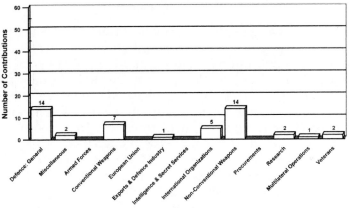

Subject

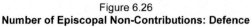

Figure 6.26
Number of Episcopal Non-Contributions: Defence

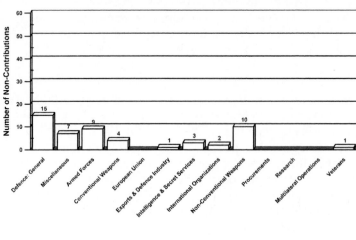

6.5.4 *Education and Employment*

The number of contributions made by the bishops to debates which involved the subjects of Schools (54 contributions), Higher Education & Research (45 contributions) and Further Education (36 contributions) are a clear indication of the priority which the bishops placed on education (Figure 6.27). This is emphasised further when the proportionally low number of non-contributions to debates on these three subjects is taken into account (Figure 6.28). These contributions were fairly evenly spread over the 1980s, though there was a particular glut of contributions during the 1987/88 Parliamentary session during which the Government's Education Reform Bill (1988), which covered each of these subjects, made its passage through the House of Lords. Episcopal contributions were also noticeably high during the 1979/80 Parliamentary session during which the Government's Education No.2 Bill (1980) was considered in the Upper House. The subject of Teachers drew far fewer contributions from the bishops (10 contributions) compared to the subjects mentioned above. However, the bishops did not register any non-contributions in debates covering the subject of Teachers during the Thatcher years. The bishops also missed no opportunity to speak on Special Needs Education which drew only two episcopal contributions but which saw no non-contributions.

Figure 6.27
Number of Episcopal Contributions: Education & Employment

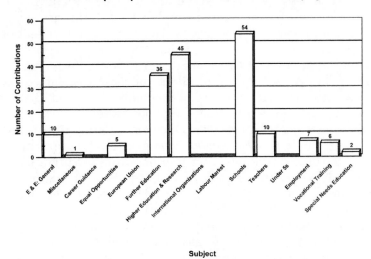

Figure 6.28
Number of Episcopal Non-Contributions: Education & Employment

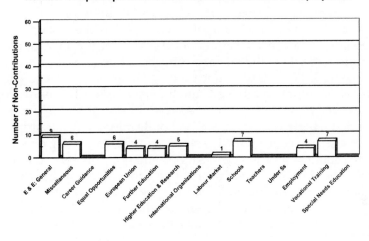

6.5.5 Environment, Transport and the Regions

Housing & Homelessness (39 contributions) and Local Government (43 contributions) were the subjects within this subject group which received by far the greatest attention from the bishops during the Thatcher years (Figure 6.29). On both subjects the episcopal attention that they received was relatively well spread throughout the period. The most striking peak occurred in the 1984/85 Parliamentary session during which bishops spoke in debates covering the subject of Local Government on 14 occasions. This peak was the result of the Government's Local Government Bill (1985) which received episcopal input at every stage from Second Reading through to Third Reading. Episcopal non-contributions for these two subjects were, however, also high (18 for Housing & Homelessness and 23 for Local Government) (Figure 6.30). Only nine contributions were recorded for the subject of Urban Regeneration. Considering the media fuss which surrounded the *Faith in the City* report this is surprisingly few, though the bishops did miss only four opportunities to speak on this matter. It is noticeable, however, that all of those contributions which did occur were made from December 1985 onwards – the *Faith in the City* report was published in September 1985.

The data relating to episcopal non-contributions leaves the reader in little doubt that the bishops as a whole were largely uninterested in the transport-related subjects. On each of these subjects there were a large number of missed opportunities for Christian input. It is also clear that the bishops were uninterested in contributing to debates relating to the Environment & Pollution or Conservation. Bishops made speeches in debates on Conservation only once, missing six opportunities which one might have expected the bishops to take up. More stark are the figures for debates on the Environment & Pollution, to which the bishops contributed on only four occasions, squandering 30 further opportunities. This is surely representative of a wider failure within the Church to take seriously environmental issues even once they began to receive widespread public and media attention. Hugh Montefiore (Bishop of Birmingham), a forerunner in environmental concern (active since the 1950s in writing on environmental matters and in organisations such as Friends of the Earth), recalls the response to environmental concerns from the Church of England during the 1980s: 'I did raise the matter. I mean I had a little group at the Board of Social Responsibility, an environmental group, and we did produce a report, twice, but I can't say that it had any effect really. People just absented themselves from the debate really.'[30] Christian doctrines of God as creator and humanity's role as the stewards of that creation should have placed the Church as a whole, not just a few of its leaders, at the forefront of public concern over environmental issues. Environment & Pollution as a subject is also found

---

30   Hugh Montefiore (Bishop of Birmingham), in an interview with the author, 21st May 2002, Appendix 3.

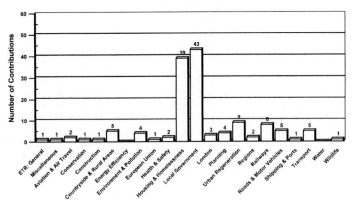

Figure 6.29
**Number of Episcopal Contributions: Environment,
Transport & the Regions**

in the Foreign & Commonwealth Office, Scottish Office and Welsh Office subject groups. In these subject groups the bishops' record on environmental issues was no more impressive, with the bishops contributing on one occasion, and missing seven opportunities.

The European Union (European Community as it then was) is another subject to which the bishops' input was similarly lacking over the course of the Thatcher years. The European Union received the greatest number of episcopal non-contributions (31) in the Environment, Transport & the Regions subject group, as opposed to just one contribution. The bishops' record in other subject groups where the European Union came up for discussion (Defence, Education & Employment, Foreign & Commonwealth Office, Health, Social Security, H.M. Treasury) was no better. In total there were 90 episcopal non-contributions in comparison to only nine contributions. The same is true of the specific EU Agricultural (one contribution and 23 non-contributions) and EU Fisheries (no contributions and two non-contributions) subjects within the Agriculture, Fisheries & Food subject group. This record is concerning. Surely some greater input from the Bench of Bishops was warranted on a subject of such profound national and international significance.

6.5.6 Foreign and Commonwealth Office

Bishops spoke in debates which considered a wide range of the business of the Foreign & Commonwealth Office (Figure 6.31). The great-

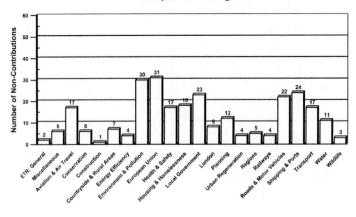

Figure 6.30
**Number of Episcopal Non-Contributions: Environment,
Transport & the Regions**

est number of contributions made were to debates on the subject of Sub-Saharan Africa (21 contributions) in which the high profile issues of apartheid in South Africa and poverty were the focus. The high number of non-contributions in debates covering the subject of the European Union has already been discussed. Otherwise, the bar-chart of episcopal non-contributions supports the conclusion that the episcopal contribution within the Foreign and Commonwealth subject group was evenly balanced between the various subjects (Figure 6.32).

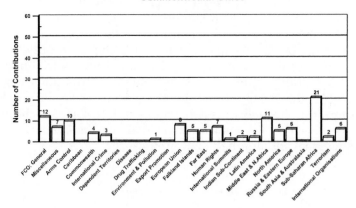

Figure 6.31
**Number of Episcopal Contributions: Foreign &
Commonwealth Office**

Figure 6.32
**Number of Episcopal Non-Contributions: Foreign &
Commonwealth Office**

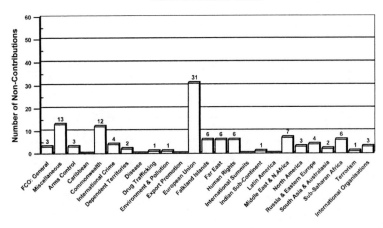

Subject

6.5.7 Health

Debates relating to the subject of Embryology and Fertilisation received the greatest number of episcopal contributions (17 contributions) within the Health subject group during the Thatcher years (Figure 6.33). No episcopal non-contributions are recorded for the same subject (Figure 6.34). Ten of these 17 contributions related to the Government's Embryology and Fertilisation Bill (1990) including 11 contributions at the Committee stages. The bishops also contributed on nine occasions to debates covering the subject of Abortion (seven of which were Private Members' Bills) and missed only one opportunity to contribute to the subject in Second Reading debates, debates on Motions, and debates on the Address. Mental Health is another subject within the Health subject group on which the record of the bishops is impressive. Here they made ten contributions but registered no non-contributions. On the wider issue of the National Health Service the bishops made only 13 contributions to debates, missing 14 opportunities to speak.

6.5.8 Home Office

Immigration & Nationality (32 contributions), Marriage & Family (33 contributions) and Prisons, Probation & Aftercare (15 contributions) were manifestly the primary areas of interest for the bishops during the 1980s (Figure 6.35). These subjects received not only high numbers of contributions but also low numbers of non-contributions

Figure 6.33
Number of Episcopal Contributions: Health

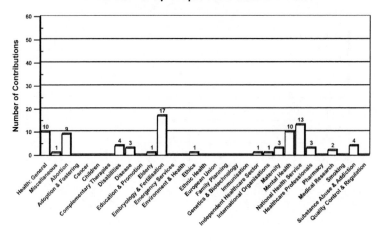

Subject

Figure 6.34
Number of Episcopal Non-Contributions: Health

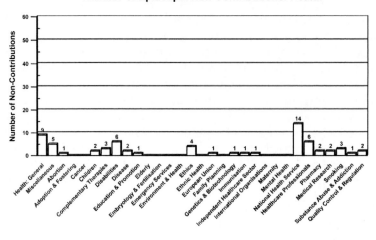

Subject

(five for Immigration & Nationality, eight for Marriage & Family, and eight for Prisons, Probation & Aftercare) (Figure 6.36). Consideration in the Upper House of the Government's British Nationality Bill (1981) accounts for a particular peak of 14 contributions in debates covering the subject of Immigration & Nationality during the 1980/81 Parliamentary session.

Also of considerable interest was the subject of Trading for which we have a record of 20 episcopal contributions and only five non-contributions. Deliberative debates on Sunday trading and the debates surrounding the Government's Shops Bill (1986) during the 1985/86 Parliamentary session largely account for this interest. The number of contributions recorded for the subject of Charities (10 contributions), Criminal Law & Policy (17 contributions) and Political & Constitutional matters (19 contributions) were also quite high. Yet, in the context of the number of episcopal non-contributions recorded for each of these subjects, this does not seem to represent a particular emphasis in the bishops' speech-making. It is, however, interesting to observe that the bishops missed 15 opportunities to speak in debates covering the subject of Gambling and 13 opportunities to speak on Licensing. Instead they made only three contributions on Gambling and two on Licensing.

Figure 6.35
Number of Episcopal Contributions: Home Office

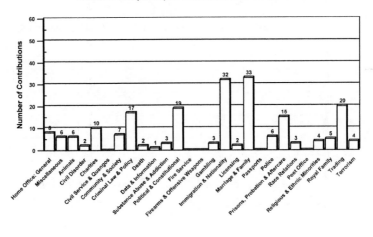

Subject

6.5.9 International Development

The bishops greatest contribution to the International Development subject group was made in debates which fell within the International Development: General subject (14 contributions) (Figure 6.37). Of these contributions, 11 were made in debates on the Address and overall just four opportunities to contribute to debates which covered international development issues at a general level were missed

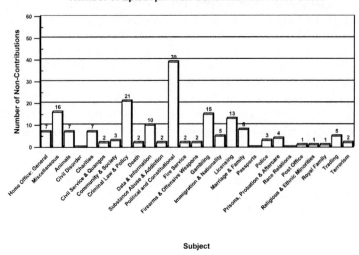

Figure 6.36
Number of Episcopal Non-Contributions: Home Office

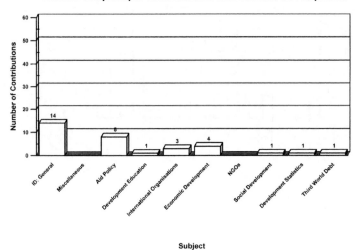

Figure 6.37
Number of Episcopal Contributions: International Development

(Figure 6.38). The bishops' primary focus was otherwise in debates covering the subject of Aid Policy, to which they made contributions on eight occasions and registered only one non-contribution. Further comment cannot be made on the International Development subject group because it came before the House on so few occasions.

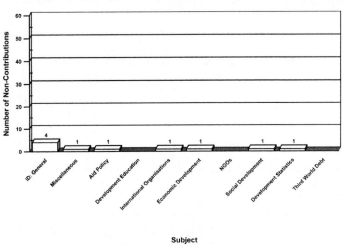

Figure 6.38
Number of Episcopal Non-Contributions: International Development

6.5.10 Social Security

The main emphasis of the bishops' contribution to the debates of the House which related to the Social Security subject group were general overarching policy discussions. This is clear from their emphasis upon contributing to debates in the Social Security: General subject (15 contributions), as opposed to the other more specific subjects within the group (Figure 6.39). The only exceptions are debates

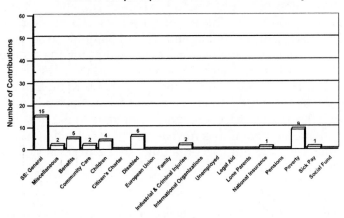

Figure 6.39
Number of Episcopal Contributions: Social Security

which tackled Poverty which received notable interest from the bishops, with nine contributions made and only two non-contributions (Figure 6.40).

Figure 6.40
Number of Episcopal Non-Contributions: Social Security

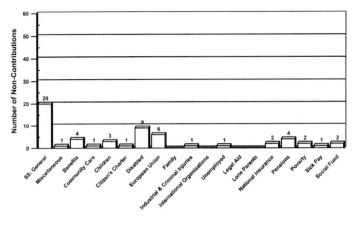

6.5.11 Trade and Industry

As already mentioned the bishops made a limited contribution to House of Lords discussion within this subject group. Their greatest contribution was in debates covering the subject of Employment (15 contributions), but even this was in the context of 14 non-contributions. (Figures 6.41 & 6.42). The subject of Employment also arose in the Education & Employment, H.M. Treasury, and Northern Ireland subject groups. Overall the bishops spoke 23 times in debates which discussed Employment and missed 24 opportunities to contribute to Second Reading debates, debates on Motions and debates of Address on Employment. This record reveals a lesser commitment from the bishops to the debates of the Lords relating to the unemployment problem than one would have expected, a problem on which the *Faith in the City* report comments thus: 'It is the steep rise in unemployment in recent years above all else that has significantly increased the number of families living in poverty in Britain today.'[31]

---

31   Archbishop of Canterbury's Commission on Urban Priority Areas, *Faith in the City: A Call for Action by Church and Nation* (London: Church House Publishing, 1985), 197 (9.13).

The bishops record in other areas of the Trade & Industry subject group was far worse. On the subject of International Trade they made one contribution and 15 non-contributions. In debates covering the subject of Competitiveness & Productivity the bishops failed to make a single contribution to the House (whereas on the subject of Space they managed two speeches). In fact the bishops missed a total of 13 opportunities to be involved in debates on the matter. On the similar subject of Privatisation the bishops fared little better. They made two contributions yet missed 14 opportunities to speak in debates on matters such as: 'Industrial Production' (during May 1983) and 'Privatisation and Wealth Creation' (during June 1985). Unfortunately, whilst Church of England policy documents acknowledged that 'the process of wealth creation must be supported wholeheartedly' alongside an emphasis on the fair distribution of the wealth created,[32] the bishops' record in the Lords communicated a different message. It could be argued that the bishops' failure to contribute to debates on these matters in the House implicates them in a silent endorsement of left-wing solutions to economic difficulties, solutions which focused on public spending and interventionist government.

Figure 6.41
Number of Episcopal Contributions: Trade & Industry

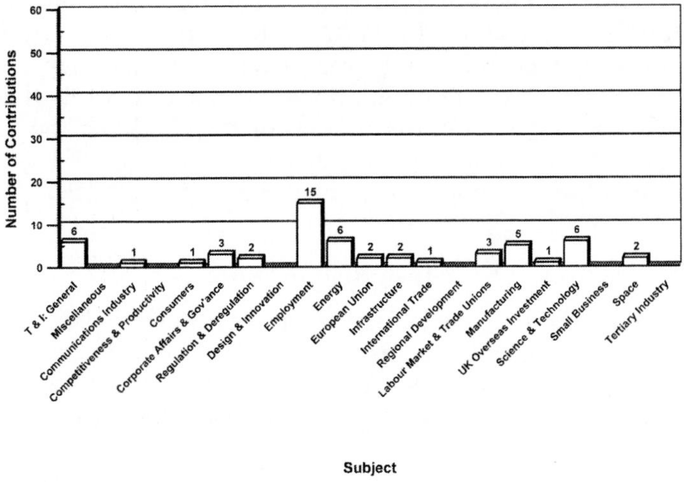

---

32 Commission, *Faith*, 204 (9.28).

Figure 6.42
Number of Episcopal Non-Contributions: Trade & Industry

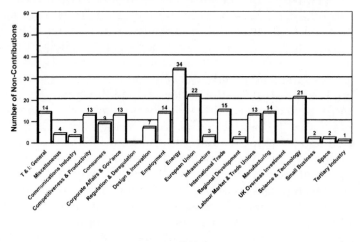

Subject

6.5.12 H.M. Treasury

A similar picture to that described above appears when the figures for episcopal contributions and non-contributions to the H.M. Treasury subject group are explored. Bishops made no contributions to broad discussions on the subject of The Economy, allowing 16 opportunities to pass them by. Perhaps this represents a recognition by the bishops of the limits of their knowledge and experience in this area. However, those same limitations did not prompt the bishops to excuse themselves from discussions of the House on the subject of Taxation (12 contributions), nor fit with the Church of England's publication of several policy documents on economic affairs.[33]

6.6 Which Bishops Spoke

During Margaret Thatcher's time as Prime Minister speeches were made in the debates of the House of Lords by 51 of the 58 individual bishops eligible to contribute to the House, four of whom contributed from two different bishoprics.[34] Only 17 of these 51 individual

---

33   For example: D. Edwards, *The State of the Nation* (London: Church House Publishing, 1976); R. Harris, *Morality and Markets* (London: Church House Publishing, 1986); Board for Social Responsibility, *Church and Economy* (London: Church House Publishing, 1989).

34   Graham Leonard contributed whilst Bishop of Truro and then London, Eric

Figure 6.43
Number of Episcopal Contributions: H.M. Treasury

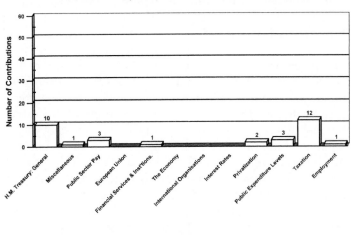

Subject

Figure 6.44
Number of Episcopal Non-Contributions: H.M. Treasury

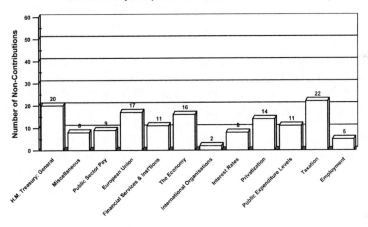

Subject

bishops made more than 10 contributions, with these 17 individuals making 577 of 768 (75%) of the bishops' speeches to the House during

James contributed whilst Bishop of Wakefield and then Winchester, Ronald Bowlby contributed whilst Bishop of Newcastle and then Southwark, John Habgood contributed whilst Bishop of Durham and then York.

the 1980s. Of the eligible dioceses only the diocese of St Edmunds-
bury & Ipswich saw none of its bishops make a contribution to the
business of the House. As with episcopal attendance, the number of
contributions made by each diocesan bishop varies a great deal (Figure 6.45). The bishops from the Canterbury province made 72% of
the total episcopal speeches during the 1980s, the bishops from the
York province 28%. Whilst the bishops from the Canterbury province undertook the greater share of the burden for making verbal
contributions to the House, relative to the number of dioceses within
each, the bishops from the provinces of Canterbury and York undertook an equal share of speech-making at the House of Lords.[35] Considering the additional distance of the bishops serving in the York
province from Westminster, this is an admirable record. It is a record
which needs to continue in order to justify the Church of England's
claim that, in their role at Westminster, the bishops act as representatives for the communities and regions of England.[36]

The greatest number of verbal contributions to the debates of
the House were made by Maurice Wood (Bishop of Norwich) (93
contributions), Stanley Booth-Clibborn (Bishop of Manchester) (82
contributions), and David Say (Bishop of Rochester) (65 contributions). David Halsey (Bishop of Carlisle), who attended the House
on more occasions than any other bishop during the Thatcher years,
spoke in the debates of the House on only six occasions. This fits
with his explanation of his approach to contributing to the House
(Section 5.4 above) in which he notes that, because his return train
to Carlisle left London before 6.00pm, he was unable to be present
for evening debates and 'virtually debarred from speaking' by the
protocol of the House which expects that 'if you speak in a debate
you are expected to stay to the end for the formal summing-up of the
final two speeches.'[37] John B. Taylor (Bishop of St Albans) makes it
clear, however, that this protocol need not stop a bishop from speaking in the House. Asked if a change to this aspect of the procedures
of the House would help the bishops to speak more in the House he
comments thus:

---

35 The Canterbury province contains 29 dioceses and made a combined total
    of 554 contributions. The York province contains 13 dioceses and made
    a combined total of 214 contributions. For a comparison with episcopal
    attendance and voting see Section 5.4 above.

36 Council, *Role*, 6. 'The pastoral role of the bishops is rooted in their diocesan
    responsibilities and the ministry they extend there to many aspects of local
    life... In that capacity, bishops also bring a representative voice different
    from any likely form of purely political (including elected) representation.'

37 David Halsey (Bishop of Carlisle) in a letter to the author, 27th April 2002.

I don't think so, no. They [the Lords Temporal] understand. They're very understanding towards you but you obviously try to fulfil the requirement as you can. And there are other peers who will apologize. Courtesy more than law. Everything is courtesy in the House of Lords.[38]

Figure 6.45
Number of Contributions to House of Lords Debates by Individual Bishops

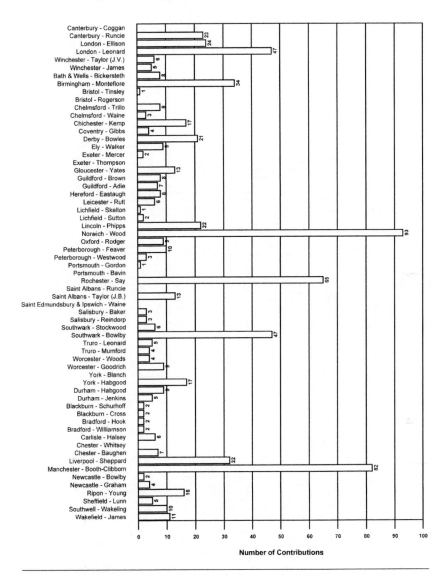

Number of Contributions

38   John B. Taylor (Bishop of St Albans) in an interview with the author, 29th July 2002, Appendix 5.

The greatest number of contributions in any one Parliamentary session was made by Maurice Wood (Bishop of Norwich), who made 40 contributions during the 1983/84 Parliamentary session. His time was particularly taken up with contributing to the Government's Matrimonial and Family Proceedings Bill (1984) and a Private Members' Video Recordings Bill.

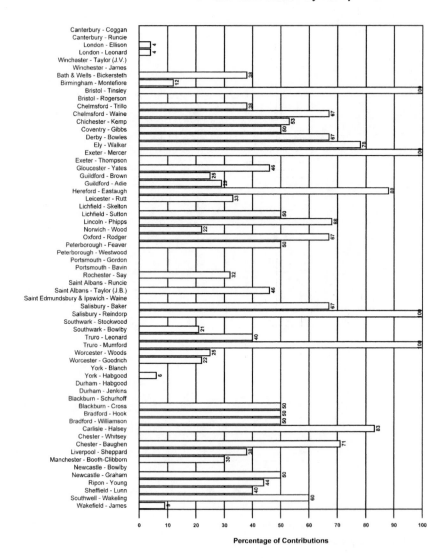

Figure 6.46
Percentage of Individual Bishops' Contributions to House of Lords Debates made whilst Duty Bishop

The limited attendance of David Jenkins (Bishop of Durham) at the House of Lords (Section 4.3 above) is mirrored by just five speeches in the House during the Thatcher years. Of the three men (Graham Leonard, Robert Runcie, and John Habgood) who were eligible to attend the House throughout the Thatcher years, Leonard recorded the greatest number of contributions to the House. As Bishop of Truro, and then London, he spoke in the House on a total of 52 occasions. Runcie and Habgood, even with the particular additional responsibilities of their archiepiscopates to contend with for the majority of the 1980s, managed a considerable level of input into the debates of the Lords. Robert Runcie spoke on 23 occasions as Archbishop of Canterbury, John Habgood on 17 occasions as Archbishop of York. The additional influence exerted by the holders of these two titles, particularly in capturing media attention, mean that it is essential to the ongoing effectiveness of the Bench of Bishops that they continue to make a similar or greater number of speeches in the House of Lords in the future.

Of the 768 speeches made by the bishops during the 1980s, 236 (31%) were delivered by the designated duty bishop of the day.[39] Each of the bishops who made a large proportion of their contributions whilst duty bishop made, overall, a small number of verbal contributions to House of Lords. Indeed, each of the four bishops who made all of their contributions whilst duty bishop spoke, in total, on less than eight occasions in the Upper House (Figure 6.46). Conversely, the three bishops who spoke on the most occasions during the Thatcher years did so whilst duty bishop on a minority of occasions: Maurice Wood (Bishop of Norwich) made only 22% of his speeches as duty bishop, Stanley Booth-Clibborn (Bishop of Manchester) made 30% whilst duty bishop, and David Say (Bishop of Rochester) made 32% whilst duty bishop. That no incumbent of the dioceses of Canterbury, York, London, Winchester and Durham made more than a handful of speeches to the Lords whilst duty bishop is explained by the fact that they are not required to be on the rota of duty bishops.

The number of contributions made by each individual bishop to Government Bills reveals that the greater proportion of the bishops' response to the Thatcher Government's legislation was made by a small group of just seven bishops (Figure 6.47). This group made 65% (150 out of 230) of the episcopal speeches during the consideration of Government Bills during the Thatcher years. This group consisted of:

---

39   The designated duty bishops also cast 31% (290 out 933) of the total votes cast by bishops during the 1980s (Section 5.3 above).

Figure 6.47
**Number of Contributions by Individual Bishops to Debates on
Private Members' & Government Bills**

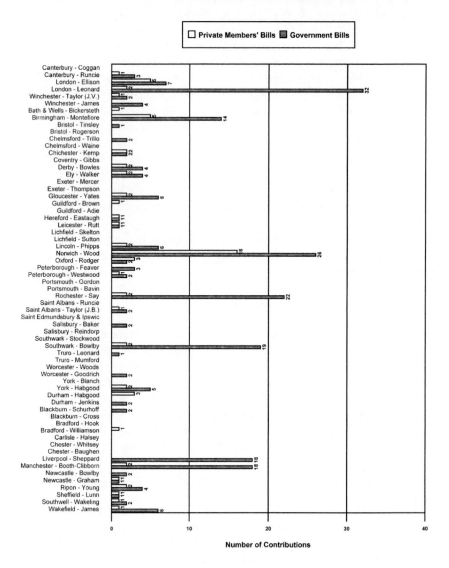

Number of Contributions

- Graham Leonard (whilst Bishop of London) who made 32 speeches.
- Hugh Montefiore (Bishop of Birmingham) who made 14 speeches.[40]

---

40   Hugh Montefiore's contribution rate is all the more impressive in view of

- Maurice Wood (Bishop of Norwich) who made 26 speeches.
- David Say (Bishop of Rochester) who made 22 speeches.
- Ronald Bowlby (whilst Bishop of Southwark) who made 19 speeches.
- David Sheppard (Bishop of Liverpool) who made 18 speeches.
- Stanley Booth-Clibborn (Bishop of Manchester) who made 18 speeches.

Each of these seven bishops made a high number (between 12 and 33) of contributions to debates at the Committee stages of Bills (Figure 6.48). Together they also made 44% (47 out of 106) of the episcopal contributions to Second Reading debates. Six of the bishops in this group of seven are also listed in the group of seven bishops who cast 42% of the bishops' total votes during the 1980s. Only Hugh Montefiore (Bishop of Birmingham) and Eric Kemp (Bishop of Chichester) are not included in both groups.

The extent of the contribution of some of these individual bishops is accounted for by the length of their eligibility to attend and contribute to the House. Graham Leonard, Ronald Bowlby and David Sheppard were eligible to contribute from the particular diocese noted in the list above for in excess of nine full Parliamentary sessions of the Thatcher years. Not all of these bishops had such long periods in which to contribute to the debates of the House. Hugh Montefiore was eligible to contribute for less than three full Parliamentary sessions, Maurice Wood and Stanley Booth-Clibborn for only around six Parliamentary sessions. None of the bishops outside of this group (whose eligibility to contribute to the House during the 1980s ranged from a few months to more than 11 full Parliamentary sessions) made more than seven contributions to debates on Government Bills.

The 201 contributions made by bishops to debates on Motions are more evenly spread among the different diocesan bishops (Figure 6.48). Whilst Booth-Clibborn, Bowlby and Wood are again amongst the highest contributors, several other bishops made a good number of contributions to this type of debate including: Robert Runcie (whilst Archbishop of Canterbury) who made 9 contributions, Eric Kemp (Bishop of Chichester) who made 7 contributions, Cyril Bowles (Bishop of Derby) who made 6 contributions, and John Habgood (whilst Archbishop of York) who made 7 contributions. A total of seven individuals were responsible for all of the bishops' contributions to the debates on Church of England Measures, with the bulk

---

the fact that he was only eligible to attend the House from December 1984 to November 1987.

Figure 6.48

Number of Contributions by Individual Bishops to the Different Debate Types

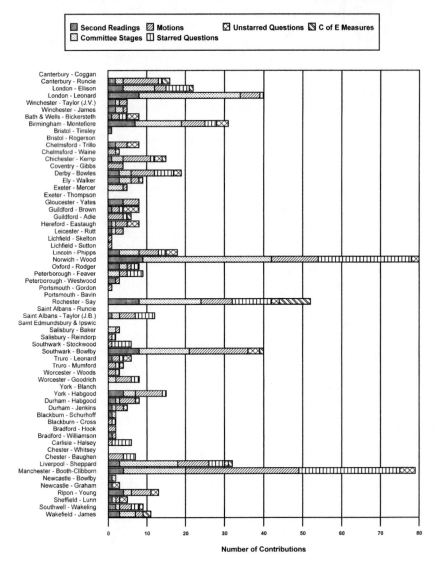

of work undertaken by David Say (Bishop of Rochester) who made 8 contributions to debates on this type of business (Figure 6.48).

By far the greatest number of contributions within the subject group Culture, Media and Sport were made by Maurice Wood (Bishop of Norwich) (Figure 6.49). The subject of Broadcasting which, as already mentioned, was of particular interest to Wood, comes within this subject group. Wood also spoke more than any other bishop in debates within the Defence, Health, and Home Office subject groups. Close behind Wood in Defence subject groups came David Say (Bishop of Rochester) who made five contributions (Figure 6.50). Overall, the contributions to the Defence subject group were distributed fairly evenly amongst a good number of bishops. The same can be said of the bishops' contribution in debates covering the subject of Education & Employment, though it was Graham Leonard (Bishop of London) who was the greatest contributor (19 contributions) (Figure 6.51).

During the Thatcher years the Environment, Transport & the Regions subject group was given most attention by Ronald Bowlby (whilst Bishop of Southwark) who made 20 contributions and Stanley Booth-Clibborn (Bishop of Manchester) who made 18 contributions (Figure 6.52). David Sheppard (Bishop of Liverpool) and Maurice Wood (Bishop of Norwich) made ten contributions each. That the bishops of Southwark, Manchester and Liverpool should each contribute heavily in this area is accounted for by the fact that most of these contributions related specifically to Housing & Homelessness and Local Government (and more particularly the abolition of the Metropolitan City Councils), all issues of special import in urban dioceses.

Robert Runcie (whilst Archbishop of Canterbury) spoke in debates on Foreign & Commonwealth Office business six times (just over a quarter of his total contribution to the debates of the House) (Figure 6.53). Three of these contributions were made at times of national 'crisis' (the Falklands conflict and the Gulf war) and two as Tributes (on the assassination of Mrs Ghandi and on the 40th Anniversary of the United Nations). Each of these situations show the Archbishop operating in his national leadership role and as leader of the worldwide Anglican Communion. By a considerable margin the greatest contributor to the Foreign & Commonwealth Office subject group was Stanley Booth-Clibborn (Bishop of Manchester) who spoke on 18 occasions. Clearly, this was an area of special interest to him. He spoke considerably more on this subject than any other except the Environment, Transport & the Regions. None of his time was taken up with the Committee stages of Bills but rather with a whole variety of subjects within the subject group, particularly relating to racism and poverty in Africa. It is this kind of approach which, it is argued in Section 6.4 above, is most suitable for the bishops to adopt at the House of Lords.

A good number of bishops made contributions on the Health subject group, with the particular subject of Embryology & Fertilisation appearing to account for the interest of John Habgood (whilst Archbishop of York) (Figure 6.54). Similarly, four of Graham Leonard's seven contributions were on this matter. The bishops' contribution to the Home Office subject group is dominated by the names of Graham Leonard (whilst Bishop of London) who made 11 contributions, Hugh Montefiore (Bishop of Birmingham) who made 15 contributions, Maurice Wood (Bishop of Norwich) who made 24 contributions, David Say (Bishop of Rochester) who made 21 contributions, and Stanley Booth-Clibborn who made 18 contributions (Figure 6.55). Most noteworthy is the record of Cyril Bowles (Bishop of Derby) who made ten contributions (his greatest contribution to a subject group) and Robert Runcie who, whilst Archbishop of Canterbury, made 11 contributions (his greatest to a subject group). Bowles was also involved in making the bishops' contribution to the House on International Development, making four contributions (Figure 6.56). Stanley Booth-Clibborn (Bishop of Manchester) also made four contributions David Say (Bishop of Rochester) made five. Overall, only 16 individuals spoke in debates covering the subject of International Development.

Ronald Bowlby (whilst Bishop of Southwark) was the greatest episcopal contributor, with six speeches, to debates within the Social Security subject group (Figure 6.57). It is likely that the character of his diocese, covering most of London south of the Thames including a great number of individuals dependent on state provision for their needs, accounts for this level of interest. Hugh Montefiore (Bishop of Birmingham) was the greatest episcopal contributor to the Trade & Industry subject group, making 11 contributions (Figure 6.58). Four of these speeches were made in debates relating to the use of animals in scientific procedures. The 15 contributions on the subject of Employment (specifically unemployment) within the subject group were made by a variety of bishops. Robert Runcie (whilst Archbishop of Canterbury) and John Habgood (whilst Archbishop of York) did not contribute at all to the debates in the Trade & Industry and H.M. Treasury subject groups. Simon Phipps (Bishop of Lincoln) made four contributions to the Trade & Industry, and six to the H.M. Treasury, subject groups (Figure 6.59). He was the highest contributing bishop to the latter subject group, though only seventeen individuals contributed altogether. A comparison of the Trade & Industry and H.M. Treasury subject groups (the 'economic' groups) reveals that it was the same four bishops who made the majority of the bishops' contributions to both. Those four bishops were: Hugh Montefiore (Bishop of Birmingham), Simon Phipps (Bishop of Lincoln), Maurice Wood (Bishop of Norwich), and Stanley Booth-Clibborn (Bishop of Manchester).

In line with comments made during our analysis of which bishops spoke in debates on Church of England Measures, we see that David Say (Bishop of Rochester) led the Church of England's input into the consideration of all the debates which came within the Ecclesiastical Affairs subject group during the 1980s (Figure 6.60). He was supported by the contributions of 21 other diocesan bishops including Gerald Ellison (Bishop of London) who made six contributions – a quarter of the speeches he made between the beginning of Thatcher's premiership and his retirement in July 1981.

6.7 Conclusion

How positively one responds to the episcopal contribution record depends, in part, to which figures one refers. To say that a bishop made a speech in the House of Lords, on average, every other sitting day during the Thatcher years sounds more impressive than to say that bishops spoke, in total, on 20% of sitting days. Whichever way the data is presented, it seems reasonable to conclude that there was plenty of room for greater episcopal involvement in the socio-political debate of the House, particularly on those matters on which the Church of England was well known to have been critical of the policies of the Thatcher Government.

There is evidence to indicate that there was a growing reaction from the Bench of Bishops to the Thatcher Government's failure to abide by the policies and the style of the post-war political consensus. In parallel with an increasing consideration of social questions in the General Synod after 1983 the level of episcopal contributions to the House of Lords increased between 1983 and 1987. At the heart of this negative response were the bishops from the largely urban dioceses whose attitude would appear to have been driven, not by a specific decision to oppose the Government, but in response to the increasing number of specific Bills and issues which came before the House which were affecting the communities within their dioceses, and on which they therefore felt compelled to speak.

As a group the bishops did make contributions on a wide-range of legislative and deliberative debates. Shell's claim that 'in almost any area of legislation an episcopal contribution may be forthcoming' is a fair one.[41] The bishops were found speaking during the Thatcher years on subjects from telecommunications to Hong Kong, from airports to local government finance. However, whilst a contribution may have been forthcoming on almost any area of legislation, Shell is right to assert that the episcopal preference was for contributing to debates where a 'moral dimension was self-evident'.[42] However, the sheer number of deliberative debates in which they were silent

---

41   Shell, *Lords*, 54.
42   *ibid*, 55.

(458 debates on Motions) does suggest that the number of debates with a moral dimension which did not receive an episcopal contribution was not insignificant. Indeed, a scan of the non-contribution debates on Motions reveals a number of debates with a self-evident moral dimension, such as a debate on 'World Hunger' (during July 1983), a debate on 'Housing' (during November 1983), and a debate on 'Social Deprivation' (during April 1984).

Donald Shell rightly criticizes the bishops for failing to speak regularly at the House on those subjects on which the Church had been publicly critical of the Government.[43] During the Thatcher years, particularly on economic affairs (as indicated by analysis on the Trade & Industry and H.M. Treasury subject groups) the bishops spoke very little on matters on which the Church of England was widely known to be critical of the Government. The House of Lords clearly represents the most appropriate forum for the Church of England to enter into the national debate on any socio-political matter which should be the primary vehicle for it to vocalise its position in relation to Government policies.

On first inspection, and in contrast to the conclusions of Francis Bown, our research does not reveal the bishops to have concentrated their contributions on deliberative debates. In fact, they contributed a slightly higher proportion of their speeches to legislative (39%) rather than deliberative (33%) debates. Certainly, during the Thatcher years the bishops did not avoid what Lee and Stanford describe as 'getting down to the nitty-gritty of clauses in legislation'[44] and are not open to criticism that they were unwilling to work at seeing the principles which they espoused applied to the specific clauses of Bills, communicating, on occasions, a particular depth of commitment to the issues on which they spoke. However, a closer look at the data reveals that, in the context of the House as whole (which gave, on average, twice as much time to legislative rather legislative debates), the bishops do show an appropriate relative preference for speaking in the deliberative debates which afford the Lords Spiritual their best opportunity of influencing Government policy and public opinion.

Our analysis reveals that during the 1980s there was not a high correlation between bishops' speech-making and their leading of prayers. Just under one-third (31%) of the episcopal speeches to the House during the Thatcher years were delivered by the bishop present to open the day's business with prayers. It was also noteworthy that those bishops who made a large number of contributions

---

43   *ibid*, 56.
44   Lee & Stanford, *Believing*, 31.

to the House made a small proportion of these contributions whilst duty bishop. This evidence supports Bown's argument that the bishops do not merely 'join-in' when obliged to be present at the House to read prayers.

A clear hindrance to episcopal speech-making at Westminster is the fact that many crucial debates take place in the evenings. Just 24% of the bishops' speeches were made in debates which began during the five hours of the evening period, whereas 70% of their speeches were made in debates which began during the two and a half hours of the afternoon period. It is not reasonable to expect that the procedures of the House will change in order to make attendance and speech-making for any minority group within its membership easier. As such any strategy which the Church of England formulates to seek to increase the effectiveness of the bishops' contribution to the House of Lords will need to tackle this hindrance. First and foremost such a strategy will need to set about creating a situation whereby those bishops who have been chosen to perform this aspect of the Church's public ministry have far greater flexibility to be at the House during the evenings and at short notice.

While Shell notes, with justification, that few eligible bishops never contribute to the House of Lords,[45] Medhurst and Moyser are right to describe the contributions of most of the Lords Spiritual as 'spasmodic'.[46] Only 17 of the 51 individual bishops who did speak at the House of Lords during the Thatcher years made more than 10 contributions. In fact, these 17 individual bishops made 75% of the bishops' speeches to the House. Likewise, the bulk of the episcopal input (65%) into the consideration of Government legislation during the Thatcher years was made by only seven individual bishops. There were a number of individual bishops who were, however, heavily involved in this arena: Maurice Wood (Bishop of Norwich), Stanley Booth-Clibborn (Bishop of Manchester) and David Say (Bishop of Rochester). Each made a high number of contributions to the House over the course of the 1980s. Overall the variation in the level of contribution to the House made by each individual bishop, even taking into account the varying length of their periods of eligibility to attend the House, can only be accounted for in the same way as the variation in the attendance rate of the bishops – with reference to the individual personality, experience, expertise and priorities of each individual bishop.

---

45 Shell, *Lords*, 54.
46 Medhurst & Moyser, *Secular*, 274.

Figure 6.49
Number of Contributions by Individual Bishops: Culture, Media & Sport

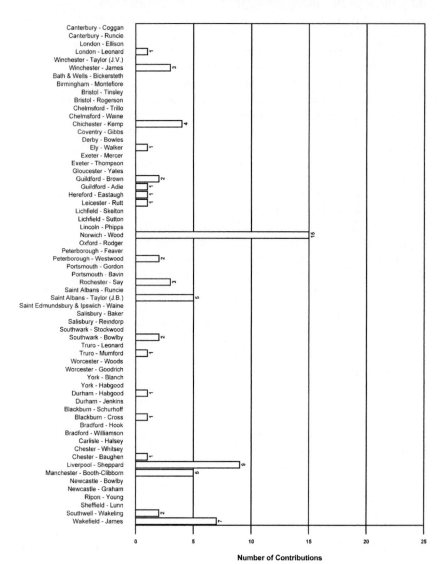

Number of Contributions

Figure 6.50
Number of Contributions by Individual Bishops: Defence

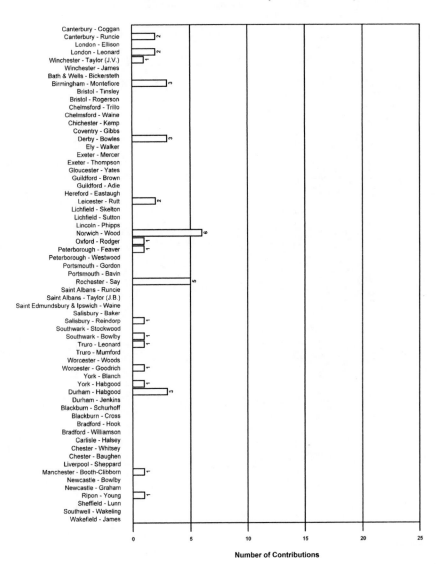

Number of Contributions

Figure 6.51
**Number of Contributions to House of Lords Debates by Individual
Bishops: Education & Employment**

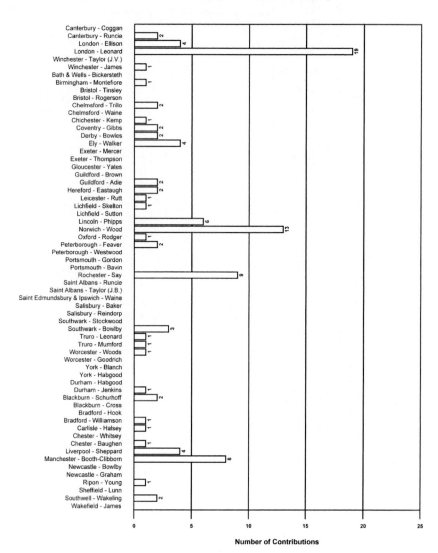

Number of Contributions

Figure 6.52
**Number of Contributions by Individual Bishops:
Environment, Transport & the Regions**

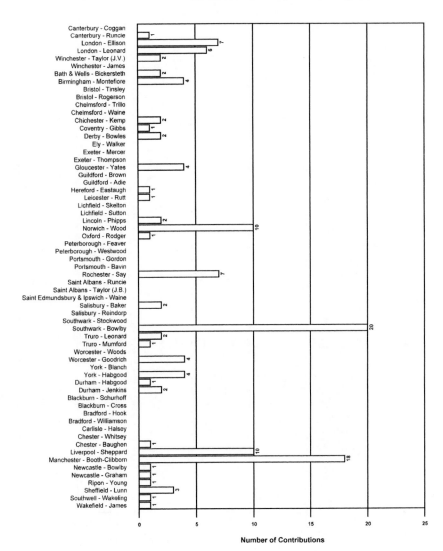

Number of Contributions

Figure 6.53
**Number of Contributions by Individual Bishops:
Foreign & Commonwealth Office**

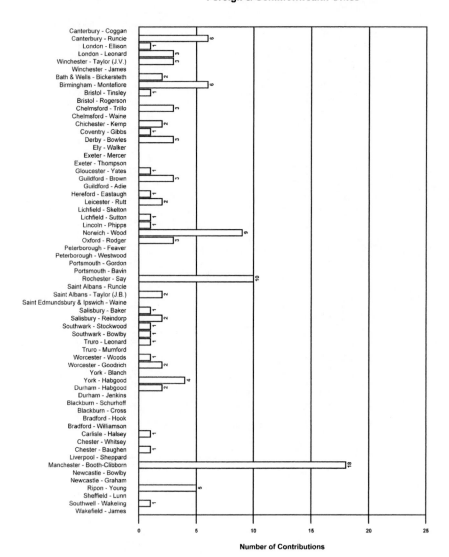

Number of Contributions

Figure 6.54
Number of Contributions by Individual Bishops: Health

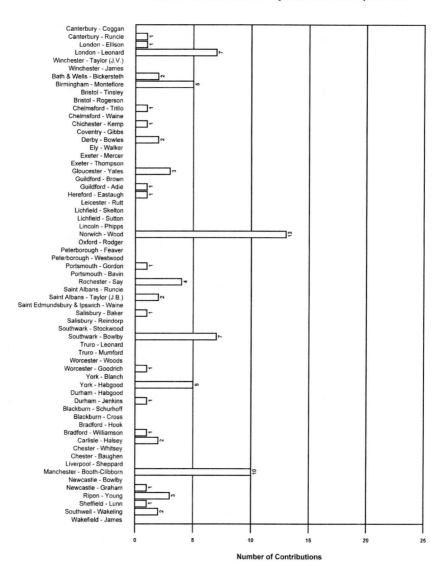

Number of Contributions

Figure 6.55
Number of Contributions by Individual Bishops: Home Office

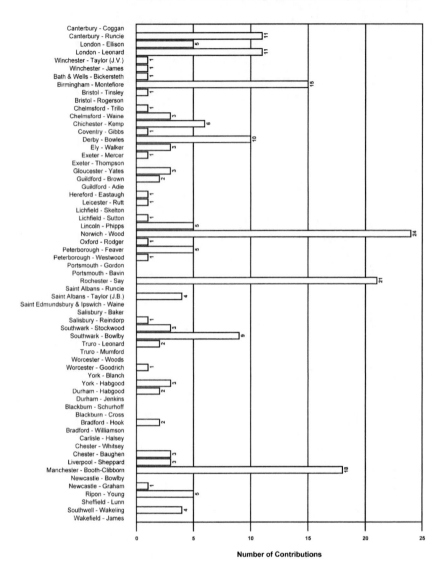

Number of Contributions

Figure 6.56
Number of Contributions by Individual Bishops: International Development

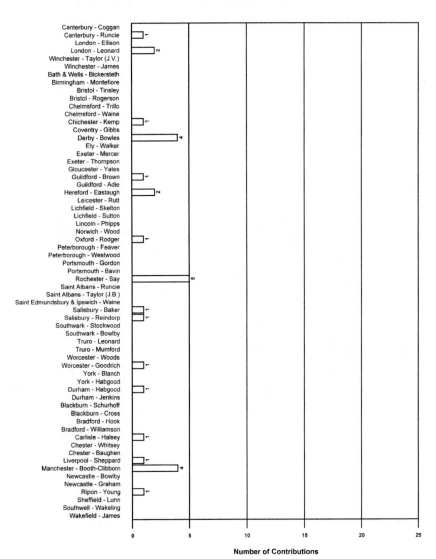

Number of Contributions

Church and State

Figure 6.57
Number of Contributions by Individual Bishops: Social Security

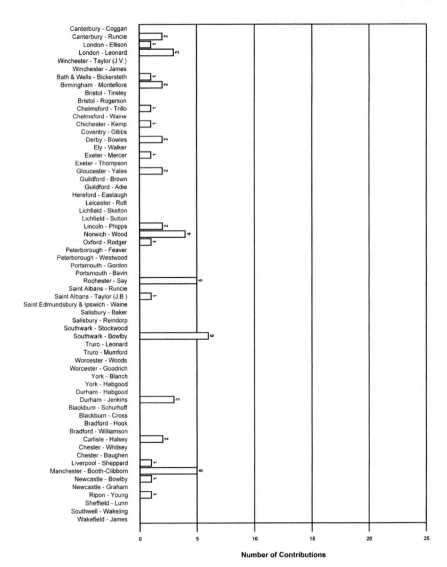

Number of Contributions

Figure 6.58
Number of Contributions by Individual Bishops: Trade & Industry

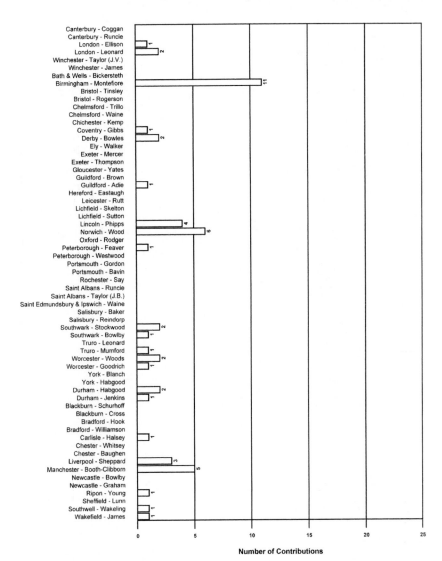

Number of Contributions

Figure 6.59
Number of Contributions by Individual Bishops: H.M. Treasury

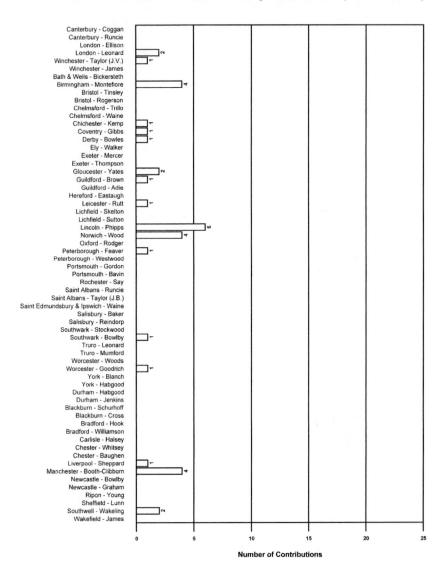

Number of Contributions

Figure 6.60
Number of Contributions by Individual Bishops: Ecclesiastical Affairs

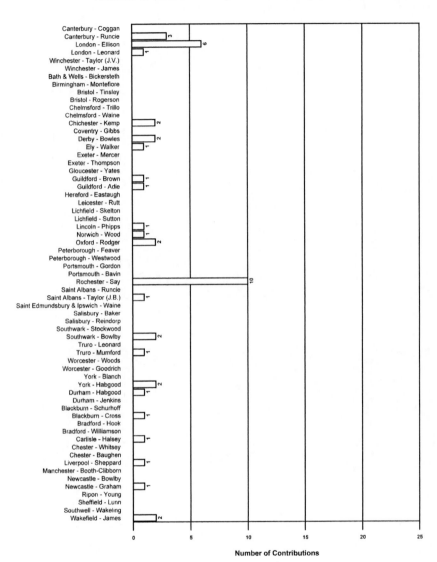

Number of Contributions

Episcopal Speech-Making: Content

7.1 Introduction

7.1.1 Introduction

When bishops do speak the note they strike tends to be thought-ful rather than campaigning, faithful in fact to the character of most Lords debates, and reflecting an awareness that the Upper House can no longer claim an overriding say in major decisions of policy.[1]

Giles Ecclestone's assessment of the speech-making of the Church of England bishops to the House of Lords, written in 1981, describes a measured and reflective contribution. Whether Ecclestone would have offered the same picture of the episcopal contribution to the House and the character of Lords debates in 1991 is open to question. Francis Bown does not offer any detailed analysis of the content of the bishops contributions to the House of Lords. He does, how-ever, give some assessment of the bishops' response to the Thatcher government. Having measured the number of words used by the bishops in speeches which were supportive and critical of the Government he concludes that:

The statistics for the 1979-1987 period do tend to support the view that the votes and words of the Lords Spiritual have tended towards criticism of rather than support for the Conservative Gov-ernment. The ratio of anti-Government: pro-Government is... 13:2 in words. Over half the pro-Government words (20,787 – 52.7%) were provided by just one bishop, Maurice Wood, Bishop of Norwich. However, it should be noted that the majority of the bishops' words was without a pro- or anti-Government content and among the anti-Government votes and words are included those of 'critical friends'.[2]

---

1   Ecclestone, *England*, 51.
2   Bown, 'Influencing', 117.

7.1.2 Methodology

The following analysis of the content of the episcopal speeches made at the House of Lords during the Thatcher years is based on House of Lords *Hansard*, the official record of House of Lords debates. Only speeches made during the period of Mrs Thatcher's time as Prime Minister were analysed. As such only the first ten days of the 1990/91 Parliamentary session were included.

Our analysis of the content of the bishops' speeches during debates considering Government and Private Members' Bills is limited to contributions which were made at the Second Reading stage.[3] This decision was based upon the fact that '...[t]he second reading is the stage at which the general principles of a Bill are considered'.[4] Thus, even where a peer makes contributions to every stage of a Bill's progression through the House, the basis for each of those contributions will, in all but the rarest of cases, have been laid out at the Second Reading. Active involvement in the Committee stages of a Bill by any peer will normally have been preceded by a Second Reading contribution. All other episcopal contributions to the House which were reported in *Hansard* have been included in our analysis, except the rare occasions where a bishop contributed to a Private Bill, a Statutory Instrument, or discussion relating to business and procedural matters (not including Tributes). In order to analyse the response of the bishops to the Thatcher Government each episcopal contribution was classified in one of four ways:

1) *For Her Majesty's Government (HMG)*. Speeches classified in this way were clearly supportive of the policies of the Thatcher Government.

2) *Against Her Majesty's Government (HMG)*. Speeches classified in this way were clearly unsupportive of the policies of the Thatcher Government.

3) *Neutral*. Speeches classified in this way were either too ambiguous to be considered either supportive or unsupportive of the Thatcher Government or were made in a debate in which for/ against judgements were largely inappropriate, such as Private Members' Bills.[5]

4) *Not Analysed*. Speeches classified in this way were made at the

---

3   However, during the course of our discussion some references will be made to the extent of episcopal contributions to the latter stages of Government and Private Members' Bills.

4   Limon & Mackay, *Erskine*, 468.

5   Whilst it was recognized that some Private Members' Bills do receive Government support, for the purposes of this analysis all Private Members' Bills were classified as 'neutral'.

> Committee stages of Government and Private Members' Bills, and also the consideration of Commons' amendments to Bills, whose content has not been analysed.

Decisions as to whether a speech was for or against the Government were based on the content of the speech itself, regardless of whether it related to a large or a small aspect of the matter under discussion. Therefore, to take a common example, in speeches where at the outset a bishop briefly notes his overall support for a piece of Government legislation but devotes the remainder of his speech to attacking a minor aspect of that legislation, the contribution would be classified as against the Government. Likewise, where a bishop spent 80% of his speech praising the Government, but made a brief criticism of the Government at its end, the speech would be classified as being for the Government. Our concern is with the content of the bishops' contribution to the House of Lords and as such our measure of their support or otherwise of the Government is based upon those thoughts to which they gave fullest voice in the House, not to their passing (though often significant) comments.

We commented previously (Section 6.6 above) that a group of just seven bishops made 65% of the episcopal contributions to debates on Government Bills.[6] In our consideration of the points which individual bishops made in their contributions to the debates of the House of Lords our attention will focus on the speech-making of those individuals. We will reflect on speeches in debates covering a variety of subjects, focusing our attention upon those issues which received the greatest episcopal attention and those subjects which, during the 1980s, were of the greatest significance. We will focus primarily on those occasions where the bishops took a clear line in support of, or against, the Government. It should be noted once more (see Section 6.1.2 above) that the subject classification of each speech relates to the subjects covered in the debate as a whole, not to the specific content of the speech of the bishop. Moreover, when each debate was classified it was given one *or more* subject classifications. As such, to take an example, a debate entitled 'NATO Policy: Deterrence and Disarmament' would be registered as being a contribution on the subjects of Conventional Weapons, International Organizations, and Non-Conventional Weapons within the Defence subject group and on Arms Control within the Foreign and Commonwealth Office sub-

---

6   These bishops were: Graham Leonard (whilst Bishop of London), Hugh Montefiore (Bishop of Birmingham), Maurice Wood (Bishop of Norwich), David Say (Bishop of Rochester), Ronald Bowlby (whilst Bishop of Southwark), David Sheppard (Bishop of Liverpool), and Stanley Booth-Clibborn (Bishop of Manchester).

ject group.

In order to facilitate analysis of the arguments employed by the bishops in their contributions an argument classification scheme was developed (Appendix 7). The argument classification scheme isolated 44 potential arguments within five categories: secular arguments, arguments based on experience, theological arguments, ecclesiastical arguments, and arguments based on morality. Where the same type of argument was used more than once in a speech it was recorded only on the first occasion that it was used.

The content of the episcopal contributions to the following subject groups have not been analysed because the number of contributions made by the bishops was not great enough to warrant this level of analysis or to provide significant contrast and comparison between each individual subject within the group: Agriculture, Fisheries & Food, the Lord Chancellor's Department, Northern Ireland, the Scottish Office, the Welsh Office, and Ecclesiastical Affairs.

7.2 The Points the Bishops Made

7.2.1 Overview

The bishops spoke in support of the Thatcher Government on 49 occasions and against the Thatcher Government on 172 occasions during the course of the Thatcher years (Figure 7.1). Expressing these figures as a percentage of the bishops' total contributions we can say that 6% of the bishops' contributions to the House of Lords were for, and 22% were against, the Thatcher Government (Figure 7.2). This is a ratio of nearly 7:2 between speeches against and speeches for the Thatcher Government. We can therefore say that where the bishops took a definite position in relation to Government policy, on the majority of occasions the position that they took was against the Government.

Of the remaining episcopal contributions, 46% were neither supportive nor unsupportive of the Government and 25% were made in debates whose content has not been analysed. Whilst it cannot be justified from this data, it is probable that those debates whose content has not been analysed (primarily contributions at the Committee stages) were no more positive towards the government than those debates that have been analysed. That almost half of the bishops' contributions were classified as being neutral is not unexpected. This is likely to be the result of the fact that many of these contributions were made in debates covering moral and ethical issues in which the bishops take a great interest and have their greatest influence. These types of discussion tend not be party-political and as such there is no defined Government position against which to compare the contributions of individual peers. Moreover, many Private Members' Bills (which are classified as neutral), to which the bishops made 46 contributions at the Second Reading stage (Figure 6.16), are used to air and consider moral and ethical issues.

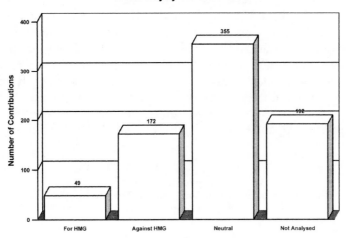

Figure 7.1
**Number of Episcopal Contributions For and Against
Her Majety's Government**

Only in the 1981/82 Parliamentary session did the bishops make a greater percentage of speeches in support of the Government than against it (19% for, 11% against) (Figure 7.3). It seems probable that this is to be accounted for by the Falkland Islands crisis. The bishops spoke on four occasions (one-third of their pro-Government speeches) in support of the Government in debates on this matter. More generally, it is likely that an atmosphere of 'national crisis' would have made the bishops cautious about speaking against the Government unless absolutely necessary. The 1988/89 Parliamentary session saw the bishops responding more negatively to the Thatcher Government than in any other Parliamentary session. Over the course of the 153 sitting days (Figure 4.2) of this Parliamentary session they made no contributions in support of the Government and 38% of their contributions against the Government. Overall, during the 1980s the percentage of episcopal contributions which were supportive of the Government decreased. Thus, from the 1979/80 Parliamentary session to the 1985/86 Parliamentary session an average of 9% of the bishops' contributions were for the Government. Yet from the 1986/87 Parliamentary session to the 1989/90 Parliamentary session an average of 4% of the bishops' contributions were for the Government. In contrast, over the course of the Thatcher years the percentage of episcopal contributions against the Government increased. Thus, from the 1979/80 Parliamentary session to the 1985/86 Parliamentary session an average of 19% of the bishops' contributions were against the Government. Yet from the 1986/87 Parliamentary session to the 1989/90 Parliamentary session an average of 28% of the bishops' contributions were against the Government. Looking at this data we can conclude that as the Thatcher years progressed the episcopal contribution became increasingly critical of the Thatcher Government. This broadly fits with the conjecture outlined above (Section 6.2) that overall the bishops attended the House more (Figure 4.3 above), voted against the Government more (Figure 5.8 & 5.9 above), and made speeches more (Figure 6.2 above), from the 1983/84 Parliamentary session onwards, for varying periods of time, in response to the emergence of a distinctly Thatcherite, New Right political agenda during the life of the 1983-87 Conservative Government.

Figure 7.2
**Percentage of Episcopal Contributions For and Against
Her Majesty's Government**

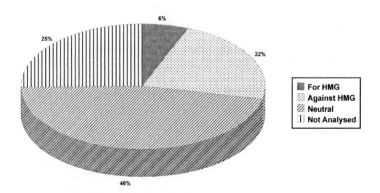

Analysis of the number of contributions made by each individual bishop for and against Her Majesty's Government indicates that there was a considerable diversity in the level of support which was given to the Thatcher Government (Figure 7.4). Maurice Wood (Bishop of Norwich) was by far the most supportive bishop, speaking for the Government on 14 occasions. This represents 29% of the bishops' speeches in support of the Government. The next most supportive episcopal contributor was David Say (Bishop of Rochester)

who spoke in support of the Government on five occasions. All 49 episcopal contributions for the Government were made by 21 individuals (with John Habgood and Graham Leonard speaking in support of the Government from two different dioceses). Thus, of the 51 individual bishops who spoke in the House of Lords during the Thatcher years, 30 never spoke in support of the policies of the Thatcher Government. Of these 30 individual bishops, only 11 also never spoke against the Government.

Figure 7.3
Percentage of Episcopal Contributions For and Against Her Majesty's Government in each Parliamentary Session

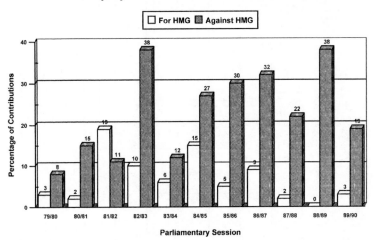

Stanley Booth-Clibborn (Bishop of Manchester) supplied considerably more speeches against the Thatcher Government than any other bishop, speaking against the Government on 46 occasions. This represents 27% of all the bishops speeches against the Government. A greater variety of individual bishops spoke against the Government than for it. The 172 speeches against the Government were made by 34 individuals (with Graham Leonard, Colin James and John Habgood speaking against the Government from two different dioceses). Thus, of the 51 individual bishops who spoke in the House of Lords during the Thatcher years, only 17 never spoke against the Government.

Analysis of what percentage of the speeches of each individual bishop were for and against the Government enables us to compare and contrast their response to the policies of the Thatcher Government with greater clarity (Figure 7.5). Maurice Wood (Bishop of Norwich) was the only bishop from the group of seven who made a

Figure 7.4
**Number of Contributions by Individual Bishops For and Against
Her Majesty's Government**

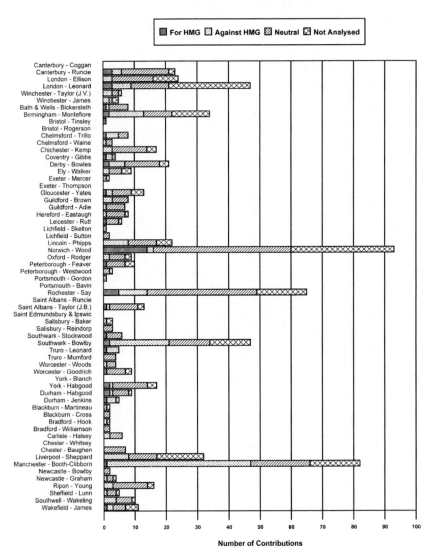

■ For HMG ⊠ Against HMG ▨ Neutral ⊠ Not Analysed

Number of Contributions

greater percentage of his speeches for than against the Government. Only 2% of his contributions (which were spread over a wide variety of subject areas) were critical of the Government, whilst 15% were supportive. Stanley Booth-Clibborn (Bishop of Manchester) made a massive 57% of his contributions against the Thatcher Government, whilst only 1% were in its support. The other five members of this group also contributed speeches to the House of Lords which were primarily negative in their content:

- Of the contributions of Graham Leonard (whilst Bishop of London), 6% were for the Government and 13% against.[7]
- Of the contributions of Hugh Montefiore (Bishop of Birmingham), 6% were for the Government and 32% against.[8]
- Of the contributions of David Say (Bishop of Rochester), 8% were for the Government and 14% against.
- Of the contributions of Ronald Bowlby (whilst Bishop of Southwark), 4% were for the Government and 40% against.
- Of the contributions of David Sheppard (Bishop of Liverpool), none were for the Government and 25% were against.

The contributions of Robert Runcie (whilst Archbishop of Canterbury) and John Habgood (whilst Archbishop of York) reflect the distinct role each plays as a national establishment (rather than purely local ecclesiastical) figure. Both registered a high percentage of contributions (65% of the total contributions of each) which were classified as neutral in their response to the Government. This was more than each of the members of the group of seven bishops. Runcie and Habgood also made the same percentage as, or a greater percentage than, each of the members of the group of seven, in support of the Government.

The greatest ratio between speeches for and against the Government was found in the Environment, Transport and Regions subject group (Figure 7.6). Here the bishops made no speeches in support of the Thatcher Government and 48 against. The difference between the number of episcopal contributions for and against the Government was also stark in the Home Office (11 speeches for HMG, 39 against),

---

7   This is an unexpectedly critical contribution in view of the fact that Margaret Thatcher was, according to Hugo Young, 'by the mid-1980s... in the habit of saying to anyone within earshot that the Bishop of London was the only man in the Church of England who made the kind of sense she was looking for.' Young, *One*, 420. Leonard also, surprisingly, cast no more votes in support of the Government than against (Section 5.4 above).

8   Montefiore recalled the response of Margaret Thatcher herself to his contributions on socio-political issues: '"That perfectly dreadful man in Birmingham". I was pleased. It was repeated to me that she said that..., and I remember once at the National Exhibition Centre when I was introduced to her she said to me, which I thought was monstrous really, "but you're always so controversial bishop". I thought, "you're the last person to..." I don't think she minded people being straightforwardly opposed to what she said.' Hugh Montefiore (Bishop of Birmingham) in an interview with the author, 21st May 2002, Appendix 3.

Church and State

Figure 7.5
Percentage of Contributions by Individual Bishops For and Against Her Majesty's Government

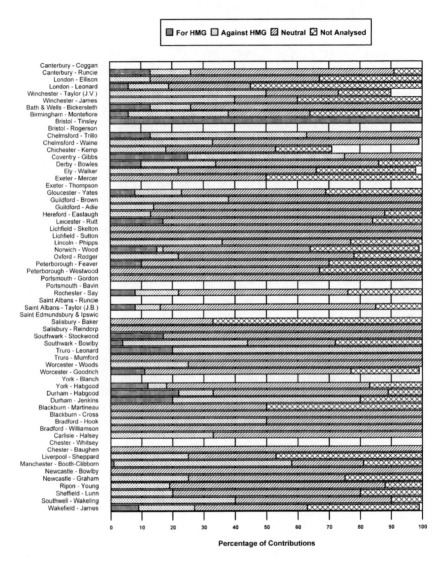

Percentage of Contributions

Social Security (three speeches for HMG, 19 against), and Trade & Industry subject groups (four speeches for HMG, 20 against). The only subject groups in which the number of contributions which were supportive of the Thatcher Government exceeded those which were unsupportive were Defence (13 speeches for HMG, nine against), Northern Ireland (two speeches for HMG, none against), and Ecclesiastical Affairs (one speech for HMG, none against). The greatest number of episcopal speeches made in support of the Thatcher Government were made in relation to the Foreign and Commonwealth Office subject group (20 speeches for HMG, 34 against).

All but one of the 40 episcopal contributions to debates covering the Ecclesiastical Affairs subject group were classified as neutral in relation to the policies of the Government. Just over two-thirds of the episcopal contributions to debates covering the Home Office subject group were also neutral in their response to the Thatcher Government. Only in the Environment, Transport & the Regions and the H.M. Treasury subject groups did the number of episcopal contributions which were against the Government exceed those which were considered to be neutral.

Figure 7.6
**Episcopal Contributions For and Against Her Majesty's Government:
Total for Each Subject Group**

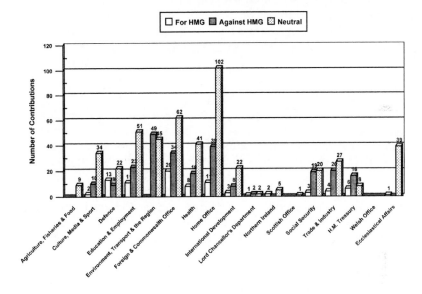

7.2.2 Culture, Media and Sport

In debates covering the subject of Broadcasting the bishops spoke against the Government on five occasions and for it twice (Figure 7.7). On ten occasions bishops contributed but in a way which was classified as neutral in its response to the Thatcher Government. Each of the contributions the bishops made against the Government (which totalled 52 minutes in length) were made during deliberative debates. Two of these contributions were made by David Brown (Bishop of

Guildford) who spoke during October 1979 and July 1981 in debates covering the subject of the BBC overseas broadcasting services.[9] On both occasions he spoke with those challenging the Thatcher Government's plans to curtail this part of the BBC's service testifying, on the basis of personal experience, that '...the BBC broadcasts have a standard of integrity and independence which make them deeply valued by audiences all across the world, and never more so than in times of crisis, danger and uncertainty.'[10] The bishops spoke three times in debates covering the subject of cable broadcasting, twice for the Government and once against. The contribution against the Government came during November 1982 when Colin James (whilst Bishop of Wakefield) spoke in a deliberative debate entitled 'Cable Expansion and Broadcasting Policy'.[11] His contribution challenged the Government for failing to make plans to safeguard sufficiently the standards of cable broadcasting and called for the establishment of a regulatory body to monitor the standard and variety of programming. James also called for greater provision for local community programming. James contributed a second time on this subject, at the Second Reading of the Government's Cable and Broadcasting Bill during December 1983.12 This Second Reading contribution was followed by a total of seven contributions at the Committee stages. He spoke in support of the Government's intention to set up a cable authority to monitor cable broadcasting:

> Many of us in this House have, I believe, not been overwhelmingly enthusiastic about the advent of cable television programmes... However, I have felt that some of those dangers are very much lessened by the safeguards in the Bill... I think the strongest of all the safeguards lies in the considerable duties and powers that are being entrusted to the cable authority; and much will depend on how these responsibilities are carried out, on the guidelines that the cable authority is given by the Home Secretary, and on who will be appointed to discharge the responsibilities that are entrusted to them.[13]

David Say (Bishop of Rochester) made a very similar point in his contribution to a debate during April 1983 in response to a Government Statement on its 'Cable Systems and Services' White Paper.[14]

---

9   *House of Lords Debates*, 25/10/79, vol. 402, col. 279-282 and 30/7/81, vol. 423, col. 816-819.

10 *ibid*, 30/7/81, vol. 423, col. 816.

11 *ibid*, 23/11/82, vol. 436, col. 809-812.

12 *ibid*, 19/12/83, vol. 446, col. 508-510.

13 *ibid*, 19/12/83, vol. 446, col. 510.

14 *ibid*, 27/4/83, vol. 441, col. 936-937.

All three contributions by the bishops to debates covering the subject of cable broadcasting therefore took the same line. They shifted from being classified as against the Government to being classified as supportive of the Government because Government policy changed in response to the arguments of a significant body of opinion (of which the bishops were only a part) arguing for the stiff regulation of cable broadcasting.

In debates covering the subject of Films and Videos each of the six episcopal contributions were classified as being neutral in their response to the Government. Two of these contributions were made at the Second Reading stage of a Private Members' Video Recordings Bill. This Bill, which came before the House during the 1983/84 Parliamentary session, proposed a classification system for video recordings and received the general support of Maurice Wood (Bishop of Norwich) and Colin James (Bishop of Wakefield).[15] After Broadcasting, the subject within the Culture, Media & Sport subject group which received the most negative contributions from the bishops was Historic Buildings and Ancient Monuments. On this matter the bishops spoke against the Government on three occasions, never speaking in their support. Three bishops spoke in an Unstarred Question debate during February 1980 covering the subject of Cathedrals and tourism with Eric Kemp (Bishop of Chichester) speaking against the Government. He challenged the suggestion that allowing cathedrals to claim a remission of VAT on its charges for admission was a valuable way of helping them arguing (in part on the basis that not all who visit Cathedrals are 'sightseers' and tourists) that it was inappropriate for cathedrals to charge the admission fee for which they could claim a VAT rebate.[16]

On the sole occasion where the subject of a National Lottery came before the House (in a deliberative debate during February 1990) Stanley Booth-Clibborn (Bishop of Manchester) spoke against the Government's plans. While admitting that '[t]he Churches simply do not have their act together over the issue of gambling... we are divided about it',[17] he emphasised, amongst other things, the danger posed by a lottery to a proper sense of the role taxation should play in the funding of the arts, sport, and care for the environment:

> It is a tragedy when leaders of political parties simply favour the idea that taxation should be kept as low as it possibly can be without emphasising the positive side of what taxation is needed for in

---

15 *ibid*, 2/4/84, vol. 450, col. 525-528, 532 and 2/4/84, vol. 450, col. 552-554.

16 *ibid*, 27/2/80, vol. 405, col. 1463-1465.

17 *ibid*, 28/2/90, vol. 516, col. 784.

order to improve life in the community... I believe that if we were to go down the road of a nationwide lottery we might be doing damage to the social fabric of this country which we cannot see at the moment, but which will become visible in later years.[18]

Figure 7.7
**Episcopal Contributions For and Against Her Majesty's Government:
Culture, Media & Sport**

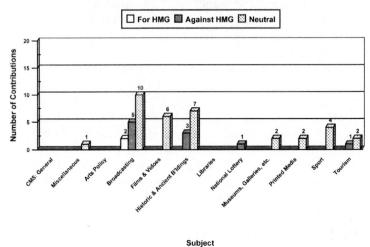

7.2.3 Defence

Defence is the most significant (in terms of the number of episcopal contributions made to it) of the three subject groups in which the number of contributions for the Thatcher Government exceeded those against it (Figure 7.8). The contributions supportive of the Government were most prevalent in debates which covered the issue of disarmament (which fell into the International Organizations and Non-Conventional Weapons subjects). In these debates the bishops spoke for the Government five times and against it three times, presenting a variety of different positions on the subject. Supportive of the Government were Graham Leonard (whilst Bishop of Truro),[19] Maurice Wood (Bishop of Norwich),[20] and John Habgood (whilst Bishop of Durham)[21] who each took a similar line which argued

18   *ibid*, 28/2/90, vol. 516, col. 788.
19   *ibid*, 23/4/80, vol. 408, col. 839-842.
20   *ibid*, 11/11/81, vol. 425, col. 233 and 16/2/83, vol. 439, col. 283, 286-290, 301, 319-320.
21   *ibid*, 16/2/83, vol. 439, col. 243-246.

that: a determination should exist to seek disarmament and peace, a nuclear deterrent should be maintained, the Government should not adopt a pacifist position (peace at any cost), the Government should not seek unilateral disarmament.

Figure 7.8
Episcopal Contributions For and Against Her Majesty's Government: Defence

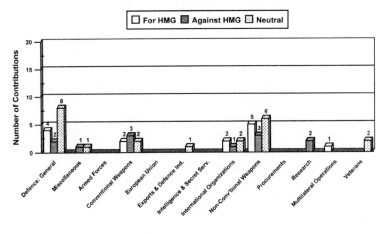

Speaking against the Government were John V. Taylor (Bishop of Winchester),[22] Patrick Rodger (Bishop of Oxford)[23] and Stanley Booth-Clibborn (Bishop of Manchester).[24] Each sought, to varying degrees, to place themselves apart from Government policy. Taylor took an essentially pacifist position, arguing for the destruction of British nuclear weapon stocks. Rodger argued similarly but in terms of working towards a chemical and nuclear-free zone in Western Europe in the near future, irrespective of the position taken by the rest of the world. Booth-Clibborn considered the variety of Christian positions before going on to express his personal perspective:

> The possession of and threat to use nuclear weapons is, I believe, utterly inconsistent with a religion of love, yet it becomes justifiable to do something that is unjust if the aim is to preserve peace... I believe that the main view taken by the report *The Church and the Bomb* is the correct one, though I can see the problems and that we ought indeed to move to the abandonment of the British inde-

---

22   *ibid*, 16/6/82, vol. 431, col. 656-660.
23   *ibid*, 16/1/85, vol. 458, col. 974-977.
24   *ibid*, 25/2/87, vol. 485, col. 215-217.

pendent nuclear deterrent in consultation with our allies but still
with continued membership of NATO and reluctant possession of
a nuclear deterrent there.[25]

7.2.4 Education and Employment

The bishops' contribution to the debates covering the subjects of
Further Education, Higher Education & Research, and Schools were
mostly neutral in relation to the policies of the Thatcher Government
(Figure 7.9). In total the bishops made 30 contributions of this sort.
Of those speeches on these subjects which did express a clear negative or positive response to the policies of the Thatcher Government
the majority were negative (five speeches for HMG, 13 against).

The episcopal contributions to the Second Reading stage of the
Government's wide-ranging Education No.2 Bill (1980) and Education Reform Bill (1988) were amongst those contributions which
were classified as neutral. David Martineau (Bishop of Blackburn)
made a balanced contribution to the Second Reading of the Education No. 2 Bill (1980).[26] His speech included a warm welcome for
various aspects of the Bill (including new procedures relating to
schools admissions policies and parental selection of schools) whilst
questioning other aspects (such as the omission of clauses on the role
of School Governors in the conduct and curriculum of schools). Two
contributions were made to the Second Reading of the Education
Reform Bill (1988). The first was by Graham Leonard (who made 12
of the bishops' 19 contributions at the Bill's Committee stages),[27] the
second by David Say (Bishop of Rochester).[28] Both expressed support
for education reform and regret that more time had not been given
for consultation. Say went on to focus on the issue of freedom of
thought and speech in Universities. Leonard proceeded to welcome
the Bill's commitment to religious education as an essential part of
the National Curriculum but, more negatively, expressed doubt over
the planned procedure for schools to become grant-maintained (not
the principle of grant-maintained schools itself) and plans to abolish
the Inner London Education Authority (ILEA):

> I must say something as the Bishop of London with regard to
> the proposal relating to the abolition of ILEA. Frankly, I view the
> future with dismay. Whatever the deficiencies or extravagances of
> ILEA, the prospect of a simple devolution to the boroughs and in

---

25 *ibid*, 25/2/87, vol. 485, col. 217.

26 *ibid*, 25/2/80, vol. 405, col. 1052-1055.

27 *ibid*, 18/4/88, vol. 495, col. 1230-1234, 1296, 1298.

28 *ibid*, 18/4/88, vol. 495, col. 1291-1293.

Figure 7.9
**Episcopal Contributions For and Against Her Majesty's Government:
Education & Employment**

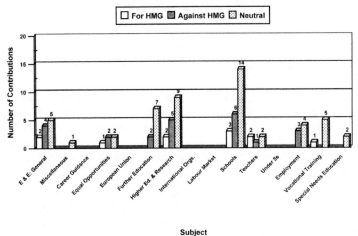

a relatively short time is most alarming. If the necessary special and advisory services are to be provided to meet the extraordinary needs of inner London, that can only be done without unnecessary and very expensive duplication by some form of unitary authority to operate in those spheres.[29]

The bishops took every opportunity available to them to contribute to debates covering the subject of Teachers. Unusually they spoke for the Government more than against it on this subject (two speeches for HMG, one against). The first contribution for the Government was made by David Say (Bishop of Rochester) during October 1986 at the Second Reading of the Government's Education Bill which related to schools and teaching staff.[30] The speech welcomed the Bill's clarification of the roles of the Head, Governing Body and Local Education Authority and the increased role for parents in school governance. This Second Reading contribution was followed by five episcopal contributions at the Committee stages. The second contribution supporting the Government was made by Graham Leonard (whilst Bishop of London) at the Second Reading of the Government's Teacher's Pay and Conditions Bill (1987).[31] Leonard broadly welcomed the provisions of the Bill but, reflecting more widely, pushed for education to be taken off the political battle-

29 *ibid*, 18/4/88, vol. 495, col. 1234.
30 *ibid*, 10/3/86, vol. 472, col. 455-457.
31 *ibid*, 12/1/87, vol. 483, col. 382-386.

field in favour of a more consensual approach to policy-making. The episcopal contribution on the subject of Teachers which was unsupportive of the Government was made by Michael Adie (Bishop of Guildford) during March 1989 in a deliberative debate on teacher shortages.[32] Adie's contribution sought to emphasise the seriousness of the teacher shortage (with particular reference to the shortage of Religious Education teachers) and the way forward for dealing with the problem:

> If the Government can acknowledge the shortage of teachers in religious education, as in some other subjects, accept that heavier responsibilities are now falling on teachers of RE, and provide more money for in-service training and shortage-subject status where initial training provision is concerned, then we may be able to move forward in confidence.[33]

The bishops also took every opportunity available to them to speak in debates covering the subject of Special Needs Education. They spoke twice and on both occasions their comments were neutral in response to the Thatcher Government. The first of the contributions, by Robert Runcie (Archbishop of Canterbury), was a 16 minute speech made during January 1981 during a debate called to mark the International Year of the Disabled.[34] In his speech Runcie argued that in order for '[a]ll the richness of educational opportunity'[35] to be available to the disabled as to other children, provision should be made for those with special needs to undertake a longer education with access to any necessary additional facilities.

7.2.5 Environment, Transport and the Regions

Over half of the bishops' 48 speeches against the Thatcher Government in this subject group were made in debates covering the subjects of Housing & Homelessness and Local Government (Figure 7.10). The bishops never spoke in support of the Government in debates covering the subject of Housing and Homelessness. On three occasions the bishops spoke against the Government at the Second Reading of Government Bills. Ronald Bowlby (Bishop of Southwark)[36] and John V. Taylor (Bishop of Winchester) spoke at this stage of the Housing and Building Control Bill during April 1983.[37]

---

32   *ibid*, 8/3/89, vol. 504, col. 1486-1488.
33   *ibid*, 8/3/89, vol. 504, col. 1488.
34   *ibid*, 14/1/81, vol. 416, col. 65-69.
35   *ibid*, 14/1/81, vol. 416, col. 66.
36   *ibid*, 9/6/80, vol. 410, col. 31-34.
37   *ibid*, 9/6/80, vol. 410, col. 46-48.

Both spoke specifically against Clause 2 of the Bill which extended the right to buy to the tenants of certain charitable housing associations. Ronald Bowlby (Bishop of Southwark) spoke against the Government again during July 1988 at the Second Reading of their Housing Bill.[38] His contribution pointed out that adequate housing for the cold-wet climate of Britain cannot be provided by the free-market alone and recommended that, alongside keeping the market free and flexible, tenants must be protected from exploitation and injustice. Bowlby also proposed that provision of adequate low-cost rented accommodation become the aim of Government policy both now and in the future, with slow and steady progress the key to a successful achievement of that aim.

On three occasions the bishops spoke against the Government in deliberative debates on Housing and Homelessness. John Bickersteth (Bishop of Bath and Wells) spoke in a debate on the homeless young during November 1982.[39] Ronald Bowlby (Bishop of Southwark)[40] and Graham Leonard (whilst Bishop of London)[41] spoke in general debates with the title 'Homelessness' during 1988 and 1989. Each bishop made essentially the same two points. Firstly, they emphasised the seriousness and significance of homelessness as a problem. Secondly, they focused on the desperate need for more affordable accommodation. Graham Leonard (whilst Bishop of London) also focused on the need for the Church to apply the gospel to family life and relationships.[42]

> The greatest cause [of homelessness], mentioned in all the papers I have read, is disputes with relatives and within the family. That presents a challenge to the Churches. While it is right for us to be concerned with housing policy, we can only involve ourselves with a clear conscience if we also seek to apply the gospel we profess to the problem of family life and personal relationships, preparation for marriage, reconciliation in the case of divorce, and guidance on the upbringing of children.[43]

The Government's Local Government Bill (1985) received episcopal contributions at every stage of its journey through the House of Lords. Both episcopal contributions to the Second Reading were unsupportive of the Government. Both contributors, Ronald Bowlby (Bishop of Southwark) and David Sheppard (Bishop of Liverpool),

---

38   *ibid*, 11/7/88, vol. 499, col. 610-614, 679.

39   *ibid*, 11/11/82, vol. 436, col. 380-382.

40   *ibid*, 11/7/88, vol. 499, col. 610-614, 679.

41   *ibid*, 7/6/89, vol. 508, col. 898-900, 920.

42   *ibid*, 7/6/89, vol. 508, col. 899-900.

43   *ibid*, 7/6/89, vol. 508, col. 900.

Figure 7.10
**Episcopal Contributions For and Against Her Majesty's Government:
Environment, Transport & the Regions**

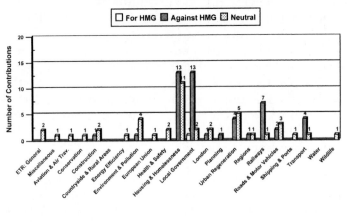

Subject

were incumbents of dioceses set to be directly affected by the provisions of the Bill which paved the way for the abolition of the seven Metropolitan City Councils (including the Greater London Council). Bowlby's contribution focused on the damaging effects that the Bill would be likely to have on voluntary agencies.[44] David Sheppard urged the Government to pay greater attention to the case against them in relation to the plan to abolish the Metropolitan City Councils, arguing that someone elected to serve the city as a whole is bound to feel a greater sense of responsibility for the whole city than a local councillor.[45] He also noted that voluntary agencies were 'alarmed' by the proposals.[46]

As one might expect in the context of the December 1985 publication of the *Faith in the City* report, none of the episcopal contributions to debates covering the subject of Urban Regeneration were supportive of the Government. In fact, the bishops spoke against the Government on four occasions and spoke neutrally on five occasions. Robert Runcie (Archbishop of Canterbury) and David Sheppard (Bishop of Liverpool) both contributed to a debate during February 1987 entitled 'Inner City Problems'. Runcie summed up the findings and recommendations of the Faith in the City report before going on to outline the ways in which the Church had responded to the

44   *ibid*, 15/4/85, vol. 462, col. 456-460.
45   *ibid*, 15/4/85, vol. 462, col. 485-488.
46   *ibid*, 15/4/85, vol. 462, col. 488.

38 recommendations made to it by the report.[47] He then made an impassioned call for national action to help inner cities:

> It seems to me that many different kinds of resources are called for if our cities are to be won back from what some of them are today, many different kinds of talent and innovation working in harmony – the financier and the architect, the businessman and the philanthropists, the legislator and the planner, the policeman and the social worker, the churchman and the educationalist, the landscape artist and the civil engineer. Such an approach has implications for housing, education, health, employment, law and order, and the creation and distribution of wealth... the length of the catalogue itself shows that no one sector of society can tackle the issues alone. They are not the responsibility of the centre, of local government, or private sector finance. They are the responsibility of all of us.[48]

Runcie ended his speech with a statement of confidence in the possibility of the rejuvenation of the cities and by sharing his belief that the national resources necessary to achieve that goal do exist (noting that public opinion favours an increase, or no decrease, in the tax burden to resource the fight against poverty). Sheppard began his contribution similarly, outlining the process of producing the *Faith in the City* report and its findings.[49] Like Runcie, he called for tackling the problem with increased public expenditure, arguing specifically for a system of progressive taxation to fund this expenditure. Sheppard also argued for a greater sense of partnership between Government departments, private and voluntary sectors, and central and local Government. In calling for increased taxation and public expenditure both Runcie and Sheppard set themselves firmly against the policies of the Thatcher Government. In the case of Runcie this constituted one of only three speeches which can be classified as against the Government.

Whilst overall the impression is that the bishops were uninterested in transport related subjects, it should be noted that bishops contributed to debates covering the particular subject of the Railways on seven occasions, each time speaking against the Government. Three of these contributions were made at the Second Reading of Government's Channel Tunnel Bill (1987). None of the episcopal contributors spoke against the concept of a fixed channel rail link. Each did, however, use their contribution to speak against the Government in some way. The first, by Stanley Booth-Clibborn (Bishop of Manchester), was a very brief speech which challenged the Government

---

47   *ibid*, 2/2/87, vol. 484, col. 34-38.
48   *ibid*, 2/2/87, vol. 484, col. 37.
49   *ibid*, 2/2/87, vol. 484, col. 67, 73-78.

claim that the Channel Tunnel was comparable as a terrorist target to a single ferry boat.[50] The second, by Ronald Bowlby (Bishop of Southwark), was more parochial in its concern:[51]

> Waterloo Station lies within the diocese of Southwark and, as a consequence, I have been approached by local residents and local clergy to ask this House to look very carefully at the likely consequences of bringing around 70% of the estimated passenger traffic to a single terminal in London.[52]

The third contribution was made by Hugh Montefiore (Bishop of Birmingham) who raised concerns over the plan to transport cars and lorries through the tunnel in addition to a simple rail tunnel.[53] He also made clear his dissatisfaction with the fact that there was no public enquiry into the scheme.

7.2.6 Foreign and Commonwealth Office

The greatest number of speeches in support of the Thatcher Government were made to debates which fell within the Foreign and Commonwealth Office subject group. The low-point in the Church-State relationship during the Thatcher years is widely considered to be the post-Falklands War Thanksgiving Service which took place at St. Paul's Cathedral on 26th July 1982. In this light it is remarkable that the bishops never spoke against the Government on the subject of the Falkland Islands in the House of Lords. Rather, the bishops spoke in support of the Government on the subject on four occasions (Figure 7.11). Robert Runcie (Archbishop of Canterbury), whose sermon was the chief cause of the tension at the St Paul's Thanksgiving Service (Section 2.3.4.4 above), made two of these four contributions. The first came in a deliberative debate on 14th April 1982 (12 days after the Argentine invasion of South Georgia) and assured the Government of the prayers of the Bench of Bishops, particularly for those Ministers making important decisions.[54] Runcie then emphasised the Church of England's support for the principles of international law and the right of self-determination for all peoples – Margaret Thatcher's preferred justifications for the British invasion of the Falkland islands.[55] Amidst these comments, however, came an indication of things to come:

---

50 *ibid*, 16/2/87, vol. 484, col. 908.
51 *ibid*, 16/2/87, vol. 484, col. 909-912.
52 *ibid*, 16/2/87, vol. 484, col. 909.
53 *ibid*, 16/2/87, vol. 484, col. 953-956.
54 *ibid*, 14/4/82, vol. 429, col. 298-299.
55 Thatcher, *Downing*, 173, 175-176.

[W]e must resist any temptation to stir up feelings of hurt national pride which would cloud our judgement or deflect us from our immediate concern in securing the well-being of a peace-loving and, I believe, God-fearing people. We need also to remember that whatever we may think of the Argentine Government, the Argentinians are a Christian people with whom we have many ties. I am especially aware of this, since there are two Anglican dioceses in that country.[56]

Runcie's second contribution to the House came on the 20th May, the day before British troops landed at San Carlos on the Falkland Islands.[57] It counselled that the (by then inevitable) use of force should remain focused on achieving a political solution, not a military victory as an end in itself, and that the force used be the minimum necessary to achieve this objective. Runcie proceeded to argue that reconciliation with Argentina should remain as the primary objective of the Government, with diplomatic efforts continuing. Finally, he urged that '...none should yield to the temptation to regard the other as sub-human or themselves as superhuman.'[58]

With retrospect one can see here, and in the final comment of his first speech, a similar tone and content to that which characterised Runcie's St Paul's Thanksgiving Service sermon. At this stage, how-

Figure 7.11
**Episcopal Contributions For and Against Her Majesty's Government:
Foreign & Commonwealth Office**

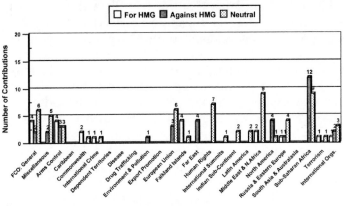

---

56 *House of Lords Debates*, 14/4/82, vol. 429, col. 299.
57 *ibid*, 20/5/82, vol. 430, col. 814-815.
58 *ibid*, 10/5/82, vol. 430, col. 815.

ever, they can only be interpreted as words of advice and caution by the Archbishop to a Government whose actions he fundamentally supported. There was no indication in either his speech near the start, or his speech near the end, of the war that his comments were made because he was dissatisfied with the Government's approach. None of the other episcopal contributions to the House of Lords on the subject of the Falkland Islands added anything of substance to those points made by Runcie.

Within the Foreign & Commonwealth Office subject group the bishops spoke most negatively on the subject of Sub-Saharan Africa. Here they made no speeches in support of the Government and 12 against. Seven of the 12 speeches against the Government were made specifically on South Africa and the apartheid issue. Three were made during brief discussion in response to Starred Questions and each time the contributor was Stanley Booth-Clibborn (Bishop of Manchester). The remaining four negative contributions were made by three bishops: Stanley Booth-Clibborn (Bishop of Manchester), Hugh Montefiore (Bishop of Birmingham), and David Young (Bishop of Ripon).

Booth-Clibborn's second negative contribution was made during March 1988 in an Unstarred Question debate on apartheid.[59] His speech specifically called on the Thatcher Government to bring more pressure to bear on South Africa. 'I think it is true,' he asserted, 'that ritual condemnations of apartheid are no longer enough in this very grave and serious situation that faces South Africa, the world and our own country.'[60] More specifically he pushed for British disinvestment in, and sanctions against, South Africa – countering the Government argument that sanctions would primarily harm the black South African population by pointing to the fact that the majority of black South Africans themselves supported sanctions. He also countered the Government argument that sanctions would not achieve the goal of changing the policies of the South African Government directly: 'As to whether sanctions would be effective, no one can really answer that until sanctions have been tried.'[61] Montefiore contributed to a general deliberative debate on the subject of South Africa during July 1986.[62] He began his speech powerfully:

It seems to me that the situation for a black African in South Africa today is not altogether unlike that of a Jew in pre-war Nazi Ger-

---

59 *ibid*, 24/3/88, vol. 495, col. 356-358, 372.
60 *ibid*, 24/3/88, vol. 495, col. 356.
61 *ibid*, 24/3/88, vol. 495, col. 358.
62 *ibid*, 4/7/86, vol. 477, col. 1170-1173.

many: liable to arbitrary arrest, subject to violence and sudden disappearance without trace. We must think of what the situation looks like from their point of view and not just from ours.[63]

Montefiore also noted the special concern of the Churches over the situation because of South Africa's claim to be a Christian country. Montefiore called, as Booth-Clibborn did, for the Thatcher Government to assert more economic, moral, and political pressure on the South African Government. In response to Government arguments against sanctions, Montefiore argued that in this country unemployment as a result of such sanctions could be avoided, and that the majority of black South Africans supported sanctions.

David Young (Bishop of Ripon) spoke on the apartheid issue during an Unstarred Question debate during March 1990.[64] He began his speech by reflecting upon reasons behind the considerable policy changes in South Africa which had taken place and the basis for hope which had begun to take root there (and which would lead to the repeal of apartheid laws in July 1990). However, he went on to emphasise the priority of keeping pressure on the South African Government to end apartheid, describing its removal and the emergence of a democratic society as an '...essential prerequisite for a proper attack on poverty'[65] and noting the influential role played by sanctions in bringing about those encouraging changes which had already taken place. The bishops presented a united voice on the subject of South Africa. Each of the individuals who spoke on the subject emphasised the need for the British Government to put more pressure upon South Africa than they were doing, specifically by giving support to sanctions.

7.2.7 Health

In the Health subject group the bishops' contributions to debates covering the subject of Embryology and Fertilisation were, except on one occasion (which was for the Government), neutral in their response to the policies of the Thatcher Government (Figure 7.12). Closer investigation reveals that the episcopal contribution which gave support to the Government was followed by 11 further Committee stage episcopal contributions. This positive speech was made in December 1989 at the Second Reading stage of the Government's Human Fertilisation and Embryology Bill (1990) by John Habgood

---

63   *ibid*, 4/7/86, vol. 477, col. 1170-1171.
64   *ibid*, 22/3/90, vol. 517, col. 484-486.
65   *ibid*, 22/3/90, vol. 517, col. 485.

(Archbishop of York).[66] Focusing on the issue of embryo experimentation (which he described as 'the moral heart of the Bill'[67]) Habgood threw his support behind the 14-day rule as the most workable basis for a consensus on the matter, commenting thus:

> It is no more possible to set it up as a totally clear moral dividing line than it is to do the same for the moment of conception. But to make it a cut-off point is morally and biologically defensible. The fact that it is based on an identifiable biological transition will, I believe, protect it against future argument for extending the limits of research.[68]

Figure 7.12
Episcopal Contributions For and Against Her Majesty's Government: Health

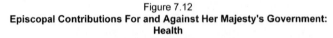

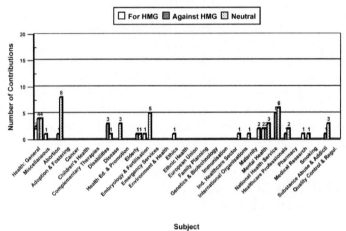

Subject

In debates covering the subject of Abortion the bishops' contributions were, except on one occasion (which was against the Government), neutral in their response to the Government. Seven of the nine episcopal contributions were, however, made to debates on Private Members' Bills which (for the purposes of this analysis)[69] are always classified as being neutral. During the Thatcher years three Private Members' Bills came before the House which sought to amend the law on abortion. The bishops spoke twice during the Second Reading of each of these Bills and each of the contributions was, in its

---

66 *ibid*, 7/12/89, vol. 513, col. 1019-1022.
67 *ibid*, 7/12/89, vol. 513, col. 1019.
68 *ibid*, 7/12/89, vol. 513, col. 1022.
69 See Section 7.1.2 above.

content, similar to the others. We shall, therefore, only look at the episcopal contributions to one of the Bills, the Abortion (Amendment) Bill, whose Second Reading took place in December 1982. The stated aim of the Bill to outlaw 'abortion on demand' was supported in a short speech by Maurice Wood (Bishop of Norwich).[70] Graham Leonard (whilst Bishop of London) contributed to the debate more fully, speaking for 26 minutes, expressing concern that changes in the law be followed by action within the medical profession (to ensure that attempts to evade its intentions are not allowed to prosper) and called for the confrontation of the underlying social causes of the need for abortion. He also aligned himself with those calling for changes to the law on the basis of the problems which had arisen as a result of the implementation of the Abortion Bill (1967),[71] describing his position:

> I believe that the foetus has a right to live and to develop as a member of the human family. Therefore I see abortion and the termination of that life by the act of man as a great moral evil... I do not believe that the right to life, as a right pertaining to persons, admits no exceptions whatever. I never have been an absolutist in this matter, but I do believe that the right of the innocent life admits very few exceptions indeed. I will not seek to elaborate those exceptions, but I will say that in abortion we are faced with a choice between two evils, and we have to decide which is the lesser evil. The Bill before us helps us to make that responsible but very difficult judgement.[72]

In debates covering the subject of Mental Health, on which the bishops contributed on every opportunity available, the bishops spoke both for and against the Government on two occasions. Maurice Wood (Bishop of Norwich) spoke during December 1981 in support of the Government's Mental Health (Amendment) Bill (1982) at its Second Reading stage.[73] In his contribution he welcomed the general emphases of the Bill and especially its underlying emphasis on opening up society to the mentally disabled. He did, however, voice concern that the links which exist between Churches and Chaplains within institutions should not be lost with a move towards care in the community. John B. Taylor (Bishop of St Albans) also spoke in support of the Thatcher Government on the subject of Mental Health. His contribution came in a deliberative debate on the care of the mentally ill during December 1985.[74] Taylor commu-

---

70   *ibid*, 6/12/82, vol. 437, col. 93-94.
71   *ibid*, 6/12/82, vol. 437, col. 70-75.
72   *ibid*, 6/12/82, vol. 437, col. 73.
73   *ibid*, 1/12/81, vol. 425, col. 960-963.
74   *ibid*, 4/12/85, vol. 468, col. 1327-1330.

nicated the support of the Church of England for the principle of moving care of the mentally ill into the community and its commitment to helping make it work in practice. He noted three particular ways in which this could happen. Firstly, through contributing to the process of educating ordinary people not to be afraid of the mentally handicapped. Secondly, by enlisting volunteers to help in those neighbourly acts which homes for the mentally handicapped may require. Thirdly, by providing its own care homes.

The two contributions on the subject of Mental Health against the Government both came from Ronald Bowlby (Bishop of Southwark) during deliberative debates during 1988.[75] Both speeches argued that no shortcuts exist to the effective care of the mentally ill and challenged the Government not to consider care in the community as an economy drive. 'In this, as in so many other things,' he said, 'there are no short cuts or cheap solutions. I am not just talking about money but even about human care and, I would want to say, prayer.'[76] Indeed, both speeches emphasised the need for more resources, particularly in terms of personnel, to enable proper care to be provided and the transition from institutional to community care to take place.

The greatest ratio between contributions against and for the Government was found in debates covering the subject of the National Health Service. Here the bishops never spoke in support of the Government but spoke against it five times. Two of these negative contributions were made in the short discussions surrounding Starred Questions. The first, during January 1985, was on drug prescribing and the second, during November 1986, was on hip replacement operations. Two bishops contributed in deliberative debates covering the NHS. David Jenkins (Bishop of Durham) contributed to a debate on the NHS and reform of the social security system during November 1985.[77] His twenty minute speech attacked the Government's reform proposals rather less diplomatically than most episcopal contributions:

> I fear that it certainly seems to me that the Green Paper proposals do not look like a satisfactory basis for the sort of social security system we need to take us into the 21st century and do not give us much encouragement that either the social security service or the National Health Service is safe in their present hands. This is regrettable – and very political of a bishop. Unfortunately,

---

75   *ibid*, 18/5/88, vol. 497, col. 342-345 and 7/12/88, vol. 502, col. 631-634.
76   *ibid*, 18/5/88, vol. 497, col. 342-345.
77   *ibid*, 20/11/85, vol. 468, col. 577-582, 588.

commonsense overtakes my ecclesiastical prudence.[78]

Jenkins went on to attack the Government proposals for their lack of vision, their failure to consider wider questions relating to the organization of society and unemployment, and the inherent message of their policies that the poor are a burden to be maintained at the lowest possible level of subsistence. This last point attacked the fundamental New Right belief that the people who are losers in the market game should be stigmatised in order to drive them to become winners. Jenkins also pressed for more money, personnel, training and time to be invested in the NHS and the social security system to enable them to run effectively.

Stanley Booth-Clibborn (Bishop of Manchester) was the second bishop to contribute to deliberative debates covering the subject of the NHS. He spoke twice on the matter, in April 1987 and December 1989.[79] The second of these contributions engaged most directly with the Government. It expressed grave doubts over the value of bringing competition into the NHS and sought increased overall funding for it from taxation. Booth-Clibborn also widened his attack to the general philosophy that private is always better than public in a variety of fields including education, health, and social security. He described as 'utterly deplorable' the claim by recently appointed Chancellor of the Exchequer, John Major, that 'money is better left in the pockets of the people where they will use it properly rather than in government hands.'[80]

7.2.8 Home Office

Within this subject group the subject of Political and Constitutional matters received the greatest episcopal input. Each of the episcopal contributions were classified as being neutral in their response to the Government (Figure 7.13). Half of these contributions were made in debates of tribute to retiring peers, or peers who had recently passed away. The bishops also contributed on two occasions to deliberative debates which considered aspects of their own role in the House of Lords. Both speeches were classified as neutral in relation to the Thatcher Government. The first was made by David Say (Bishop of Rochester) during the brief exchange which followed the asking of a Starred Question on the clergy and politics by Lord Bishopston

---

78   *ibid*, 20/11/85, vol. 468, col. 579.

79   *ibid*, 1/4/87, vol. 486, col. 599-601 and 6/12/89, vol. 513, col. 884-886.

80   *ibid*, 6/12/89, vol. 513, col. 885-886. Booth-Clibborn quoted the Chancellor of the Exchequer directly, citing 'a radio broadcast' as his source.

on 20th March 1984. His light-hearted contribution expressed confidence in the influence exerted by the bishops:

> My Lords, would the Minister [Viscount Whitelaw] not agree that life for him and other spokesmen for Her Majesty's Government, and indeed for spokesmen of her Majesty's loyal Opposition, would be much duller were it not for occasional clerical competition? Even the activities of certain bishops sometimes have encouraging results in other places.[81]

The second contribution was made during a debate on 18th May 1988 surrounding an Unstarred Question by Lord Tanlaw '...to ask the Leader of the House whether it is now appropriate for the bishops to continue to have to wear robes and sit and speak from the spiritual Benches when taking part in the proceedings of the House of Lords.' Ronald Bowlby (Bishop of Southwark) spoke for ten minutes, commenting on the role of the bishops in the House of Lords generally and the specific points raised by Lord Tanlaw's question. He opened by stating unequivocally the difference between politics and party politics, and the position of the Lords Spiritual in relation to both:

> We do not regard ourselves, any of us, in any sense as party politicians... We may occasionally make a speech or cast a vote this way or that which will support or criticise a policy, be it of government or of opposition. But few of us are card-carrying members of any party and still fewer of us, if any, would ever wish to be bound by some kind of party Whip... But I want to stress that politics, as distinct from party politics, is about the science and art of government, and it is difficult to see why Her Majesty should summon us here at all if she then requests us to be silent after Prayers. So the issue is and always has been how and where to draw the line between the principles of justice, moral considerations and the assessment of human consequences – all of which must be our primary concern as spiritual Peers – and those details of legislation and administration about which we are certainly as fallible as anyone else.[82]

It is noticeable that Bowlby does not close the door to episcopal contributions relating to the details of legislation and administration but rather emphasises the bishops' fallibility on such matters and the fact that they are not their primary concern. He goes on to respond to Lord Tanlaw's question, offering an essentially pragmatic reflection on the issues raised:

> I believe it is true that, if one asks most bishops, they will say that it is a bit of a nuisance to have to keep taking off one's robes and putting them on again every time one wants a cup of tea or some-

---

81   *ibid*, 20/3/84, vol. 449, col. 1108.
82   *ibid*, 18/5/88, vol. 497, col. 410-412.

thing a little more fortifying, or to go into the Library. I do not believe that we have a sense of changing our personality, character or concern by putting our robes on and taking them off.

It is true that robes belong more naturally to the sphere of church and worship and one feels a little out of place wandering about in them here... However, I should not wish to exaggerate that. They are perfectly appropriate for the prayers. They identify us and, with television in your Lordships' House, that may be more important than it was.

If robes went I believe there would then be an even stronger case for continuing to sit here. In any event, I believe that there is a strong case for sitting here because we are near the Throne. It reminds us and noble Lords that we are here by courtesy of a royal choice and summons of long standing and have a particular loyalty to the Crown. We are near the Government Benches because the Christian faith requires us to pray for and support good rulers.[83]

The bishops were most negative towards the Government in debates covering the subject of Immigration and Nationality, never speaking for the Government and speaking against it on 11 occasions. At the heart of this negativity towards the Thatcher Government were the debates on their British Nationality Bill which took place during June, July and October 1981. The bishops made twelve contributions at the Committee stages following two speeches at the Second Reading by Robert Runcie (Archbishop of Canterbury) and Graham Leonard (whilst Bishop of Truro). Runcie spoke first, making a number of points.[84] Firstly, and arguably most significantly, he noted that the Bill failed to encourage a sense of belonging amongst the British immigrant community: 'Belonging is a basic human need and it is one of the tragedies of the world we live in that there are so many people today who are, either formally or effectively, stateless; without rights in the country in which they live.'[85] Secondly, he argued that the Bill failed to recognise the increasingly free movement of people internationally for the purposes of education, work and experience. Thirdly, he suggested that the provisions of the Bill would inject uncertainty into the social life of the nation. Leonard took a similar line to Runcie, focusing particularly on the damage the Bill would do to the sense of belonging of many which he described as a fundamental human need.[86]

The bishops were also negative in all their contributions to debates

---

83   *ibid*, 18/5/88, vol. 497, col. 411.
84   *ibid*, 22/6/81, vol. 421, col. 875-878.
85   *ibid*, 22/6/81, vol. 421, col. 876.
86   *ibid*, 22/6/81, vol. 421, col. 901-906.

Figure 7.13
Episcopal Contributions For and Against Her Majesty's Government:
Home Office

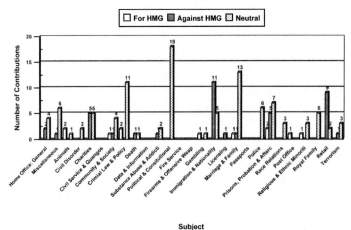

Subject

covering the subject of Retail, each of which focus specifically on the subject of Sunday trading. The most significant and influential of these contributions were made during December 1985 and February 1986 in debates considering the Government's Shops Bill (1986) at which four Second Reading and eight Committee stage speeches were made. The Second Reading contributions were made by Hugh Montefiore (Bishop of Birmingham), who made two contributions,[87] Colin James (Bishop of Winchester),[88] and Ronald Bowlby (Bishop of Southwark).[89] Together their speeches totalled 65 minutes in length. Montefiore made the first contribution and began by proposing an amendment: '...that this House considers that the law should be amended so as to rationalise restrictions on trading hours without such extensive deregulation as the Bill proposes.'[90] In other words, the amendment pushed for substantial deregulation, but not total deregulation (what the bishops described as a 'balance' or 'compromise'). Each of the other episcopal contributions spoke in support of this amendment presenting what was the collegial contribution from the Bench of Bishops during the Thatcher years. Each made it clear that their position was not a blind Sabbatarianism[91] but a concern

---

87   *ibid*, 2/12/85, vol. 468, col. 1069-1076, 1110-1111 and 2/12/85, vol. 468, col. 1172-1175.
88   *ibid*, 2/12/85, vol. 468, col. 1102-1105.
89   *ibid*, 2/12/85, vol. 468, col. 1114-1117, 1133.
90   *ibid*, 2/12/85, vol. 468, col. 1069.
91   Montefiore stated the point bluntly: 'It is not sinful to work on Sundays'. *ibid*, 2/12/85, vol. 468, col. 1070.

over the likely social effects of total deregulation. They worked with an assumption that there is a fundamental human need for individuals and communities to enjoy a day of rest each week. Colin James (Bishop of Winchester) emphasised this point:

> The trouble with total deregulation is that it isolates the freedom of the consumer; it isolates the freedom of big business as being the supreme good, as being the determining factor of what should happen in society and how the law should be reformed. I should want to hold these freedoms of the consumer and the freedoms of the retailer in a wider and more generous framework of what makes for the good of the family and the common good of the community... We are dealing here with subtle, sensitive, intangible issues bound up with our particular history and culture and our religious tradition, where changes could have far-reaching implications for our community life, for those who work in the retail trade and for the future pattern of the retail trade itself.[92]

In debates covering the subject of Prisons, Probation and Aftercare the bishops spoke for the Government twice, against the Government on five occasions, and neutrally seven times. Ernest Tinsley (Bishop of Bristol) made the more substantial of the two contributions in support of the Government, speaking during December 1983 at the Second Reading of the Government's Repatriation of Prisoners Bill.[93] His short speech offered support for the Bill's provisions for foreign prisoners to be transferred to their own countries. Only one of the speeches against the Government was made in a deliberative debate. This contribution by Hugh Montefiore (Bishop of Birmingham) was made to a debate on prison conditions during February 1987 and pushed for a reduction in the prison population, particularly those on remand. Montefiore argued in support of the policy of prison-capping to facilitate the achievement of this reduction.[94] The probation service was the specific focus of one of the episcopal contributions which was neutral in relation to the Thatcher Government. This contribution was made by Maurice Wood (Bishop of Norwich) during June 1983 in a deliberative debate.[95] Wood made it clear that he considered the probation service to be one of the caring professions, and a profession worthy of encouragement for its work '...at the very sharp point of confrontation with humanity in its weakness and in its sinfulness; and yet as a Christian one must say at its possibility of redemption.'[96] In line with this Wood also outlined

---

92   *ibid*, 2/12/85, vol. 468, col. 1103.
93   *ibid*, 21/12/83, vol. 446, col. 766-767.
94   *ibid*, 25/2/87, vol. 485, col. 256-258.
95   *ibid*, 30/6/83, vol. 443, col. 409-412.
96   *ibid*, 30/6/83, vol. 443, col. 410.

his belief that the best approach for dealing with the criminal will involve a short period of punishment followed by a real attempt at reclamation.

As one would expect the bishops spoke a great deal in debates covering the subject of Marriage and Family, making one contribution in support of the policies of the Thatcher Government, one against, and 13 which were neutral. The one contribution recorded as being against the Government was made by David Say (Bishop of Rochester) during November 1983 at the Second Reading of the Government's Marriage and Matrimonial Proceedings Bill.[97] It was followed by a further six contributions at the Committee stages. Say opened his Second Reading speech by explaining the importance of the Church distinguishing, to a certain degree, between the teaching about marriage which it is appropriate to give to its members and the comments which it is right to make in relation to the laws of the state on divorce.[98] In so doing he quotes T.A. Lacey's *Marriage in Church and State*, published in 1912. Writing about the duty of the Christian called to the reformation of the laws of the State, Lacey notes:

> In doing this he has no right to put aside what he has learnt as a Christian, and in the quality of citizenship to act as a mere natural man... But neither is he bound to insist that the laws of the State, in regard to marriage or in regard to anything else, shall conform exactly to Christian teaching. Not all subjects of the State are Christian and the State must legislate for all.[99]

Say went on to focus on the lack of an emphasis on reconciliation within the Bill's provisions. Subsequently he sought to challenge the ease with which divorce occurs, particularly where no significant enquiry into the causes of the marital breakdown has taken place. Focusing on specific ways of tackling this Say made note of the shortcomings of the three-year rule, but in so doing questioned '...whether the alternative proposed [reducing the time limit for divorce to one-year and abolishing all exceptions] is the right one at this time.'[100] He ended by calling for more professional support to be made available for struggling marriages.

7.2.9 International Development

In debates covering the subject of Aid Policy the bishops spoke

---

97   *ibid*, 21/11/83, vol. 445, col. 45-49.
98   *ibid*, 21/11/83, vol. 445, col. 45.
99   T.A. Lacey, as cited by David Say (Bishop of Rochester), *ibid*, 21/11/83, vol. 445, col. 45.
100 *ibid*, 21/11/83, vol. 445, col. 48.

against the Government once and were neutral in their comments seven times (Figure 7.14). The contribution against the Government was made by David Say (Bishop of Rochester) during August 1980 who challenged the Government for reducing the UK contribution to the United Nations Children's Fund.[101] Three contributions stand-out from those which were classified as neutral. Together they focused on specific issues relating to UK aid policy, doing so in a tone which was clearly intended to be perceived not as 'against' the Government. George Reindorp (Bishop of Salisbury) encouraged the Government to increase its spending on development education in the UK, and to fight against the EU Common Agricultural Policy being allowed to damage the agricultural programmes of developing countries.[102] Eric Kemp (Bishop of Chichester) emphasised the role of Non-Governmental Organisations (NGOs) and governmental 'partnership' with NGOs.[103] Stanley Booth-Clibborn (Bishop of Manchester) argued the case for not running-down the UK's bilateral aid programme.[104]

Figure 7.14
Episcopal Contributions For and Against Her Majesty's Government: International Development

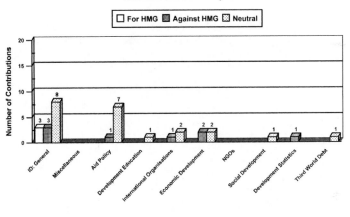

---

101 *ibid*, 6/8/80, vol. 412, col. 1488.
102 *ibid*, 3/6/81, vol. 420, col. 1251-1254.
103 *ibid*, 6/6/84, vol. 452, col. 644-646.
104 *ibid*, 18/12/85, vol. 469, col. 850-854, 861.

7.2.10 Social Security

We have already considered David Jenkins' speech on the NHS and reform of the Social Security system during November 1985 (Section 7.2.7) which was arguably the most critical episcopal contribution in the Social Security: General subject.[105] The bishops' contributions to other debates in the Social Security: General subject were more balanced (Figure 7.15). Three bishops contributed to a deliberative debate on Social and Economic Policies during January 1985. One spoke for the Government, one against, and one neutrally. The neutral contribution came from Hugh Montefiore (Bishop of Birmingham) in an 11 minute long speech.[106] His challenging, but not directly critical speech reflected on the changing, pluralist nature of society and the role of work, employment, welfare and the state within it. He argued that the unity of society is not dependent on material success but rests at the level of fundamental aims and values. Maurice Wood (Bishop of Norwich) made it clear that he intended to offer an optimistic contribution to the debate, which he duly did.[107] He praised the Government for a number of achievements: the control of inflation, the ongoing provision of social security, the Youth

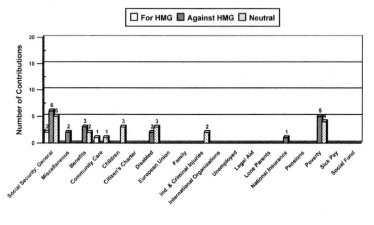

Figure 7.15
Episcopal Contributions For and Against Her Majesty's Government: Social Security

105 *ibid*, 20/11/85, vol. 468, col. 577-582, 588.
106 *ibid*, 23/1/85, vol. 459, col. 243-245.
107 *ibid*, 23/1/85, vol. 459, col. 268-271, 352.

Training Scheme, the Enterprise Allowance Scheme, and the Community Programme. The contribution against the Government was made by Cyril Bowles (Bishop of Derby).[108] His speech challenged the Thatcher Government at a number of levels. He described a far-reaching mood of hopelessness and despondency amongst the employed and unemployed alike about which, he argued, the Government were failing to speak hope and take action. He also made a blanket call for increased spending on the welfare state and attacked the Government for ignoring poverty and assuming that individual effort was enough to lift all of the poor out of their poverty.

The episcopal contributions to debates more specifically covering the subject of Poverty followed a tack similar to that made by Bowles, with five contributions against the Government and none in its support. Only one of the contributions against the Government was made in a debate which did not also cover the subject of Urban Regeneration (whose content has been summarised in Section 7.2.5). This one contribution was made by John Yates (Bishop of Gloucester) during March 1990 in a deliberative debate entitled 'Rich and Poor in Society'.[109] Yates argued that the poor in society had become poorer still during the 1980s and therefore that the trickle-down effect and private charitable giving could not be trusted to provide for their needs. He also sought to widen the definition of wealth: 'Wealth,' he asserted, 'is not just money although money is a part of it. Wealth, says the dictionary, is the happiness and the prosperity of the people. Wealth creation is the increase of true well-being in the community – fulfilment, health, and a good environment.'[110]

7.2.11 Trade and Industry

The subject of Employment received the largest share of the bishops' contributions to the Trade and Industry subject group (Figure 7.16). Most of these contributions were made in debates which covered employment issues (particularly unemployment) alongside a number of other social and economic issues. Of the four episcopal contributions made to debates which did have employment as their sole focus, three were against the Government and one was neutral in relation to the Government. All three of the contributions against the Government were made by David Sheppard (Bishop of Liverpool).[111]

---

108 *ibid*, 23/1/85, vol. 459, col. 304-307.
109 *ibid*, 14/3/90, vol. 516, col. 1557-1559.
110 *ibid*, 14/3/90, vol. 516, col. 1558.
111 *ibid*, 3/3/81, vol. 417, col. 1400-1403; 25/11/81, vol. 425, col. 822-824 and 28/11/84, vol. 457, col. 913-917.

Taken together they emphasised the deep hurt caused by unemployment to those communities affected by it, set out the case for various
solutions to the unemployment problem (including increased public
spending and job creation programmes), and powerfully challenged
the assumption that unemployment was a price worth paying for
improvements in national efficiency and competitiveness:

> Our greater efficiency and national competitiveness, which I read-
> ily say is vital to our national life, is being bought at a very great
> cost. We see that cost in the waste of individual talents, in the stress
> on families and on children, in the alienation of whole groups from
> feeling that they have any stake in the affluent consumer society
> which all-pervasive advertising proclaims to be the right of nor-
> mal British people. That alienation is the seed bed for apathy, for
> a great deal of ill-health, for drug abuse... and for destructive mili-
> tancy. It is destroying the sense of fellowship and companionship
> of our nation.[112]

Colin James (Bishop of Wakefield) made the neutral contribution
during November 1983 in a deliberative debate on job creation ini-
tiatives.[113] Focusing on society's fundamental attitude to work he
argued that efforts should be made to generate a 'contribution ethic',
as opposed to a 'work ethic', throughout society.

Figure 7.16
Episcopal Contributions For and Against Her Majesty' Government:
Trade & Industry

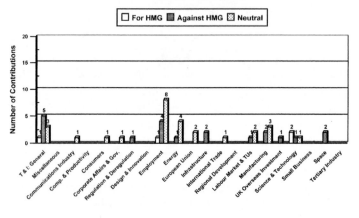

112 *ibid*, 28/11/84, vol. 457, col. 914.
113 *ibid*, 2/11/83, vol. 444, col. 578-581.

7.2.12 H.M. Treasury

We have already considered three contributions made by the bishops to debates relating to the Government's social and economic policies (Section 7.2.10). These speeches together gave a twofold response to the Thatcherite economic programme.[114] Firstly, they challenged the use of material prosperity as the yardstick of national success. Secondly, they called for the Government to provide more help for the economically weak. In so doing they placed the bishops firmly with those opposing the Thatcher Government's economic policies. The bishops' contributions to debates covering the H.M. Treasury: General subject were also overwhelmingly negative, with seven speeches which were against the Government, two in support of the Government, and two which were neutral. The speeches which were against the Government called for a greater emphasis on justice, greater effort in tackling unemployment, and increased investment in Youth Training Schemes. The lone speech which offered support for the policies of the Thatcher Government was made by Maurice Wood (Bishop of Norwich) in the debate on the Address at the beginning of the 1984/85 Parliamentary session. The opposition of the bishops to the economic policies of the Thatcher Government was such, however, that even in Wood's contribution there was, hidden behind supportive language, a veiled call for the plight of the poor to move further up the Governmental agenda.[115]

The Lords Spiritual were primarily negative in their contributions to debates covering the more specific subject of Taxation. They made two contributions for the Government and four against (Figure 7.17). The contributions for the Government were made during the exchanges following Starred Questions on taxation and marriage[116] and the VAT rating of Easter eggs. Stanley Booth-Clibborn (Bishop of Manchester) made the contribution to the latter, pressing the argument for increased taxation to fund increased public spending. Noting that the Easter egg is a symbol of new life, he commented (no doubt tongue-in-cheek) that '...it is entirely appropriate that VAT should be charged as a sign of the importance of taxation in the life of our country.'[117]

The episcopal contributions against the Government were all made at the Second Readings of Government Bills. Graham Leonard

---

114 *ibid*, 23/1/85, vol. 459, col. 243-245; 23/1/85, vol. 459, col. 268-271, 352 and 23/1/85, vol. 459, col. 304-307.

115 *ibid*, 13/11/84, vol. 457, col. 280-284.

116 *ibid*, 16/3/88, vol. 494, col. 1134.

117 *ibid*, 25/3/88, vol. 495, col. 380.

Figure 7.17
**Episcopal Contributions For and Against Her Majesty's Government:
H.M. Treasury**

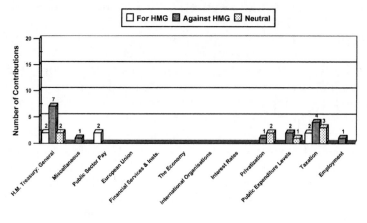

Subject

(Bishop of London) and John Wakeling (Bishop of Southwell) both
contributed to the Second Reading of the Rates Bill (1984). Leonard
responded to the Bill most directly, speaking against it because, he
argued, it failed to take sufficient account of the principle of sub-
sidarity:[118] 'I do not say that the rating system does not need drastic
reform. That is not the point at issue. I believe it does need to be
reformed and reformed in a way which increases responsibility and
realism in the face of local needs, rather than the reverse.'[119] Leonard
also argued that the provisions of the Bill would lead to both the
centralisation of control over education and would have a number
of detrimental effects on voluntary agencies. John Yates (Bishop of
Gloucester) spoke during May 1988 at the Second Reading of the
Local Government Finance Bill.[120] He attacked both the rating system as constituted and the planned Community Charge for not tak-

---

118 *ibid*, 9/4/84, vol. 450, col. 926-930. Leonard unpacks this principle of
    subsidarity: 'This principle states that social institutions, which include
    those of the state, have an auxiliary and complementary function concerning
    the tasks and needs of smaller groupings or individuals. That means to
    say that on the one hand institutions must leave to smaller groupings and
    individuals what they can do by their own proper power, and that on the
    other hand they must assist the smaller groupings or individuals where
    they are unable to accomplish a necessary or socially desirable aim.' *ibid*,
    9/4/84, vol. 450, col. 927.
119 *ibid*, 9/4/84, vol. 450, col. 928.
120 *ibid*, 9/5/88, vol. 496, col. 844-846.

ing the ability to pay into account in the setting of charges.

7.3 The Arguments the Bishops Employed

Over the course of the Thatcher years the bishops drew on a wide range of arguments to justify their perspective on the great variety of issues which came before them in House of Lords (Figure 7.18). The arguments that the bishops employed most often were those based on their Diocesan and Vocational Experience (used on 217 occasions). This is in line with the Church of England's own claim, expressed more recently, that the value of its contribution to the House of Lords is built upon the bishops ability to '...draw with a special authority upon the realities of life in their parishes, including in areas abandoned by most other institutions.'[121] Michael Baughen described the way in which local knowledge, relationships and experience enabled him to bring a distinctive perspective to the House in his contributions during an interview with the author in May 2002:

> One of the [reasons] why bishops could be so powerful is that, as they would say to me when I spoke on poverty and things like that, 'you can quote chapter and verse of what's actually happening today'. You see, and I would quote from them about Loan Sharks... for instance one couple came to see one of our vicars and said that they had taken up this offer that all your different sort of debts were taken on board, you know, under one and then they had their first repayments and they couldn't believe it. So they went to the vicar in great distress and he said, 'well what interest are you paying?'. And they said, 'well what's interest?'. Now see you could quote that... I would write to my vicars in these days when I was on such a debate and they would write, you know, give me chapter and verse of what happened in the last few weeks. Now we could

---

121 Council, *Role*, 7. A similar assessment, emphasising the additional authority which came with being based in the diocese, was made by Hugh Montefiore when asked whether the local rooting of the bishops is essential to the value they bring to the House of Lords: 'Well, it depends on the Bill. I mean if it was a Bill concerned with space travel or something then obviously they wouldn't be more specialised in it than anybody else. But if it was something which concerned social life and economic life, certainly they could speak with authority whereas few others could. I don't mean all of them. Someone like Lord Ezra who has been in charge of the coal, he could say something, but you know, in a place, in a conurbation like Birmingham where there was a lot of industry one could speak with some authority... and one could say what one had actually seen.' Hugh Montefiore (Bishop of Birmingham) in an interview with the author, 21st May 2002, Appendix 3.

do that because we have a network that nobody else has.[122]

The extent of the bishops' use of arguments based on their experiences in the diocese certainly supports the view that any evolution of the Church's approach to episcopal contribution to the House of Lords should not involve the total severance of the Lord Spiritual from his diocesan role. Nonetheless, it is clear from Baughen's comments that the local experience which the bishops are able to bring to Parliament is just as dependent on their network of relationships with the vicars in their care as it is on direct personal involvement on the ground in the diocese. This suggests that, were the Lords Spiritual to be released from a greater proportion of their diocesan work whilst maintaining their role as 'chief pastor in the local church',[123] they would be able to speak with no less authority on the realities of life in their parishes than they do at present.

The second most commonly employed arguments were those based on Facts and Statistics (used on 197 occasions) and Academic and Professional Advice (used on 149 occasions), suggesting an emphasis amongst the bishops on contributing to the debate of the House on the basis of a competent understanding of the issues under discussion. It is also noteworthy how often the bishops justified their positions on the basis of arguments relating to Community, Society and Family (used on 116 occasions), and the Economy and Finance (used on 92 occasions). In the context of the above, the number of occasions on which the bishops justified the points they made on the basis of moral and theological arguments were few. Particularly striking is the fact that the bishops employed arguments relating to Personal Morality (its significance and the need to encourage it) on only 12 occasions. The theological and moral arguments which were used most were those relating to Doctrine and Theology (used on 77 occasions) and Social Morality and Ethics (used on 54 occasions).

Overall it is significant that the arguments employed most by the bishops are rooted in experience and are essentially 'secular' in their basis. It is clear that in using these arguments the bishops are straying from those theological and moral arguments which they are most competent to employ and from which other peers (particularly Christians) want them to speak. To a great extent this is true. None-

---

122 Michael Baughen (Bishop of Chester) in an interview with the author, 21st May 2002, Appendix 2.

123 Avis, *Understanding*, 55. Avis is at pains to point out that: 'In Anglicanism, as in Roman Catholicism and Eastern Orthodoxy, the diocese, as the community united in its bishop and as the bishop's sphere of ministry, is regarded as the *local church...*' Avis, *Understanding*, 64.

Figure 7.18
Arguments Employed by the Bishops

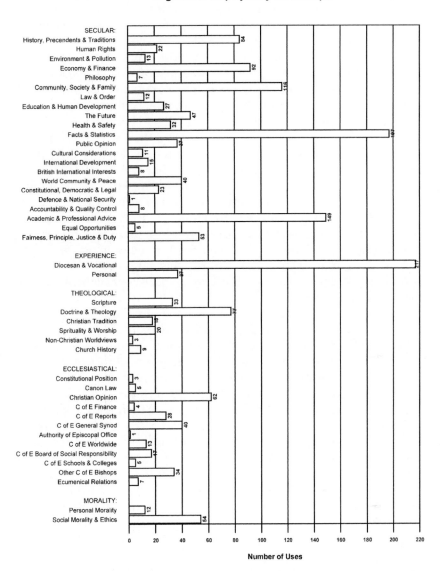

Number of Uses

theless, we must avoid dichotomizing too sharply between the secular and the spiritual. Whilst there is obvious value in distinguishing between these two types of argument it must not be forgotten that a sense of right and wrong (of morality) can be implicit in a secular argument and therefore may be implicitly communicated through the use of these arguments.

In the bishops' use of ecclesiastical arguments the impact of the ecumenical movement and ecumenical thinking is clearly discernible. Arguments relating to Christian Opinion (covering all denominations), often referred to by the bishops by reference to the view of 'the Churches', were used on 62 occasions. David Say's conclusion is that the bishops were little interested in drawing support for the points which they made by reference to the debates of the Church of England General Synod: 'I don't think that, with the exception of when one was presenting a Measure which had been through Synod and one was quoting what had been said and the voting there, I don't think on other issues the Synodical thing was really very prominent at all.'[124] Our research suggests, however, that arguments relating to General Synod (used on 40 occasions) were employed considerably by the Lords Spiritual. This indicates that the bishops were keen to draw upon Synod's democratic credentials to justify the points they made in the House and to assert themselves as representatives of the Church of England's active membership, even if, as David Say argues, the replacement of the Church Assembly with the General Synod did not increase the authority of the episcopal contributors to the House of Lords.[125]

The use of arguments relating to Church of England Reports (used on 28 occasions) and the Board for Social Responsibility (used on 17 occasions) tie in with the use of arguments based on Facts & Statistics and Academic & Professional Advice as indicative of an intention amongst the bishops to be seen as competent, well-informed contributors to the socio-political debates of the House. The Lords Spiritual referred to the comments and view of their fellow Church of England bishops on 34 occasions to justify the points that they made. This clearly does not indicate that the bishops adopted a full-scale collegial approach to contributing to the House. It does, however, certainly indicate a recognition that their authority in the House is increased if they are perceived to be speaking not just from an individual point of view but in line with the views of other bishops.

7.4 Conclusion

Our analysis of the speech-making of the Lords Spiritual during the

---

124 David Say (Bishop of Rochester) in an interview with the author, 29th May 2002, Appendix 4. John Taylor's memory of the 1980s led him to the same conclusion: 'We never referred to Synod. Very, very rarely.' John B. Taylor (Bishop of St Albans) in an interview with the author, 29th July 2002, Appendix 5.

125 *ibid*.

Thatcher years paints a broadly similar picture to that provided by Francis Bown of the period from 1979-1987 – of an episcopate whose verbal contributions '...tended towards criticism of rather than support for the Conservative Government'.[126] The data reviewed also indicates that almost half of the bishops' speeches to the House did not, however, take a definite position in relation to Government policy, supporting Ecclestone's suggestion that episcopal contributions tend to be '...thoughtful rather than campaigning'.[127] Of those speeches which were analysed and which took a definite position in relation to Government policy (28% of the 768 contributions) there was an average of seven speeches whose content was critical of the Government for every two which offered the Government support. The only bishop to consistently speak warmly and positively in response to the Thatcher Government was Maurice Wood (Bishop of Norwich). Of the 51 individual bishops who did speak in the House of Lords during the 1980s, 30 never spoke in support of the Government. On plans for a national lottery, on homelessness, on the abolition of the Metropolitan City Councils, on the inner cities, on South Africa and apartheid, on the National Health Service, on the British Nationality Bill (1981), on Sunday trading, on unemployment, and on economic policy the bishops opposed the Government.

As the Thatcher years progressed the content of an increasing number of the bishops' speeches was critical of the Government. From the 1979/80 Parliamentary session to the 1985/86 Parliamentary session an average of 19% of the bishops' contributions were classified as being against the Government. In contrast, from the 1986/87 Parliamentary session to the 1989/90 Parliamentary session an average of 28% of the bishops' contributions were classified as being against the Government. As stated already, this supports the conjecture outlined above (Section 6.2) that overall the bishops attended more and spoke more often as the Thatcher years progressed in response to the emergence of a distinctly Thatcherite, New Right political agenda during the 1983-87 Parliament.

On most occasions where more than one bishop contributed to the same debate their contributions were independent (bringing differing points to the issue under discussion), but rarely conflicting. This was the case with the episcopal contributions to the discussion of the Government's Education Reform Bill (1988), aid policy, abortion, and the Channel Tunnel Bill (1987). There were, of course, occasions when the bishops spoke with a clearly united voice on a particular issue. On apartheid and on Sunday trading this was particularly

---

126 Bown, 'Influencing', 117.
127 Ecclestone, *England*, 31.

the case, and a well-researched and pre-prepared 'party-line' could be detected in the episcopal contributions. Equally, there were occasions, such as on the subject of disarmament, where conflicting messages emanated from the Bench of Bishops. This record fits with John B. Taylor's description of how being present at the House of Lords as an individual Lord of Parliament, not a corporate spokesmen for the Anglican Church, affected the manner in which he approached his role: 'You were aware that you had total freedom to say what you wanted to say. But essentially the things that you wanted to say would be representing the Church's view and you wanted to know what the Church's line was on a particular subject...'[128]

On occasions, the bishops certainly spoke politically in the House, stepping beyond statements of broad principle to make specific policy recommendations. Most notably they did this on the subject of taxation (where they consistently and repeatedly called for increased public spending, funded by increased taxation, during discussions on a number of issues). Throughout the Thatcher years, on a range of different subjects, the bishops made their own specific recommendations, and supported and attacked specific Government policies. It should also be noted once more (see Section 6.7 above) that the bishops spoke considerably in the Committee stages of legislation where, in view of the clause-by-clause analysis which is taking place, it would be very difficult not to enter into detailed policy discussion.

Two significant findings emerge from our analysis of the arguments used by the bishops to support the points that they made during their speeches in the House. Firstly, the bishops' considerable use of experience-based arguments indicates how significant the link between the episcopal contributor and the local church is in generating episcopal contributions which are authoritative in tone and distinctive in perspective. Secondly, the bishops' considerable use of arguments based on facts, statistics, and academic and professional advice indicates a strong emphasis on influencing debates through the presentation of a well-informed and credible assessment of the issues under discussion.

---

128 John B. Taylor (Bishop of St Albans) in an interview with the author, 29th July 2002, Appendix 5.

CHAPTER EIGHT

The Bishops and the Bible

8.1 Introduction

8.1.1 Introduction

Having seen how relatively little the Lords Spiritual made use of moral and theological arguments during their speeches it is of special interest to consider how often, and in what manner, the bishops made use of the Bible in their contributions to the House of Lords.[1]

> The Bible is the central source for the furnishing of the Christian moral universe, the source of our moral vision. In its drama, its characters, its themes, its struggles, its beauty, and its complexity we are supplied with much of our vision of life in the world lived in relationship to God...
>
> The Bible points beyond itself in testimony to the power and presence of God in the experience of the biblical communities. Thus, authority rests in the church's affirmation of the Bible as a mediating witness to a God who was gracefully active in the experience of the ancient community, but is still gracefully active in our own experience.
>
> In Christian ethics our character and our conduct are shaped by many different sources of authority in our lives – our family, our culture, our education, our immediate context, as well as our faith. What is the position of the Bible as authoritative alongside these other sources of authority? It is our view that in Christian ethics the Bible is always primary but never self-sufficient...
>
> With the Bible as a constant reference point the church can and must enter into active dialogue with other sources of authoritative moral insight in our world, forging out the models of God's new activity in continuity with the Bible's witness to God's previous activity. Often the authority of Scripture is as much in its modelling of a process as in its mediating of a content. In attending to the discernment of God's will by the biblical communities we become sensitised to God's will in our own time.[2]

---

1   The use of the Bible is, of course, of particular interest to those who describe their churchmanship as evangelical.

2   B.C. Birch, *Let Justice Roll Down: The Old Testament, Ethics, and Christian Life* (Louisville, KY: Westminster John Knox Press, 1991), 33, 34.

In this confession the American Old Testament scholar Bruce C. Birch affirms the significant and primary role that should be played by the Bible in the process of ethical deliberation, decision and pronouncement in which the Church of England bishops engage as part of their role as Lords Spiritual. It is a confession which could sit comfortably within an Anglican tradition which similarly affirms the Bible as 'primary but never self-sufficient' in relation, not only to our modern context, but to other sources of ecclesiastical authority. In *The Anglican Understanding of the Church: An Introduction*, Paul Avis discusses three sources for Anglican ecclesiology: the Church in history, the Bible, and reason.[3] He is clear in stating that the role played by the Bible in shaping Anglicanism is the authoritative one:

> Anglicanism is a reformed faith. Though the English Church long predated the Reformation, it was decisively marked by the events of the sixteenth century. They gave it its biblical centre of gravity... Since, however, Rome also claimed the authority of Scripture and antiquity [the early Church], it is important to remind ourselves that the Reformers asserted the authority of Scripture and antiquity over and above the contemporary empirical church with its accumulated traditions.
>
> Thanks to biblical and historical scholarship, we are far more conscious today than the Reformers were of the intimate interconnection between Scripture and tradition, and are able to see Scripture as set within the context of tradition, or as the authoritative element in tradition, as well as the paramount criterion for interpreting tradition.[4]

Likewise Henry Chadwick asserts: 'Within the Anglican Communion the accepted norms of authority are located first in the faith

---

3   Avis, *Understanding*, 33-44.
4   Avis, *Understanding*, 36, 38. Having briefly summarised the interconnection between Scripture and tradition it is appropriate to mention the interconnection between reason and both Scripture and tradition. A.S. McGrade offers a succinct explanation: 'Reason has served Anglicans, and has often been explicitly invoked by them, as a counterpoise to unthinking biblicism or unthinking conformity to historical precedent. The Reformation principle that "Scripture containeth all things necessary to salvation" did not prevent bitter controversy under Elizabeth I about scripture's meaning and the Church's discretionary authority in matters of liturgy and governance. In the culminating contribution to this debate, Richard Hooker's *Of the Laws of Ecclesiastical Polity*, reason is defended as not only as necessary for an accurate understanding of Scripture but as competent to determine a broad range of issues not explicitly covered in Scripture.' A.S. McGrade, 'Reason', in Sykes & Booty (eds.), *Anglicanism*, 106.

declared in Scripture, then in the safeguard of interpretation provided by the Catholic Creeds, and finally in the liturgical tradition of Prayer Book and Ordinal.'[5] The Church of England has a biblical centre of gravity. In parallel it also operates with a restricted understanding of the purpose of Scripture:

> [T]he English Reformers refrained from taking Protestant principles to their logical conclusion. For example, they did not claim that everything done in the Church must be justified by explicit reference to Scripture. Neither Luther nor Calvin, and certainly not the English Reformers, insisted on a biblical blueprint for detailed patterns of worship or detailed structures of ministry... There was a consensus, though of varying degrees, that holy Scripture had a God-given but restricted purpose... to show the way of salvation.[6]

The Bible is at the very heart of the Anglican way of being Church, including those priestly, pastoral and prophetic activities of the Church which are performed through engagement in socio-political debate in Parliament. It is not claimed that everything done in the Church[7] which is not to do with 'the way of salvation' must be justified by explicit reference to Scripture. However, the silent assumption underlying this recognition of the limitations of Scripture is that, wherever it does have something to say about what is being done in the Church, its voice should be heard. We might also interpret the role of Scripture to 'show the way of salvation' in a wide sense and conclude that when the bishops are contributing to House of Lords debates they are seeking to show how national affairs can best be conducted to help, not hinder, individuals and communities along the way of salvation. Indeed, the Church of England's contribution to the Wakeham Commission on the reform of the House of Lords

---

5   H. Chadwick, 'Tradition, Fathers and Councils', in Sykes & Booty (eds.), *Anglicanism*, 96. In the same collection of essays Reginald Fuller takes the same position: 'The primacy of Scripture means that Scripture is the norm of faith and the norm by which other norms (creeds, traditions, confessions of faith) are judged.' R.H. Fuller, 'Scripture', in Sykes & Booty (eds.), *Anglicanism*, 83.

6   Avis, *Understanding*, 39, 40. Article VI of the Articles of Religion states that: 'Holy Scripture containeth all things necessary to salvation: so that whatsoever is not read therein, nor may be proved thereby, is not to be required of any man, that it should be believed as an article of the Faith, or be thought requisite or necessary to salvation.'

7   We interpret 'in the Church' broadly, not limiting it to what takes place in a particular building or when only confessing Christians are present.

argued that: '[t]he Church believes that its potential arises out of its belief in God and the moral law, and its concern to establish how that moral law should be worked out in human life.'[8]

There is an appreciation in Reginald Fuller's discussion of the role of Scripture within Anglicanism of the significance of the contribution that the Bible has to bring to the resolution of all ethical decisions.

> The Bible, as well as being a norm for theology, is also a norm for ethical behaviour. Modern Anglicans do not regard it as a code-book of law. Rather, the specific ethical commands of the Bible are illustrations of the kind of behaviour God requires in specific situations. They are derived from what God has done for us in his saving acts. We have many situations to face today which are not covered by the specific demands of Scripture, and therefore we have to go beyond the confines of the canon. But always we have to ask, what kind of imperative does the indicative of the gospel (what God has done) imply?[9]

In the Church of England the Bible is accepted as being the primary source of moral authority. Differences of approach exist with regard to the extent to which tradition and reason should be given an authoritative voice in the search for ethical direction. Similarly, differences of opinion exist with regard to what the Bible counsels on a whole range of issues from capital punishment to divorce and remarriage. Nonetheless, the basic authority of Scripture is questioned by few. However, when the bishops enter the Palace of Westminster they enter an arena in which few would deviate, at least publicly, from the Wakeham Report's acceptance that the House of Lords reflects the relativism of a plural society:

> In considering whether the faith communities should have specific, explicit representation, we do not in any way imply that they are the sole source of philosophical, or spiritual insight or that their insights are necessarily more valuable than those contributed by people without a religious faith... We... recommend that the reformed second chamber should continue to include people capable of articulating a range of philosophical, moral and spiritual viewpoints, both religious and secular.[10]

In the Church, but even more so in a plural society, moral direction cannot be given by command or prescription. Hermeneutically it would be erroneous to expect Scripture to provide clear-cut direc-

---

8   Council, *Role*, 6.
9   Fuller, 'Scripture', 84.
10   Royal, *Future*, 151 (15.4, 15.6).

tion relating to the moral ethical challenges of the twenty-first century.[11] Pragmatically, to be heard within the 'moral conversations'[12]
of a plural society the Church has to speak from alongside its partici-
pants, not from above them. The challenge is to do so in a manner
which remains true to its belief in the unique wisdom and authority
of God's revelation. The form of address that Oliver O'Donovan suggests the Church should use towards the individuals within its own
membership provides an indication as to how the Church might
address those individuals who corporately make many of society's
decisions:

> Counsel, indeed, is the church's most characteristic form of address
> to the individual... It is not, however, that the church pretends to
> know nothing about rights and wrongs of individual decision.
> When the church counsels, it points to the authority of God's rev-
> elation in Christ and to the moral teaching of Jesus, the prophets
> and the apostles; for it knows that right attitudes and decisions,
> however hidden and inscrutable in their detail, are those which
> come from a thoughtful obedience to that revelation. Thus the
> church counsels with authority. Its counselling is not fashioned on
> the non-directive model popularly favoured in a pluralist society,
> in which the counsellor's role is limited to helping the client dis-
> cover and articulate his own convictions... but then neither is it
> a veiled appeal to its own political authority as a society which,
> having made rules, expects obedience and loyalty. It is a didactic
> moral authority, appealing to the authority of a truth which stands
> above it and seeking to place the hearer in an equality of perspec-
> tive with the teacher. The church commends its case by argument,
> persuasion and the exposition of Scripture... Its counsel, therefore,
> is authoritative without being coercive.[13]

The exposition of Scripture is just one of the methods through
which the Church can commend its case. There are those who would

---

11 'Biblical materials never make moral decisions for us nor do they lay out
strategies or courses of action. Simply put, the Bible cannot be used as a
prescriptive code-book. Many issues requiring moral decision were never
imagined by the biblical communities (e.g., bio-ethical issues), and others
appear for decision and action in such radically altered socio-economic
circumstances that faithful response may still be unclear and complex.'
Birch, *Justice*, 32. See also: P. Baelz, *Ethics and Belief* (London: Sheldon Press,
1977), 93 and Fuller, 'Scripture', 83.

12 Submission of the Chief Rabbi, Professor Jonathan Sacks, to the Royal
Commission on the Reform of the House of Lords. Cited in Royal, *Future*,
151 (15.5).

13 O. O'Donovan, *Resurrection and Moral Order: An Outline for Evangelical Ethics*
(Leicester: IVP, 1986), 171.

argue, however, that in a society which has undergone a century-long process of secularization the proclamation of Christian truth only has limited value in influencing the shape of public policy. The Relationists of the Jubilee Centre, Cambridge argue that, '[t]he closer one gets to Whitehall and Westminster and the closer one gets to matters of policy rather than simply principle, the more appropriate – indeed essential – is translation'.[14] Translation is the 'endeavour to convey, as far as possible, Christian truth in secular language using secular concepts' where 'the language of the Bible is avoided and the biblical drama of creation – fall – redemption – glory is not mentioned.'[15] The Relationists are right to assert the importance of contextualizing the Christian message when contributing to socio-political debate in a secular context. However, they are also shrewd to recognise that for resisting the secularization process more broadly, and for challenging the principles which underlay public policy, it would be ill-advised to attempt to avoid the language of the Bible and the biblical drama completely:

> Nonetheless, public policy debate would lose a vital component if the churches' contribution was all through the medium of translation. The pubic arena needs to be reminded of the transcendent and modern culture needs theology as well as morality.[16]

Whereas translating Christian truth into secular language is an appropriate tool for communicating Christian truth to an increasingly secularly-minded audience, avoiding all reference to the Bible and the biblical drama inadvertently implies that the secularization of the public realm is complete, that Christian truth is only truth for those who acknowledge it to be so, and that Christianity has nothing distinctive to contribute to public debate other than that which is also contained in the canon of secular wisdom.[17] Tackling this same

---

14 Jubilee Policy Group, *Political Christians in a Plural Society: A New Strategy for a Biblical Contribution*, (Cambridge: The Jubilee Policy Group, 1994), 53.

15 *ibid*, 52.

16 *ibid*, 53.

17 It is interesting that St. Paul's meeting with the Areopagus in Athens (recorded in Acts 17:16-34) is considered by many to offer a biblical basis for a contextualized approach. Such an interpretation is clearly true to the record of Acts 17 which records Paul starting his speech to the Areopagus with reference to their altar 'To an Unknown God'. However to argue for a translational approach (in which reference to the Christian message and the salvation-historical drama recounted in Old and New Testaments is 'avoided') on the basis of Acts 17 is inappropriate. Paul does directly quote the Hebrew scriptures to his audience (Deuteronomy 30:20 in Acts 17:28) even though one might assume that for Paul to quote the holy book

issue Duncan Forrester considers there to be a necessary role for the language of transcendence in politics:

> If what theology has to say in no significant way differs from what most people are saying anyway, theology and the church lose credibility; they should either have kept silent, or said something distinctive, rooted in their own convictions about God, human beings and fellowship.[18]

In the particular context of the House of Lords, an approach which sought to avoid any explicit reference to the Bible and theological viewpoints would not only cause the Church to lose credibility, it would also undermine its efforts to bring the kind of distinctive spiritual contribution to the House of Lords which the bishops' membership (alongside others) is intended to generate:

> Religious belief... is an important part of many people's lives and it is desirable that there should be a voice, or voices, in the second chamber to reflect that aspect of people's personalities and with which they can identify... the reformed second chamber should continue to include people capable of articulating a range of philosophical, moral and spiritual viewpoints, both religious and secular.[19]

The best approach to the use of the Bible in the socio-political contributions of the bishops would seem to embrace fully the need to translate Christian truth into secular language and concepts whilst acknowledging the authority of the Bible as a source of moral direction and wisdom by making explicit reference to it.[20] Such an approach aims to give as robust as possible a secular justification for the points

---

of the Jewish people to a Greek audience would have been of no value in convincing them of the significance of his message. Moreover, Paul does give unequivocal voice to the message concerning the Christ and the salvation-historical drama found in the Torah. He refers to his God as the Creator of the world, to God's promise to Abraham (and the fulfilment of that promise). He then also proclaims the coming judgement of God and the resurrection of Christ.

18 Forrester, *Beliefs*, 81.

19 Royal, *Future*, 151 (15.5, 15.6).

20 Such an approach might, for example, quote and give a brief exposition of Jesus' injunction to 'love your neighbour as yourself' (Matthew 22:39) whilst also asserting the value in consequentialist and rationalist terms of the outworking of such an ethic for individuals and communities.

being made whilst maintaining a firm and confident[21] belief that the insights of theology, and more specifically Scripture and the gospel it proclaims, are both relevant and authoritative for all mankind. Lesslie Newbigin argues persuasively that '...the church today cannot without guilt absolve itself from the responsibility, where it sees the possibility, of seeking to shape the public life of nations...', asserting that Christians who accept this responsibility must muster:

> ...the courage to hold and to proclaim a belief that cannot be proved to be true in terms of the axioms of our society... The church needs to be very humble in acknowledging that it is only a learner, and it needs to pay heed to all the variety of human experience in order to learn in practice what it means that Jesus is the King and Head of the human race. But the church also needs to be very bold in bearing witness to him as the one who alone is that King and Head. For the demonstration, the proof, we have to wait for the end. Until then we have to be bold and steadfast in our witness and patient in our hope. For 'we are partakers of Christ if we hold our first confidence firm to the end' (Hebrews 3:14).[22]

8.1.2 Methodology

The use of the Bible is only one possible index which could be used to assess the moral and spiritual distinctiveness of the contribution of the bishops to the House of Lords. However, because of the centrality of the Bible to Anglicanism and the Christian faith (in both the worldview of the Church's membership and the perception of those who observe it from outside of its membership) and the ease of finding references to the Bible within the bishops' contributions, it is was

---

21 'I want to suggest', writes Lesslie Newbigin, 'the word "confidence" as the one which designates the proper attitude. In a pluralist society, any confident attitude of the truth is met by the response, "Why should I believe this rather than that?" Every statement of ultimate belief is liable to be met by this criticism, and - of course - if it is indeed an ultimate belief then it cannot be validated by something more ultimate... And if, as always happens in a pluralist society, we are asked: "But why start with Jesus? Why not start somewhere else?" we have to answer that no rational thought is possible except by starting with something which is already given in some human tradition of rational thought and discourse. Our immediate answer may well be, "Why not?" For the ultimate answer we have to wait for the end of all things.' L. Newbigin, *The Gospel in a Pluralist Society* (London: SPCK, 1989), 243.

22 L. Newbigin, *Foolishness to the Greeks: The Gospel and Western Culture* (London: SPCK, 1986), 148-149.

considered to be the best method for assessing the distinctiveness of the episcopal contribution.

The following analysis is based on House of Lords *Hansard*, the official record of House of Lords debates and covers the every sitting day of the House of Lords for which Margaret Thatcher was Prime Minister (9th May 1979 – 22nd November 1990). Each of the bishops' 768 contributions to the House which occurred during this period were searched for both explicit and implicit references to the Bible. The extent and the nature of this use of biblical material was then analysed. An explicit reference to the Bible is taken to refer to an occasion on which a bishop quoted the Bible, referred to a specific biblical text, or made reference to 'the Bible', 'Scripture', or the like. An implicit reference to the Bible is taken to refer to an occasion on which a biblical concept was contained in an episcopal contribution to the House without any explicit reference being made to the Bible. Whilst not explicitly referring to the Bible these concepts are clearly biblical and brought a definitely biblical perspective to bear on the debates of the House. Such concepts may not, of course, be exclusively biblical, either because they have been translated into other contexts or because they are shared with other traditions. It can be assumed though that, in the context of a bishops' speech, a meaning concurrent with the biblical concept is intended, even if a detailed explanation is not given by the bishop in his speech.

8.2 The Extent of the Bishops' Explicit Use of the Bible

The Church of England bishops made 768 speeches to the House of Lords during the Thatcher years (Section 6.2 above). Just fifty-one of these speeches made explicit reference to the Bible (Figure 8.1). Expressed as a percentage we can say that only 7% of episcopal contributions to the House made explicit reference to Scripture. Thus, Scripture was not given an explicit voice in 93% of the episcopal contributions to the House of Lords. Of the fifty-one explicit references to Scripture, 23 involved direct quotations from the Bible, 19 referred to the content of specific texts of the Bible, and nine referred to an aspect of the teaching of 'the Bible' or 'the Scriptures' as a whole.

Each of the eleven Parliamentary sessions analysed contained two or more episcopal contributions containing a reference to Scripture (Figure 8.2). The 1984/85 Parliamentary session contained the most speeches which referred to the Bible with eleven of the bishops' seventy-one speeches (Figure 6.1 above) containing a reference. The 1982/83 and 1985/86 Parliamentary sessions contained the least number of speeches which referred to Scripture. During the 1982/83 Parliamentary session only two of the 39 episcopal speeches contained a biblical reference. For the 1985/86 Parliamentary session the figure was just two references to the Bible in 99 episcopal contributions. Twice, therefore, a whole season of Parliamentary life passed-by with the bishops of a self-confessed Reformed denomination making just two references to the Bible in their speeches.

Of the bishops' references to the Bible, 39 were made during contributions to deliberative debates (Figure 8.3). Three of these were in

Figure 8.1
Number of Explicit Episcopal References to the Bible

Figure 8.2
**Number of Explicit Episcopal References to the Bible
in each Parliamentary Session**

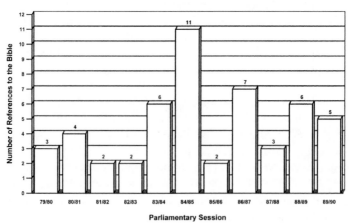

the debates on the Queen's speech, three during debates surrounding an Unstarred Question, and 33 during debates on Motions. Only on ten occasions did the bishops refer to Scripture during their contributions to legislative debates and it was, on every occasion, at the Second Reading stage (Figure 8.4). Thus, on none of the 191 occasions when a bishop made an intervention at the Committee stage of a Bill (Figure 6.18 above) did they refer to Scripture. Deciding to place an explanation of relevant biblical principles within debates which were intended to focus upon the general principles of Government policy and legislation, rather than during discussions relating to the individual clauses of the legislation, is surely an entirely appropriate approach.

Just 24 of the 51 individual bishops who spoke in the House of Lords during the Thatcher years made a speech which contained an explicit reference to the Bible (Figure 8.5). Ronald Bowlby, as Bishop of Newcastle and later Southwark, was eligible to attend the House for the entire length of Thatcher's premiership, made 49 verbal contributions to the House during that time, yet failed to make reference to the Bible on any occasion. John Habgood, author of *Church and Nation in a Secular Age*, was eligible to speak in the Lords throughout the Thatcher years (as Bishop of Durham and then York), yet considered referring to the Bible to be worthwhile just once. In fact only six bishops made more than two speeches containing a reference to the Bible during the 1980s. They were: Robert Runcie (whilst Archbishop of Canterbury), Hugh Montefiore (Bishop of Birming-

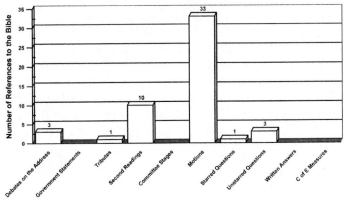

Figure 8.3
**Number of Explicit Episcopal References to the Bible during Contributions
to Different Debate Types**

Debate Type

ham), Maurice Wood (Bishop of Norwich), David Sheppard (Bishop of Liverpool), John Yates (Bishop of Gloucester), and Stanley Booth-Clibborn (Bishop of Manchester). The greatest number of references to the Bible were made by the evangelical Maurice Wood who was already present in the Lords when Thatcher came to power and left the House in August 1985. Seven of his 93 speeches (Figure 6.45) to the House of Lords made explicit reference to the Bible.

Figure 8.4
**Number of Explicit Episcopal References to the Bible during Contributions
to Private Members' and Government Bills**

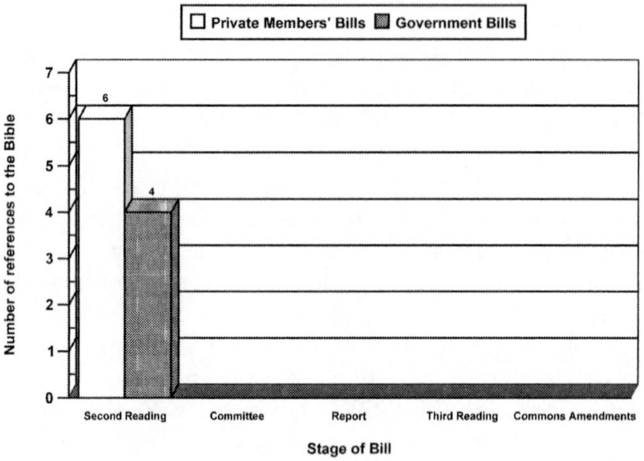

8.3 The Nature of the Bishops' Explicit Use of the Bible

8.3.1 The Biblical Sources Used

On the 51 occasions when the bishops made explicit reference to the Bible during their contributions to the House of Lords they used a wide variety of biblical sources. They made reference to the Old Testament (or a portion of it) on 21 occasions and to the New Testament (or a portion of it) on 32 occasions.[23] The bishops referred to all the main biblical genre, with the exception of Apocalyptic (Table 8.1). Texts as diverse as Ecclesiastes 11:4 ('He who studies the rain shall not sow and he who regards the clouds shall not reap') and Sam-

---

23 Some speeches referred to more than one portion of the Bible. For example John B. Taylor (Bishop of St Albans) referred to the Ten Commandments, Genesis 1-2, Amos, Isaiah, and 'the Gospels' during his speech on Sunday Trading during February 1989. *House of Lords Debates*, 8/2/89, vol. 503, col. 1572-1574.

Figure 8.5
Number of Explicit References to the Bible by Individual Bishops

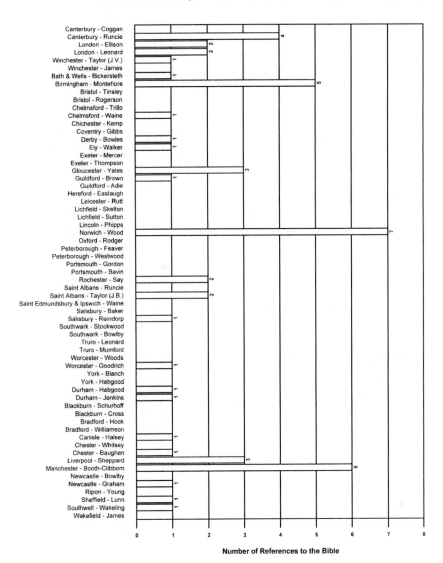

Number of References to the Bible

son's riddle ('Out of the eater, something to eat; out of the strong, something sweet')[24] were employed in the bishops' attempts to win

---

24 Judges 14:14. Unfortunately George Reindorp (Bishop of Salisbury) mistakenly locates this riddle in the story of Samson and Delilah (Judges 16). The two episodes are unconnected in the Judges narrative.

the battle of ideas in the House. The Gospels received the greatest episcopal attention, accounting for 20 of the 21 references to the New Testament Narrative genre. The bishops quoted the words of Jesus eight times:[25]

- '...to whom much is given much will be required...' (Luke 12:48)[26]
- 'But man does not live by bread alone...' (Matthew 4:4/Luke 4:4)[27]
- 'Look up, for your redemption draws near.' (Luke 21:28)[28]
- '...the gates of hell shall not prevail against it.' (Matthew 16:18)[29]
- 'Judge not lest ye be judged. For with what judgement ye judge ye shall be judged, and with what measure you mete it out it shall be measured to you again.' (Matthew 7:1-2)[30]
- 'Blessed are you poor, for yours is the Kingdom of God.' (Luke 6:20)[31]
- 'Feed my sheep.' (John 21:17)[32]
- 'You shall know the truth and the truth will make you free.' (John 8:32)[33]

Table 8.1

Number of Explicit Episcopal References to the Different Biblical Genre

Biblical Genre	Number of Episcopal References
Old Testament History	6
Old Testament Law	2
Old Testament Prophecy	5
Psalms	7
Wisdom Literature	2
New Testament Narrative (Gospels & Acts)	21
Epistles	11
Apocalyptic	0

25 All quotations are rendered using the exact words used by the particular bishop in his speech. As such the particular version of the Bible used varies from reference to reference and is not given here.

26 Gerald Ellison (Bishop of London), *House of Lords Debates*, 29/4/81, vol. 419, col. 1185.

27 Graham Leonard (Bishop of London), *ibid*, 12/5/82, vol. 430, col. 269.

28 Maurice Wood (Bishop of Norwich), *ibid*, 16/2/83, vol. 439, col. 287.

29 Maurice Wood (Bishop of Norwich), *ibid*, 30/1/84, vol. 447, col. 532.

30 John Wakeling (Bishop of Southwell), *ibid*, 9/4/84, vol. 450, col. 950.

31 David Sheppard (Bishop of Liverpool), *ibid*, 28/11/84, vol. 457, col. 915.

32 Robert Runcie (Archbishop of Canterbury), *ibid*, 23/11/88, vol. 502, col. 39.

33 Stanley Booth-Clibborn (Bishop of Manchester), *ibid*, 26/4/89, vol. 506, col. 1285.

Amongst those portions of Scripture which received the most episcopal use was the parable of the Good Samaritan (Luke 10:30-37). The bishops referred to it on three occasions. It also happened to be one of Margaret Thatcher's favourite political texts. John Campbell outlines how she understood its message to apply to twentieth-century man, with reference to her upbringing in Grantham:

> There is in Mrs Thatcher's descriptions of her parents' good works a strong sense of moral condescension, the Christian duty owed by the virtuous and hard-working to those less fortunate... From this starting-point she developed the philosophy that private charity – an individual voluntarily spending his own money – was morally better than collectivised welfare financed by taxation. From quite early in her political career one of her favourite texts was the parable of the good Samaritan – who could help the robbed traveller only because he had his own money.[34]

Contrastingly, the episcopal use of the passage consistently drew a less individualistic application from the example of the Samaritan. On each of the three occasions when the bishops made use of the passage it was to add support to a collectivised, statutory approach to improving the well-being of individuals and communities. Even Maurice Wood (Bishop of Norwich), the bishop most supportive of the Thatcher Governments in the Lords division lobby (Section 5.4 above), used it in this way during his contribution to the Second Reading of the Criminal Injuries Compensation Bill (1979):

> By the action of giving a Second Reading to this Bill we can do what the Good Samaritan did, which was to draw close and with sympathy and sensitivity, and incidentally with financial help also, if you read the parable closely; he poured in oil and wine and sought to care for the victim of violence.[35]

Cyril Bowles (Bishop of Derby) began his use of the parable by setting it in the context of its increasing political currency:

> In conclusion, in these days when the parable of the Good Samaritan is becoming part of the stock in trade of political speeches, perhaps I may be allowed to make some reference to that. The parables of Jesus are not allegories, although they have frequently been interpreted in this manner, so that we cannot argue that the priest and Levite passed by because they were having to cut their personal expenditure.[36]

Bowles then gave a neat exegesis of the parable to add authority to his call that support be given to the recommendations of the Brandt

---

34 Campbell, *Thatcher*, 17.
35 *House of Lords Debates*, 3/7/79, vol. 401, col. 257.
36 *ibid*, 12/3/80, vol. 406, col. 1116.

Report (particularly regarding the quality and quantity of development aid):

> The parable was told in response to the question, 'Who is my neighbour?', asked by the lawyer wanting to vindicate himself. But, as always with parables, the way in which Jesus deals with them at the end is the crucial point, and what he does is to turn the question right around. He does not answer the question 'Who is my neighbour?', but asks, 'Which do you think was neighbour to the man who fell into the hands of the robbers?' It is always our response to the situation that matters, and not our attempting to decide who the limited group of people are to whom the help must be given... Charity, love of neighbour, expresses itself corporately in justice which is brought about by a mutual sharing of resources, and this in general and in particular is what this splendid report urges us to do.[37]

David Lunn (Bishop of Sheffield) turned to the example of the Good Samaritan to give authority to his support for a Second Reading to be given to a Private Members' Bill which sought to ensure that appropriate after-care is provided for those discharged from hospital after having received medical treatment for schizophrenia:

> The piece of Scripture I wish to refer to is curiously politically controversial. It concerns the parable of the Good Samaritan. I see the schizophrenic as the person who has indeed fallen asleep among thieves and who is the most desperate need of help. I hope we are not among those who pass by on the other side.[38]

The Apostle Paul's image of the body in 1 Corinthians 12 was also popular material for episcopal speeches. It was used on three occasions, twice by David Sheppard (Bishop of Liverpool) and once by Stanley Booth-Clibborn (Bishop of Manchester).[39] Sheppard, opposing the second reading of the Government's Local Government Bill (1985) which legislated for the abolition of the Greater London Council and seven Metropolitan County Councils, argued for the maintenance of strong links within a city between '...those who are stronger economically and those who are weaker economically'.[40] He urged that individuals and communities should act '...in one world as members of one another', continuing, '[t]he phrase comes from St

---

37   *ibid*, 12/3/80, vol. 406, col. 1116-1117.
38   *ibid*, 12/4/89, vol. 506, col. 334.
39   *ibid*, 14/1/87, vol. 483, col. 564. Booth-Clibborn was contributing to a deliberative debate entitled 'Regional Policy: Imbalance in Prosperity'.
40   *ibid*, 15/4/85, vol. 462, col. 486.

Paul's picture of the body, in which the greatest honour is to be given to the weakest member. That picture of the body is very relevant to a great city. Is one weak, then all are weak. We are to be members of one another.' Two years later, during his speech in a debate on inner-city problems Sheppard recalled to the House a recurring theme of the Archbishop's Commission on Urban Priority Areas:

> On the Commission we repeatedly told each other that we were examining not just what was happening in urban priority areas but also the health of the whole church and nation. We often quoted to each other St Paul's words on the body: 'We are members of one another'.[41]

In fact, Sheppard and Booth-Clibborn's particular use of the image of the body owes more to Plato than Paul. In his letter to the Corinthians Paul borrows the image of body, which was common currency in Greek political thought,[42] and uses it to teach the Corinthian Christians about the spiritual unity of the Church which results from the baptism by the Spirit of its members and the resultant need for the Church's members to work together and honour one another.[43] In contrast the two bishops take the image of the body and use it more generally to illustrate the economic interdependence of rich and poor. This more closely resembles the use of the image of the body as a 'rhetorical appeal for harmony and interdependence in political life from the fifth and fourth centuries BC (including Plato's *Republic*) through to the first and second centuries AD (including Dio Chrysostom's *Orations*).'[44]

The only other portions of Scripture to which the bishops referred more than once were also New Testament passages: the parable of the Sheep and Goats (Matthew 25:31-46) and Paul's words in Philip-

---

41 *ibid*, 2/2/87, vol. 484, col. 75.

42 'A term or turn of phrase loaded with a political history'. A.C. Thiselton, *The First Epistle to the Corinthians*, (Carlisle: Paternoster Press, 2000), 992.

43 'The body is a unit, though it is made up of many parts; and though all its parts are many, they form one body. So it is with Christ. For we were all baptised by one Spirit into one body... God has combined the members of the body and has given greater honour to the parts that lacked it, so that there should be no division in the body, but that its parts should have equal concern for each other. If one part suffers, every part suffers with it; if one part is honoured, every part rejoices with it. Now you are the body of Christ, and each one of you is a part of it.' (1 Corinthians 12:12-13, 24-27)

44 Thiselton, *Corinthians*, 992-993.

pians 4:8.[45] David Say (Bishop of Rochester) gave attention to the former during the second day of the Debate on the Address at the beginning of the 1984/85 Parliament in a speech which focused on overseas development. He made reference near the end of his speech to the 1983 Philip Noel-Baker lecture given by Professor John Ferguson (then Chairman of the United Nations Association):

> [A]fter detailing the horrifying number of millions of people who do not have safe water to drink, who suffer from hunger and malnutrition, who are illiterate or who are blind... Professor Ferguson went on to say that as a Christian he shuddered each time he read the parable of the Sheep and Goats, because by that parable the nations are under judgement according to whether they have or have not fed the hungry. No excuses were allowed in the Gospel story and he said that there can be no excuses allowed in today's world. We must not say that 'we first have to make the world a safe place for democracy' or 'we have to deter the Communists' or whatever. If we have not fed the hungry we have turned our back on the Lord who told the parable in order to challenge the hearts and minds of his hearers.[46]

Hugh Montefiore (Bishop of Birmingham) was the second bishop to use the parable of the Sheep and Goats. He began his contribution to a deliberative debate on prison conditions during February 1987 by stating unequivocally: 'Christians have plenty of reasons to be concerned with prisons, whether they think of the parable of the Sheep and Goats; of a clause in the litany; or what is written in the Epistle to the Romans, concerning the duty of the state in punishing offenders.'[47]

On both occasions when Philippians 4:8 was used by the bishops it was in the context of asserting the need to look to the renewal of society based on Christian principles, not only legislation, as the answer to pressing social problems. Gerald Ellison (Bishop of London) ended his contribution to a 1980 deliberative debate on obscenity and film censorship by noting that:

> [B]ecause indulgence in pornography is sterile and joyless, it is bound to lead to an unhappy society... the only solution to the problem... is to be found in a rediscovery of sounder social principles, of true family life and of sacrificial self-discipline...

---

45 '...whatever is true, whatever is noble, whatever is right, whatever is pure, whatever is lovely, whatever is admirable - if anything is excellent or praiseworthy - think about such things. Whatever you have learned or received or heard from me, or seen in me - put it into practice. And the God of peace will be with you.' (Philippians 4:8).

46 *House of Lords Debates*, 7/11/84, vol. 457, col. 50.

47 *ibid*, 25/2/87, vol. 485, col. 256.

St Paul got things right when in commending men to seek peace, he told them that the way to do it was to think on things true, honest, pure and of good report.[48]

John Waine (Bishop of Chelmsford) took a similar line in a wide-visioned speech to a deliberative debate proposed by Lord Rodney '...to call attention to the effect of pseudo-religious cults on family life and young people':[49]

[F]or the ultimate answer to these pseudo-religious cults it is not sufficient to look only for new legislation. The ultimate answer to these movements is a revitalising of society and a renewing of the Christian Church and the other older religious movements... It is our task in the Church to work for such a renewal of the Church and I believe that that is going on. Moreover, I believe that all of us together have to commit ourselves to seeking to create a society which is not about the pursuit of arid materialism but is a society in which ideas and ideals can flourish; a society where whatever things are true, honest and just and whatever things are pure, lovely and of good report may be safeguarded, nurtured and allowed to fill the thoughts and aspirations of those in all age groups who look for purpose, direction and meaning.[50]

8.3.2 The Impact of the Bible

The bishops allowed the Bible to impact their speeches to varying degrees (Table 8.2). Their explicit references to Scripture can be divided into three types: insubstantial references, brief references, and 'unpacked' references.[51] On four of the 51 occasions on which the bishops referred to Scripture explicitly the reference was insubstantial, making no serious or relevant contribution to the content of the speech in terms of the points being made or the arguments being used to justify those points. In these cases the Bible was mentioned not in order to share its teaching, but simply to add colour to the speech. Robert Runcie's opening remarks to the debate which he tabled to mark the 40th anniversary of the United Nations were one such occasion:

After the spate of speeches and articles on the subject during the

---

48   *ibid*, 16/1/80, vol. 404, col. 182-183.
49   *ibid*, 10/2/88, vol. 493, col. 247.
50   *ibid*, 10/2/88, vol. 493, col. 257.
51   Where a bishop made reference to more than one portion of the Bible in his contribution the classification of the extent to which they allowed the Bible to impact their speech was based on their use of the part of Scripture to which they gave most attention.

Table 8.2

Episcopal Contributions Containing an Explicit Reference to the Bible

Bishop	Subject of Debate	Date	Location of Biblical Reference
Insubstantial References			
Reindorp (Salisbury)	Development Aid Policy	3/6/81	Psalm 23:4
Bickersteth (Bath & Wells)	Straw & Stubble Burning Prohibition Bill	14/2/84	John 4:35
Halsey (Carlisle)	Health & Welfare Provision	13/2/85	Psalm 91:3
Runcie (Canterbury)	UN: 40th Anniversary	29/10/85	Ruth 2:17
Brief References			
Ellison (London)	Obscenity & Film Censorship	16/1/80	Philippians 4:8
Habgood (Durham)	Marriage Enabling Bill	25/2/81	Book of Leviticus
Ellison (London)	Equality in Society	29/4/81	Luke 12:48/Mark 9:35
Brown (Guildford)	BBC External Services	30/7/81	Isaiah 2:4
Leonard (London)	Child Upbringing & Social Influences	12/5/82	Matthew 4:4/Luke 4:4
J.V. Taylor (Winchester)	Disarmament	16/6/82	James 3:17-18
Wood (Norwich)	NATO Policy: Deterrence & Disarmament	16/2/83	Luke 21:28
Runcie (Canterbury)	Crimes of Violence	15/11/83	The Gospels
Say (Rochester)	Tribute to Lord Byers	7/2/84	Psalm 15:2
Wakeling (Southwell)	Rates Bill	9/4/84	Matthew 7:1-2
Wood (Norwich)	Human Fertilisation: Warnock Report	31/10/84	Genesis story
Sheppard (Liverpool)	The Unemployed	28/11/84	Luke 6:20
Wood (Norwich)	Social & Economic Policies	23/1/85	1 Timothy 2:1-2
Wood (Norwich)	School Morning Assembly	7/2/85	Psalm 145:4
Montefiore (Birmingham)	Immigration Control	6/3/85	The Bible
Jenkins (Durham)	Training for New Technologies	25/3/85	The Bible
Sheppard (Liverpool)	Local Government Bill	15/4/85	1 Corinthians 12:12-26
Walker (Ely)	Marriage: Degrees of Relationship	9/12/85	The Bible
Montefiore (Birmingham)	Home Affairs	18/11/86	The Bible
Booth-Clibborn (Manchester)	Regional Imbalances in Prosperity	14/1/87	1 Corinthians 12:12-26
Graham (Newcastle)	Prayer Book	22/1/87	Proverbs 25:11
Sheppard (Liverpool)	Inner City Problems	2/2/87	1 Corinthans 12:12-26
Montefiore (Birmingham)	Prison Conditions	25/2/87	Matthew 25:32 & Rom. 13:4
Booth-Clibborn (Manchester)	Relations with US and Soviet Union	25/3/87	Ephesians 4:15
Booth-Clibborn (Manchester)	National Health Service	1/4/87	The Bible, 1 Corinthians 12:12-26
Yates (Gloucester)	Alcohol Abuse	25/11/87	The Prophets, Psalm 104:15
Waine (Chelmsford)	Pseudo-religious Cults	10/2/88	Philippians 4:8
Booth-Clibborn (Manchester)	Poverty in Africa	8/6/88	The Prophets, Teaching of Jesus
Runcie (Canterbury)	International Affairs	23/11/88	John 21:17
J.B. Taylor (St Albans)	Broadcasting in the 1990s	13/12/88	Luke 11:17-26
Booth-Clibborn (Manchester)	Crimes of Violence: Public Protection	15/3/89	Galatians 5:19-26
Lunn (Sheffield)	Schizophrenia After-Care Bill	12/4/89	Luke 10:30-37
Booth-Clibborn (Manchester)	The Press & the People	26/4/89	The Prophets, John 8:32
Yates (Gloucester)	The Family	29/11/89	The Bible
Baughen (Chester)	The Family	29/11/89	The Bible
Yates (Gloucester)	Rich & Poor in Society	14/3/90	The Bible
Goodrich (Worcester)	Environmental Protection	20/12/89	Genesis 1, Ecclesiastes 11:4
Runcie (Canterbury)	The Gulf	6/9/90	The Bible
Unpacked References			
Wood (Norwich)	Criminal Injuries Compensation Bill	3/7/79	Luke 10:30-37
Bowles (Derby)	International Development	12/3/80	Luke 10:30-37
Leonard (London)	Abortion (Amendment) Bill	6/12/82	The Gospels
Wood (Norwich)	Nuclear Weapons	30/1/84	Matthew 16:18
Say (Rochester)	Overseas Development	7/11/84	Matthew 25:32
Montefiore (Birmingham)	Hong Kong Bill	19/2/85	Philippians 3:20, Acts 22:28
Wood (Norwich)	Industry Year 1986	8/5/85	1 Timothy 6:10
Montefiore (Birmingham)	Animals (Scientific Procedures) Bill	28/11/85	Genesis 1:26
J.B. Taylor (St Albans)	Sunday Trading	8/2/89	10 Commandments, Genesis 1-2, Amos, Isaiah, The New Testament

past fortnight I may be thought to cut a figure rather like Ruth gleaning after a combine harvester; but it would seem to me to be a grave omission if this House did not have the opportunity to mark this anniversary with a short debate...[52]

Similarly, John Bickersteth (Bishop of Bath & Wells) made reference to John's Gospel in pressing for urgent action relating to the procedure for straw and stubble burning, but not to bring any serious biblical influence to bear on the debate: 'We do not have long before this season's conflagration. To alter one word of Scripture – that is, the numeral – "You have a saying, there are yet five months and then cometh the harvest".'[53]

The large majority of the bishops' explicit references to the Bible were 'brief references' in which a relevant piece of biblical teaching was brought to bear on the subject under discussion but where the reference was not explored or unpacked. The bishops made reference to the Bible in this manner on thirty-eight occasions. In May 1982 Baroness Ewart-Biggs moved a Motion '...to call attention to the difficulties encountered by those responsible for the upbringing and care of children at home, at school and at leisure.'[54] In his contribution to the ensuing debate Graham Leonard (Bishop of London) focused one of his points on the pressures created in a consumer society by the desire for 'immediate results, for getting things quickly and without cost'.[55] In making this point he made the words of Jesus (Matthew 4:4/Luke 4:4) his own:

> But man does not live by bread alone, and there are human needs that cannot be met by material things and which cannot be bought quickly and without cost. We do not see advertisements to enable us to acquire fidelity, integrity or honesty, partly because these qualities are not for sale but partly because they cannot be acquired in a moment and they need time to grow.[56]

Leonard moved directly from the words of Jesus to the application of their meaning without stopping (possibly due to the familiarity of the words and the assumption that their meaning is self-evident) to offer any explanation as to what Jesus was communicating to his audience.

Similarly, Hugh Montefiore (Bishop of Birmingham) brings an undeveloped biblical point of reference at the end of his input to a 1985 debate in response to a Commission for Racial Equality Report on immigration control:

> The scriptures say that there is much need to show consideration and kindness to the poor and to the deprived, and especially to

---

52 *ibid*, 29/10/85, vol. 467, col. 1454.

53 *ibid*, 14/2/84, vol. 448, col. 213.

54 *ibid*, 12/5/82, vol. 430, col. 251.

55 *ibid*, 12/5/82, vol. 430, col. 269.

56 *House of Lords Debates*, 12/5/82, vol. 430, col. 269.

the strangers within the gates. This is one of the reasons why the Church of England in General Synod has called the nationality law and the immigration rules in many ways unchristian.[57]

Stanley Booth-Clibborn (Bishop of Manchester) provided a brief biblical rooting for his comments on the role of truth in the media during a deliberative debate on the 1989 Annual Report of the Press Council entitled: 'The Press and the People'.

> Deep issues lie behind any discussion of the press. We are con-
> cerned with issues of truth and the way in which it is presented in
> our society. I need hardly say that in the religious tradition from
> which I come truth is fundamentally important. Much is said in the
> Bible about truth. It ranges from what was said by the prophets of
> old, and how on occasions it was costly for them to stand for what
> they saw as being truth, to the words of Jesus, who said: 'You shall
> know the truth and the truth will make you free.'[58]

References to the Bible such as those examples reported above would seem to constitute the minimum degree to which the Bible should impact any episcopal contribution to the Upper House. Such references assert the relevance of the Bible to public affairs and act as a reminder to all who deliberate and legislate in the House that, as the Parliamentary prayer also reminds them, it is Almighty God '...by whom alone Kings reign, and Princes decree justice; and from whom alone cometh all counsel, wisdom and understanding.'[59] It is surely remiss of a Church of England bishop to provide less than this kind of brief reference to the biblical teaching which is relevant to the subject at hand. It could equally be argued that, in an age in which an increasing majority of people have not been nurtured as children and adults in the teaching of Scripture, bishops can no longer assume that their audience at Westminster (and in the dio-cese too) share in their fundamental understanding of the Bible or their willingness to act in response to a brief, passing reference to its teaching. Margaret Thatcher's interpretation of the parable of the Good Samaritan, which many of the bishops found to be self-serving and overly individualistic, should alert all Christian contributors to public debate that operating with any kind of assumed understand-ing of the meaning of biblical texts on the part of one's audience is a risky business.

Of the bishops 768 verbal contributions to the House of Lords, nine (just over 1%) contained explicit references to the Bible which 'unpacked' the context and meaning of the biblical material men-

---

57   *ibid*, 6/3/85, vol. 460, col. 1420.
58   *ibid*, 26/4/89, vol. 506, col. 1285.
59   The Parliamentary Prayer (1661) reproduced in Rogers, *Parliament*, 12.

tioned. Among them were three of the episcopal contributions discussed above: the use of the story of the Good Samaritan by both Maurice Wood (Bishop of Norwich)[60] and Cyril Bowles (Bishop of Derby),[61] and the reference of David Say (Bishop of Rochester) to the parable of the Sheep and Goats.[62] On these occasions the episcopal contributor did more than simply state the biblical story or phrase to which they were referring, they also offered some explanation of its meaning. The same was true of Graham Leonard (Bishop of London) when he unpacked the teaching of 'the Christian Gospels' on freedom in his speech during the Second Reading of the 1982 Abortion (Amendment) Bill (1983):

> One aspect of human life is that a human being is a responsible person. I would say that the greatest gift which God gives to us is our freedom... I believe that this freedom is uniquely reflected in the Christian gospels. It is a fact that God chose to redeem us on the Cross in a way which leaves every one of us still free to choose; the Cross does not compel but only recognises our freedom – but if we respond, it then liberates us even further. I believe that when we come to an issue such as this, we have to consider society as a whole – because society can help or hinder the freedom which the individual possesses.[63]

Likewise, when Maurice Wood (Bishop of Norwich) referred to Matthew 16:18 in a debate on Nuclear Weapons during January 1984 he gave some brief exegesis of the verse he quoted:

> My second comment is particularly about the Motion of the noble Lord, Lord Jenkins of Putney, which refers to the termination of the human race... I believe that the Church has a responsibility not to be complacent but to proclaim the fact that when Our Lord said, 'the gates of hell shall not prevail against it', he was taking the long view and that the Church will be here when Our Lord comes again in power and great glory. I believe there is a strong theological hope in the fact that the human race will not be terminated, that Our Lord will come again and that it is the Christian Church's duty, whatever view about pacifism or not pacifism it takes, to lift the people's thoughts and minds to the hope of God's long-term plan for his world with the hints that one day there will be new heavens and a new earth where dwells righteousness.[64]

---

60 *House of Lords Debates*, 3/7/79, vol. 401, col. 257.
61 *ibid*, 12/3/80, vol. 406, col. 1116.
62 *ibid*, 7/11/84, vol. 457, col. 50.
63 *ibid*, 6/12/82, vol. 437, col. 72-73.
64 *ibid*, 30/1/84, vol. 447, col. 532.

The fullest use of Scripture in an episcopal contribution to the
House of Lords during the Thatcher years came from John B. Taylor
(Bishop of St Albans).[65] Taylor spent well over half of his speech on
Sunday Trading (delivered during February 1989) offering a biblical
background to the issue, referring to and unpacking the content of
various parts of Scripture. He began with the fourth of the commandments given to Moses by God on Mount Sinai (Exodus 20:8-11):

> [T]he Hebrew people who adopted the Sabbath principle saw in
> it much more than a social institution. To them it was a gift from
> God for all mankind. So in the earliest historical reference to the
> Sabbath day, which must date back to Moses in the 13th century
> before Christ, the Ten Commandments are insistent in saying that
> keeping the seventh day holy to God is as important as honouring
> parents and not committing murder or adultery. They are regula-
> tions given by God to a people who had been freed from slavery so
> that they could live well in the land to which they were going.[66]

Taylor then looked at God's day of rest on the seventh day of creation (Genesis 1-2) before quoting oracles given by the prophets Amos
and Isaiah:

> [A]lthough the day of rest was God's gift to His people, it none-
> theless needed to be protected and enforced. Human nature being
> what it is, people would always be tempted to reject the gift and
> so deprive themselves and others of its benefits... That theme was
> taken up by the prophets, who fulminated against those who
> wanted to trade on the Sabbath. Listen to Amos: 'Woe to those who
> say, "When will the new moon be over that we may sell grain? And
> the Sabbath, that we may offer wheat for sale?"' What he was say-
> ing, in effect seven centuries before Christ was that when the profit
> motive or commercial values encroached upon this protected area
> the gift was destroyed, the benefits lost and the soul of the nation
> was in jeopardy. It was that serious. Or less negatively, in prophecy
> of Isaiah there is this: 'If you turn back your foot from the Sabbath,
> from pursuing your business on my Holy day, and call the Sabbath
> a delight and the Holy day of the Lord honourable... then you shall
> take delight in the Lord and I shall make you ride upon the heights
> of the earth'.[67]

The final stage of Taylor's theological excursus provided some
context for what the New Testament appears to say (albeit silently)
about the Sabbath:

> There is no point in denying the fact that nowhere in the New Tes-

---

65 Taylor's extensive use of Old Testament material fits with his background
    as an Old Testament scholar.

66 *ibid*, 8/2/89, vol. 503, col. 1571-1572.

67 *ibid*, 8/2/89, vol. 503, col. 1572.

tament is working on a Sunday or a day of rest condemned. That is partly because the Sabbath still remained a protected day in places where Jews were numerically strong and partly because the transition from the seventh day to the first day of the week was only just beginning and was strictly reserved for worship and to celebrate the resurrection.[68]

In analysing the bishops' explicit use of the Bible it was interesting to note that on a number of occasions they made reference to the Bible at the end of their speech. This was the case in 14 (27%) of the 51 Scripture-referencing speeches. A number of the bishops' references to the Bible began with phrases such as: 'In conclusion...',[69] 'May I end by saying...',[70] and 'Finally...'.[71] In contrast only three speeches began with a reference to the Bible. This may be due to a tendency among the bishop to see the role of Scripture within his speech as being to provide, to use Robert Runcie's words, '...some wider religious justification for his words.'[72] Such an approach begins with comments made on the specific issue under discussion and then offers a biblical legitimation for those comments. The alternative approach, to start with the biblical perspective and work outwards towards contextualized comments relating to the specific issue under scrutiny, arguably communicates a greater confidence in the message of the Bible. It was favoured by Hugh Montefiore (Bishop of Birmingham) for his speech at the Second Reading of the Hong Kong Bill which he began thus:

> My Lords, St. Paul wrote to Christians in the Roman colony of Philippi, 'Our citizenship is in heaven'. But if their spirit was in the heavens, their bodies were very much on earth – and the same holds good for the inhabitants of the British colony of Hong Kong. Earthly citizenship means that we belong to a country; we have inalienable rights. It is a matter of identity, and it affects our self-esteem, our rights, our inmost being.
>
> At Philippi, Paul, after he had been beaten up by the authorities, took pleasure in informing them that he was a Roman citizen. 'I am a citizen of no mean city', he said when he was arrested. The chief captain said, 'I bought my citizenship with a great sum of money'; but Paul said, 'I am a Roman born'. Because he was a Roman citizen he was able to appeal to Caesar. But, as I understand it, the new class of British citizen whom it is proposed to inaugurate will not have an equivalent privilege.

---

68   *ibid*, 8/2/89, vol. 503, col. 1573.
69   *ibid*, 12/3/80, vol. 406, col. 1116.
70   *ibid*, 16/1/82, vol. 431, col. 660.
71   *ibid*, 6/9/90, vol. 521, col. 1810.
72   *ibid*.

St. Paul put great value on his earthly citizenship, and, indeed, citizenship is very important to us all. It is for this reason that I should like to draw attention to some of the provisions of the Bill.[73]

By referring to the Bible at the end of their speeches it would seem that the bishops were seeking to add moral authority to their comments and, in so doing, to challenge their listeners to respond actively, rather than passively, to the points made. This was clearly the intended purpose of the final remarks of a speech by David Say (Bishop of Rochester) on overseas development policy during the Debate on the Address at the opening of the 1984/85 Parliament (to which we referred above). Having discussed the parable of the Sheep and Goats he concluded his speech thus:

> If we have not fed the hungry we have turned our back on the Lord who told the parable in order to challenge the hearts and minds of his hearers. We all know in our hearts that we must not acquiesce in world hunger and world poverty, but we need a bold, imaginative and consistent lead if words are to give place to action. Dare we hope that a Government who say that they will work continuously for a greater atmosphere of trust between East and West, that they are committed to playing a constructive role at the United Nations, to maintaining a substantial aid programme and to contributing to arms control and disarmament, will surprise the world and delight the members of all parties and of none by giving issues of world hunger and world poverty a higher priority than ever before?[74]

David Lunn (Bishop of Sheffield) used the parable of the Good Samaritan to the same effect at the end of his contribution to the second reading of a Private Members' Schizophrenia After-Care Bill (also quoted above):

> We cannot help everyone, but this Bill could help some. I hope it may be able to do so. Like the noble Earl, Lord Longford, I dare to refer to Scripture. The piece of Scripture I wish to refer to is curiously politically controversial. It concerns the parable of the Good Samaritan. I see the schizophrenic as the person who has indeed fallen among thieves and who is in the most desperate need of help. I hope we are not among those who pass by on the other side.[75]

8.4 The Bishops' Implicit Use of the Bible

The Lords Spiritual made 108 implicit references to the Bible during

---

73 *ibid*, 19/2/85, vol. 460, col. 493-494.
74 *ibid*, 7/11/84, vol. 457, col. 50-51.
75 *ibid*, 12/4/89, vol. 506, col. 334.

the course of 77 speeches in the House of Lords. On many occasions two or more implicit references were made in the same episcopal speech. Thirty-one of the fifty-one individual bishops who spoke in the House of Lords during the Thatcher years made speeches which contained one or more implicit reference to the Bible (Figure 8.6).

A number of those bishops who failed to refer to the Bible explicitly during the Thatcher years did make such implicit references. For example, Ronald Bowlby made implicit reference to the Bible during six of the contributions he made to the House whilst Bishop of Southwark. Likewise, John Habgood made reference to biblically-based theological concepts in one of his speeches whilst Bishop of Durham and in three of the speeches he made as Archbishop of York. The six bishops who made the greatest number of speeches which made implicit reference to the Bible were: Robert Runcie (whilst Archbishop of Canterbury), Maurice Wood (Bishop of Norwich), Ronald Bowlby (whilst Bishop of Southwark), Stanley Booth-Clibborn (Bishop of Manchester), Graham Leonard (whilst Bishop of Truro and London), and Hugh Montefiore (Bishop of Birmingham). Of these bishops only Bowlby and Leonard were not also amongst the six bishops who made most explicit references to the Bible. Of the fifty-one individual bishops who made verbal contributions to the House during the 1980s,[76] fifteen made no reference to the teaching of the Bible, either explicitly or implicitly.[77] For most of these the

---

76 Those individual bishops who did not make a verbal contribution to the House during the Thatcher years were: Donald Coggan (Archbishop of Canterbury), Barry Rogerson (Bishop of Bristol), Geoffrey Thompson (Bishop of Exeter), Timothy Bavin (Bishop of Portsmouth), Stuart Blanch (Archbishop of York), and Hubert Whitsey (Bishop of Chester).

77 Those individual bishops who made no reference to the Bible whatsoever in their speeches to the House of Lords during the 1980s were:
   – Ernest Tinsley (Bishop of Bristol), who spoke once in the Lords during the Thatcher years.
   – John Gibbs (Bishop of Coventry), who spoke four times in the Lords during the Thatcher years.
   – Michael Adie (Bishop of Guildford), who spoke seven times in the Lords during the Thatcher years.
   – Kenneth Skelton (Bishop of Lichfield), who spoke once in the Lords during the Thatcher years. - Keith Sutton (Bishop of Lichfield), who spoke twice in the Lords during the Thatcher years.
   – Douglas Feaver (Bishop of Peterborough), who spoke ten times in the Lords during the Thatcher years.
   – William Westwood (Bishop of Peterborough), who spoke three times in the Lords during the Thatcher years.
   – Archibald Gordon (Bishop of Portsmouth), who spoke once in the Lords

limited number of occasions on which they spoke to the House during Thatcher's premiership explains this lack of biblical references. For others, however, the lack of references to the Bible is more surprising because they made a good number of speeches to the House during our period of study.

Those bishops who did refer implicitly to the Bible during their contributions to the House of Lords referred to more than thirty different biblically-based theological concepts (Table 8.3). They applied biblical concepts such as the fundamental value of humans, the fatherhood of God, and human responsibility to the subject of their speeches a number of times, in addition to other concepts such as compassion, judgement and forgiveness which were mentioned only once. Often a bishop would touch on a number of these theological concepts together. Michael Baughen (Bishop of Chester) referred to a whole range of theological beliefs which have proved significant in the development of the United Kingdom during a debate entitled 'Prisons and Alternatives to Custody':

> This country is founded on Christian principles, with a belief in justice, yet also of mercy; a belief in mankind's bias to evil yet also mankind's enormous potential for good; a belief in the essential value of every human being. But how far do we apply those principles? ...It was Winston Churchill who once remarked that the standards of society can be judged by the standards of its prisons.[78]

Justice was the concept most often used, being referred to on ten occasions. It was touched upon by Maurice Wood (Bishop of Norwich) during a deliberative debate on the Probation Service, commenting: 'I believe that there is a sense in which, in Christian justice,

---

    during the Thatcher years.
- John Baker (Bishop of Salisbury), who spoke three times in the Lords during the Thatcher years.
- Mervyn Stockwood (Bishop of Southwark), who spoke six times in the Lords during the Thatcher years.
- Peter Mumford (Bishop of Truro), who spoke four times in the Lords during the Thatcher years.
- Robert Schurhoff (Bishop of Blackburn), who spoke twice in the Lords during the Thatcher years.
- David Cross (Bishop of Blackburn), who spoke twice in the Lords during the Thatcher years.
- Ross Hook (Bishop of Bradford), who spoke twice in the Lords during the Thatcher years.
- Robert Williamson (Bishop of Bradford), who spoke twice in the Lords during the Thatcher years.

78   *ibid*, 30/11/88, vol. 502, col. 327.

someone who has done something wrong has a just sense of knowing that he deserves punishment.'[79] John Waine (Bishop of Chelmsford), contributing to another debate regarding prison care, sought to place justice in the context of mercy: 'This debate is about a particular prison [Wandsworth]. I therefore wish to observe, only very briefly, that Christian principles require us to hold together a belief in justice and values with a belief in mercy, because God is merciful and we all need his mercy.'[80]

The fatherhood of God and man's creation in the image of God was another theological concept referred to repeatedly by the bishops. Robert Runcie (whilst Archbishop of Canterbury) emphasised God's fatherhood of all people during his contribution to a debate considering the Falkland Islands on 20th May 1982:

> A member of that much maligned species, a BBC correspondent, said the other day that the Christian message behind all this is that politicians, journalists, soldiers and relatives everywhere are level under the fatherhood of God. None should yield to the temptation to regard the other as sub-human or themselves as superhuman.[81]

During his contribution to the Second Reading of the Government's Social Security Bill (1986) Ronald Bowlby (Bishop of Southwark) referred to three connected but nonetheless distinct theological concepts:

> [E]very person is made in the image of God, and so all should be respected and valued. In that sense we are all interdependent and have a shared responsibility for one another, which includes meeting the genuine spiritual, mental and physical needs of those who are poor or handicapped.[82]

The same biblically based belief in the fundamental value and worth of every individual human being led Robert Runcie to support the bottom up approach to the provision of social care:

> Our voluntary sector has never been larger or more flourishing. The phrase which has been used – build from the bottom up – is in danger of becoming a cliché, but that is because of repetition, not because it is wrong. For me, such an approach reflects a profoundly Christian understanding about the infinite value and dignity of each individual human being, whatever their outward circumstances.[83]

---

79   *ibid*, 30/6/83, vol. 443, col. 410.
80   *ibid*, 14/11/89, vol. 512, col. 1286-1287.
81   *ibid*, 20/5/82, vol. 430, col. 815.
82   *ibid*, 2/6/86, vol. 475, col. 614.
83   *ibid*, 2/2/87, vol. 484, col. 38.

Figure 8.6
Number of Implicit References to the Bible by Individual Bishops

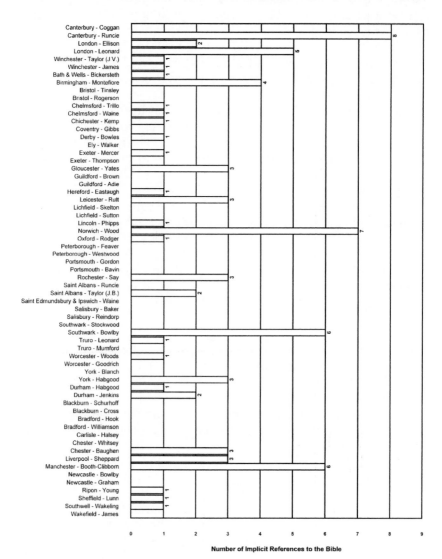

Number of Implicit References to the Bible

References to vision and hope were twice used to charge the House with the need to assume a positive attitude towards difficult matters. John Trillo (Bishop of Chelmsford) emphasised the need for vision during the Second Reading of the Government's Northern Ireland Bill (1982), which laid out a framework for devolution:

I recognise also that these proposals, even if fully implemented, will not of themselves deal with the pressing and tragic matters of unemployment and violence which loom so large in the Province, or dispel overnight the deep-rooted suspicions which are a feature of the religious and communal life of the Province. These are but first steps on the road that we are taking, in the realistic recognition that there are no instant solutions to such intractable and long-term problems.

Realism is necessary in everything to do with politics – but so also is vision. The American theologian Reinhold Niebuhr, himself a strenuous critic of all forms of unrealism, in religion or politics, spoke of the 'the relevance of an impossible ethical ideal'. Without such an ideal, without a vision, our politics becomes simply a matter of keeping out of trouble; of standing pat. In the setting of Northern Ireland, our ideal, the goal for all of us, must be the gradual development of self-governing institutions which have the support of the whole community there.[84]

An emphasis on hope was also part of Archbishop Runcie's speech with which he opened a debate he tabled to '...call attention to the 40th anniversary of the United Nations and the need to increase the effectiveness of the organisation'. 'Defeatism about the United Nations,' he asserted, 'as in other matters, ensures defeat. The theological virtue of hope, as in other matters, shapes the future.'[85]

David Sheppard (Bishop of Liverpool) reminded the House of humanity's need to exercise their God-given stewardship over creation responsibly and with an awareness of the interdependence of all people during his speech to a debate starkly entitled 'Third World Starvation', during March 1985:

As I have read about third world famine, an unwelcome phrase has kept coming to mind. Five years of drought, the never-ending queues in the relief camps – it all seems beyond human control. But disaster is not inevitable. If we start talking about acts of God, we need to ask rather more about how God has made the world. He has put the responsibility into our hands. He teaches us that we are members one of another in his world.[86]

Contrary to what some might expect, reference to 'sin' was by no means absent from the episcopal contributions to the House. One such reference was made by Stanley Booth-Clibborn (Bishop of Manchester) to bring a biblical perspective to bear on a discussion about drug trafficking:

[W]arning lights always flash in my mind when I hear made in the debate a reference to drug traffickers as 'thoroughly evil'. This

---

84   *ibid*, 8/7/82, vol. 432, col. 915-916.
85   *ibid*, 29/10/85, vol. 467, col. 1458.
86   *ibid*, 27/3/85, vol. 461, col. 1085.

raises problems for those of us brought up in the Christian tradition, because we are taught to distinguish between the sin and the sinner. While it is legitimate to refer in the strongest possible terms to the actual evil of trafficking in drugs, when one speaks about the men involved it becomes more complex, because within the Christian tradition good and evil are mixed up in individuals in ways in which it is quite inappropriate to refer to people as 'wholly evil' in that way... the point is that we must combat the sin and the evil in society and at the same time retain a sense of compassion and attempt to understand those who fall into these great evils and very sinful actions.[87]

Table 8.3

Episcopal References to Biblically-Based Theological Concepts

Theological Concept	Number of Episcopal References
Justice	10
Fatherhood of God	9
Fundamental dignity & value of individuals	9
Personal responsibility	7
Sin	6
God as Creator	5
Love	5
Peace & Reconciliation	4
Freedom	4
Family	4
Human potential and ability	4
Human stewardship of creation	4
Human interdependence	4
The Incarnation	4
Evil of aggression & violence	3
A day of rest	3
Vision & Hope	2
Truth	2
Marriage	2
Dignity of work	2
Community	2
Sanctity of life	2
Forgiveness	1
The Cross	1
Judgement	1
Charity	1
Compassion	1
Worship	1
Redemption	1
Prayer	1
Chastity	1
Kingdom of Heaven	1
Mercy	1

The Incarnation was twice used to support the contention that human life should be ascribed fundamental value. Graham Leonard (Bishop of London) stated it thus during his contribution to the Second Reading of a Private Members' Abortion (Amendment) Bill (1982): 'As a Christian, I am committed to the sanctity of human life. By the incarnation and by the fact that God took our human nature

---

87   *ibid*, 12/11/85, vol. 468, col. 205.

upon him, human life was given an eternal blessing.'[88] The Incarnation was also referred to by David Sheppard (Bishop of Liverpool) in order to bring an astute theological perspective to an issue to which, some might assume, biblical teaching has little to contribute. The occasion was as part of comments made 'as a Christian to Christians' during a speech at the Second Reading stage of the Government's Broadcasting Bill (1990), regarding possible changes in the viewing habits of Christians which might result from the launch of Christian cable television channels:

> Much of the debate has centred around the question of broadcasting or narrowcasting. It will be possible for those who own cable stations to use their religious networks to encourage their friends to watch their channel. That is fine, but I should be sorry if a significant part of the Christian body turned away as a regular practice from mainline channels which are part of the united life of our nation. That would follow the philosophy which sees the Church as a fortress of light, calling individuals to separate themselves from the darkness of the world around. In contrast, I believe that the Incarnation, by which I believe God in the person of Jesus Christ entered into the thick of life, calls us in the direction of broadcasting not narrowcasting.[89]

David Sheppard (Bishop of Liverpool) demonstrated the ability to apply biblical teaching meaningfully to important issues during his speech at the Second Reading of the Government's Football Spectator's Bill (1989), brought before Parliament to 'deal with the problem of hooliganism associated with football, in this country and abroad, in so far as it involves English and Welsh people.'[90]

> As I reflected on this Bill I asked myself whether there was such a thing as a theology of football. I do not mean the kind of theology which asks whether God cares if England has a goal-scoring striker, or even a successful pair of opening batsmen, important though such questions may be to some of us. My question goes a little deeper and is, I think, more serious... Many people feel very alone. In other centuries or cultures the large extended family, the tribe or village had and has its celebrations and excitements. Many people have little sense of belonging, of counting, or of identity. I do not wish to exaggerate, but following a football team gives one many of those experiences: it is something to be proud of; it is a

---

88   *ibid*, 6/12/82, vol. 437, col. 72. Norwich Wood (Bishop of Norwich) reference to the incarnation made the precisely the same point: '...man's divine value was derived from the incarnation of Christ which had given worth to all human life.' *ibid*, 20/6/84, vol. 453, col. 352-353.

89   *ibid*, 5/6/90, vol. 519, col. 1320.

90   *ibid*, 2/2/89, vol. 503, col. 1217.

success that is yours to share in. Indeed, sometimes laps of honour and bringing the cup home have the feel of a liturgy of resurrection. All that is worth having and perhaps more significant than we sometimes think.[91]

Overall, it is noticeable that in the bishops' explicit and implicit references to the Bible there were just two references to eschatological hope, both of which were made by Maurice Wood (Bishop of Norwich).[92] When mention of the Kingdom of Heaven was made in the speech of David Lunn (Bishop of Sheffield) it focused on 'the vision of the Kingdom of Heaven on earth' and made no reference to the future aspect of its inauguration.[93] Likewise, references to the theological concepts of vision and hope in the speeches of John Trillo (Bishop of Chelmsford) and Archbishop Runcie drew no attention to the eternal perspective. Attention was given in the bishops' speeches to the Incarnation of Christ and to his moral teaching. Only once, however, was reference made to the salvific work of Christ on the Cross. It is noteworthy that this reference, by Graham Leonard (Bishop of London), emphasised not the saving work of the Cross but the freedom which God gives us to choose how we respond to it.[94]

8.5 Conclusion

The Church of England's biblical 'centre of gravity'[95] was not always in evidence during the bishops' outings to Westminster. Indeed, a detailed consideration of the use of the Bible by the bishops in the House of Lords during the 1980s does not reveal an episcopate entirely convinced of the relevance of the Bible to the public life of an increasingly un-churched and secular nation. Biblical material was explicitly referred to in only 7% of episcopal contributions to the House, and just 1% of the bishops' speeches offered a thorough examination of biblical material. During the 1985/86 Parliamentary session only two of the 99 episcopal contributions to the Upper House made reference to Scripture. Less than half of the 51 bishops who spoke in the House during the Thatcher years made any reference to the Bible, and only six bishops referred to the Bible more than twice during the Thatcher years. The bishops implicit references to biblical teaching were more commonplace. It was still the case, however, that only 10% of the episcopal contributions to the House of

91 *ibid*, 2/2/89, vol. 503, col. 1233-1234.
92 *ibid*, 30/1/84, vol. 447, col. 532 and 16/2/83, vol. 439, col. 287.
93 *ibid*, 4/4/90, vol. 517, col. 1417.
94 *ibid*, 6/12/82, vol. 437, col. 72-73.
95 Avis, *Understanding*, 36.

Lords contained an implicit reference to the Bible. This record raises the question of what, if anything, the Lords Spiritual contributed to House of Lords debates which could not have been delivered with greater authority and insight by the Lords Temporal? The answer to this will, for many, determine whether they consider the continued presence of the bishops in the House of Lords to be a worthwhile use of the time and energies of the Church of England's human resources. For others the answer to this question will determine whether they consider the continued episcopal membership of the House to be an unfortunate fact of history which no-one has had the time or inclination to undo or a unique opportunity which sees the socio-political issues which are at the heart of British life considered in the light of the truth and wisdom of the Christian tradition.

Archbishop Robert Runcie, contributed to a debate concerned with the growing tensions in the Gulf during June 1990, commenting that '...the Christian churchman who contributes to a debate of this grave character may be expected to give, albeit briefly, some wider religious justification for his words.'[96] We might agree with him that, at the very least, a brief religious justification is to be expected from churchman contributing in socio-political debates of significance. We should, however, add a short rider to his comments to note that almost every debate which takes place in Parliament is, in relation to the lives of some of the nation's individuals and communities, grave in character. Social, economic, health and overseas development policies which are unjust or oppress the voiceless have every bit as much potential for the destruction of lives as does British military involvement in international violent conflicts.

Some might seek to argue that during the period under consideration there was evident in the speeches of the bishops a lack of confidence that the Bible contains anything of relevance to the complex issues under consideration in the debates of the House. For example, David Lunn (Bishop of Sheffield) introduced his only reference to the Bible in a House of Lords debate with the defensive words 'I *dare to* refer to scripture' [italics mine].[97] Similarly, Stanley Booth-Clibborn (Bishop of Manchester) appeared to lack confidence because he was uncertain that his biblical reference was of any value in the well-informed to and fro of a House of Lords debate. 'My last word,' he states, 'comes from a manual of *perhaps* a personal and even a national instruction over 2,000 years ago' [italics mine].[98] It

---

96 *House of Lords Debates*, 6/9/90, vol. 521, col. 1810.

97 *ibid*, 12/4/89, vol. 506, col. 334.

98 *ibid*, 14/1/87, vol. 483, col. 564.

may be argued that what we have here are turns of phrase, examples of the traditional English understatement or a clergyman's reserve. Whether that is the case nor not, such comments potentially communicate a lack of confidence in the public relevance of the Bible to the House.

The House of Lords is not, of course, the Lambeth Conference, the General Synod, or a service of worship in an Anglican Cathedral. It is almost a truism to state that to speak in exclusively biblical terms when seeking to bring an influential Christian perspective to bear in any kind of socio-political debate in a largely secular context is of limited worth. Speaking in secular language and with reference to the respected secular wisdom available was not, however, something the episcopal contributors to the House of Lords struggled to do. Our analysis of the content of the speeches of the bishops (Chapter 7 above) revealed an episcopate at home drawing upon academic and professional advice, facts and statistics, and the experiences of those in their parishes. Whereas the bishops made speeches which made use of theological arguments on 77 occasions, they referred to facts and statistics to support their points on 197 occasions, and academic and professional advice on 149 occasions (Figure 7.7). It is entirely appropriate that the larger part of any contribution to the House of Lords should be focused upon all the practical and detailed concerns which are its business. Nonetheless, in assessing the contribution of the bishops to the House of Lords, we must conclude that their failure to refer explicitly or implicitly to the Bible in the vast majority of their speeches suggests that the strength of Anglicanism's biblical centre of gravity does not extend to this aspect of the Church of England's witness in the socio-political realm. Moreover, we must conclude that their speech-making may have unintentionally contributed to the secularization of public life. Considering the contribution of the bishops to the House of Lords in the light of the thoughts of Oliver O'Donovan quoted above we observe that, in seeking to offer moral direction to the nation's Parliamentarians, the bishops who sat in the House of Lords during the Thatcher years commended their case by argument and persuasion but not, for the most part, by the exposition of Scripture.[99]

---

99   O'Donovan, *Resurrection*, 171.

CHAPTER NINE

Conclusion

9.1 Introduction

Our consideration of the contribution of the Church of England bishops to the House of Lords during the Thatcher years has yielded a considerable amount of empirical data relating to the bishops' attendance, voting and speech-making. In seeking to analyse and interpret this data we have drawn a number of conclusions. Considered together these conclusions paint the picture of a Bench of Bishops whose contribution can be characterized as critical, insignificant, inefficient and indistinct. We will explore each of these characteristics below, giving particular attention to their relevance in the event of any attempt being made to evolve the Church of England's approach to episcopal involvement at the Palace of Westminster. Before we do this, however, we must reflect critically on the methodology employed by this research project.

9.2 Methodological Critique

9.2.1 General Comments

Overall, this exploration of the contribution of the Lords Spiritual during the 1980s was well served by the methodological approach employed. Each of the four main purposes of the analysis outlined in Section 1.1 above were fulfilled through engagement with primary and secondary documentary evidence and interviews with bishops who served as Lords Spiritual during the 1980s.

When studying elites George Moyser and Margaret Wagstaffe advocate the observation of subjects *in situ* and extended contacts with subjects.[1] One drawback of studying the contribution of the bishops during the Thatcher years was that it was not possible for any participant observation to take place. There would be much to gain from future research projects in this area which analyses, over a period of years, the contribution of a small number of bishops to the

---

1   Moyser & Wagstaffe, 'Studying Elites: Theoretical and Methodological Issues', in Moyser & Wagstaffe (eds.), *Research Methods for Elite Studies*, 19.

House of Lords more closely. Such research would benefit greatly from regular access to the bishops under scrutiny (through regular interviews and more informal correspondence relating to more specific matters which arise) and regular attendance at the House of Lords to hear debates to which episcopal contributions are made.

9.2.2 Primary and Secondary Sources

House of Lords *Hansard*, House of Lords *Sessional Statistics*, and the House of Commons *Weekly Information Bulletin* provided data on the bishops attendance, voting, and speech-making which, when analysed using database software, produced a comprehensive body of empirical data on the contribution of the bishops to the House of Lords during the Thatcher years. Engagement with a generous quantity of published material enabled our subject to be considered within its political and ecclesiastical context, and in the light of the process of reform of the Second Chamber which began in January 1999. A far lesser quantity of published material focused directly on the subject of the contribution of the bishops to the House of Lords during the 1980s. This literature did, however, prove valuable in the process of analysing and interpreting the empirical data.

9.2.3 Episcopal Interviews

Gathering oral evidence through conducting interviews with four bishops with experience of serving at the House of Lords during the period under consideration was worthwhile. It added the colour and insights of experience to the thesis. Of particular worth was the information it generated on the practical working of the House of Lords and the role of the Lord Spiritual. It also highlighted the practical obstacles which confront bishops who attempt to take their role in the House seriously. Full transcripts of the interviews conducted with Michael Baughen, Hugh Montefiore, David Say and John B. Taylor have been included as appendices two to five of this thesis.

The interviewing approach adopted did achieve its aims (outlined in Section 1.2 above). The danger of purely anecdotal and irrelevant material using up precious interviewing time, which Medhurst and Moyser suggest is a potential danger when using open-ended questions, was largely avoided.[2] The exception to this was the first interview, conducted with Michael Baughen, in which the subject of the shipbuilder Cammell Lairds received a little too much attention. It is noteworthy that this was the interview which was arranged at such

---

2   Medhurst & Moyser, 'Studying', in Moyser & Wagstaffe (eds.), *Methods*, 94.

short notice that interview questions could not be sent in advance of the interview date.

Consideration was given to writing an individual chapter, entitled 'Episcopal Reflections', comparing and contrasting the responses given by the four bishops interviewed. The decision was taken not to write such a chapter for two main reasons. Firstly, and least significantly, out of a concern not to give the subject of the thesis too influential a voice in the formulation of the conclusions of the thesis. To have committed a whole chapter to the reflections of the bishops may have given too much attention to the views of individuals whose particular experience, whilst giving them tremendous insight, also makes it likely that they will hold a fairly strong and well-thought through view of the issues under discussion. Secondly, a chapter considering the interview data produced was not written because the sample of four bishops was considered too small for comparisons and contrasts of real significance to be generated. Unfortunately attempts, begun in January 2000, to arrange an interview with Rt Rev Robert Runcie were unsuccessful due to his illness and subsequent death in July 2000. An attempt was also made to organize an interview with Lord Sheppard of Liverpool but, though a date was set for a meeting, it did not work out. Had these two interviews been possible, perhaps in addition to interviews with one or two other bishops who served on the Bench of Bishops during the 1980s, then a useful chapter could have been written.

A little time, however, should be given here to remark on the major areas of similarity and disparity between the responses elicited from the four bishops who were interviewed. It will be noted below (Section 9.3.2) that each of the interviewees emphasised the extent to which the workload and responsibilities resultant from being a diocesan bishop posed genuine obstacles to them making a considerable and consistent contribution to the House of Lords. David Say's pithy remark (also quoted below) captured the perspective of each of those interviewed: 'I always used to say that if 12 months ahead you said you would go to St Agatha's in the Mud, then to St Agatha's in the Mud you must go.'[3] Each of the bishops, except Baughen (in whose interview the matter was not discussed), also emphasised the importance of being present in the Lords as individual Lords of Parliament, not as corporate spokesmen for the Church of England.

On other matters the bishops presented differing perspectives. Michael Baughen took a more positive view of the level of influence bishops are able to wield in the House – though he noted repeat-

---

3   David Say (Bishop of Rochester) in an interview with the author, 29th May 2002, Appendix 4.

edly that he only had limited experience of Margaret Thatcher's premiership. He described specific occasions where both on and off the floor of the House he was able to make an influential contribution to public affairs, describing the episcopal influence as 'very, very wide underneath'.[4] The other bishops were less positive in their tone and failed to given precise examples of influence. They did, however, clearly share Baughen's belief that there is an important and worthwhile role for the Lords Spiritual in the House of Lords. Both Michael Baughen and David Say noted the potential and the importance of behind the scenes, informal influence available to the Lords Spiritual. In contrast Hugh Montefiore and John B. Taylor made it clear that '[t]here wasn't time for it'.[5] Hugh Montefiore was the only bishop who indicated a distaste for the whole idea of bishops lobbying and influencing affairs informally at Westminster, commenting thus: 'I am not at all sure I would have wanted to lobby very much really. I might ask people to be present but they've got to be persuaded by what I say in the House.'[6]

9.3 Findings

9.3.1 A Critical Contribution

[I]f we attend to the example of Jesus, his solace and encouragement was for the most part given to the weak and poor and marginalized. The powerful and the decision-makers tended to find him a disturbing and a disconcerting presence. Theology's public statements should probably reflect the same qualities.[7]

The Bench of Bishops was overwhelmingly critical of the Thatcher Government over the course of the 1980s. Overall the bishops' voting was clearly intended to register opinions rather than alter outcomes. Nonetheless, the bishops voted against the Government twice as many times as they voted in their support and, in divisions which resulted in a Government defeat, were ten times as likely to vote with those seeking to bring about a Government defeat as with the Government. Whilst nearly half of the bishops' speeches to the House of Lords were neither supportive nor unsupportive of

---

4   Michael Baughen (Bishop of Chester) in an interview with the author, 21st May 2002, Appendix 2.
5   John B. Taylor (Bishop of St Albans) in an interview with the author, 29th July 2002, Appendix 5.
6   Hugh Montefiore (Bishop of Birmingham) in an interview with the author, 21st May 2002, Appendix 3.
7   Forrester, *Beliefs*, 62-63.

the Government, in those speeches which did take a definite position in relation to Government policy there was an average of seven speeches which were critical of the Government for every two which offered the Government support. Moreover, as the Thatcher years progressed the content of an increasing number of bishops' speeches was critical of the Government.

9.3.2 *An Insignificant Contribution*

You see the worst thing that happened was, we'd have a bishops meeting at Lambeth which would end at lunchtime and quite a lot of the chaps would come into the Lords in the afternoon... and they would be discussing salmon fishing. The next day, the very next day, all the bishops have gone back for their jobs and there would be an absolute cracker debate on some social service and there would be just the duty bishop there. 'Whoa, you were all here for salmon fishing, why weren't you here today?'[8]

The episcopal contribution to the House of Lords was neither sufficiently considerable nor consistent to wield significant influence in the public realm during the Thatcher years. The bishops did not play a sufficient enough role in the life of the House for them to be able to argue convincingly (if they wished to) against those who would assert, with Lord Orr-Ewing, that they are 'visitors rather than contributors'.[9] Only one in four of the divisions of the House saw a bishop entering the division lobby. The bishops made speeches in the House of Lords on just 20% of its sitting days and failed to speak consistently during debates on those subjects of which they were publicly critical of the Government.

In view of the real obstacles that the bishops face in playing a full part in the House of Lords, this was an admirable record. The bishops are, first and foremost, Anglican pastoral-managers with a full load of ecclesiastical responsibilities with which to contend. The procedures of the House (not least the emphasis on evening sittings)[10] militate against fitting attendance and speaking at the House into a busy diary. The reflections of Michael Baughen, Hugh Montefiore,

---

8   David Say (Bishop of Rochester) in an interview with the author, 29th May 2002, Appendix 4.

9   Lord Orr-Ewing goes on to comment: 'If you were to ask me whether the work and the decisions of the House would be significantly different if they were not here, I would have to say, "No".' Lord Orr-Ewing as cited by Bown, 'Influencing', 106.

10 Just 24% of the bishops' speeches were made during the five hours of the evening period as opposed to 70% during the two and a half hours of the afternoon period.

David Say and John B. Taylor each emphasise the hindering effect of these obstacles:

> [Y]ou see the trouble is everything is last minute, you don't know what's coming up for next week. People used to say, 'so how disgraceful that only five of the bishops were there to vote', but what do you think I'm going to do? I've got a year's diary ahead of me already booked for the next year as it were. I was at this church this night, do I say to them when I've been booked for a year to go to their 150th anniversary that 'sorry, I've got to go down and vote at the House'?[11]

> I was in Birmingham, you know it took two and a half hours by the time you left home to get into the House and it was very difficult to attend the House at all because my diary was made up one year ahead and the business with the House is made up one month ahead and you can't just cancel things simply, 'Oh, I'm terribly sorry I can't, I'm in the House of Lords... And so finding time to lobby that was out of the question really.[12]

> I always used to say that if 12 months ahead you said you would go to St Agatha's in the Mud, then to St Agatha's in the Mud you must go.[13]

> [Y]ou tried every excuse to get off a bit early because you'd got to get back for something or another or if you knew very well there were a pile of problems waiting on your desk needing to be dealt with.[14]

An admirable record is not, however, the same as a significant record. At present the bishops are required to work around these obstacles. If the bishops are to serve both Church and Nation in Parliament effectively, more needs to be done to remove these obstacles so that there is no longer a ceiling on the extent to which the bishops can contribute to the House of Lords. The House of Lords represents a genuine opportunity for the Church of England to bring authoritative, non-coercive counsel close to the centre of national socio-political decision-making.[15] The Church needs to consider more carefully

---

11   Michael Baughen (Bishop of Chester) in an interview with the author, 21st May 2002, Appendix 2.

12   Hugh Montefiore (Bishop of Birmingham) in an interview with the author, 21st May 2002, Appendix 3.

13   David Say (Bishop of Rochester) in an interview with the author, 29th May 2002, Appendix 4.

14   John B. Taylor (Bishop of St Albans) in an interview with the author, 29th July 2002, Appendix 5.

15   Hugh Montefiore is quick to note, however, that the loss of the Lords Spiritual from the House of Lords would not equate to the complete loss of Christian influence in Parliament. 'It would be a category error. It would

how it can capitalize on this opportunity and the general respect which the bishops' contributions to the House elicit. Donald Shell is confident in the potential of the bishops to have an impact through their speeches to the House: 'Given the large cross-bench element and the independent-mindedness of peers generally, individual speeches can sway votes in the Lords, and the contributions made by bishops in general have an impact out of proportion to their numerical strength.'[16] John B. Taylor describes his personal experience of the same sense of welcome and respect at the House of Lords:

> By and large they [Lords Temporal] very much appreciated what the bishop had to say. Because the bishops usually spoke sense. Because the bishop didn't speak with a party political card and steered very often through an argument and raised an issue that needed to be raised but was not a party-political ding-dong battle. I remember one saying to me: 'In my opinion a bishop ought to speak in every debate'. That was one of the younger ones.[17]

The bishops also have an opportunity to influence the life of the nation through informal 'lobbying'[18] and friendship at Westminster.[19] To the mind of Michael Baughen '[t]he main exchanges of value were

---

be totally wrong because I mean the lay people are just as important as the bishops and a lot of them have practical experiences where bishops haven't.' Hugh Montefiore (Bishop of Birmingham) in an interview with the author, 21st May 2002, Appendix 3.

16 Shell, *Lords*, 55.

17 John B. Taylor (Bishop of St Albans) in an interview with the author, 29th July 2002, Appendix 5. See also Hugh Montefiore (Bishop of Birmingham) in an interview with the author, 21st May 2002, Appendix 3, who recalls: 'I was surprised. I was quite surprised, what a welcome one had.' See also Michael Baughen (Bishop of Chester) in an interview with the author, 21st May 2002, Appendix 2, who commented thus: 'I found, and I think it's quite genuine, that there was a huge appreciation of what was said by most of the bishops because they were earnest in what they were doing.'

18 The term 'lobbying' is used throughout this chapter not in narrow sense to refer to an assertive and well-organised drive to achieve certain political outcomes, but to refer to a more general sharing of views and ideas with policy-makers and opinion-formers.

19 Michael Baughen describes one aspect of this informal opportunity: [W]hen you go for a meal at the House of Lords, if you don't have guests you go into what is called the Members sort of dining place and it is one long table, you have to sit at the next available seat, you can't go and choose... And I found it always very stimulating because you've got all sorts of people who voiced what they felt and then you could deal with it and it was a very, very useful PR place...' Michael Baughen (Bishop of Chester) in an interview with the author, 21st May 2002, Appendix 2.

not in the Chamber, they were outside the Chamber'.[20] Lord Longford points to the bishops' failure to get involved in the informal
lobbying and manoeuvring which takes place in the corridors, bars
and restaurants of the Palace of Westminster ('perfectly respectable
features of political life') as crucial to understanding their lack of
influence in the House.[21] Asked whether he spent time off the floor
of the House building informal relationships with decision-makers, John B. Taylor gave a simple reply: 'There wasn't time for it'.[22]
Hugh Montefiore responded in the same manner: '...one didn't have
time'.[23] The Lords Spiritual simply need more time, both on and off
the floor of the House, to make speeches, to vote, to do research and
preparation, and most importantly to simply be present at the Palace
of Westminster in order to engage informally with policy-makers.

A powerful case exists for the Church of England undertaking a
review of its approach to episcopal Parliamentary involvement in
order to overcome those obstacles which hinder it from being a significant and influential voice in the House of Lords. Such a review
would do well to listen to aspects of the proposal which Archbishop
Geoffrey Fisher made to Prime Minister Clement Attlee in 1949
(which has received endorsement more recently from Trevor Beeson).[24] Edward Carpenter outlines Fisher's proposals in detail:

> The upshot of these consultations was a letter to the Prime Minis-
> ter from the Archbishop in which he confirmed that those he had
> consulted were in general agreement with the proposals in respect
> of a reformed House of Lords so far as bishops were concerned.

---

20   Michael Baughen (Bishop of Chester) in an interview with the author, 21st
     May 2002, Appendix 2. He continues: It's true in the ordinary House. It is
     outside as much as anything, or what triggers from a debate and what you
     can do because you're in the House. You can get access to information, you
     can put questions down or you can see people and get action...'
21   Longford, *Bishops*, 116.
22   John B. Taylor (Bishop of St Albans) in an interview with the author, 29th
     July 2002, Appendix 5. Taylor refers to one bishop who did manage to get
     involved in this aspect of Parliamentary life (crucially he notes that '...he
     was always around'): 'There are some bishops who are remarkably good
     at hobnobbing and socialising. The best one was Maurice Wood, when he
     was bishop of Norwich and they loved him. He was the kind of bishop they
     loved. He was always around. He was in the bar chatting with them. He
     was caring for them pastorally, he was asking after their wives. He knew
     them by their Christian names, he spent a lot of time... He spent quite a lot
     of time there.'
23   Hugh Montefiore (Bishop of Birmingham) in an interview with the author,
     21st May 2002, Appendix 3.
24   Beeson, *Bishops*, 65.

They approved that: (1) the two Archbishops, together with the bishops of London, Durham and Winchester should without question, retain their seats ex officio; (2) five other diocesan bishops should sit in the Lords; (3) these should not have their place in the Upper House merely on the grounds of seniority, but in terms of the likelihood of their making a useful contribution. Amongst these there should be younger bishops.[25]

Whether the number of Lords Spiritual was reduced to ten or to 16 (as proposed in the Government's November 2001 White Paper *The House of Lords: Completing the Reform*), Fisher's suggestions make considerable sense if they were combined with the decision to release those bishops with seats in the House from a greater number of their diocesan responsibilities, through the appointment of additional suffragans to serve the diocese.[26] This would mean that whilst fewer bishops are eligible to sit on the Bench of Bishops, those who are have sufficient time and energy to play a consistent part in its life – both on and off the floor of the House. John B. Taylor's response to this suggestion sets it in the context of the present role of suffragans and, in contrast to the report of Owen Chadwick (Section 3.1.1 above),[27] the value placed by the diocese itself on its bishop's wider ministry:

> You do leave others to run the diocese. A diocesan bishop is there to lead the diocese, someone else can run the diocese. There are expectations on you being present at this, that and the other. And you want to because you are very much the Father of the family and you don't want to be out too frequently. But it has to be said that the diocese usually recognises that they get back in benefits what they lose in time. Because you are bringing something back into your diocese from your contribution outside there in the world. And when they hear what you're doing they're glad that their man is involved. Very, very few dioceses resent the time that bishops spend in the House of Lords, or episcopal meetings or Church bodies, because they know very well that they are privileged to have a wider insight when they are talking with their bishops.[28]

---

25 Carpenter, *Fisher*, 396.

26 In view of the Church of England's initial response to the recommendations of the Wakeham Commission these recommendations operate with the assumption that it is unlikely that the Church of England would propose that its representation at the House of Lords should be undertaken by anyone other than its bishops. See Archbishops' Council, *Comments from the Church of England on the Government's White Paper* (Unpublished: January 2002).

27 Chadwick, *Ramsey*, 129-130.

28 John B. Taylor (Bishop of St Albans) in an interview with the author, 29th July 2002, Appendix 5.

The total severance of the link between the Lord Spiritual and the diocese is unlikely to be to the benefit of the bishops' contribution to the House. It was considered by the Church of England's submission to the Wakeham Commission and the Wakeham Commission itself to be crucial to the value of the bishops' contribution to the House of Lords[29] and analysis of the content of the bishops' speeches to the House indicates that they used arguments based on their diocesan and vocational experience more than any other.

9.3.3 An Inefficient Contribution

The episcopal contribution to the House of Lords during the Thatcher years was inefficient, the bulk of the bishops' voting and speech-making being undertaken, as it was, by a minority of those eligible to sit on the Bench of Bishops. A significant proportion of the 26 bishops eligible to contribute to the House of Lords during the Thatcher years played no real part in its work. During the 1980s a group of just seven bishops cast 42% of the bishops' votes, and another group of seven bishops (including all but one of the vote-casting group of seven) made 65% of the bishops' speeches. Three-quarters of the speeches made from the Bench of Bishops were made by 17 individual bishops. The sheer variety in the record of the attendance, voting and speech-making of each individual bishop is best accounted for with reference to the individual personality, experience, expertise and priorities of each bishop.

This data adds weight to the case in support of Archbishop Fisher's suggestion that the number of bishops with seats in the Lords be reduced[30] and that selection to fill these places should no longer be based on seniority. Selection, whilst maintaining a geographical spread, should rather take account of the individual personality, experience, expertise and priorities of the individuals within the available pool of bishops. In the context of a reduction in the number of places for the Church of England bishops to 16, this would ensure that each of the places on the Bench of Bishops would be occupied by individual bishops committed, and able, to make use of the opportunity to contribute to the House. Equally, it would ensure that bishops ill-equipped to contribute to Parliamentary life would be protected from expending their energies away from their calling within their

---

29   Council, Role, 6-7 and Royal, *Future*, 158 (15.27).
30   'My own, fairly strong view is that the bishops have not helped by insisting upon the numbers [26 Lords Spiritual] being maintained.' David Say (Bishop of Rochester) in an interview with the author, 29th May 2002, Appendix 4.

diocese and the national structures of the Church. In view of the data presented on the voting and speech-making of the bishops during the 1980s, it is reasonable to argue that if the number of places for Church of England bishops is reduced to 16, the extent of the total episcopal contribution would be unlikely to drop significantly if the right individuals are filling those places. Indeed, if those bishops were given greater time to devote to their role at Westminster one could expect an increase in their voting and speech-making to take place.

9.3.4 An Indistinct Contribution

It can be argued that the bishops' contribution to the House of Lords during the Thatcher years was not sufficiently distinctive. The Lords Spiritual made use of facts and statistics to support their points on 197 occasions and academic and professional advice on 149 occasions. Meanwhile reference was made to theological arguments on just 77 occasions, and explicit reference was made to the Bible during just 7% of their speeches. Only 1% of the episcopal contributions to the House of Lords explored biblical material in detail.

It is entirely appropriate that the bishops bring a contribution to the House of Lords which communicates a competent understanding of the issues under discussion. In so doing it will rightly depend on and refer to insights from science, political theory, sociology, economics, anthropology, history and whatever disciplines might be relevant to the debate in hand. Indeed reference to this body of knowledge is an intrinsic part of theology and biblical exposition itself. 'Hearing the Bible and observing human society must interact, creating what is often referred to as a hermeneutical spiral.'[31] Nonetheless, in not making sufficient implicit and explicit use of the Bible the bishops are open to two particular accusations. Firstly, that they were unwitting contributors to the secularization of public life. Secondly, that their contributions contained little which could not have been presented to the House with far greater authority by Lords Temporal; that they failed to provide the particular voice, reflecting religious belief in people's lives, which is increasingly the *raison d'être* for their membership of the Second Chamber;[32] in short, that they failed to bring a distinctive contribution to Parliament:

> If what theology has to say in no significant way differs from what most people are saying anyway, theology and the church lose credibility; they should either have kept silent, or said something distinctive, rooted in their own convictions about God,

---

31 Jubilee, *Plural*, 30.
32 Royal, *Future*, 151 (15.5).

human beings and fellowship.[33]

9.4 Recommendations

In the light of the evidence outlined above, and the likely reduction of the number of places available for Church of England bishops in a fully reformed Second Chamber, a considerable case exists for an evolution in the Church of England's approach to the service of its bishops in the House of Lords. Such an evolution must overcome the obstacles which at present hinder busy diocesan bishops from bringing a significant moral and spiritual contribution to the debates of the House of Lords and to the life of its restaurants, bars, offices and corridors. In order to achieve this aim it is therefore recommended that:

1) The Church of England should cease to resist the Government's intention to reduce its numerical representation in a reformed Second Chamber to 16.

2) Those bishops who do serve on the Bench of Bishops should, through the appointment of additional suffragan bishops, be released from a greater number of their diocesan responsibilities so that they are able to play a more consistent and considerable part in the life of the Second Chamber.

3) The selection of diocesan bishops to sit in the Second Chamber should no longer be based on seniority. Rather, whilst maintaining a geographical spread of diocesan bishops (possibly, in part, through the retention of the five *ex officio* seats), attention should be given to the particular personality, experience, expertise and priorities of individuals within the available pool of bishops. This will ensure that seats on the Bench of Bishops are occupied by individuals willing and able to contribute to the life of the House of Lords.

4) Those serving on the Bench of Bishops should be encouraged to consider how they can bring a more distinct moral and spiritual contribution to the House of Lords. In this context particular attention needs to be given to considering what role the Bible and the perspectives of theology should in their contribution.

---

33   Forrester, *Beliefs*, 81. See also Lee & Stanford who argue that '...it is precisely the theological input that the church should be offering, whatever the topic on the table, for faith and the interpretation of Christian teaching is the church's distinctive contribution'. Lee & Stanford, *Believing*, 31-32.

Interview Questions

Co-ordination

- Were the bishops' contributions to the House of Lords during the 1980s co-ordinated in any way from Church House or Lambeth?
- Did any bishop carry a form of 'departmental brief'?

Individual Peers of the Realm?

Medhurst & Moyser (*Church and Politics in a Secular Age*, 97) note that 'the bishops are officially present there [at the House of Lords] as individual peers of the realm rather than corporate spokesmen.'

- Did this fact having any outworking in the way in which you approached your role at the House of Lords?

Synodical Government

- Do you think that the shift to Synodical government reduced or increased the authority with which you were able to contribute to the House of Lords?

Influence

Donald Shell (*The House of Lords*, 55) claims that 'bishops, in general, have an impact out of proportion to their numerical strength'.

- Do you feel that as bishops you had any real influence in Parliament during the 1980s?

Informal Lobbying

Lee & Stanford, writing in 1990, argued that: 'Given that the majority of the present Government are Christians, and to different degrees practice their faith, they have a natural predisposition to listen rather more attentively to bishops than the general public is led to believe.' (*Believing Bishops*, 29).

- What opportunities were open to you for informal lobbying off the floor of the House?
- What level of influence were you able to achieve through informal lobbying?

Procedure

- If a bishop was allowed to speak in a debate without having to stay to the summing-up, and if more notice was given of forthcoming debates, do you think that the bishops would be more effective in performing their role?

Margaret Thatcher

- To what extent do you think that it was Mrs Thatcher's style, more than the substance of her policies, which led to much of the tension between Church and State during the 1980s?

H.M. Opposition

- Did episcopal opposition to the Thatcher governments increase as a conscious response to the ineffective opposition being offered by the Labour Party?

The House of Lords

- Would your experience support the conclusion that bishops are generally well-respected by other peers?

Prayers

- What is the ongoing significance of a bishop being in attendance to read prayers at the House?

Transcript of Interview with Michael Baughen (Bishop of Chester)[1]

(AP) My focus is on the Thatcher years, but with your experience of both Thatcher and Major as Prime Minister I wonder if I might start by asking you if, as a bishop, you saw a big difference between the Thatcher and Major years?

(MB) I'm not so sure if I can help because I was there at the end. I was one of the bishops who went to Chequers. Do you know that she called the bishops to Chequers? I was one of the ten that went so I do know about that. That was just about the moment that I was going in because my maiden speech was just after that, but I went in any case. Robert Runcie asked me to go to that, and that was quite interesting. I mean the impression at the time was that she was very much against what was going on because of 'Faith in the City' – 'Faith in the City' was the breakpoint – and the rubbishing business that went on about that was quite disgraceful really and I think that really set, sort of, teeth on edge. I think it was brave of her in a way. An interesting thing to do to ask us to go and meet her and she did it in style. I mean we went to Chequers and had a meal and everything but the actual conversation afterwards was frank and honest. It was not... I mean during my maiden, after my maiden speech actually, I made my maiden speech on the growing gap between the poor and the rich. After that (of course only when you made your maiden speech can you intervene) and on the same day as I had made my maiden speech one guy got up and said, 'very glad to hear the prime minister has hauled the bishops in to tell them off at Chequers'. So I immediately intervened on the very day that I made my maiden and he sat down and I said well I was one of the bishops who went Chequers and it wasn't that at all. It was a sharing of views and was frank and honest but that in no way was it sort of calling the bishops in to tell them off. So I sat down and he got up and said, 'well that's what I read in the *Daily Telegraph*.' Everybody went 'blaaah'.

And it was. I mean I think there was some straight talking and not least of course from David Sheppard and I think David Jenkins, I think David Jenkins was there. But it was an honest thing and I said to her in the course of the thing, I said, 'if you really came to see what the Church is doing in these areas and you came to Birkenhead in my diocese, or Wallasey, or to parts of Winchester or so on where they are in the inner city, they are the only professionals who live there after 5.30 at night or on the weekends. There is no doctor, no policeman, no administrative person from the council and no teacher, nobody lives there. They all come in. The only people who live there are the clergy and their fami-

---

1   Conducted at Bishop Baughen's home on 21st May 2002.

lies and they know what's going on and this is why our network is picking up what's going on, it's honest and real. It isn't from an outsider's point of view. They know what it's like not to be able to get to the post office and all the rest of it with problems with the doctor and so on,' and I said, 'really and honestly the fact that they stay there and work there and live there and we're in the inner city for Christ, that they are pure gold, they are absolutely pure gold Prime Minister'. And afterwards she asked me for the names and addresses of a number of them so that she could write and wish them well and thank them for what they were doing. To my knowledge I never heard anybody tell me that she'd written but I guess the intention was there.

Yes quite.

So I mean that was where you could do it. The main exchanges of value were not in the Chamber, they were outside the Chamber.

That was one of my major questions.

This is always so. It's true in the ordinary House. It is outside as much as anything, or what triggers from a debate and what you can do because you're in the House. You can get access to information, you can put questions down or you can see people and get action so that because I was in the House and we were in the thick of it at Cammell Lairds, the ship building company who were about to go to the wall and because we met with the Shop Stewards and we constantly had this personal contact we really knew the place and the Managing Director was an amazing guy. I thought, we thought because of that I could ask to see the minister and I went but it was outside as much as anything I think. Bitston Steel was closed down and taken over by a Scandinavian or some company abroad and I wrote to Norman Tebbitt (and again because you write as a member of the House of Lords they must reply to you) and wrote earlier on about the principle of the thing, about their getting the right benefits or whatever it was you know sort of payments that they needed and I got this letter back from him and as the thing progressed this company wriggled, I've forgotten how they wriggled now, so that they weren't responsible for these payments at all and so I saw the Shop Steward. He was a communist and he was wonderful – Charlie his name – and they came to see me at Bishops House and he sat there and he said, 'never thought I'd sit here'. And so he said, 'what do I call you', so I said Michael. So we were then Michael and Charlie and we got on very, very well from then on but because I got the Tebbit letter I actually was able to force the issue and they did get the payment and it was really thanks to my intervention.

Really, do you have other examples of that? Where that kind of behind the scenes... that's the thing I find hard to track.

Well that's a definite example and it was Tebbit in fact who was the person who was whatever he was, responsible for employment or something at the time, and although I haven't got the specifics I didn't keep all this, I didn't keep diaries like that. Because the main thing that we could do was to operate on the care of people and argue for that. Well, Cammell Lairds was a disgraceful thing and I really do think that there were some very bad dealings going on in the Government over that. Cammell Lairds was taken over by DSL at Borrowin-Furness and once they had taken it over it wasn't just what DSL was doing it was the lack of support from the Government's side and I really get very upset about Cammell Lairds, the way they treated them and I still don't know to this day because I never did get to the bottom of what was going on, but they had the biggest shed anyone had got. I mean it was absolutely huge, you could build big destroyers inside under cover, it was an enormous facility and so the possibility was they were going for these big Hydrofoil sort of modern big things, you know. They could build all this under cover like no one else could and other things they were contending for and they got cut, undercut by France. I think there is probably little doubt that the French Government was subsidising in order to do it and it was this that the ministers wriggled. They simply would not face it. They got very cocky, they deserved to be removed from power, they really did. They got so cocky and so, um, they just put people down, the put you down and just this sort of voice of pomposity and you really felt you wanted to go... hit them almost. There were exceptions to that. Men like Earl Ferrers was exceptional and some of the women who came onto the bench were brilliant. They were honest and if they didn't know the answer or were going to think about what you said they would do it, but the others would never give an inch. And over Cammell Lairds I am convinced that the thing was a very poor, something happened between the Government and between the rest of us over it and I wish we could have forced it further than we did. The manager of Cammell Lairds he was absolutely outstanding, resigned and went to another job and that was it then. That's what they wanted to do, get him out.

Do you think that that was Government dogma basically overriding common sense or just bad, bad practice almost?

I think they didn't care, frankly. I mean I felt that the Thatcher Government didn't care. My own feeling was that in spite of her defending herself these days saying they were a caring Government they weren't and it was the lack of care everywhere down the line. So the lack of care for employees and the readiness to let something go rather than bother to argue with the French I think as much as anything and not being bothered about who lived in Birkenhead because they lived in London. It was very much a geographical thing. The Camel Laird thing was a great disgrace of a very fine plant that had all the facilities to beat anybody in Europe and a very fine workforce and very fine Shop Stewards who were willing to work with it and it was exceptional. So I think that care is probably the key to it really and it was someone in the, with somebody from official circles, let's put it like that, early on in my ministry and looking at the state there and there were three of our churches in inner Birkenhead that were in a dreadful state of dry rot they had all been not cared for really and the times and results of the war and also being in the inner city and this chap said, 'well why doesn't the church pull out of this area'. And I said, 'the church pulls in'. And you don't pull out, that's the Church of England. Others may have to pull out because they can't finance their church but we are the Church of England, we're responsible for the whole of this land and so we in fact raised a million pounds to build and rebuild one of the churches, that's what it costs all that. The Queen came and opened it, but I mean it was that attitude, 'why do you bother with it?', you know, and it was that attitude of these sort of fractious masses and the idea that they would never face up to poverty being a cause of unrest.

Now again do you think that was because they had this kind of level of New Right thinking that was 'this is how it is' and they wouldn't sway from it or was it more of a personal kind of, like you say, lack of care more like personal ambition?

Yeah, I think so. I think it was very much living in the nice areas of this world. One of the [reasons] why bishops could be so powerful is that, as they would say to me when I spoke on poverty and things like that, 'you can quote chapter and verse of what's actually happening today'. You see, and I would quote from them about loan sharks for instance and the way the church could pioneer a credit union and all the rest of it. And how people in these areas, for instance one couple came to see one of our vicars and said that they had taken up this offer that all your different sort of debts were taken on board, you know, under one and then they had their first repayments and they couldn't believe it. So they went to the vicar in great distress and he said, 'well what interest are you paying?'. And they said, 'well what's interest?'. Now see you could quote that. You could quote actually, I would write to my vicars in these days when I was on such a debate and they would write, you know, give me chapter and verse of what happened in the last few weeks. Now we can do that because we have a network that nobody else has.

Now do you think, one of my questions is, if there's reform, if the bishops had possibly wanted to contribute even more in the House and have more time there, one of the options is to have full-time bishops in the House. I don't know to what extent that is a reasonable option, but if that was an option, do you think one of the big problems would be they would lose that local link or could they still maintain it through that network?

You are quite right to say it's swings and roundabouts. My own belief is that it shouldn't be attached to the See, to your diocese. Now thus it would be possible to retire and go on in the House, if you wanted to, to give real attention to the House. Now you're going to see Hugh Montefiore who was sort of foaming at the mouth that he was only in for what, two years or something like that, because he was never afraid to speak about anything and he would have been certainly a stirrer if he had been able to get another five years. So I think that either to go to seventy or seventy-five would have been a real option. Certainly to seventy anyhow and for those living near enough to London to give it the time. I mean I don't know if I would have done that or not but I was always frustrated because the weeks we were on duty (you know you're on three weeks duty or two weeks duty) you really got into things but then that was it, certainly for Chester.

Definitely. And I guess particularly for those behind the scenes conversations, not only time in the chamber.

That's right. No you really got into people and with people and there was a lot of interplay during that week and then that was it. If you were there more permanently and wanting to do that. I mean originally we were there for five months of the year, as you know. All the bishops had houses in London. The bishop of Chester had one where the BBC now is, next door to All Souls, Langham Place. He was involved in the building of All Souls, Langham Place of all things. So they were here for five months. So if you look at the pictures. Have you been to the House of Lords?

Yes.

Well if you've seen the picture there, you'll see serried ranks of bishops on the wall there, because they came for basically five months. So they were a real Lord Spiritual. But I think the problem is this, that if you narrowed it down to just a few bishops you'd have to be a little bit careful about who you put in. At least you get the range that the bishops are by the present system and so I mean I will contend against Oxford over divorce to his absolute fury. And we will not necessarily take the same line and so we are, you'd have to try and work out how you select the bishops to do it because, but I do think that certainly if we could retain the same sort of numbers we could have made a much better contribution by being in for longer and that could have been by retirement.

And do you see that as an option which could come into being over the next few years, is that a widely held perspective?

Only if you remove it from the See. But this is probably what they're talking about when they talk about sort of individual nominations of bishops to be in the House but yeah you only get certain people in and the sort of people they want in. They are going to be a bit selective. I mean some bishops don't want to be in the House. The last thing on earth they want to do is to be in the House, so they drag their feet about everything about it. I enjoyed it. I found it stimulating. Very, very hard sweat because often it's wet-tail around the head. When you were on duty you had to handle the debates that were happening unless there was a specialist bishop coming in for it, like education or one of the moral issues. So often you know I would get the Board of Social Responsibility to come and on one occasion when they wouldn't brief me properly I made them come over to the House to sit down and said, 'now I'm going to ask you the questions because you are expecting me to speak tonight and you can't be clear over the phone about it so come here'. They accepted that and it was very useful and I was able to make an effective speech. But even then you see, where we lose out Andy, is that, for instance in one of those debates I am thinking about that particular night. There were two debates we were involved in. One about provisions for homeless people who were in hotel rooms who couldn't cook and therefore the costs of living were far higher than if they were in something else. It was on that line. So you had a really good debate with about, in the evening 80 or something in the Chamber, and you won the debate really basically and we were very influential in winning it. And then of course there would be a division and they all appeared and it would just go the Government's way. So speaking is not enough. It's much more persuasion really.

Yeah, based on those relationships.

Yeah, I mean after all, even if you had all 26 bishops present what's that against so many?

In fact in my research I don't think I recall one occasion where the bishops even numerically would have swung a division, and even then I'm sure back-up would have arrived.

Well we know that.

And that's part of the system isn't it?

Well it's part of it but I mean I found, and I think it's quite genuine, that there was a huge appreciation of what was said by most of the bishops because they were earnest in what they were doing. But obviously as you rightly said the moral issues are sort of major issues that we wade in on but you were able to do, there was a debate on charity law for instance and the Roman Catholics asked me when I was on duty to speak on contemplative communities, the fact they weren't allowed to be charitable. So they gave me the gist of their speech that they wanted and I delivered it for them and on that occasion do you know that in the long debates however many people want to speak, divides up the time, so if you have 20 people into three hours you have a 20th of three hours and if there's 60 people and you might only have three minutes. I remember Oxford coming down once and he had all this big speech prepared and he had three minutes. He was fuming. He came all the way from Oxford for it. I quite agree. I quite understood it, but you can still be quite effective in three minutes if you want to be and on one occasion, on that occasion, I looked and I saw I still had about a minute left. Well, there was a major issue right in my own diocese where way back in the first World War, just after the first World War, there was a shooting, firing sort of range set up in a hall built to give the young people something useful to do after the first World War. It lasted about four years I think and then collapsed and it was handled then by the Luco Trust who'd handled it ever since and here this thing was sitting in prime position being used, temporarily it was being used as a builders place you know. Anyhow it came up, the builder sort of getting out of it and so on and so we applied to be able to sell it and for the trust to put it to educational, actually to build a hall for one of the schools and they refused on the grounds, charity law refused and said it was built as a firing range you've got to put it back as a firing range and that was in this age. And just after someone had been shot dead on the M62 at the service station, someone with a gun you know, before some of the other incidents. So I took the minute to shoot it. I immediately had the head of the Charity Commission onto me, within an hour.

And they turned the whole thing upside down and took the chap apart in Liverpool. He conceded as much as he could I mean he knew he had to and we got the money. So you could do something just quite quickly like that just to stir but you didn't have to do it in the House you can do it without that, so that was again one of the things that we did and obviously things like Broadcasting Bills and Embryology, the Education thing which Graham Leonard carried through was brilliant what he did on that. I think to lose that, to lose this from the House would be a very serious loss. When I went to, this might interest you, when I went to New Zealand because we were linked to Christchurch, New Zealand and I went out to visit and the bishop of Christchurch in New Zealand asked me to go and speak to the local Rotary which has 250 members (so much bigger than ours) on 'What on earth is a bishop doing in the House of Lords?' So I did and I listed all the votes, I listed all the influence we had been able to, I had the whole information at my fingertips so I have it now. And at the end she was very wistful and she said, 'now I realise what we lost'. She said we have no ear of the Government at all. We have no access to the Government, but we have just because we're there and we have it for everybody for all denominations.

And this is interesting. I can't remember who it is, but they'd done some interviews with some Muslim and Jewish leaders and again even they were saying, 'this is a good thing for what you might call the fibre of the nation. We need this.'

Well I think that's right and if there is an anti-church thing, 'get the bishops out, the bishops shouldn't be there and why should they be there', and all that sort of stuff at the moment. Well, that's the secular nation we're in, it's very anti-church. But I believe that to throw that away and to throw our influence away from there, which is very, very wide underneath, and some bishops are very much better at it than I was, and people particularly nearer London.

It's a whole network of relationships.

Yeah, yeah and if you, you know I didn't, I mean I left school at 15 and began to work, I never had the sort of Oxbridge sort of background but the Oxbridge background has a sort of network of its own and you see them relating and talking and greeting and inter-playing with them a lot – much more than I did, although I got to know a lot of people. The other thing is that I don't know whether you know this, but when you go for a meal at the House of Lords, if you don't have guests you go into what is called the members sort of dining place and it is one long table, you have to sit at the next available seat, you can't go and choose.

I didn't know that.

And I found it always stimulating because you've got all sorts of people who voiced what they felt and then you could deal with it and it was a very, very useful PR place to sort things out really and to really be at the grassroots. So those sort of influences.

You say there are those who deal with it naturally, but do you think there's a need for more cohesion in terms of the PR of the bishops in public policy.

Well there's a chap at Lambeth of course who does that and they don't tell you what to do but they do ask you whether you would do this and... There was a debate on noise in national parks and people who wanted to put speed boats on Ullswater or somewhere to do speed racing and there was a great deal of opposition to this and they said this is something we really want to speak about and they wrote me the speech, which is very kind of them because it was a very good speech and I actually delivered it, I didn't usually do that, but I delivered basically their speech. I mean I made it my own but I mean it was recorded this turned the whole thing and I got the credit for this chap. They tended to co-ordinate to some extent. Not enough I didn't think in my day but a certain amount. But you see the trouble is everything is last minute, you don't know what's coming up for next week. People used to say, 'so how disgraceful that only five of the bishops were there to vote', but what do you think I'm going to do? I've got a year's diary ahead of me already booked for the next year as it were. I was at this church this night, do I say to them when I've been booked for a year to go to their 150th anniversary that 'sorry, I've got to go down and vote at the House?' In any case, it takes three and a half hours at least to come down by train to get to the House and three and a half hours back and if you do come you are supposed to stay until the end of the debate but how do I get back at nine o'clock at night? I don't. It's another day.

And again there are things on that side that I think need to change or somehow there's got to be an evolution there.

Well it's partly that the home... the home county bishops were able to do it because they could pop up and pop back and they would often apologise perhaps they couldn't stay and we had to do that before the summing up of the Ministry for the three hour debate. But they did, they were the main people. In a sense who you appoint to the home counties is pretty significant. On the other hand if you do that and they're the only people who speak you've lost the north of England and the north really has...

Quite, which is one of those main areas that needs that voice.

This is what we do. So it's swings and roundabouts there.

You talked earlier about some of the guys who had a specialism in education, obviously Graham Leonard had that. Was that in any way formalised or did it just again evolve somewhat?

Well the Chairman of the Board of Social Responsibility in the Synod, the General Synod, if he was in the House would take on that issue because he'd been into them all. So he would normally be your lead runner in that. It didn't mean the rest of you weren't going to be there and be involved.

But clearly that was his area of expertise.

Yes, and he would therefore have to alter his timetable to be there and education was a case in point. Graham Leonard only had to walk across the road, it was only five seconds. But he was often up to two or three o'clock in the morning and took it through with great detail and with great success. So yes it's specialist sort of areas, I mean if it's, what other areas might there be? There might be people who've got these specialisms from their own backgrounds. Environment would be more general.

Economic matters?

Yes, probably, although again it's rather broad in a way. One difficulty is that you don't know about everything and therefore you can't really contend with some of these speakers and they are very informed people and you don't do it lightly. I once got taken apart and that's because I was pressed hard by some youth organization, club, charity project, something in Manchester. They were being badly hit by having their grass removed or something, I've forgotten what it was now. I went into this as thoroughly as I could with them but because it was last minute I didn't check, I didn't have time to cross-check and of course

I was decimated because they only fed me their side of the story, which is the trouble and when I went to see the minister about Cammell Lairds, BSL had only fed me what they wanted me to hear and he took me apart. It was very embarrassing when he had his, all his assistants there, and I just went alone. I didn't take anyone from Cammell Lairds but I put the points to him and he said that it wasn't true and after about five minutes I said well I am obviously wasting your time and I apologise and I had been wrongly informed and on the basis of that came to see him and that was it.

Now, would that be an example of where you were perhaps under-trained for that specific role? You know, taking someone with you, from that point onwards I guess...
I think that's quite true. I ought to have... I ought not to have gone without someone from Cammell Lairds because they would have been exposed.

Yeah, yeah and let them do the talking.
I mean, I've learnt since that that's what you do, you take two or three people if possible. Although sometimes you've got to be alone like the Chancellor, the previous Chancellor, in his Divorce Bill, knew I was opposing him and he asked me to come and see him because he was a Christian and we got on very well and he was a very nice guy and I went. I had to go on my own and he had all his team around him and that was quite an interesting ding-dong because he didn't give way particularly and we really had a good exchange of views, not acrimonious, but I admired him for asking me to go and talk to him about why I was opposed to it.

He asked you?
He asked me to go and see him.

You've learnt these lessons and often lessons are learnt that way. Did you feel like you could be better resourced? Do you think that's an area in which bishops should be given initial training let alone kind of...
Well I think initial training, I think when you go into the House you need to have someone take you through much more than we are. Well you do big brother but it's more than that. I think there are some guidelines but they're not adequate enough for everything and there are certain things about how you do things and how you don't do things, so you don't put your foot in it, how you address people and all the rest of it. You need the confidence, it takes a while to get used to it and get the atmosphere before you would dare to do very much. But then you learn how to put questions down and then you learn how to handle it because you have to keep asking questions, you know you can't explain anything after that and all the rest of it. There are techniques you have some information about, and they may be better informed now than they were, but I think things like the meeting with the Minister was a mistake on my part.

No quite.
I was obviously a bit cocky but perhaps I thought I could do it. I think I felt that as a bishop with that information that they needed to answer me. Well I was

very upset about it, I felt I had done everything under the sun for Cammell Lairds and that someone there... let me go to the slaughter really. They knew I was going.

Which when you've bent over backwards and more...

It was after the good manager had been sacked and after the dirty sort of double-dealing stuff was going on. I think going back to the issue over France it was also the Government who wanted the money and I'm very convinced that there was something happening over Cammell Lairds that wasn't honest. But we never got to the honest truth out on the floor of the House and that Cammell Lairds should not have gone to the wolves as it did. There was every reason to intervene to say that in regards to what they said the French were doing badly, undoubtedly doing deals behind the scenes.

Can I just ask you again about the things about the Thatcher Government, just that sense of not caring. Did you detect a change with the Major Government and did you detect a change in the relationship between the bishops and the Major Government?

Well as I say, I don't think my experience with the Thatcher Government was long enough to really to get other than the frustration over that but certainly in the years I was mainly in would have been the Major years there were, who's the person who was the Overseas, the woman. I should know what her name was, she was an MP in Wallasey at one point so I ought to know. Well, she was marvellous and she was honest. In fact there were several of the women that they brought on at that point who I felt were outstanding and a real honour to integrity and one or two of the men like Earl Ferrers and so on – I respected his integrity. If there was anything raised in debate about the home, he would always come immediately to me and say, 'let me have a word with you about that'. I admired his integrity. And he would write to me afterwards. So I think there was a sort of change in some of them on the front bench. Not all of them, they retained some who I could have socked in the jaw. I felt they were so pompous and you knew you were just going to get these sort of pompous answers to try to put you down. So it probably was a change on the front bench of atmosphere but I mean people like Lord Wakeham, which one was he under? Lord Wakeham was wonderful. He was a wonderful leader of the House. I admired him enormously. I altered those rules to the House on one occasion when I, there was a thing going through a Bill with about 500 clauses, and that's the thing you can't handle by the way, that's when we can't do it because, it's too big. That's when your lost, when that's going on in your week, but there was one clause that Lambeth said you ought to try and vote on that if you possibly can and I had to go on to Harley Street for a medical check or something and I came back into the House through the door and the bells were ringing for the division and I looked and saw it was amendment, whatever it was. So I mean our robes were downstairs and tables upstairs it's only two minutes from the bell but I belted up the stairs just as I was and threw my jacket down and raced up the stairs and said to one of the Flunkeys: 'Can I vote without robes?' And he said, 'I don't know I'll go ask'. So he went and asked and the chap said 'Yes', but I voted the other side of the House. I crossed over and then in this packed voting lobby which was mixed in parties, this Flunkey exercised all his authority: 'Stop!' You can't vote without your robes you see. There was mayhem and the whole thing was passed or lost with two votes or something so it was a near, it could have been a very near thing if it had proved much more crucial. But immediately, they all intervened, point of order, 'Disgraceful. He was prohibited from voting just because of robes and this is not democracy', etc, etc... And Labour and Liberal and the cross-benches all came in on it and Lord Wakeham suddenly got up and said, 'I never cease to wonder about the strange things of this House, we'll look into it', and they altered it.

And the famous unwritten constitution of the United Kingdom is changed. That's brilliant.

Yes, so now you can in an emergency, but it's always an emergency!

Do you have any of those kind of personal memories of Margaret Thatcher or any other things that just really stand out from your time in the House?

No, because she was only, she came into the House, I mean she doesn't come much to the House, but when she comes she walks through like a queen, then she sits and she doesn't like sitting down on the bench really. She expects to be running it doesn't she? When she does speak there isn't a great deal of credence. I mean there's not a lot of respect for her really in the House.

But of course in the years when she was Prime Minister, I mean while she wasn't in that House, I only got the back end of it really.

So I think it would be a tragic loss. I think that, I mean we both agree that there should be longer opportunity and I think releasing it from the See is one way of doing that. On the other hand I'm very chary about, I really would prefer it not too shortened down from the number of bishops because it does give this geographical spread across the whole nation in a way which the House is not spread in the same way.

And you do need someone who is personally rooted, not just got the connections.

That's right. I mean we are, we are living, well we've lived in draughty great places that are very impractical but you were actually out on the job the whole time. I was on the road most of the time. I worked, I had an office in the back of my car. Talk about you know these posh bishops having drivers, I couldn't have done the job without a driver.

Yeah, practically speaking.

I remember he was ill one weekend and it cost me 6 hours behind the wheel that I'd planned in to prepare in the back of a car. So you saw everything. I mean I was 1000 square miles, I had inner city, I had country, I'd got the lot. It gives you a real touch for people. So I think it's been a huge loss to the whole nation right the way through. Disestablishment would be awful.

Can you see it happening in any sense. It is certainly not impossible. It's always up for question but...

There's a growing mood towards it isn't there? But if we became disestablished then what's the next move? The next coronation would be in a Mosque. I mean they start talking about fair religions, I mean it would be absolutely disastrous. It's not very large in this country, it's just voluble and people are leaning over backwards about it.

Which is admirable to some extent, but then beyond that...

That's right. I mean proportionally it's so small and I just think they've leant over so far, it's quite worrying from my angle. So I don't know. I mean I think I can see why people argue against establishment but New Zealand was a salutary experience for me.

And of course you get disestablished and still have religious representation in the Lords but whether we have that same...

It wouldn't be the same.

No, I guess you would... this is the interesting thing for me, once you have lost the hereditary peers, the Queen ultimately comes into question, the hereditary principle. Well at what point do we shift?

We used to take people around the House of Lords and show them the pegs that the Prince of Wales and the Duke of Edinburgh used. So I mean, you said that the speeches were not pusillanimous and that's probably true to some extent because nothing is achieved by being pusillanimous. Not in the Lords. You can be in the Commons but you can't in the Lords so much. And when people are, there's a real kickback really, it doesn't influence. You've got to do it by persuasion. You've got to do it by clear argument and facts and not by bellyaching and they are, there were bellyachers particularly on the opposition bench, on the Labour bench. I've noticed they're a little bit more moderate now they're in government, the same people. Because I can still go you see. I can still sit on the steps at the front.

Do you do that often?

Every now and again. Particularly when we take guests to show them around and lunch or something. And we were able to go to the receiving of the coffin of the Queen Mother and stand on the steps. Lots of privileges.

Yes, definitely.

I hope they don't throw those out, because they're quite nice! And the other thing of course. General Synod meets across the road and there's nowhere in General Synod buildings where you can go to prepare a speech, but all you have to do is walk across to the bishops rooms at the House of Lords. It's a very, very useful place for us. So there are side benefits we wouldn't want to lose but I hate wearing robes but then if we didn't wear robes we wouldn't have to have rooms to put them on, and so we wouldn't have anywhere.

And you probably don't know this. When a man becomes a diocesan bishop, it's probably going to be five years at the moment before he comes in, because it's only twenty-six out of forty-three. But you are allowed to go and sit on the steps of the throne, from the word go.

Which is something probably that needs to be taken advantage of.

Well absolutely, and I took a bishop in with me once but the Flunky threw him out and I was absolutely furious with him. He wouldn't admit that he had to in the end. He had to write and apologise to me. I said 'I expect a letter of apology.'

Transcript of Interview with Hugh Montefiore (Bishop of Birmingham)[1]

(AP) Reading 'Christianity and Politics' something that struck me was the significance of being the Chairman of the Board of Social Responsibility. Did that make a big difference in terms of your role in the House?

(HM) Role in which House?

In the House of Lords, sorry.

No, I don't think so. It enabled me to speak perhaps with more authority and perhaps with more knowledge than other bishops but I don't think they would have, I don't know that they had more respect for me because I was Chairman of the Board of Social Responsibility.

Did it add to your workload so to speak and the things you were asked to cover in the House of Lords?

I was never asked to cover anything. You see you're not there in the House of Lords as a representative of the Church. It's a very important point. Nowadays I think the present Archbishop has somewhat changed it and given bishops responsibility for making themselves aware of certain subjects. That's what happens at the moment. That certainly didn't happen in my day and you are not chosen to go to the House of Lords because you are a representative. You go in your own right as a bishop, a rather important distinction. There are certain subjects that I was interested in and certain subjects I had to deal with when I was Chairman of the Board so that I knew more about them. I wasn't there for very long, though I made the most of my time. No one would die or retire for five years after I was a bishop so it took me some time to get in.

I've certainly picked up from my research that you contributed a great deal when you were in. Was it a disappointment when...

It was only about three or four years.

Yeah, it was '84 to '87 wasn't it?

Well, you know better than I do. Yes, I'm sure you're right. Yes I did and I very nearly got, you know, I had to retire before I could take through a Bill on abortion. A very modest bill saying that it was wrong to kill an embryo that was capable of being born alive because they were killing them off. I found this out when I went to the maternity hospital in Birmingham and there they said 'this baby was nearly aborted'. And so I had a modest Bill but it was looked on suspiciously by the pro-abortionists and rather by disdain by the totally against

---

1   Conducted at Bishop Montefiore's home on 21st May 2002.

abortion but however I got it through Second Reading, but then it went through a select committee because I left the House, I retired.

I don't think the bishops had actually proposed a Bill for a long time. I didn't think I could but I asked and they asked the Clerk of Parliaments to come and Lord Denham did and said, 'Oh yes' and so he said, 'well you do it'.

Now did you find that often was the case? That those who disagreed with you would just disagree blankly and that those who potentially should have supported you were consistently saying, 'you're not going far enough'. But you were trying to work within the confines of what was possible, not what was ideal?

Yes, yes. That's right. I didn't want to overhit my Bill on abortion because I knew it could be amended in such a way that it would produce the opposite result. Yes, I suppose so, the Roman Catholic peers were very good. They supported me, although they were totally against all abortion. Didn't have much support from my fellow bishops, I hasten to add.

Did you find you've got this three year time in the House of Lords? Did you find that actually was only by the last six months, year, that you'd actually got a grip on how the House was working and the details involved in being there. Would you look back and say I actually needed to have been better prepared, or was that something that you found easy to adapt to?

No, I found that easy. Contrary to what most people think, the bishops were greatly welcomed in the House of Lords and we were treated with great friendship and of course we were the only people who had a constituency and that was very important because the other people could only generalise and we could speak out of our own experience and knowledge. No, I had to pick up the way the House worked and so on and pick up the details of committees and when you could speak and when you can't speak, and so on. I remember once I made a hash of it. When there's a Statement by a Minister you can only ask questions, you couldn't go and say anything. The House of Lords is a funny place anyhow so you're always called to order by your fellow peers, not by anyone on the Woolsack.

Now, something that has been intriguing me is the extent to which what happens in the Chamber can have an influence on the Government but, moreover, the extent to which what goes on behind the scenes can. Was your experience that actually most of your influence was through informal lobbying behind the scenes?

No, I never engaged in that.

Really?

Yes, yes. Well partly because one didn't have the time. I was in Birmingham, you know it took two and a half hours by the time you left home to get into the House and it was very difficult to attend the House at all because my diary was made up one year ahead and the business with the House is made up one month ahead and you can't just cancel things simply, 'Oh, I'm terribly sorry I can't, I'm in the House of Lords'.

Absolutely.

And so as for finding time to lobby that was out of the question really, there just wasn't time. I'm not at all sure that I would have wanted to lobby very much really. I might ask people to be present but they've got to be persuaded by what I say in the House.

Now do you think your experience is representative of the bench at that time?

Well I can't imagine that the other bishops had a chance, had opportunity to lobby. I think perhaps one exception was on the subject of education. The then Bishop of London, now Monsignor Leonard, he I think did some lobbying when they were revising the Education Bill about the assembly and whether it should be Christian and so on. I think probably he did consult quite widely in that respect. Anyhow he was in London and he could do that.

So we've got this House of Lords and I think one of the big things I've picked up is that for you there was a very great limitation particularly when you lived outside of London on how much you could get to the House. Partly that was due to the House itself and the set up there, like you say the release of timetables only a month in advance and having to stay to the end of debates.

There was another problem and that was the last train home because if you contribute to a debate you're supposed to stay 'til the end. The last train home for Birmingham was just before midnight so it was very tricky.

So how do you think the House of Lords develops to facilitate more episcopal involvement of a higher quality? Do you think there's a need for that?

Well it's different from when I was there. After all you've only got 93 hereditaries now haven't you and you've got about five (not quite) hundred, you've got masses of life peers. How do I think it develops? Well I am very clear you see if you want to get something through you do it before five o'clock when all the people on a job come in. I thought sometimes the old trade union people were rather stupid when they spoke late in the afternoon when all their opponents from the city would have arrived. You learn that sort of thing. How does it develop? Well, I found that I never dare to speak unless I was master of my subject because there would usually be some internationally known expert there and one didn't want to be put down. Whether that is so at the moment I don't know. Whether it will be there when it's reformed I don't know. If people are elected I fear they'll be second-raters, people who couldn't get into the Commons, not necessarily people with tremendously wide experience. How is it developing did you say?

For example, some people talk about having bishops whose primary focus is the House of Lords.

Oh no, no. You're not appointed a bishop to be a legislator. No, bishops are welcomed to speak at Second Reading. Did you know that? You know at Second Reading, the general idea of the Bill is discussed and the bishops are particularly welcomed there because they can at that time apply a moral and spiritual perspective to the particular Bill in question. That seems to me proper. I don't think it is the job of bishops to engage in detailed committee work. I don't think that's their job but I think that they have important influence on the State's legislation by intervening at Second Reading over the general, moral and spiritual implications of the Bill. Occasionally they may be particularly interested and follow the Bill all the way through. This was certainly so as far as I was concerned over the Shops Bill and it was certainly true over the Animal, over the regulations about treating animals, but that was a business and that was almost impossible to see it all the way through because committees would meet on awkward days and I do think that bishops on the whole should confine themselves, except on certain very contentious matters, to Second Reading.

Would you say that the bishops' local rooting in the diocese is essential to the value they bring to the House because they have hands on experience?

Well, it depends on the Bill. I mean if it was a Bill concerned with space travel or something then obviously they wouldn't be more specialised in it than anybody else. But if it was something which concerned social life and economic life, certainly they could speak with authority where as few others could. I don't mean all of them. Someone like Lord Ezra who has been in charge of the coal, he could say something, but you know, in a place, in a conurbation like Birmingham where there was a lot of industry one could speak with some authority and also at that stage there was terrible unemployment, about 10%, one could speak with some authority about that and one could say what one had actually seen. That's of housing too. Whereas I felt that most of the other peers (some of them were experts on the subject) would vote on what they felt rather than what they knew.

Now, Mrs Thatcher, to what extent do you feel that it was her style, you know the way she did things, that created some of the tensions?

Well I have quite an admiration for Margaret Thatcher. Some people forget the hell of a mess this country was in when she first came and there was appalling inflation, about 25% per annum, you know, and she stopped that by being very determined admittedly. When I went to Birmingham, for example, I remember one of the first things I did was to see the person, dear what's he called, who looks after industry?

CBI?

The local CBI man and I said how much over-manning is there and he said, 'about 33%', and I mean she did put an end to that but a lot of factories were closed down because they couldn't cope and it was a very necessary thing to have done, but it was done a bit brutally. She was never very interested in individual people and she thought that they should sink or swim and also her style did initiate a great deal of selfishness, there's no doubt about that. People were out for the money which they weren't before, they saw that they had social responsibilities as well as the need to, well perhaps try and make a fortune. So she was good, I would say she was like the curate's egg, good in parts.

Because I think her policies actually, certainly early on, were significantly important but the style with which they were implemented and the lack of

kind of consensus involvement, discussions, maybe created some of the, and I guess again the weakness of the opposition, the Labour opposition?

Well we were the only opposition. Labour were hopeless at that stage, I really did think that, they didn't seem to have any cutting edge and the Liberals were very feeble too.

Was there a conscious decision at any stage do you think, taken amongst bishops to say, 'this opposition in the House, the official opposition isn't working, we need to up the gear?'

No, no I don't think so. I think that quite a lot of people, I used to belong to a little, we started an urban bishops group actually of the largest conurbations in the country and we were literally, we were terribly appalled at what was happening to people and also over immigration. At that stage people were stateless in the country and we were generally concerned and needed to express our concern but the point was that the bishops were the only people who were doing that really and therefore the Press seized on and tended to inflate what was said I think because we generally tried to be respectful in what we said.

I certainly picked that up reading your speeches, there's a kind of reserve to it, that you maybe would assume wasn't there reading the Press and the media.

Yes, I think that's true and I mean that led to Faith in the City. I was heavily involved in setting up that Commission. We thought that the only way really we could draw attention to what was happening was to set up a really good Commission and in the end we thought the only way that that would have any force was if it was appointed by the Archbishop of Canterbury because that is a name which still commanded some attention and I think that was very successful.

I mean some would say that the *Faith in the City* report, part of its success was it did push beyond broad principles and it did start to really hammer home some details of what needed to happen, but there's obviously this big debate over how political the bishops should be. Now it seems like the greatest success was on an occasion when they did actually get their hands very much dirty. Is that fair?

Well, I don't know, I mean if you look at the number of recommendations that were made in *Faith in the City* precious few of them were implemented and personally I believe that the job of the Church is to do what William Temple called middle axioms. Do you know what I mean by that?

Yes.

I won't go and explain what it is and I'm doubtful as to whether it's appropriate that the Church should give detailed recommendations on what a government should do in particular situations, though I appreciate in a report like that, that unless you had some detailed recommendations, the whole thing would collapse and not be taken seriously. But, by and large, I am not, I don't approve of clergymen getting involved in political details because it's not their job.

Now, I detected an increase in physical attendance and an increased extent of interventions, you know more contributions being made, as the 1980s pro-

gressed. From the 1983/84 to 1987/88 sessions there was a kind of peak in those things. Now I don't know, it's difficult to know whether that was due to specific Bills that went through or whether it was a result of, as a Thatcherite agenda became clearer and maybe some of the New Right policies began to be implemented, that there was an increased response?

Well I'm interested, I didn't know that. You've obviously gone into the statistics of attendance. I retired in '87 and therefore I don't know what happened afterwards really.

There's just that kind of, and it's very difficult because it's out of context, it's just the Thatcher years. But there's a peak for the first two Parliamentary sessions which I wonder if that's just due to the interest of a new government. Again, I'd be interested to know your perspective on that. And then it dips and then it increases again and that's for attendance (and for voting less so) but certainly for the number of speeches that were made.

I find that very interesting. I've never really thought that because I always think the bishops attend because they have something to contribute on a particular subject and if the legislation is controversial or if they think even that it offends against Christian principles then I think they make an effort to attend, and I don't really know what legislation was being put forward in the latter half of '87 or '88. I took a break when I retired so I don't think that I can really comment on that but I don't think that there was a sort of increasing momentum of opposition to the Parliament. I don't think that is the case.

It's interesting, as I've looked at the figures more and more, I've started to think that it was my initial conclusion but looking back at it I think it comes down to specific bills, you know the British Nationality Bill was at the start of the 80's, the Shops Bill...

I have to say that there were, here I must actually go into personalities. It so happened that there were a lot of local bishops who were more concerned with the distribution of wealth than with its creation. This I certainly found in the urban group bishops. Living as I did in Birmingham I was inevitably brought up against the fact that you can't distribute before you create. But I found that that was rather brushed aside by some of my colleagues and I think that this group of bishops, all of whom went on longer than me, probably were more vocal than you would usually find.

Interesting.

People like Booth-Clibborn, who sadly is now dead, and David Sheppard too and the Bishop of Bath, the retiring Bishop of Bath and Wells. But then of course that man who wrote that book, what was his name? You quoted him didn't you?

Medhurst?

That's right, he tends to say the bishops belonged to a sort of middle-class elite which tended to be more left wing than most.

It's interesting to hear you say that they did seem to be more left wing because

also to some extent I think the whole political playing field shifted to the right so far that actually when people took a kind of centre left position they appeared to be far more left wing than they were.

I believe that to be true. I believe that to be true, and there was a certain bias against more liberal-minded people, like Habgood for example was not made Archbishop of Canterbury. Well, I think that Thatcher would have taken the second person on the list rather than putting Habgood there.

Now do you have any particular memories of Thatcher and that relationship?

'That perfectly dreadful man in Birmingham'. I was pleased. It was repeated to me that she had said that.

Really, say it again, I didn't...

'That perfectly dreadful man in Birmingham', and I remember once at the National Exhibition Centre when I was introduced to her she said to me, which I thought was monstrous really, 'but you're always so controversial bishop'. I thought, 'you're the last person to...' I don't think she minded people being straightforwardly opposed to what she said.

I think she thrived on it.

I mean I was invited to dinner in Downing Street which rather surprised me on one occasion.

Now when you went into the Lords, you know you go in '84, what did you see your role as when you went in, you know what were your two, three aims. 'This is why I'm here?'

Oh you receive, have you seen the summons the bishops receive from the Queen? Oh, it's a remarkable document. 'We demand your presence', you know, 'to consult with us on the major affairs of state'. It's most remarkable. Try and get hold of it if you can. So you're summoned with this you see and I thought well I better do this, I better go.

You might be in trouble if you don't !

Yes, and I was clear that my job was not to legislate in a sense, I didn't mean, I mean I did vote occasionally but one was to contribute to the debate as a bishop. And as a bishop that meant to look at the effect on people, on individual people, what the legislation was going to do to them, whether it would further their own, their own situation or not and to talk on broader matters, just say like the nuclear threat, to speak in moral terms. In those days the nuclear argument was very strong and I persuaded the Synod to accept an amendment to the report Bishop Baker produced on this which was all against any kind of nuclear response and I persuaded the Synod to put: 'no first use' instead of that and, but I don't think I ever had occasion to bring that, I can't remember, I don't think there was a nuclear debate in my time in the Lords.

But again so if you found yourself in a position where you actually were quite substantially able to influence church policy on nuclear weapons.

Oh yes. I mean my amendment carried the day. The only time that the, Margaret Thatcher was frightened of the Church. She thought it would go pacifist against the all nuclear mood and this debate was regarded as so important. It's the only time there's been all-day television of the General Synod. It was a very important debate.

Now in your book you've got a whole chapter on the environment. Something I picked up was that the environment was an issue that really didn't get a lot of attention in the House of Lords.

It didn't get a lot of attention anywhere. I've been concerned with the environment since the 1950s. Which is a long time. I wrote the first book really, which was said by *New Scientist* to be the first to produce details on it all and I couldn't get the General Synod interested and the Lords wasn't interested in those days. I mean, nowadays everyone takes it for granted that you've got to be interested in the environment, though no one takes it much for granted that you've got to do something about it! I chaired the Independent Commission on Transport for example, and I was very interested in transport matters and again I chaired the Friends of the Earth. I have been heavily involved in these matters and I've written on it but I don't recollect anything in the House of Lords in my day on the environment, in my three or four years, I don't think there was or I'd have been there. And I did raise the matter. I mean I had a little group at the Board of Social Responsibility, and environmental group and we did produce a report, twice, but I can't say that it had any effect really. People just absented themselves from the debate really.

Prayers. The bishops reading the prayers at start of the day. Do you think that is something which is significant in the life of the House?

Yes, I do. It sets a tone even if people don't go to it. You see a very large number of the members of the House are walking about in the lobby during prayers, not everybody goes there. No one else is allowed in, largely because you really can't see a lot of bottoms! Prayers are very formal prayers but nonetheless I think that, just as the Speaker's Chaplain says prayers in the Commons, I don't say it has a great effect but it does, it does, it is a symbol really that there are, there are moral and spiritual implications. I wouldn't say more than that, and of course I accept that the people who attend it do no doubt pray very genuinely.

How many people would attend them in your experience? Was it, were there many there?

Oh you'd find 30 or 40 probably, but you must remember that you see you only get your daily allowance of course if you come into the Chamber and so most people come in if possible at half past two after prayers to listen to questions and then they pile out. And then they've earned their daily allowance.

Something which very much intrigued me was to learn that the bishops were originally present in the House of Lords because actually they had, they were land owners.

That's right. They were almost the first people in the House of Lords, though I think they're likely to be chucked out now.

Really?

Well, they're talking about it now under the, you know under the new, the latest, well they've got a Parliamentary Committee, a joint committee now haven't they, and I know that people are opposed to any bishops being in there.

Really. You know my expectation has always been that they would reduce the number of bishops to maybe 16 but they would invite other representatives more formally.

Well there's a problem you see with other representatives. First of all the Roman Catholics aren't allowed to be in a legislature. Forbidden by the Pope, except in particular circumstances. Cardinal Hume was certainly offered a life peerage. And secondly, the other officials are not in it for life and the House of Lords is hardly likely to put someone in for five years. You know the Moderator of Methodists and so on, and so there are actually problems. And then there's another problem and that is the bishops are only in the House of Lords because they were actually appointed by the State. Now if others can come in by right who aren't appointed by the State then the State is letting itself in for decision-making by people who have no, who haven't been elected and who haven't been chosen by the State. Do you see the trouble?

Yeah. You can't have one President of the Methodist Conference and then not have another one because maybe their views don't quite fit, you haven't been able to vet them in that sense.

Well they, it puts the power in the hands of the Methodist Church. This is the problem. Not, not the views might be different but the power at the moment is in the hands of the State by nomination of bishops or by creation of life peerages. But once you have, let us say, someone from the Methodist Church comes in, then the Methodist Church would decide who that person was.

Absolutely.

You see the point?

Yes, absolutely.

And this is a great problem for having them. So they have had a few people in but I do see it needs to be more widely shared.

So you seriously think it might be that the bishops would lose their role?

Well I've read this in the paper. Yes, you know in the last week or so. Its only come out lately.

Now, do you think when the General Synod was created in the 70s, do you think because bishops (although you know constitutionally they're not speaking for the church) do you think because they could keep referring back to this slightly more democratic body, do you think that gave them more weight in the House, or do you think it actually reduced it?

I don't think it made any difference at all. No.

No, okay.

I think a person was taken on his own merit. I don't think, as I say I don't think what happened within the Church had any effect on what bishops said. People judged it on its own merits.

And they were warmly welcomed and with good relationships between bishops and the other peers?

Very friendly, no really very friendly. Yes, yes. I was surprised. I was quite surprised, what a welcome one had.

On reflection how much influence do you think the bishops had during the 80s? Are there particular instances you can recall to mind?

No I can't. For instance, I led the opposition to the Shops Bill and it was got through. They wheeled up all the old Dukes and Earls and they all sat in the bar until it came to voting and then they all voted against it.

Goes against the spirit of the thing a bit, doesn't it?

That's right, I'll never forget that. I can't think it had a great deal of influence in specifics. I think on one occasion it did, however, was the Bishop of London over the Education Bill, but then in a way you see a third of all schools are church schools.

A little bit firmer ground.

But you know, it's a bit different. I must be honest, I think it has an influence but I don't think it's an influence of the results really.

Some would say that unless it's influencing the results that's a bad thing but what you could argue is that actually the Christians simply being there and speaking the Word of God or speaking Truth into situations, that's all you can do. You can't force the issue further.

No you can't. It's not as though everyone there is a Christian, and all you can do is to make them aware of the spiritual and moral aspects of the situation as you see it and also through your knowledge in your diocese to make people aware of the implications of what they are doing to individual people and they have to make their own decisions. There's no sort of religious lobbying. No bishops lobby there. We're not there for that purpose.

No, absolutely.

And I think that it's very important that they should hear that, really important they should hear it, whatever decision they make and I wouldn't ask for more than that.

So success to some extent is being heard. After that...

People have to make up their own minds. See the House of Lords is not whipped in the way in the same way as the House of Commons. Did you realise that?

Yes, yes.

It is whipped but no-one minds very much if you vote according to conscious.

Definitely.

Except on a matter like sort of the Shops Bill where they come up from the country. The one thing I think that is very difficult is the Ecclesiastical Committee. It is a very important part of the establishment of the Church of England. When General Synod makes a decision other than on faith and order and doctrine, it has to go before the Ecclesiastical Committee of both the, a joint committee of both Houses. It can't amend it. It can only say to the Houses, this is appropriate or inappropriate and then the Houses have to vote on it. This is rather ridiculous because if you look at the Measures that have gone before the Houses, only those, only those speak who have a bee in their bonnet. So I do think the Ecclesiastical Committee have sometimes helped by saying something is inappropriate. The Synod has then looked at it again and I think once or twice made a more sensible decision.

They've refined it.

But it is an odd situation, really.

The final area really is collegiality and bishops speaking with one voice. Again some would say that the real influence, that the most effective the bishops are, is when they unite and when they speak together. Do you think collegiality is something bishops should work towards in the House?

I'm interested you say that. I remember the Archbishop thinking there should be more collegiality when I was there, giving the impression there had been none before really and this was my impression of bishops meetings, they decide this and that and then all the bishops go off and do whatever they thought best. I think it would be unfortunate if the bishops turned out en-masse and voted en-masse. I don't think they'd be welcomed in the House for so doing and I think it might hasten their decline. Because then there would be a kind of bishop lobby and people would say, you know, 'we're really past this having a lobby from the church', and so on. But secondly, it's utterly impractical. You could never possibly get them all because people have to make a big effort and so they were only on certain occasions. They couldn't make a big effort all the time.

Definitely. There was 18 on one occasion.

Yes, there were. Yes. There have been occasions when people have felt very strongly and there has been strong-line about it. I forget who it was but there were a vast number on one occasion.

I'm not sure whether it was, I think it might have been one of your Shops Bill debates.

Yes, we did have a great, we had a great rally once at that, yes. Yes, that was very interesting because I'd only just come into the House really and I was so enraged by this and I thought that, I was told I couldn't oppose it. I could only say that this Bill be read six months hence. Yes, because if it's read six months hence, then of course it fails because it has to come in the Session. So I moved this Bill be read six months hence.

That's excellent.

Your thesis is what?

The title would be: 'The Contribution of the Church of England Bishops to the House of Lords during the Thatcher Years'.
Yes, that's very interesting.

I'm hoping, I think we're all hoping that, there will be continued religious representation. What one would hope would be reflecting on that period...
You mean, I mean there would be a religious, people with strong convictions. You see one of the things that surprises me about the House of Lords was this, and I don't think this is true of the Commons, but it's true of the House of Lords, is the very strong Christian convictions of large numbers. It's a much more Christian House than the House of Commons and this is very clear. There's a Christian prayer group, for example.

So it would be easy to mistake the loss of the bishops to be the complete loss of Christian influence.
It would be a category error. It would be totally wrong because I mean the lay people are just as important as the bishops and a lot of them have had practical experiences where bishops haven't.

Yes, absolutely. Well, thank you.
No, you mustn't think that to sack the bishops from the House of Lords would mean that it had become a non-Christian body. It wouldn't. Well, whether that would continue with the non-hereditaries, that I'm more doubtful about. You see, the hereditaries do tend to be rather religious strangely enough. So I'm rather uncertain as to whether that would necessarily continue in a reformed House. I may be wrong about that, I'm just uncertain.

Transcript of Interview with David Say (Bishop of Rochester)[1]

(AP) Medhurst and Moyser note that bishops are officially present at the House of Lords as individual peers of the realm rather than corporate spokesmen. Did this fact have any outworking in the way in which you approached your role at the House of Lords?

(DS) The bishops are, we are not peers, we are always referred to as Prelates. We are the only group who are not there for life – at least life! We are there really as cross-benchers, as individuals. The archbishops lay officer at Lambeth Palace keeps an eye on the programme and Lambeth arranges the rota of prayers and if you can't go you have to find someone else. But we are very much present as individuals, in no sense are we an organised party. Some people find it very hard. It's quite important that.

The other thing to be said of course. With the best will in the world the bishops are a group who have very heavy responsibilities – many of them a long distance from London. I should say the majority of people were very understanding of our position. There were the minority who weren't. You see the worst thing that happened that was, we'd have a bishops meeting at Lambeth which would end at lunchtime and quite a lot of the chaps would come into the Lords in the afternoon... and they would be discussing salmon fishing in the Lords. The next day, the very next day, all the bishops have gone back for their jobs and there would be an absolutely cracker debate on some social service and there would be just the duty bishop there. 'Whoa, you were all for salmon fishing, why weren't you here today?'. So that's always been a problem but, as I think I hinted to you in the papers I sent to you, there were occasions when we did turn out in pretty good force which has never been really acknowledged as it should be.

On the whole the lay peers were always glad if we were there and taking part. I always made a special point of trying to be there for big international debates and that was always appreciated. They certainly didn't like it if you only turned up for Ecclesiastical Measures. That leads me to one of your other questions about the chap who says prayers. The importance of that, you see, is that he's around the whole week. There were those who had genuine concerns about faith, about decisions the church was making and one had a personal relationship which was very valuable, very valuable indeed. Dear old Donald Soper who was a great man and always wore a cassock in the House of Lords was never invited.

Your first question was co-ordination and my notes on that are 'not co-ordinated, but kept informed', and that was the role of the lay secretary at Lambeth

---

1   Conducted at Bishop Say's home on 29th May 2002.

to make sure that bishops who were thought to be knowledgeable on various subjects were informed if there was going to be a debate to which they might contribute and the duty bishop was sort of kept in touch of what was likely to come up and if he, sometimes he had no intention of coming, another bishop would be rustled up for it. Now we had no official brief but bishops who were chairman of various Synodical committees, especially education and social responsibility, they always tried to cover the more important legislation and the major general debates. I always used to say that if 12 months ahead you said you would go to St Agatha's in the Mud, then to St Agatha's in the Mud you must go.

Is there any way of getting round that, whilst maintaining strong diocesan links?

It has been to some extent improved by the fact that, for instance the education council or the social responsibility boys will prepare a brief and very often the bishop concerned has been involved in the thought process before, but that is a great help. I used to sometimes refer back to the British Council of Churches, especially on international and ecumenical things. But I think there is really no proper co-ordination. Informing the bishops and stimulating those who might be on the ball.

Individual peers of the realm. I think the fact that we were there as individuals but there was a very real sense in which, unlike the temporal peers, we did have a constituency we had a diocese and I always made a point of any sort of major thing I would consult fairly widely. And also of course we had the responsibility of representing leaders of other Churches, particularly the Free Churches. The Duke of Norfolk would like to claim to be the representative of the Catholic Church so we had to be a bit careful on that one. I had very close relationships with my Roman Catholic neighbours and I didn't hesitate to say so at times and also to bring out when the Roman bishops had acted alongside us and that wasn't always popular with some of the Roman Catholic laymen. I think that the rather distinctive role, the fact that we were only there while we held our jobs and the only group who were not there for life, the Law Lords can stop sitting on the bench but they can go on in the Lords until they die.

Do you think the shift to Synodical government reduced or increased the authority with which you could contribute to the House of Lords?

I really don't think it made any difference. Because you see in the earlier days we had the Church Assembly behind us. I don't think that, with the exception of when one was presenting a Measure which had been through Synod and one was quoting what had been said and the voting there, I don't think on other issues the Synodical thing was really very prominent at all. You've got to face the fact that some of the bishops were pretty bolshy about the Synod anyway. Perhaps one of the things one was able to do at times was to reflect the difference of opinion, that we weren't all lined up... There were people with minds of their own and didn't hesitate to take a different view from the Archbishop of Canterbury.

Some people would say having one voice, a collegiality, is really significant

and inflates the power of your voice. How do you respond to that? Because I am picking up a definite sense that, as far as you are concerned, difference is healthy.

On some of the big issues that we had on housing, the GLC, the Shops Bill, there was a very strong opinion and we were able to quote what others had said and the way others had voted but they were on what I would call the great issues. One of the things a lot of people don't realise is that a very large part of the time in Parliament is extraordinarily dull and the amount of basic homework that has to be done. The revision of legislation that comes up from the Commons where the Commons have not looked even at the commas in the sentences. You'd have 40 pages come up from the Commons which because the guillotine has come down has not been discussed at all. We had no guillotine in the Lords and if we went on till the beginning of August while the Commons were on the beach we did. And the revising role of the Lords, especially now with a great pressure of legislation, a great pressure on the timetable and of course the new boys and girls want to get home for 10pm and can they feed their babies at the bar. There is undoubtedly a change of attitude. I think the reform of the House of Commons is much more important than the reform of the House of Lords. There's no sign that it will happen.

Donald Shell claims that 'bishops, in general, have an impact out of proportion to their numerical strength'. Would you agree with that assessment?

I think that's probably true. I mean there are only 21 of us plus the two archbishops and London and Durham, 21 of us who are doing the work really. Well you put that alongside the numbers of Tories and Labour and Liberal Democrats and certainly cross-benchers. The cross-benchers in the Lords are a very important group. They are very much larger than usually understood. And I believe the situation is so different from when I was there and I believe now the cross-benchers are even more significant than they were before.

Lee and Stanford, writing in 1990, argued that '[g]iven that the majority of the present Government are Christians, and to different degrees practice their faith, they have a natural predisposition to listen rather more attentively to bishops than the general public is led to believe'.

I wouldn't make too much of that. I think that an awful lot of speech-making goes on in the Lords. And a great deal of it from all sides is not very high quality. What I would say is that on a big issue, with a bishop who knows his stuff he can have quite an important influence and is respected as such and appreciated for being there. I think that is all that I would say.

When you step out of the Chamber and you are milling around at the bars, or wherever, is there a power there, is there an opportunity there?

That is why it is important that the bishops should not be governed by their other commitments too much. I used to say very firmly that the week you are on duties for prayers you really must give it priority and not start arranging seeing curates every half hour. I look back now and I've got a fairly full diary, of events rather than comments, and I really am amazed at the intensity of the programme I had to go through. The good Lord was extraordinarily good, that's all I can say, you see. And I went on for longer than most because I wasn't covered by the rule on compulsory retirement. It was a very intensive life. I go back very occasionally now, but I'm always amazed by the chaps, lay peers who stop and greet me and remember things that we did together and that sort of thing. And now, of course, all or most of the hereditaries have been what they call 'pruned'.

If a bishop was allowed to speak in a debate without having to stay to the summing-up and if more notice was given of forthcoming debates do you think that the bishops would be more effective in performing their role?

No, I don't think so because provided you give notice when you begin your speech that you have got to be at so and so at seven o'clock or eight o'clock and unlikely to be able to there for the summing-up. As long as you give notice on that and accept that probably in those circumstances the Minister will not bother to make any comment on what you say. And that's the disadvantage of not staying. If you are still sitting there he can't altogether ignore you, unless he's had fifty speeches and has had to be really selective.

Do you think that, particularly for some of those bishops who live further afield, more notice would make a difference?

It does make a bit of difference. Sometimes one had an advance notice without the details, that Wednesday in three weeks time will be an international debate. Wouldn't get much more notice than that. But then you see the programme is settled on the previous Thursday and all lots of things can blow up in between and there's no guarantee that it will go through as planned.

To what extent do you think it was Mrs Thatcher's style, more than the substance of her policies, which led to much of the tension between Church and State during the 1980s?

No. I think it was the policies that we were opposed to, for the most part. The style, if anything, enabled her to get away with quite a lot. Partly because she was a woman and partly because she was very skilled in playing her cards. But no, I really don't think it was her style, it was the substance of her policies. She was like Tony Blair, she consulted those she wanted to and no one else, that was her way.

Did episcopal opposition to the Thatcher Government increase as a conscious response to the ineffective opposition being offered by the Labour Party?

I don't think it was a conscious response. I think it was later interpreted as such by the lay peers but I don't think the bishops set about to be an organised opposition. But by their reaction to various things like the GLC and the housing and so on, and marriage and divorce, by their reaction to those proposals they built up this role of being a rather more effective opposition than the other around.

Would your experience support the conclusion that bishops are generally well-respected by other peers?

Yes, provided you give it time, provided that you are not always in a hurry and can listen as well as speak.

When you think over particularly the Thatcher years, the 1980s, what would your assessment be of the level of influence you were able to wield?

I don't think this was a thing we were much conscious of, or dare I say concerned about. One turned up, did one's stuff, and took part in what was a a developing pattern of relationships. I was there from '69. I was there in the Harold Wilson Government, the Ted Heath Government, Alec Home, Wilson and Callaghan, and then Margaret Thatcher the rest of the time. As I hinted to you in a reply to one of the earlier questions we weren't really very conscious of setting ourselves up over against the Margaret Thatcher Government any more than anybody else's. It's interesting how in subsequent writing and commentaries and so on that the idea has grown up that the Labour opposition was very weak. I think it was because of that as much as anything else that the role of the bishops was perhaps enhanced by those who were looking for it. Others would have been the last to agree. I'm bound to say we had a fairly active group of bishops around and I think that made a difference too.

The media role. I wonder whether, when the cameras came into the Lords at the start of that period, the bishops and the Thatcher confrontation was enhanced simply because suddenly the world was opened to the spectacle of the House.

Yes, I think you're right there. The Lords were televised several years before the Commons... It was remarkable really, people said that chaps played to the gallery, but the number who did that were very, very few. It tended to underlie how routine and almost dull a lot of the business was. The Commons changed their view very largely because they saw the Lords getting away with it.

The bishops attendance and the number of interventions they were making in debates increased from about 1983/84 onwards to the later part of the 1980s. Do you think that was the result of an accident due to the legislation that was going through or because there was this growing response to a number of Thatcherite policies and lack of social care and neglect of the underprivileged?

As I said to you already I don't think it was a conscious organised thing about opposing Mrs Thatcher. What I think is that the legislation that came up and the debates which we were precipitated into, they did raise very important questions of principle which we did, by and large, take pretty seriously. The GLC debates were, the education debates, the Lords turned down two or three propositions which rocked the boat no end. I haven't thought about it before but I think it is just possible that you had a fairly vigorous, well-informed number of bishops, not the total lot, but a number of them, at a time when the leadership in the Commons was not very strong. The leadership in Parliament was not very strong in both Houses.

I noted in some of the papers you sent to me your proposal that bishops become life peers and thus have an ongoing role in the House of Lords after their retirement from the diocese. In the current reform situation do you see that as one of the possibilities?

It's very sad the way that things have gone. My own, fairly strong view is that the bishops have not helped by insisting upon the numbers being maintained. I have always regretted that there wasn't much more emphasis on the matter being treated ecumenically. You may have seen in one of my letters that I refer back to 1974 when I had made a speech just on that subject. You see the Wakeham Report was really quite good on that and came up with 16 bishops and the other 10 places should go to representatives of other faiths. There is always this bogey that is produced that I tried to deal with in the last letter I wrote to the paper about it. Because the leadership of the free churches changed every year. That is always used to make the excuse that there is no one who can continue in a position of authority and be such in the Lords. Of course what has happened in recent years is that the lady of, who was President of Methodist Conference was made a life Baroness, Mrs Richardson. So she's on the cross-benches, but of course there is considerable pressure about the other faiths. Which is equally difficult to handle because they are not all of one mind. You can get one lot of Moslems being bloody-minded about the others. That would almost inevitably lead to neither of them getting a place. I think it will have to happen in the same way Moslem schools have begun to happen when even 10 years ago that was ruled right out. It's difficult to see what the final pattern is going to be. There's quite a lot of feeling now that the Church of England should no longer have its privileged position. And it could so easily have been handled differently but there are those who are very, very hesitant to extend the reins of leadership. I remember after I made one speech old Hailsham from the Woolsack made quite a humorous crack about the wide variety we might be landed with should the Rt Rev Prelate's ideas should by any chance be followed up. It's going to be very interesting to see. The danger is nothing will happen and they will cruise on with these 92 hereditaries that they've left in. What is so fascinating is that, one of their real problems at the moment is how to get rid of some of the life peers who just haven't pulled their weight. They say that life peers were appointed on the understanding that they were to give time and I think quite a number of them just haven't. Partly because they're getting older and partly because it just hasn't appealed to them. And a chap who has been very good in running his business or some international global concern is not going to sit down day after day and cope with legislation in the Lords.

Do you miss involvement in the House?

Yes, It's the only part of my previous life I do miss. I have always said that it was the one part that I missed. Again, you see, it's no good pretending that it's as it was. And it's not going to be. It's going to be more different still but it's very important and I think quite significant, that the Government have got themselves into such a tizzy over House of Lords reform that they've had now to virtually say we leave it to Parliament to a joint committee of both Houses and we'll see what they come up with. That is an indication of not only how important the Upper House, the revising House is, but also of its independence.

Transcript of Interview with John B. Taylor (Bishop of St Albans)[1]

(AP) Are there any 'departmental briefs', a co-ordination and management?

(JB) A number of bishops have their own portfolios. The Chairman of the Board for Social Responsibility is the obvious person, the Chairman of the Board of Education is another. I had one that related, which was when I was for five years Chairman of Communication and therefore when the Broadcasting Bill came through it was expected that I would, but there was also of course the Bishop of London, as he then was, who was the Chairman of CRAC (Central Religious Advisory Council) so he had an input and there were other people who had been broadcasters (the David Sheppard's of this world) all wanted their five penny worth, quite rightly so. Essentially, the Chairman of the Board is the person who will be there if he can be there, but of course, he may not be on duty. You know the system of duties whereby you do two weeks or three weeks depending on your seniority, and of course several of the weeks are out of sitting time, so you can have a bit of a holiday some of your weeks from the House of Lords. It goes round in order of seniority the list that you sign-up for so those nearer the top can choose their two weeks if they want it to be holiday time or if they would actually like the rough and tumble and they like to be in the House of Lords for its meetings. That's for prayers and for any other business and allegedly you're supposed to be there all day for any business right up to closing time at ten o'clock or whenever it is which is only possible for the bishops of Newcastle or Durham who come and stay in their clubs. Then they can do that more readily than those of us who commute from St Albans, etc.

That takes me on to the last question I've got. The future, how you best operate the bishops' role. One of the things that has struck me is this business of bishops reading prayers and having to be present. What do you think the effect would be if it wasn't the exclusive reserve of the bishops to read prayers? We'll allow the Christian Lords temporal and other Christian denominational leaders in the House when they are there.

Well that does happen occasionally, as you know. When they can't get anyone, and ultimately the Lord Chancellor does prayers and had to do it once for me. But they used... the Methodist Lord Soper. I think he did it on one occasion. And there was another clergyman, priest, member of the House of Lords who I think was once called upon. Actually they don't want to do it and they reckon that if bishops are there than it's their job to do it and so they would not presume to seek to do that because after all you have no choice in it. You go through exactly the set text, all you can do is choose one of the different Psalms that there are.

---

1   Conducted at Bishop Taylor's home on 29th July 2002.

But everything else you've got to go through. There's a collection of Psalms that you choose from. Sometimes you can actually find one slightly appropriate to the debate – in your mind, if not in anyone else's.

It would be decided not by the bishops. It would be decided by the Whips and the Leader of the House. There would be no sympathy for it all. 'If they're not going to do that they may as well not be here' is probably what some of them would say. So if anyone suggested they ducked the one duty they were visibly present for then people would say what's the point. It's not going to feasibly come from the bishops. It would only come if it was part of a concealed hostility towards the bishops.

Going back to your original question about briefings, clearly the Board for Social Responsibility men can't be there very often. For a major thing he might get a fortnights notice if he's lucky. And may just have to clear his diary for it. But if he can't then the duty bishop really is under some obligation to take the brief and he will be briefed by the Secretary of the Board concerned. Now I was briefed on two or three occasions. I was briefed actually by a Roman Catholic body because they were very anxious that someone should speak on the GATT [General Agreement on Tariffs and Trade] Uruguay round, well I'm not an economist but they gave me the things they wanted said and I duly said them and the other occasion was the Board of Social Responsibility on the War Crimes Bill. There was pressure on me to speak. I think I was on duty. I think I was. I spoke to the Secretary of the Board and said actually, 'what is the Board's view?' He said well we had a weekend away looking at this and we came to such and such a conclusion. I said, 'If I wanted to put it more strongly than that how would you mind?' He said, 'not in the slightest. You speak what you want.' But clearly it was in the same direction but probably going a bit further. They were a bit cautious in the area of reactions. I was a bit more diffident. I duly prepared my speech. I may have some sentences from them. Yes, probably I did. But I made it my own and I did do my homework on that. Broadcasting Bill, obviously I was briefed well when I was Chairman of Communication by the Broadcasting officer at Church House and he put some nice phrases in that I was able to use. He didn't write the speech but he wrote material that becomes a speech. But that's how it works.

Now in terms of organising it, the person who organises it is the Archbishop's Secretary for public affairs who was Andrew Perkins who was the best one. He was the last one I worked under. He got the papers immediately at Lambeth. He was first to know when anything was coming up and he immediately started phoning round to the Board Secretaries just weighing up the importance of it. From time to time other organisations, CAFOD or whatever would say, 'for Pete's sake we can't let this one go by default, something must be said', and 'could the bishop do it?' And they would just do their best and see if they could comply. Or perhaps realise it is something the Church of England bishops should say something on behalf of the nation.

Did you feel the fact that you were there in your own right, not as spokesmen or a voice for the Church?

No. You were aware that you had total freedom to say what you wanted to say. But essentially the things that you wanted to say would be representing the Church's view and you wanted to know what the Church's line was on a particular subject, though you may well diverge from it. In point of fact some of us did diverge from it over the Education Bill. We wanted to tighten it up and I think I incurred a bit of the displeasure of the then Bishop of London, Graham Leonard, who was Chairman of the Board of Education because a number of us, particularly evangelicals, we signed a letter to The Times or something which asked for more than we were likely to get. And I think he rather wished we hadn't. But in point of fact there was quite a bit of feeling on the back benches amongst other godly minded peers and this was useful pressure to bring to bear. We thought it would be helping the bishop of London in his negotiating. But anyway he was aware that there was this body of opinion which he was able to align with the Moslem body of opinion who were lobbying him too and the Jewish people so that in the end he was able to say to the Government, 'well this is what the Jews and Moslems as well as the Church of England and others believe, so it's a strong platform can we get some consensus on this so it's not going to be a voting issue?' The main aim in the House of Lords is not to have to vote. And if you're arguing a case the last thing you want is a vote. Because a vote, if you're defeated, means you're dead. So you put a point and simply hope that the Minister will consider it and maybe modify things next time and perhaps you'll write in between whiles and you'll talk to some of his civil servants and he'll be anxious to find out what your case is and to give it consideration, and if it's a strong point, to meet it. So, if at an early stage you tried an amendment to a vote you wouldn't do well because the Whip would make sure it was defeated and you wouldn't have got anything whereas you might get a quarter of a cake... In my early stages I said to one person on an issue that I was quite supportive of: 'Why did you withdraw the amendment?' 'Because they've heard what I wanted to say and now we'll see further so that maybe we'll get an amendment written into a Bill then I shan't have to take it to a vote.'

Lee and Stanford, writing in 1990, argue that: 'Given that the majority of the present Government are Christians, and to different degrees practice their faith, they have a natural predisposition to listen rather more attentively to bishops than the general public is led to believe'. Is that true?

I don't know things since the end of the Tory government. I know when I was there was a fair amount of poo-pooing of the bishops when it came to our constant opposition of the Sunday Trading Bill. They sneered a bit and we had to tick them off. And the Labour peers ticked them off roundly, 'the Rt Rev Prelates are doing their job as Christian leaders'. By and large they very much appreciated what the bishop had to say because the bishop usually spoke sense, because the bishop didn't speak with a party-political card and steered very often through an argument and raised an issue that needed to be raised but was not a party-political ding-dong battle. I remember one saying to me: 'In my opinion a bishop ought to speak in every debate'. That was one of the younger ones. They know exactly what the other side are going to say. And it's only the bishops who will say something different. Or sometimes the Law Lords. You do listen to someone who has a different slant. And you also of course listen to someone who has an expertise. When the head of the MI6 stands up you listen to her... or where the former Chief of the Defence Staff stands up, he may be a bit of an old soldier, he may have been out of office for about fifteen years, but I think he's respected because he's done the job and knows what it's about.

Off the floor of the House did you spend a lot of time meeting with Ministers, meeting with other peers, seeking to put across a point of view, or did you see that amongst the other bishops?

There wasn't time for it. There are some bishops who are remarkably good at hobnobbing and socialising. The best one was Maurice Wood, when he was Bishop of Norwich and they loved him. He was the kind of bishop they loved. He was always around. He was in the bar chatting with them. He was caring for them pastorally, he was asking after their wives. He knew them by their Christian names, he spent a lot of time. He did nearly all his diocesan work from there. He spent quite a lot of time there. And being an Irishman and being very quick on his feet he could stand up and speak on anything very well. They liked him. There was quite a move when he retired to get him a Barony which would be exceptional because only Archbishops get Baronies, except more recently David Sheppard was, which really was breaking new ground. There's a lot to be said, but you know David is hardly ever there. Can't be. He's had cancer I believe and so forth so he's not doing all that well and he's right up in the Wirral. And John Habgood hardly ever shows up from Yorkshire and of course Robert Runcie's dead. So though you would have more time than the average diocesan bishop you just have an incredibly packed diary.

Making it possible for more bishops to have an additional five years in House after they retire from their diocese duties makes a lot of sense.

Everything is decided not by the Church of England but by everybody else. I think by and large they'd like to have a bishop there who actually does represent a constituency. It's like asking an MP to carry on four years after he has been deselected, even though from a practical point of view they would have more time to be available, though there's no compulsion to be there. One of the problems that the Blair Government or any government have is they appoint political peers and the chaps don't show up. They just enjoy the kudos and don't do the donkey work. So a person who does the donkey work is a person who is very much appreciated on all sides of the House. But bishops can't be expected to do that because their donkey work is in the parish.

Did you feel in the House the burden of literally not having enough time?

Oh yes, you tried every excuse to get off a bit early because you'd got to get back for something or another, or if not you knew very well there were a pile of problems waiting on your desk needing to be dealt with. Sometimes you had to go back. My most embarrassing one was when of all things on Ash Wednesday they decided to have one of the readings of the Sunday Trading Bill on which I was leading. Well, I've got a service in the evening, I've got to get back to it. And normally if you speak in a debate you are supposed to stay 'til the end. And I had to apologise to the House but I got a tart comment from one of the Lords who ought to have known better. You spend your time going in and out. You don't listen to it all. After you have spoken you are supposed to stay for the next one or two speeches. It's only your maiden speech you are supposed to stick it out and you're allowed to go out for natural needs, and I did sneak out for a cup of tea... You nip out and do a telephone call, you nip out and talk to your secretary, you nip out and look at anything in today's post. You're always in and out.

Did you feel that you had an influence in the 80s? It's a broad question. Did you feel that when you made the effort to go down there, you spent that time, you crushed your diary to make it happen? Do you think that changed anything? If you had it again would you be there more because you feel like you'd have more influence or would you be there less because you were really just going through the motions?

I quite enjoyed going, and part of it was just being sociable and talking with your friends. I am not sure that great changes took place as a result of what you did or said, though if the Church took a specifically contrary or divergent view and it was recognised that they did then civil servants had to listen to them because that's what they're paid to do and bring it to the Minister's attention and if necessary, on some bills more than others, I mean the education ones particularly – the vast influence of Church schools. They had to do a lot and the Chairman of the Board of Education, not just Graham Leonard who did good work, but more particularly Michael Adie, Bishop of Guildford – you'll recall that he got an OBE for his work which is a rare thing for a Board of Education. That really is because he spent hours on that bill and hours in discussions with the Ministers and they talked to him man to man and knew that they had to got to come up with something that was going to be reasonably acceptable to the Churches. As far as my issues, the War Crimes Bill was concerned, well most of the people were very sceptical about the War Crimes Bill. The only people who were speaking for it apart from Lord Tonypandy were Jews interestingly. But then you see most of the House of Lords remembered the Nuremburg trials and they remembered that actually by the time we had hanged quite a number of them we were just feeling that enough is enough and this could go on forever so it was deliberately called a halt to. And of course the House of Commons went for it because they were younger by thirty years and it was definitely a generational thing. And in point of fact from a Christian point of view I wanted to put in my view. We don't have to go on securing vengeance right to the last drop because every one of these people is going to have to stand before the judgement seat of God and that's far more terrifying than going through this. As well as the truly practical matter. If they're from Lithuania and now living in England what chance are you going to have of getting a reasonable defence mounted, what chance are you going to have of reliable identification evidence fifty years on, and the fact that what you are going to do is harry a few old men who maybe have seen things in a better light and whose children and grandchildren knew nothing of this. Anyway, they went for it. I think they produced one conviction. They've had one or two trials.

Do you think that the shift to synodical government reduced or increased the authority with which you could contribute to the House?

We never referred to Synod. Very, very rarely. On a particular issue we might say as part of our argument: 'Your Lordships will appreciate there has been quite a head of steam in the General Synod over this and so this represents the view of the clergy and laity in the Church as well as of the episcopate', and so you'd draw that to their attention. But only rarely do you mention how things went in the General Synod if its a thing going to the Ecclesiastical Committee and then going on before the House of Lords after that. So if a thing is a bit divided in the General Synod as many issues were then maybe the Ecclesiastical Committee will know what the voting is, will know what the debate said, because they'll have read the report of the debate and they may say 'well, you're not clear in your mind about this', and so you're onto a hiding to nothing. But you've got to have a very clear mandate if you're going for Measures to go through this House of Parliament. Mostly measures are called Miscellaneous provision measures which are tiddly-widdly little things.

If a bishop was allowed to speak in a debate without having to stay 'til the summing-up as a matter of procedure do you think that would encourage more bishops to speak in the House?

I don't think so, no.

You can leave I guess?

Oh you can, oh yes. They understand. They're very understanding towards you but you obviously try to fulfil the requirement as you can. And there are other peers who will apologise. Courtesy more than law. Everything is courtesy in the House of Lords.

Do you think the tension between Church and State during the '80s was due to a contrast of style between the Church of England led by Runcie and the Thatcher government, rather than the substance of her policies?

Oh, no I don't think it's quite that. Margaret Thatcher came to power really with her first thing to beat the power of the Unions and therefore she took on the troublemakers. Having beaten the power of the Unions she said now who next shall we take on and then it began to be professional associations – the BMA and the NUT and people like that who she thought was getting a bit uppity. And the local council, the local authority, the GLC, she took them all on and weakened their power considerably. I think she over did it. Robert Runcie's role. I mean there was no Labour opposition to speak of at all. Robert Runcie's role was that he was reminding the Government of where these issues were hurting people. That was his only concern, not to be against the Government, but to say to the Government: 'hold on do you realise what you're doing, do you realise what's going on in the inner cities. You may have achieved your successes but these are crying shames'. And it was quite a while before Margaret Thatcher suddenly realised that the inner cities, this is what we must do something about. So the ignored areas of policy I think the Church was speaking on behalf of. Clearly, the politicians didn't like this. They didn't like the opposition to the Sunday Trading Bill in particular. I remember being taken to task by Lord Hailsham in a long letter because I happened to say when that came forward that I could no longer give my support to the Government who attacked the institution of the Sunday. And I got a personal letter from Lord Hailsham telling me what a, well, what a chump I was. It was at a time when they were always telling the bishops not to meddle with politics, to which my reply was, 'well let the politicians not meddle with religion'. And I said it very strongly and they knew they couldn't answer. Then of course they brought out the argument that's it's totally illogical, you can't buy a Bible on a Sunday whereas you can buy pornography. And they tried to find every cathedral bookshop that was open on a Sunday. But I recognised that Sunday Trading laws were totally anomalous and what do you do about it. If you're trying to be a radically reformist government then you can understand them wanting to do that. But then they'd have done it far better if they had done it with consensus, or with the understanding of the religious authorities. But there we are.

So Robert Runcie took this particular line. In terms of relationship with Margaret Thatcher I think it fairly cool. They knew each other at Oxford but didn't get on as chums... And there was the famous occasion when she invited the bishops for lunch at Chequers. She suggested that Robert Runcie brought some of the bishops with him. And he put up some names and she vetoed some and the net result was about eight or ten of us went. But I was invited and Robert Runcie got those of us together after a House of Bishops meeting to decide what we would do. 'It would be rather a good idea if we finished up with some prayer and a bible study. Now John would you do the bible study?'

She was jolly good. She had two key advisors, both of them evangelical minded. Michael Allison was her Parliamentary Private Secretary and Robin Catford was her Ecclesiastical Appointments Secretary and I think these two had probably hatched the idea of suggesting it to her so they were very anxious for it to succeed and actually they were extraordinarily pleased with the way it turned out. So we duly went there on a Saturday lunchtime and I prepared my, 'what are you going to speak on? Romans 13?' 'No, I'm going to start where they are, I'm going to take the Sermon on the Mount.' But anyway, after lunch we went into the dining room and she sat down, we all sat down, and she was very gracious. She's a very gracious person. She said, 'now come on bishops, I've got no toes, you can't tread on anything that hurts, you say what you want and I'll say what I want'. So Robert Runcie I think started out and then we moved on and I can't remember how the conversation went, all I remember was I had the job of giving a little homily at the end, an opening-up of scripture, and leading in prayer. But as I say, the advisors were not just pleased with it, they said 'this is history'. And it happened in November and she said at the end of it, 'well let's not pretend this hasn't happened'. But no-one knew anything about it until February or March and then I was in Jerusalem and I got a telephone call from a Times correspondent or someone saying, 'Is it right that this happened?' I said, 'how did you hear?' He said, 'the Bishop of Peterborough mentioned it and we're surprised we didn't know. I said, 'yes it did happen, there's no secret of that'. So then it came out as a piece of news three months late. She was quite concerned that she didn't want to have the Church obviously against her. And around about that time also she took to (again it may been Michael Allison's influence) she took to inviting the odd stray bishops to a lunch or a dinner at Downing Street. After the Brighton Bomb, because he was the area bishop, Peter Ball, the Bishop of Lewes did a marvellous job caring for the injured and the bereaved and actually she wrote and asked me if I would write a reflection on the Brighton Bomb to pass round a lot of people concerned and was much appreciated. And then she turned up at Prom Praise. Michael Baughen or Richard Bewes must have invited her. Getting into the evangelical community I think. Then she invited me to a lunch when the Japanese Prime Minister came. So she got the idea of getting the odd bishop in to say grace or to be a part when she was entertaining which was her way of I think, part olive branch, part seduction. Political move.

Do you think she had a sincere and real faith?
Oh yes. Oh yes. But it was a rather Methodisty one and I don't think she had much sympathy with the eucharistic nature of so much Anglicanism which she came across. But she knew the Church of England was the established Church. She had her judgements about different bishops...

Was there ever a point at which the bishops said, consciously, we need to up the ante because there just isn't an opposition voice?
No. It was just a vacuum and therefore people were wanting another voice and then they turned to a bishop, the media did.

So the level of interest didn't increase, the focus shifted?
I mean Runcie was a very good media man and he was much sought after and he had a good number of people around him. And the BBC suddenly got the idea that bishops were available, bishops were articulate, bishops had a degree of authority. Michael Foot had none at all and Neil Kinnock not very much. So that was the weakness, there was no opposition of that sort and therefore you didn't want to get in a half-baked politician. You didn't want an opposition point of view, you wanted a different point of view.

How can you see things developing in terms of the bishops role?
I think, their wings are going to be trimmed quite a bit which will be a pity. Not so much because they won't be able to do so much, but it will fall on fewer and fewer shoulders. And that's the trouble when there's a very heavy burden... you've got to work very hard to give that time commitment and if you've got to give even more time commitment then your senior bishops are going to do their jobs less well. So it's all a matter of choices and priorities. So that's the trouble and you're very glad there are twenty-six of you so you can share things around tolerably well. There was always a bishop who was, as it were, the whipper-in of the other bishops. I did it with Roy Williamson, Southwark for a time and also did it with Michael Adie for a time. Mainly because all of us were within reach of London and therefore we could either bring a bit of influence to bear upon our brother bishops and say, 'this really is important do your very best chum'. Or alternatively we might have to stand-in ourselves. And just occasionally they wanted to consult with a bishop, for instance about changing the bishops' arrangements, and they wanted someone they could talk to other than the Archbishop of Canterbury and we did a certain amount of negotiating over changing the bishops' rooms, things to do with whether bishops always have to wear robes to vote. So you did have, I think they call them, 'pack leaders'.

Is that a term that's used officially?

Certainly I was asked by Robert Runcie 'would you be one of the pack leaders?' And I would hold meetings for the bishops in the House of Lords occasionally when you wanted to discuss a particular issue and get their mind on it or give them a bit of a jog or tell them 'hang on you mustn't play around in the prayers' or pass them things through to them if we've got them from the usual channels.

If numbers are reduced could it be that those bishops who are eligible to do it are released from more of their local duties so that they would have the time?

Well, they'll just have to get their suffragan to do more. Work has to be done. Richard Harries is ideally placed because he has three suffragans and no real episcopal area of his own. You do leave others to run the diocese. A diocesan bishop is there to lead the diocese, someone else can run the diocese. There are expectations on you being present at this, that and the other. And you want to because you are very much a Father of the family and you don't want to be out too frequently. But it has to be said that the diocese usually recognises that they get back in benefits from what they lose in time. Because you are bringing something back into your diocese from your contribution outside there in the world. And when they hear what you're doing they're glad that their man is involved. Very, very few dioceses resent the time that bishops spend in the House of Lords, or episcopal meetings or Church bodies, because they know very well that they are privileged to have a wider insight when they are talking with their bishops. Therefore, leadership is very much to do with networks and when a person whose slogging it out in a parish or as a diocesan social responsibility advisor gets a real problem he goes to his bishop and his bishop will immediately now four or five people he can put him in touch with that he was not aware of. So it really is opening doors. It's not old boyism. It's actually knowing people and knowing where the resources are, where the people with ideas are and putting people together.

Subject Classification Scheme

1.00	**Agriculture, Fisheries and Food**
1.01	Miscellaneous
1.02	Agriculture
1.03	Animal Welfare
1.04	Biotechnology
1.05	Diversification
1.06	Environment
1.07	EU Agricultural
1.08	EU Fisheries
1.09	Food
1.10	Fisheries
1.11	Forestry
1.12	Horse Industry
1.13	Land Tenure
1.14	Land Use
1.15	Organic Farming
1.16	Pesticides
1.17	Veterinary Medicine

2.00	**Culture, Media and Sport**
2.01	Miscellaneous
2.02	Arts Policy
2.03	Broadcasting (TV & Radio)
2.04	Films and Videos
2.05	Historic Buildings & Ancient Monuments
2.06	Libraries
2.07	Millennium Commission
2.08	National Lottery
2.09	Museums, Galleries & Music Venues
2.10	Printed Media
2.11	Sport
2.12	Tourism

3.00	**Defence**
3.01	Miscellaneous
3.02	Armed Forces
3.03	Conventional Weapons
3.04	Disaster Relief
3.05	Environmental
3.06	European Union
3.07	Exports & Defence Industry
3.08	Health & Safety
3.09	Intelligence & Secret Services
3.10	International Organizations
3.11	Non-Conventional Weapons
3.12	Procurements
3.13	Research
3.14	Terrorism
3.15	Multilateral Operations
3.16	Veterans

4.00	**Education and Employment**
4.01	Miscellaneous
4.02	Career Guidance
4.03	Equal Opportunities
4.04	European Union
4.05	Further Education
4.06	Higher Education & Research
4.07	International Organizations
4.08	Labour Market
4.09	Schools
4.10	Teachers
4.11	Under 5s
4.12	Employment
4.13	Vocational Training
4.14	Special Needs Education

Argument Classification Scheme

Secular

S1	History, Precedents & Traditions
S2	Human Rights
S3	Environment & Pollution
S4	Economy & Finance
S5	Philosophy
S6	Community, Society & Family
S7	Law & Order
S8	Education & Human Development
S9	The Future
S10	Health & Safety
S11	Facts & Statistics
S12	Public Opinion
S13	Cultural Considerations
S14	International Development
S15	British International Interests
S16	World Community & Peace
S17	Constitutional, Democratic & Legal
S18	Defence & National Security
S19	Accountability & Quality Control
S20	Academic & Professional Advice
S21	Equal Opportunities
S22	Fairness, Principle, Justice & Duty

Experience

E1	Diocesan & Vocational
E2	Personal

Theological

T1	Scripture
T2	Doctrine & Theology
T3	Christian Tradition
T4	Spirituality & Worship
T5	Non-Christian Worldviews
T6	Church History

Ecclesiastical

C1	Constitutional Position
C2	Canon Law
C3	Christian Opinion
C4	C of E Finance
C5	C of E Reports
C6	C of E General Synod
C7	Authority of Episcopal Office
C8	C of E Worldwide
C9	C of E Board for Social Responsibility
C10	C of E Schools & Colleges
C11	Other C of E Bishops
C12	Ecumenical Relations

Morality

M1	Personal Morality
M2	Social Morality & Ethics

Bibliography

Primary Sources

House of Lords Debates (Hansard), Volumes 400-414 (1979/80 Session) (London: Her Majesty's Stationery Office).

House of Lords Debates (Hansard), Volumes 415-424 (1980/81 Session) (London: Her Majesty's Stationery Office).

House of Lords Debates (Hansard), Volumes 425-435 (1981/82 Session) (London: Her Majesty's Stationery Office).

House of Lords Debates (Hansard), Volumes 436-442 (1982/83 Session) (London: Her Majesty's Stationery Office).

House of Lords Debates (Hansard), Volumes 443-456 (1983/84 Session) (London: Her Majesty's Stationery Office).

House of Lords Debates (Hansard), Volumes 457-467 (1984/85 Session) (London: Her Majesty's Stationery Office).

House of Lords Debates (Hansard), Volumes 468-481 (1985/86 Session) (London: Her Majesty's Stationery Office).

House of Lords Debates (Hansard), Volumes 482-487 (1986/87 Session) (London: Her Majesty's Stationery Office).

House of Lords Debates (Hansard), Volumes 488-501 (1987/88 Session) (London: Her Majesty's Stationery Office).

House of Lords Debates (Hansard), Volumes 502-512 (1988/89 Session) (London: Her Majesty's Stationery Office).

House of Lords Debates (Hansard), Volumes 513-522 (1989/90 Session) (London: Her Majesty's Stationery Office).

House of Lords Debates (Hansard), Volume 523 (1990/91 Session) (London: Her Majesty's Stationery Office).

House of Lords Sessional Statistics for the 1979/80 Session (House of Lords Journal and Information Office).

House of Lords Sessional Statistics for the 1980/81 Session (House of Lords Journal and Information Office).

House of Lords Sessional Statistics for the 1981/82 Session (House of Lords Journal and Information Office).

House of Lords Sessional Statistics for the 1982/83 Session (House of Lords Journal and Information Office).

House of Lords Sessional Statistics for the 1983/84 Session (House of Lords Journal and Information Office).

House of Lords Sessional Statistics for the 1984/85 Session (House of Lords Journal and Information Office).

House of Lords Sessional Statistics for the 1985/86 Session (House of Lords Journal and Information Office).

House of Lords Sessional Statistics for the 1986/87 Session (House of Lords Journal and Information Office).

House of Lords Sessional Statistics for the 1987/88 Session (House of Lords Journal and Information Office).

House of Lords Sessional Statistics for the 1988/89 Session (House of Lords Journal and Information Office).

House of Lords Sessional Statistics for the 1989/90 Session (House of Lords Journal and Information Office).

Secondary Sources

Anderson, D. (ed.), *The Kindness That Kills* (London: SPCK, 1984).

Archbishops' Council, *The Role of the Bishops in the Second Chamber: A Submission by the Church of England*, GS Misc. 558 (London: Church House Publishing, 1999).

— *Comments from the Church of England on the Government's White Paper* (Unpublished: January 2002).

Archbishop of Canterbury's Commission on Church and State, *Church and State* [The Chadwick Report] (London: Church House Publishing, 1970).

Archbishop of Canterbury's Commission on Urban Priority Areas, *Faith in the City: A Call for Action by Church and Nation* (London: Church House Publishing, 1985).

Avis, P., Church, *State and Establishment* (London: SPCK, 2001).

— *The Anglican Understanding of the Church: An Introduction* (London: SPCK, 2000).

Badham, P., 'Some Secular Trends in the Church of England Today', in P. Badham (ed.), *Religion, State and Society in Modern Britain* (Lampeter: Edwin Mellen Press, 1989), 23-34.

— 'Introduction', in P. Badham (ed.), *Religion, State and Society in Modern Britain* (Lampeter: Edwin Mellen Press, 1989), vii-xiv.

Badham, P. (ed.), *Religion, State and Society in Modern Britain* (Lampeter: Edwin Mellen Press, 1989).

Baelz, P. *Ethics and Belief* (London: Sheldon Press, 1977).

Baldwin, N.D.J. 'The House of Lords: Behavioural Changes – A New Professionalism and a More Independent House', in P. Norton (ed.), *Parliament in the 1980s* (Oxford: Basil Blackwell, 1985), 96-113.

— 'The House of Lords', in M. Rush (ed.), *Parliament and Pressure Politics* (Oxford: Oxford University Press, 1990), 152-177.

— 'The Membership of the House', in D. Shell & D. Beamish (eds.), *The House of Lords at Work: A Study Based on the 1988-1989 Session* (Oxford: Clarendon Press, 1993), 33-60.

Baldwin, N.D.J. & Shell, D.R., *Second Chambers* (London: Frank Cass, 2001).

Barth, K., *Church and State* (London: SCM Press, 1939).

Batsford, B.T., *The Whitehall Companion 1998-99* (London: DPR, 1998).

Bauckham, R., *The Bible in Politics: How to Read the Bible Politically* (London: SPCK, 1989).

Beeson, T., *The Bishops* (London: SCM Press, 2002).

Berger, P., *Noise of Solemn Assemblies* (Garden City, NY: Doubleday & Co., 1961).

Biddis, M., 'Thatcherism: Concept and Interpretations', in K. Minogue & M. Biddis (eds.), *Thatcherism: Personality and Politics* (London: Macmillan, 1987), 1-20.

Birch, A.H., *The British System of Government* (London: Routledge, 1998).

Birch, B.C., *Let Justice Roll Down: The Old Testament, Ethics, and Christian Life* (Louisville, KY: Westminster John Knox Press, 1991).

Board for Social Responsibility, *Not Just for the Poor: Christian Perspectives on the Welfare State* (London: Church House Publishing, 1986).

Bown, F., 'Influencing the House of Lords: the Role of the Lords Spiritual 1979-1987', *Political Studies*, XLII (1994), 105-119.

— 'The Defeat of the Shops Bill', in M. Rush (ed.), *Parliament and Pressure Politics* (Oxford: Oxford University Press, 1990), 213-233.

Brierley, P. & Wraight, H., *UK Christian Handbook 1996/1997* (London: Christian Research, 1995).

Brierley, P. & Longley, D., *UK Christian Handbook 2000/2001* (London: Christian Research, 1999).

Bruce, S., *Religion in Modern Britain* (Oxford: Oxford University Press, 1995).

— *Religion in the Modern World: From Cathedrals to Cults* (Oxford: Oxford University Press, 1996).

Campbell, J., *Margaret Thatcher: The Grocer's Daughter* (London: Jonathan Cape, 2000).

Carpenter. E., *Archbishop Fisher: His Life and Times* (Norwich: The Canterbury Press, 1991).

Carpenter, H., *Robert Runcie: The Reluctant Archbishop* (London: Hodder & Stoughton, 1996).

Chadwick, H., 'Tradition, Fathers and Councils', in S. Sykes & J. Booty (eds.), *The Study of Anglicanism* (London: SPCK, 1988), 91-104.

Chadwick, O., *Michael Ramsey: A Life* (Oxford: Clarendon Press, 1990).

Clark, H., *The Church Under Thatcher* (London: SPCK, 1993).

Cohn-Sherbok, D. & McLellan, D., *Religion in Public Life* (New York: St Martin's Press, 1992).

Constitution Unit, *Reforming the Lords: The Role of the Bishops* (London: 1999).

Cornwell, P., 'The Church of England and the State: Changing Constitutional Links in Historical Perspective', in G.H. Moyser (ed.), *Church and Politics Today: The Role of the Church of England in Contemporary Politics* (Edinburgh: T & T Clark, 1985), 33-54.

Davie, G., *Religion in Britain Since 1945: Believing Without Belonging* (Oxford: Blackwell, 1994).

— 'From Obligation to Consumption: Patterns of Religion in Northern Europe at the Start of the 21st Century' (Forthcoming).

Davies, C., 'Religion, Politics, and "Permissive" Legislation', in P. Badham (ed.), *Religion, State and Society in Modern Britain* (Lampeter: Edwin Mellen Press, 1989), 321-342.

De Gruchy, J.W., *Christianity and Democracy* (Cambridge: Cambridge University Press, 1995).

Dobson, E., 'The Bible, Politics, and Democracy', in R.J. Neuhaus (ed.), *The Bible, Politics and Democracy* (Grand Rapids: Eerdmans, 1987), 1-18.

Drewry, G. & Brock, J., 'Prelates in Parliament', *Parliamentary Affairs*, 24 (1970-71), 222-250.

Dyson, A., '"Little Else But The Name" Reflections on Four Church and State Reports', in G.H. Moyser (ed.), *Church and Politics Today: The Role of the Church of England in Contemporary Politics* (Edinburgh: T & T Clark, 1985), 282-312.

Ecclestone, G., 'Church Influence on Public Policy Today', *The Modern Churchman*, 28 (1986), 36-47.

— 'The General Synod and Politics', in G.H. Moyser (ed.), *Church and Politics Today: The Role of the Church of England in Contemporary Politics* (Edinburgh: T & T Clark, 1985), 107-127.

— *The Church of England and Politics* (London: Church House Publishing, 1981).

Elford, J., 'The Church and Nuclear Defence Policy', in G.H. Moyser (ed.), *Church and Politics Today: The Role of the Church of England in Contemporary Politics* (Edinburgh: T & T Clark, 1985), 176-200.

Eliot, T.S., *Christianity and Culture: The Idea of a Christian Society* (New York: Harvest, 1949).

Evans, B., *Thatcherism and British Politics 1975-1999* (Stroud: Sutton, 1999).

Field, F., 'The Church of England and Parliament: A Tense Partnership', in G.H. Moyser (ed.), *Church and Politics Today: The Role of the Church of England in Contemporary Politics* (Edinburgh: T & T Clark, 1985), 55-74.

Fogarty, M., 'The Churches and Public Policy: The Case for a Review', *Policy Studies*, 9.4 (1989), 43-48.

Forrester, D.B., *Beliefs, Values and Policies* (Oxford: Clarendon Press, 1989).

— 'The Ecumenical Renovation of the Gospel', in H. Willmer (ed.), *Christian Faith and Political Hopes: A Reply to E.R. Norman* (London: Epworth Press, 1979), 34-46.

Freedland, J., *Bring Home the Revolution* (London: Fourth Estate, 1998).

Fuller, R.H., 'Scripture', in S. Sykes & J. Booty (eds.), *The Study of Anglicanism* (London: SPCK, 1988), 79-90.

Furlong, M., *C of E: The State It's In* (London: Hodder & Stoughton, 2000).

Giddens, A., 'Elites in British Class Structure', in P. Stanworth & A. Giddens (eds.), *Elites and Power in British Society* (Cambridge: Cambridge University Press, 1974), 1-21.

Gill, R., *Prophecy and Praxis* (London: Marshall, Morgan & Scott, 1981).

Gilmour, I. & Garnett, M., *Whatever Happened To The Tories: The Conservatives*

Since 1945 (London: Fourth Estate, 1998).

Gould, J. & Anderson, D., 'Thatcherism and British Society', in K. Minogue & M. Biddis (eds.), *Thatcherism: Personality and Politics* (London: Macmillan, 1987), 38-54.

Government White Paper, *Modernising Parliament: The Reform of the House of Lords*, Cm 4183 (London: The Stationery Office, January 1999).

— *The House of Lords: Completing the Reform*, Cm 5291 (London: The Stationery Office, November 2001).

Griffith, J.A.G. & Ryle, R., *Parliament: Functions, Practice and Procedures* (London: Sweet & Maxwell, 1989).

Guy, J.R., 'Church in Wales', in J. Cannon (ed.), *The Oxford Companion to British History* (Oxford: Oxford University Press, 1997), 207.

Habgood, J., *Church and Nation in a Secular Age* (London: Darton, Longman & Todd, 1983).

Hamilton, M., *The Sociology of Religion: Theoretical and Comparative Perspectives* (London: Routledge, 1995).

Harries, R., 'Why we need faith in the Lords', in *Church Times* (24th May 2002).

Hastings, A., *A History of English Christianity 1920-1985* (London: William Collins, 1986).

— *Robert Runcie* (London: Mowbray, 1991).

— *Church and State: The English Experience* (Exeter: University of Exeter Press, 1991).

Haynes, J., *Religion in Global Politics* (London: Longman, 1998).

Hays, R., *The Moral Vision of the New Testament* (Edinburgh: T & T Clark, 1996).

Hennessy, P., 'The Prime Minister, the Cabinet and the Thatcher Personality', in K. Minogue & M. Biddis (eds.), *Thatcherism: Personality and Politics* (London: Macmillan, 1987), 55-71.

— *The Prime Minister: The Office and its Holders since 1945* (London: Penguin, 2001).

Hinchcliff, P., 'Religion and Politics: The Harsh Reality', in H. Willmer (ed.), *Christian Faith and Political Hopes: A Reply to E.R. Norman* (London: Epworth Press, 1979), 15-33.

— 'Church-State Relations', in S. Sykes & J. Booty (eds.), *The Study of Anglicanism* (London: SPCK, 1988), 351-362.

Jenkins, Daniel, 'Faith and Politics in Britain Today', in H. Willmer (ed.), *Christian Faith and Political Hopes: A Reply to E.R. Norman* (London: Epworth Press, 1979), 65-79.

Jenkins, David, 'Doctrines Which Drive One to Politics', in H. Willmer (ed.), *Christian Faith and Political Hopes: A Reply to E.R. Norman* (London: Epworth Press, 1979), 139-155.

Jones, B., 'Conservatism', in Jones et al., *Politics UK* (London: Philip Allan, 1991), 125-138.

Jones et al., *Politics UK* (London: Philip Allan, 1991).

Jubilee Policy Group, *Political Christians in a Plural Society: A New Strategy for a*

Biblical Contribution (Cambridge: The Jubilee Policy Group, 1994).

Kavanagh, D., *British Politics: Continuities and Change* (Oxford: Oxford University Press, 1985).

— *The Reordering of British Politics: Politics After Thatcher* (Oxford: Oxford University Press, 1997).

Lee, S. & Stanford, P., *Believing Bishops* (London: Faber & Faber, 1990).

Leech, K., 'The Church and Immigration and Race Relations Policy', in G.H. Moyser (ed.), *Church and Politics Today: The Role of the Church of England in Contemporary Politics* (Edinburgh: T & T Clark, 1985), 201-220.

Limon, D. & McKay, W.R., *Erskine May's Treatise on The Law, Privileges, Proceedings and Usage of Parliament*, 22nd Edition (London: Butterworths, 1997).

Longenecker, R., *New Testament Social Ethics for Today* (Grand Rapids: Eerdmans, 1984).

Longford, F., *The Bishops: A Study of Leaders in the Church Today* (London: Sodgwick & Jackson, 1986).

Machin, G.I.T., *Churches and Social Issues in Twentieth-Century Britain* (Oxford: Clarendon Press, 1998).

Major, J., *The Autobiography* (London: Harper Collins, 1999).

Mark, J., 'Politics and the Religious Dimension', in H. Willmer (ed.), *Christian Faith and Political Hopes: A Reply to E.R. Norman* (London: Epworth Press, 1979), 80-91.

Marr, A., *Ruling Britannia: The Failure and Future of British Democracy* (London: Penguin, 1996).

Marshall, W.M., 'Church of Ireland', in J. Cannon (ed.), *The Oxford Companion to British History* (Oxford: Oxford University Press, 1997), 209-210.

Martin, D., 'The Churches: Pink Bishops and the Iron Lady', in A. Seldon & D. Kavanagh (eds.), *The Thatcher Effect: A Decade of Change* (Oxford: Clarendon Press, 1989), 330-342.

— *Reflections on Sociology and Theology* (Oxford: Clarendon Press, 1997).

Mawhinney, B., *In the Firing Line: Politics, Faith, Power and Forgiveness* (London: Harper Collins, 1999).

McGrade, A.S., 'Reason', in S. Sykes & J. Booty (eds.), *The Study of Anglicanism* (London: SPCK, 1988), 105-120.

McLellan, D. (ed.), *Political Christianity: A Reader* (London: SPCK, 1997).

Medhurst, K.N. & Moyser, G.H., *Church and Politics in a Secular Age* (Oxford: Clarendon Press, 1988).

— 'Studying a Religious Elite: The Case of the Anglican Episcopate', in G.H. Moyser and M. Wagstaffe (eds.), *Research Methods for Elite Studies* (London: George Allen & Unwin, 1987), 89-108.

— 'Lambeth Palace, the Bishops and Politics', in G.H. Moyser (ed.), *Church and Politics Today: The Role of the Church of England in Contemporary Politics* (Edinburgh: T & T Clark, 1985), 75-106.

— 'From Princes to Pastors: The Changing Position of the Anglican Episcopate in English Society and Politics', *West European Politics*, Vol. 5, No. 2 (April

1982), 172-91.

Mews, S. (ed.), *Religion in Politics: A World Guide* (Harlow: Longman, 1989).

Minogue, K., 'Introduction: The Context of Thatcherism', in K. Minogue & M. Biddis (eds.), *Thatcherism: Personality and Politics* (London: Macmillan, 1987), x-xvii.

Minogue, K., & Biddis, M. (eds.) *Thatcherism: Personality and Politics* (London: Macmillan, 1987).

Modood, 'Ethno-religious minorities, Secularism and the British State', in *British Political Quarterly* (1994), 61-65.

Montefiore, H., *Christianity and Politics* (London: Macmillan, 1990).

— 'Religion and the Politics of the Environment', in D. Cohn-Sherbok & D. McLellan (eds.), *Religion in Public Life* (New York: St Martin's Press, 1992), 51-63.

Moore, P., 'The Anglican Episcopate: Its Strengths and Limitations', in P. Moore (ed.), *Bishops, But What Kind?* (London: SPCK, 1982), 127-134.

Moorman, J.R.H., 'The Anglican Bishop', in P. Moore (ed.), *Bishops, But What Kind?* (London: SPCK, 1982), 116-126.

Moyser, G.H. (ed.), *Church and Politics Today: The Role of the Church of England in Contemporary Politics* (Edinburgh: T & T Clark, 1985).

Moyser, G.H., *Politics and Religion in The Modern World* (London: Routledge, 1991).

— 'The Church of England and Politics: Patterns and Trends', in G.H. Moyser (ed.), *Church and Politics Today: The Role of the Church of England in Contemporary Politics* (Edinburgh: T & T Clark, 1985), 1-24.

Moyser, G.H. & Wagstaffe, M., 'Studying Elites: Theoretical and Methodological Issues', in G.H. Moyser and M. Wagstaffe (eds.), *Research Methods for Elite Studies* (London: George Allen & Unwin, 1987), 1-24.

Myers, K.A., 'Biblical Obedience and Political Thought: Some Reflections on Theological Method', in R.J. Neuhaus (ed.), *The Bible, Politics and Democracy* (Grand Rapids: Eerdmans, 1987), 19-31.

Neuhaus, R.J., *The Bible, Politics and Democracy* (Grand Rapids: Eerdmans, 1987).

Niebuhr, H.R., *Christ and Culture* (London: Faber & Faber, 1952).

Norman, E.R., *Church and Society in England 1770-1970: A Historical Study* (Oxford: Clarendon Press, 1976).

— *Christianity and the World Order* (Oxford: Oxford University Press, 1979).

— 'Christian Politics in a Society of Plural Values', in D. Cohn-Sherbok & D. McLellan (eds.), *Religion in Public Life* (New York: St Martin's Press, 1992), 17-28.

Norris, R.A., 'Episcopacy', in S. Sykes & J. Booty (eds.), *The Study of Anglicanism* (London: SPCK, 1988), 296-312.

Norton, P., 'The House of Lords and Parliamentary Reform', in Jones et al., *Politics UK* (London: Philip Allan, 1991), 356-372.

O'Donovan, O., *Resurrection and the Moral Order: An Outline for Evangelical Ethics*

(Leicester: IVP, 1986).

Palmer, B., *High and Mitred: A Study of Prime Ministers as Bishop-Makers 1837-1977* (London: SPCK, 1992).

Panikkar, R., 'Religion or Politics: The Western Dilemma', in P.H. Merkl and N. Smart (eds.), *Religion and Politics in the Modern World* (London: New York University Press, 1983), 44-60.

Parsons, G., 'The Rise of Religious Pluralism in the Church of England', in P. Badham (ed.), *Religion, State and Society in Modern Britain* (Lampeter: The Edwin Mellen Press, 1989), 1-22.

Peart-Binns, J.S., *Graham Leonard: Bishop of London* (London: Dayton, Longman & Todd, 1988).

Phillips, M., & Phillips, T., *Windrush: The Irresistible Rise of Multi-Racial Britain* (London: Harper Collins, 1998).

Plant, R., 'The Anglican Church and the Secular State', in G.H. Moyser (ed.), *Church and Politics Today: The Role of the Church of England in Contemporary Politics* (Edinburgh: T & T Clark, 1985), 313-336.

Preston, R.H., *Church and Society in the Late Twentieth Century: The Economic and Political Task* (London: SCM Press, 1983).

Raban, J., *God, Man and Mrs Thatcher* (London: Chatto & Windus, 1989).

Rivers, J., 'Disestablishment and the Church of England', in M. Schluter (ed.), *Christianity in a Changing World: Biblical Insights on Contemporary Issues* (London: Marshall Pickering, 2000), 63-80.

Rogers, D., *Politics, Prayer and Parliament* (London: Continuum, 2000).

Royal Commission on the Reform of the House of Lords, *A House for the Future*, Cm 4534 (London: The Stationery Office, January 2000).

Runcie, R., 'Foreword', in E. Carpenter, *Archbishop Fisher: His Life and Times* (Norwich: The Canterbury Press, 1991), vii-viii.

Rusbridger, A., 'The Likely Lords', in *The Tatler & Bystander* (April 1985).

Say, D., 'Changing the Status of Bishops', *The Times* (22nd April 1987).

— 'Nudging the Government: Runcie and Public Affairs', in S. Platten (ed.), *Runcie: On Reflection* (Norwich: Canterbury Press, 2002), 31-42.

Seldon, A., 'The Rise and Fall of the Post-War Consensus', in Jones et al., *Politics UK* (London: Philip Allan, 1991), 41-57.

Seldon, A. & Ball S. (eds.), *Conservative Century: The Conservative Party since 1900* (Oxford: Oxford University Press, 1994).

Shell, D.R., *The House of Lords* (London: Harvester Wheatsheaf, 1992).

— 'The Evolving House of Lords', *Social Studies Review*, Vol. 5, No. 4 (March 1990), 128-33.

— 'The House of Lords and the Thatcher Government', *Parliamentary Affairs*, Vol. 38, No. 1 (Winter 1985), 16-32.

Shell, D.R. & Beamish, D., *The House of Lords at Work: A Study based on the 1988-89 Session* (Oxford: Clarendon Press, 1993).

Shell, D.R. & Giddings, P., *The Future of Parliament: Reform of the Second Chamber* (London: The Hansard Society, 1999).

Sheppard, D., *Steps Along Hope Street: My Life in Cricket, the Church and the Inner City* (London: Hodder & Stoughton, 2002).

Sider, R.A., 'An Evangelical Vision for American Democracy: An Anabaptist Perspective', in R.J. Neuhaus (ed.), *The Bible, Politics and Democracy* (Grand Rapids: Eerdmans, 1987), 32-54.

Sleeman, J., 'The Church and Economic Policy', in G.H. Moyser (ed.), *Church and Politics Today: The Role of the Church of England in Contemporary Politics* (Edinburgh: T & T Clark, 1985), 256-275.

Stanworth, P. & Giddens, A. (eds.), *Elites and Power in British Society* (Cambridge: Cambridge University Press, 1974).

Stott. J.R.W., *Issues Facing Christians Today* (London: Marshall Pickering, 1990).

Sykes, S., *The Integrity of Anglicanism* (London: Mowbrays, 1978).

Sykes, S. & Booty, J., *The Study of Anglicanism* (London: SPCK, 1988).

Taylor, J., 'The Church Impotent', in *Third Way*, Vol. 23, No. 8 (October 2000).

Temple, W., *Christianity and the Social Order* (London: SCM Press, 1942).

Thatcher, M., *The Downing Street Years* (London: Harper Collins, 1993).

— Speech to the General Assembly of the Church of Scotland, reproduced in J. Raban, *God, Man and Mrs Thatcher* (London: Chatto & Windus, 1989), 7-20.

Thiselton, A.C., *The First Epistle to the Corinthians* (Carlisle: Paternoster Press, 2000).

Thompson, K.A., 'The Church of England Bishops as an Elite', in P. Stanworth and A. Giddens (eds.), *Elites and Power in British Society* (Cambridge: Cambridge University Press, 1974), 198-207.

Till, B., *The Churches Search for Unity* (Harmondsworth: Penguin, 1972).

Towler, R. & Coxon, A.P.M., *The Fate of the Anglican Clergy: A Sociological Study* (London: Macmillan, 1979).

Waddington, R., 'The Church and Educational Policy', in G.H. Moyser (ed.), *Church and Politics Today: The Role of the Church of England in Contemporary Politics* (Edinburgh: T & T Clark, 1985), 221-255.

Ward, K., 'Is a Christian State a Contradiction?', in D. Cohn-Sherbok & D. McLellan (eds.), *Religion in Public Life* (New York, NY: St Martin's Press, 1992), 5-16.

Welsby, P.A., *A History of the Church of England 1945-1980* (Oxford: Oxford University Press, 1984).

— *How the Church of England Works* (London: Church Information Office, 1985).

Wells, J., *The House of Lords* (London: Sceptre, 1997).

Whale, J., 'Bishops in the Lords', *The Listener* (8th August 1985).

— *The Anglican Church Today: The Future of Anglicanism* (Oxford: Mowbray, 1988).

Wheeler-Booth, M.A.J., 'The House of Lords', in J.A.G. Griffith and M. Ryle, *Parliament: Functions, Practice and Procedures* (London: Sweet and Maxwell, 1989), 455-514.

Wickham, E.R., *Growth and Inflation* (London: Church Information Office, 1975).

Willmer, H., 'Does Jesus Call us to Political Discipleship?', in H. Willmer (ed.), *Christian Faith and Political Hopes: A Reply to E.R. Norman* (London: Epworth Press, 1979), 123-138.

Willmer, H. (ed.), *Christian Faith and Political Hopes: A Reply to E.R. Norman* (London: Epworth Press, 1979).

Wilson, B., *Religion in Secular Society: A Sociological Comment* (London: C.A. Watts, 1966).

Wogaman, J.P., *Christian Perspectives on Politics* (Louisville, KY: Westminster John Knox Press, 2000).

Working Party of the General Synod, *The Church and the Bomb: Nuclear Weapons and Christian Conscience* (London: Hodder & Stoughton, 1982).

Young, H., *One of Us: A Biography of Margaret Thatcher* (London: Macmillan, 1989).

Young, H. & Sloman, A., *The Thatcher Phenomenon* (London: BBC, 1986).

Interviews

The Rt Rev Michael Baughen, interview with the author (London, 21st May 2002).

The Rt Rev Hugh Montefiore, interview with the author (London, 21st May 2002).

The Rt Rev David Say, interview with the author (Ashford, 29th May 2002).

The Rt Rev John B. Taylor, interview with the author (Cambridge: 29th July 2002).

Index

Studies in Christian History and Thought
(All titles uniform with this volume)
Dates in bold are of projected publication

David Bebbington
Holiness in Nineteenth-Century England
David Bebbington stresses the relationship of movements of spirituality to changes in their cultural setting, especially the legacies of the Enlightenment and Romanticism. He shows that these broad shifts in ideological mood had a profound effect on the ways in which piety was conceptualized and practised. Holiness was intimately bound up with the spirit of the age.
2000 / 0-85364-981-2 / viii + 98pp

J. William Black
Reformation Pastors
Richard Baxter and the Ideal of the Reformed Pastor
This work examines Richard Baxter's *Gildas Salvianus, The Reformed Pastor* (1656) and explores each aspect of his pastoral strategy in light of his own concern for 'reformation' and in the broader context of Edwardian, Elizabethan and early Stuart pastoral ideals and practice.
2003 / 1-84227-190-3 / xxii + 308pp

James Bruce
Prophecy, Miracles, Angels, *and* Heavenly Light?
The Eschatology, Pneumatology and Missiology of Adomnán's Life of Columba
This book surveys approaches to the marvellous in hagiography, providing the first critique of Plummer's hypothesis of Irish saga origin. It then analyses the uniquely systematized phenomena in the *Life of Columba* from Adomnán's seventh-century theological perspective, identifying the coming of the eschatological Kingdom as the key to understanding.
2004 / 1-84227-227-6 / xviii + 286pp

Colin J. Bulley
The Priesthood of Some Believers
Developments from the General to the Special Priesthood in the Christian Literature of the First Three Centuries
The first in-depth treatment of early Christian texts on the priesthood of all believers shows that the developing priesthood of the ordained related closely to the division between laity and clergy and had deleterious effects on the practice of the general priesthood.
2000 / 1-84227-034-6 / xii + 336pp

Anthony R. Cross (ed.)
Ecumenism and History
Studies in Honour of John H.Y. Briggs
This collection of essays examines the inter-relationships between the two fields
in which Professor Briggs has contributed so much: history—particularly
Baptist and Nonconformist—and the ecumenical movement. With contributions
from colleagues and former research students from Britain, Europe and North
America, *Ecumenism and History* provides wide-ranging studies in important
aspects of Christian history, theology and ecumenical studies.
2002 / 1-84227-135-0 / xx + 362pp

Maggi Dawn
Confessions of an Inquiring Spirit
Form as Constitutive of Meaning in S.T. Coleridge's Theological Writing
This study of Coleridge's *Confessions* focuses on its confessional, epistolary and
fragmentary form, suggesting that attention to these features significantly affects
its interpretation. Bringing a close study of these three literary forms, the author
suggests ways in which they nuance the text with particular understandings of
the Trinity, and of a kenotic christology. Some parallels are drawn between
Romantic and postmodern dilemmas concerning the authority of the biblical
text.
2006 / 1-84227-255-1 / approx. 224 pp

Ruth Gouldbourne
The Flesh and the Feminine
Gender and Theology in the Writings of Caspar Schwenckfeld
Caspar Schwenckfeld and his movement exemplify one of the radical
communities of the sixteenth century. Challenging theological and liturgical
norms, they also found themselves challenging social and particularly gender
assumptions. In this book, the issues of the relationship between radical
theology and the understanding of gender are considered.
2005 / 1-84227-048-6 / approx. 304pp

Crawford Gribben
Puritan Millennialism
Literature and Theology, 1550–1682
Puritan Millennialism surveys the growth, impact and eventual decline of
puritan millennialism throughout England, Scotland and Ireland, arguing that it
was much more diverse than has frequently been suggested. This Paternoster
edition is revised and extended from the original 2000 text.
2007 / 1-84227-372-8 / approx. 320pp

Galen K. Johnson
Prisoner of Conscience
John Bunyan on Self, Community and Christian Faith
This is an interdisciplinary study of John Bunyan's understanding of conscience across his autobiographical, theological and fictional writings, investigating whether conscience always deserves fidelity, and how Bunyan's view of conscience affects his relationship both to modern Western individualism and historic Christianity.

2003 / 1-84227-223-3 / xvi + 236pp

R.T. Kendall
Calvin and English Calvinism to 1649
The author's thesis is that those who formed the Westminster Confession of Faith, which is regarded as Calvinism, in fact departed from John Calvin on two points: (1) the extent of the atonement and (2) the ground of assurance of salvation.

1997 / 0-85364-827-1 / xii + 264pp

Timothy Larsen
Friends of Religious Equality
Nonconformist Politics in Mid-Victorian England
During the middle decades of the nineteenth century the English Nonconformist community developed a coherent political philosophy of its own, of which a central tenet was the principle of religious equality (in contrast to the stereotype of Evangelical Dissenters). The Dissenting community fought for the civil rights of Roman Catholics, non-Christians and even atheists on an issue of principle which had its flowering in the enthusiastic and undivided support which Nonconformity gave to the campaign for Jewish emancipation. This reissued study examines the political efforts and ideas of English Nonconformists during the period, covering the whole range of national issues raised, from state education to the Crimean War. It offers a case study of a theologically conservative group defending religious pluralism in the civic sphere, showing that the concept of religious equality was a grand vision at the centre of the political philosophy of the Dissenters.

2007 / 1-84227-402-3 / x + 300pp

Byung-Ho Moon
Christ the Mediator of the Law
*Calvin's Christological Understanding of the Law as the Rule of Living
and Life-Giving*
This book explores the coherence between Christology and soteriology in
Calvin's theology of the law, examining its intellectual origins and his position
on the concept and extent of Christ's mediation of the law. A comparative study
between Calvin and contemporary Reformers—Luther, Bucer, Melancthon and
Bullinger—and his opponent Michael Servetus is made for the purpose of
pointing out the unique feature of Calvin's Christological understanding of the
law.
2005 / 1-84227-318-3 / approx. 370pp

John Eifion Morgan-Wynne
Holy Spirit and Religious Experience in Christian Writings, c.AD 90–200
This study examines how far Christians in the third to fifth generations (c.AD
90–200) attributed their sense of encounter with the divine presence, their sense
of illumination in the truth or guidance in decision-making, and their sense of
ethical empowerment to the activity of the Holy Spirit in their lives.
2005 / 1-84227-319-1 / approx. 350pp

James I. Packer
The Redemption and Restoration of Man in the Thought of Richard Baxter
James I. Packer provides a full and sympathetic exposition of Richard Baxter's
doctrine of humanity, created and fallen; its redemption by Christ Jesus; and its
restoration in the image of God through the obedience of faith by the power of
the Holy Spirit.
2002 / 1-84227-147-4 / 432pp

Andrew Partington,
Church and State
The Contribution of the Church of England Bishops to the House of Lords
during the Thatcher Years

In *Church and State*, Andrew Partington argues that the contribution of the Church of England bishops to the House of Lords during the Thatcher years was overwhelmingly critical of the government; failed to have a significant influence in the public realm; was inefficient, being undertaken by a minority of those eligible to sit on the Bench of Bishops; and was insufficiently moral and spiritual in its content to be distinctive. On the basis of this, and the likely reduction of the number of places available for Church of England bishops in a fully reformed Second Chamber, the author argues for an evolution in the Church of England's approach to the service of its bishops in the House of Lords. He proposes the Church of England works to overcome the genuine obstacles which hinder busy diocesan bishops from contributing to the debates of the House of Lords and to its life more informally.

2005 / 1-84227-334-5 / approx. 324pp

Michael Pasquarello III
God's Ploughman
Hugh Latimer: A 'Preaching Life' (1490–1555)

This construction of a 'preaching life' situates Hugh Latimer within the larger religious, political and intellectual world of late medieval England. Neither biography, intellectual history, nor analysis of discrete sermon texts, this book is a work of homiletic history which draws from the details of Latimer's milieu to construct an interpretive framework for the preaching performances that formed the core of his identity as a religious reformer. Its goal is to illumine the practical wisdom embodied in the content, form and style of Latimer's preaching, and to recapture a sense of its overarching purpose, movement, and transforming force during the reform of sixteenth-century England.

2006 / 1-84227-336-1 / approx. 250pp

Alan P.F. Sell
Enlightenment, Ecumenism, Evangel
Theological Themes and Thinkers 1550–2000

This book consists of papers in which such interlocking topics as the Enlightenment, the problem of authority, the development of doctrine, spirituality, ecumenism, theological method and the heart of the gospel are discussed. Issues of significance to the church at large are explored with special reference to writers from the Reformed and Dissenting traditions.

2005 / 1-84227-330-2 / xviii + 422pp

Alan P.F. Sell
Hinterland Theology
Some Reformed and Dissenting Adjustments
Many books have been written on theology's 'giants' and significant trends, but what of those lesser-known writers who adjusted to them? In this book some hinterland theologians of the British Reformed and Dissenting traditions, who followed in the wake of toleration, the Evangelical Revival, the rise of modern biblical criticism and Karl Barth, are allowed to have their say. They include Thomas Ridgley, Ralph Wardlaw, T.V. Tymms and N.H.G. Robinson.

2006 / 1-84227-331-0 / approx. 350pp

Alan P.F. Sell and Anthony R. Cross (eds)
Protestant Nonconformity in the Twentieth Century
In this collection of essays scholars representative of a number of Nonconformist traditions reflect thematically on Nonconformists' life and witness during the twentieth century. Among the subjects reviewed are biblical studies, theology, worship, evangelism and spirituality, and ecumenism. Over and above its immediate interest, this collection provides a marker to future scholars and others wishing to know how some of their forebears assessed Nonconformity's contribution to a variety of fields during the century leading up to Christianity's third millennium.

2003 / 1-84227-221-7 / x + 398pp

Mark Smith
Religion in Industrial Society
Oldham and Saddleworth 1740–1865
This book analyses the way British churches sought to meet the challenge of industrialization and urbanization during the period 1740–1865. Working from a case-study of Oldham and Saddleworth, Mark Smith challenges the received view that the Anglican Church in the eighteenth century was characterized by complacency and inertia, and reveals Anglicanism's vigorous and creative response to the new conditions. He reassesses the significance of the centrally directed church reforms of the mid-nineteenth century, and emphasizes the importance of local energy and enthusiasm. Charting the growth of denominational pluralism in Oldham and Saddleworth, Dr Smith compares the strengths and weaknesses of the various Anglican and Nonconformist approaches to promoting church growth. He also demonstrates the extent to which all the churches participated in a common culture shaped by the influence of evangelicalism, and shows that active co-operation between the churches rather than denominational conflict dominated. This revised and updated edition of Dr Smith's challenging and original study makes an important contribution both to the social history of religion and to urban studies.

2006 / 1-84227-335-3 / approx. 300pp

Martin Sutherland
Peace, Toleration and Decay
The Ecclesiology of Later Stuart Dissent
This fresh analysis brings to light the complexity and fragility of the later Stuart Nonconformist consensus. Recent findings on wider seventeenth-century thought are incorporated into a new picture of the dynamics of Dissent and the roots of evangelicalism.
2003 / 1-84227-152-0 / xxii + 216pp

G. Michael Thomas
The Extent of the Atonement
A Dilemma for Reformed Theology from Calvin to the Consensus
A study of the way Reformed theology addressed the question, 'Did Christ die for all, or for the elect only?', commencing with John Calvin, and including debates with Lutheranism, the Synod of Dort and the teaching of Moïse Amyraut.
1997 / 0-85364-828-X / x + 278pp

David M. Thompson
Baptism, Church and Society in Britain from the Evangelical Revival to
Baptism, Eucharist and Ministry
The theology and practice of baptism have not received the attention they deserve. How important is faith? What does baptismal regeneration mean? Is baptism a bond of unity between Christians? This book discusses the theology of baptism and popular belief and practice in England and Wales from the Evangelical Revival to the publication of the World Council of Churches' consensus statement on *Baptism, Eucharist and Ministry* (1982).
2005 / 1-84227-393-0 / approx. 224pp

Mark D. Thompson
A Sure Ground on Which to Stand
The Relation of Authority and Interpretive Method of Luther's Approach to Scripture
The best interpreter of Luther is Luther himself. Unfortunately many modern studies have superimposed contemporary agendas upon this sixteenth-century Reformer's writings. This fresh study examines Luther's own words to find an explanation for his robust confidence in the Scriptures, a confidence that generated the famous 'stand' at Worms in 1521.
2004 / 1-84227-145-8 / xvi + 322pp

Carl R. Trueman and R.S. Clark (eds)
Protestant Scholasticism
Essays in Reassessment
Traditionally Protestant theology, between Luther's early reforming career and
the dawn of the Enlightenment, has been seen in terms of decline and fall into
the wastelands of rationalism and scholastic speculation. In this volume a
number of scholars question such an interpretation. The editors argue that the
development of post-Reformation Protestantism can only be understood when a
proper historical model of doctrinal change is adopted. This historical concern
underlies the subsequent studies of theologians such as Calvin, Beza, Olevian,
Baxter, and the two Turrentini. The result is a significantly different reading of
the development of Protestant Orthodoxy, one which both challenges the older
scholarly interpretations and clichés about the relationship of Protestantism to,
among other things, scholasticism and rationalism, and which demonstrates the
fruitfulness of the new, historical approach.
1999 / 0-85364-853-0 / xx + 344pp

Shawn D. Wright
Our Sovereign Refuge
The Pastoral Theology of Theodore Beza
Our Sovereign Refuge is a study of the pastoral theology of the Protestant
reformer who inherited the mantle of leadership in the Reformed church from
John Calvin. Countering a common view of Beza as supremely a 'scholastic'
theologian who deviated from Calvin's biblical focus, Wright uncovers a new
portrait. He was not a cold and rigid academic theologian obsessed with probing
the eternal decrees of God. Rather, by placing him in his pastoral context and by
noting his concerns in his pastoral and biblical treatises, Wright shows that Beza
was fundamentally a committed Christian who was troubled by the vicissitudes
of life in the second half of the sixteenth century. He believed that the biblical
truth of the supreme sovereignty of God alone could support Christians on their
earthly pilgrimage to heaven. This pastoral and personal portrait forms the heart
of Wright's argument.
2004 / 1-84227-252-7 / xviii + 308pp

Paternoster
9 Holdom Avenue,
Bletchley,
Milton Keynes MK1 1QR,
United Kingdom
Web: www.authenticmedia.co.uk/paternoster